Frankenstein and Its Classics

Bloomsbury Studies in Classical Reception

Bloomsbury Studies in Classical Reception presents scholarly monographs offering new and innovative research and debate to students and scholars in the reception of Classical Studies. Each volume will explore the appropriation, reconceptualization and recontextualization of various aspects of the Graeco-Roman world and its culture, looking at the impact of the ancient world on modernity. Research will also cover reception within antiquity, the theory and practice of translation, and reception theory.

Also available in the Series:

Ancient Magic and the Supernatural in the Modern Visual and Performing Arts, edited by Filippo Carlà and Irene Berti
Ancient Greek Myth in World Fiction since 1989, edited by Justine McConnell and Edith Hall
The Codex Fori Mussolini, Han Lamers and Bettina Reitz-Joosse
The Gentle, Jealous God, Simon Perris
Greek and Roman Classics in the British Struggle for Social Reform, edited by Henry Stead and Edith Hall
Imagining Xerxes, Emma Bridges
Ovid's Myth of Pygmalion on Screen, Paula James
Victorian Classical Burlesques, Laura Monrós-Gaspar
Julius Caesar's Self-Created Image and Its Dramatic Afterlife, Miryana Dimitrova
Homer's Iliad and the Trojan War, Naoise Mac Sweeney and Jan Haywood

Frankenstein and Its Classics

The Modern Prometheus from Antiquity to Science Fiction

Edited by
Jesse Weiner, Benjamin Eldon Stevens, and
Brett M. Rogers

BLOOMSBURY ACADEMIC
LONDON • NEW YORK • OXFORD • NEW DELHI • SYDNEY

BLOOMSBURY ACADEMIC
Bloomsbury Publishing Plc
50 Bedford Square, London, WC1B 3DP, UK
1385 Broadway, New York, NY 10018, USA

BLOOMSBURY and the Diana logo are trademarks of Bloomsbury Publishing Plc

First published in Great Britain 2018

Copyright © Jesse Weiner, Benjamin Eldon Stevens, and Brett M. Rogers, 2018

Jesse Weiner, Benjamin Eldon Stevens, and Brett M. Rogers have asserted their right under the Copyright, Designs and Patents Act, 1988, to be identified as Editors of this work.

For legal purposes the Preface on pp. vii–ix constitutes an extension of this copyright page.

Cover illustration by Christian Ward from ODY-C © 2014 Milkfed Criminal Masterminds, Inc. & Christian Ward

All rights reserved. No part of this publication may be reproduced or transmitted in any form or by any means, electronic or mechanical, including photocopying, recording, or any information storage or retrieval system, without prior permission in writing from the publishers.

A catalogue record for this book is available from the British Library.

Library of Congress Cataloging-in-Publication Data
Names: Weiner, Jesse, editor. | Stevens, Benjamin Eldon, editor. | Rogers, Brett M., editor.
Title: Frankenstein and its classics : the modern Prometheus from antiquity to science fiction / edited by Jesse Weiner, Benjamin Eldon Stevens and Brett M. Rogers.
Other titles: Bloomsbury studies in classical reception.
Description: London : Bloomsbury Academic, 2018. | Series: Bloomsbury studies in classical reception | Includes index.
Identifiers: LCCN 2017056915| ISBN 9781350054875 (pbk.) | ISBN 9781350054882 (hardback)
Subjects: LCSH: Science fiction—Classical influences. | Shelley, Mary Wollstonecraft, 1797–1851. Frankenstein. | Frankenstein's Monster (Fictitious character) | Frankenstein, Victor (Fictitious character) | Prometheus (Greek deity)—In literature. | Frankenstein films.
Classification: LCC PN3433.6 .F68 2018 | DDC 809.3/8762—dc23 LC record available at https://lccn.loc.gov/2017056915

ISBN: HB: 978-1-3500-5488-2
PB: 978-1-3500-5487-5
ePDF: 978-1-3500-5490-5
eBook: 978-1-3500-5489-9

Series: Bloomsbury Studies in Classical Reception

Typeset by RefineCatch Limited, Bungay, Suffolk

To find out more about our authors and books visit www.bloomsbury.com and sign up for our newsletters.

Contents

Preface	vii
List of Contributors	x
List of Illustrations	xiii

Introduction: The Modern Prometheus Turns 200
Jesse Weiner, Benjamin Eldon Stevens, and Brett M. Rogers   1

Part One   Promethean Heat

1. Patchwork Paratexts and Monstrous Metapoetics: "After tea M reads Ovid" *Genevieve Liveley*   25

2. Prometheus and Dr. Darwin's Vermicelli: Another Stir to the *Frankenstein* Broth *Martin Priestman*   42

3. The Politics of Revivification in Lucan's *Bellum Civile* and Mary Shelley's *Frankenstein* *Andrew M. McClellan*   59

4. Romantic Prometheis and the Molding of *Frankenstein* *Suzanne L. Barnett*   76

5. Why the 'Year without a Summer'? *David A. Gapp*   91

6. The Sublime Monster: *Frankenstein*, or The Modern Pandora *Matthew Gumpert*   102

Part Two   Hideous Progeny

7. Cupid and Psyche in *Frankenstein*: Mary Shelley's Apuleian Science Fiction? *Benjamin Eldon Stevens*   123

8. The Pale Student of Unhallowed Arts: Frankenstein, Aristotle, and the Wisdom of Lucretius *Carl A. Rubino*   145

9. Timothy Leary and the Psychodynamics of Stealing Fire *Neşe Devenot*   153

10 Frankenfilm: Classical Monstrosity in Bill Morrison's *Spark of Being*
    Jesse Weiner   170

11 Alex Garland's *Ex Machina* or The Modern Epimetheus
    Emma Hammond   190

12 The Postmodern Prometheus and Posthuman Reproductions in
    Science Fiction *Brett M. Rogers*   206

    Other Modern Prometheis: Suggestions for Further Reading and
    Viewing *Samuel Cooper*   228

Bibliography   238
Index   267

Preface

In his then-anonymous preface to the first edition of *Frankenstein* (1818), Mary Shelley's husband, Percy, writes about the story's beginnings some eighteen months earlier "in casual conversation" among Mary, Byron, himself, and others; this conversation took place "in the majestic region" of Switzerland's Lake Geneva, and in a "season" that was "cold and rainy." The present volume, too, began in casual conversation, and if the region was arguably less majestic—a Philadelphia department-store Starbucks—the weather was suitably gloomy. On that "wet, uncongenial" January afternoon, during a break from paper sessions at the annual meeting of the erstwhile American Philological Association, we set our own "ghost story challenge": to develop a collection of essays about classical antiquity and modern monsters. We are excited to see that project come to fruition and, like Mary Shelley in her preface to *Frankenstein*'s third edition (1831), we hope our own "hideous progeny" will "prosper."

"[T]he accomplishment of [our] toils," *Frankenstein and Its Classics: The Modern Prometheus from Antiquity to Science Fiction*, is the first collection devoted to classical receptions in *Frankenstein* and its traditions. Many of the essays found their own first "spark of being" at an international symposium, "The Modern Prometheus; or, *Frankenstein*," held in April 2016 at Hamilton College in Clinton, NY, USA. There was a charge in the air as the participants gathered not long before the two-hundredth anniversary of the novel's conception—a charge increased by other coincidences, including the conference overlapping with the two-hundred-and-first anniversary of the eruption of Tambora; a late snowfall that conjured the 'Year without a Summer'; and a location not far from a town called, of all things, Geneva.

Such historical and geographical coincidences aside, it was clear then that the subject-matter remains of great interest. Two hundred years after its first publication, *Frankenstein* continues to captivate audiences, to inform conversations about technological development and scientific ethics, to inspire futuristic art—and, perhaps surprisingly, to encourage reflection on classical antiquity. As the conference organizers and now this volume's editors, we are excited to be able to usher these essays into print here. Some are drawn from that symposium, while others were received in response to a subsequent call for papers. They range in scope from ancient myth and philosophy to Romantic neoclassicism to contemporary film and the psychedelic experiments of Timothy Leary. All together they offer an invitation—for readers of *Frankenstein* and the traditions it has inspired, for viewers of the many film versions and adaptations, for scholars and students of Romanticism, Classics, and classical receptions, and for others still—to explore some of the ancient roots of Mary Shelley's paradigmatic 'modern' monster.

Over the several years from that first conversation to the appearance of this volume, many people have played important roles in bringing *Frankenstein and Its Classics* to life. We editors wish to thank, above all, the contributors for sharing their insightful work and for allowing us to publish it here. Special thanks go to the team at Bloomsbury, including Alice Wright, Senior Commissioning Editor for Classical Studies and Archaeology; Clara Herberg, Senior Editorial Assistant, and Emma Payne, Editorial Assistant, for the same. We are also grateful to Hamilton College's Winslow Lecture Fund in Classics and to the NY6 Think Tank for supporting the conference that preceded this volume.

Weiner would like to thank his colleagues at Hamilton College—Anne Feltovich, Barbara Gold, Shelley Haley, Nancy Rabinowitz, and Carl Rubino—for their support throughout this project, especially during conference planning. Thanks are also due to the brilliant students in his courses at Hamilton on science fiction and the classics (spring and fall 2016) for their thoughts on *Frankenstein* and its classics. Special thanks are due to Julie for her steadfast love, support, and wisdom; and to co-editors and partners in *katabasis*, Ben and Brett, perfect comrades in escape from a Montréal cemetery.

Stevens would like to thank the students in his courses on classical traditions and science fiction at Bryn Mawr College (spring 2015) and Trinity University (spring 2017) for truly galvanizing discussions of *Frankenstein*. Trinity's Department of Classical Studies was enthusiastic in its support throughout, and two summer research students, Mellon fellow Ariana Fletcher-Bai and Murchison fellow Isaiah Mitchell (both Trinity '20), were inspiring interlocutors while the project neared completion. Special thanks are due to Jesse and Brett, alchemical co-editors and sublime companions on travels international as well as intellectual.

Rogers would like to thank the students in his courses on classical receptions and science fiction at the University of Puget Sound (spring 2015 and fall 2017) for their electrifying ideas about *Frankenstein* and *Prometheus*, as well as the Department of Classics for patiently tolerating such fevered madness. Special thanks are due to Jennifer and Elinor, who remained stalwart at Chamounix during his many *Frankenstein*-related journeys; and to Jesse and Ben, who worked tirelessly to find the best, most lustrous parts in our editorial charnel house. "[Our] travels were long and the sufferings [we] endured intense": may we never drink Frankenwine again.

Contributors

Suzanne L. Barnett is Assistant Professor of English at Francis Marion University. Her first book, *Romantic Paganism: The Politics of Ecstasy in the Shelley Circle* (Palgrave, 2017), considers the role of the classical world in later Romanticism. She has also published articles in the *Keats-Shelley Journal*, *Studies in Romanticism*, and *Romantic Circles*.

Samuel Cooper received his PhD from Princeton University and teaches Classics at Bard Early Colleges in New York.

Neşe Devenot is a scholar of British Romanticism and Cognitive Literary Studies. She received the 2016 award for Best Humanities Publication in Psychedelic Studies from *Breaking Convention*, and she served research fellowships with the New York Public Library's Timothy Leary Papers and the NYU Psilocybin Cancer Anxiety Study. Her research explores the function of metaphor and other literary devices in verbal accounts of non-ordinary experiences.

David A. Gapp is Hamilton College Silas D. Childs Professor of Biology, Emeritus. After postdoctoral work at the Jackson Laboratory in Bar Harbor, Maine, he joined the Biology Department at Hamilton where he retired in 2017 after 38 years. His research has focused on mouse models of diabetes, the endocrinology of the pancreas and gastrointestinal tract of reptiles, and, as of late, the effects of the 'Year without a Summer' on New York State.

Matthew Gumpert is Professor in the Department of Western Languages and Literatures at Boğaziçi University, and author of three books: *Grafting Helen: The Abduction of the Classical Past* (University of Wisconsin Press, 2001), *The End of Meaning: Studies in Catastrophe* (Cambridge Scholars Publishing, 2012), and *The Accident Waiting to Happen* (Sharjah Art Foundation, 2015), as well as numerous articles on the persistence of classicism in post-classical literature, architecture, and popular culture. He is currently working on a study of representations and imitations of the Parthenon, entitled *Parthenogenesis*.

Emma Hammond completed her PhD in Classics at the University of Bristol, where she also studied Classics as an undergraduate. The topic of her thesis is nostalgia in Ovid's *Heroides*. Her wider teaching and research interests are in narratological time and temporality, gender, and feminism.

Genevieve Liveley is Senior Lecturer in Classics at the University of Bristol. She is the author of a number of books and articles on narratology, Ovid's *Metamorphoses*, and its reception.

Andrew M. McClellan is a Postdoctoral Fellow in Classics at Florida State University. He is currently finishing a monograph on corpse abuse in Greek and Roman epic poetry.

Martin Priestman is Emeritus Professor of English at the University of Roehampton in London, specializing mainly in the Romantic Period and Crime Fiction. His relevant publications include *The Poetry of Erasmus Darwin: Enlightened Spaces, Romantic Times* (Ashgate, 2013), 'Lucretius in Romantic and Victorian Britain' in *The Cambridge Companion to Lucretius* (Cambridge University Press, 2007), and *Romantic Atheism: Poetry and Freethought, 1780–1830* (Cambridge University Press, 1999). He has also published the first fully annotated edition of Erasmus Darwin's *The Temple of Nature* (*Romantic Circles*, October 2006): http://www.rc.umd.edu/editions/darwin_temple.

Brett M. Rogers is Associate Professor of Classics at the University of Puget Sound. He has co-edited (with Benjamin Eldon Stevens) two volumes, *Classical Traditions in Science Fiction* (Oxford University Press, 2015) and *Classical Traditions in Modern Fantasy* (Oxford University Press, 2017). He has published on such topics as notions of teaching and learning in Athenian drama, classical reception in the science fiction novel *Dune* (for *Brill's Companion to the Reception of Aeschylus*, 2017), myth theory in superhero comics (for *Classics & Comics*, 2011), and (with Walter Scheidel) sex and cars in *Buffy the Vampire Slayer*.

Carl A. Rubino, Winslow Professor of Classics Emeritus at Hamilton College, has published and lectured extensively on Greek and Roman literature, comparative literature, and literary theory. A long-time collaborator of the Nobel Laureate physicist Ilya Prigogine, he is also known for his work on the connections between science and the humanities, where he has focused on complexity theory, the problem of time, and the impact of the theory of evolution on ethics.

Benjamin Eldon Stevens is Visiting Assistant Professor at Trinity University. He is the author of *Silence in Catullus* (University of Wisconsin Press, 2013) and co-editor, with Brett M. Rogers, of *Classical Traditions in Science Fiction* (Oxford University Press, 2015) and *Classical Traditions in Modern Fantasy* (Oxford University Press, 2017). He has published on such topics as ancient linguistics, the senses in literature, underworlds and afterlives, and classical receptions in authors including Jesmyn Ward, A. S. Byatt, and Dante. He is also a translator of contemporary Spanish poetry and contemporary French fiction.

Jesse Weiner is Assistant Professor of Classics at Hamilton College in Clinton, NY. He is the author of numerous articles on classical literature and its modern receptions.

Illustrations

1.1 Illustration from George Sandys, *Ouid's Metamorphosis Englished*, 1632 folio edition. 39
3.1 Napoleon as a "Modern Prometheus." *The Modern Prometheus, or: Downfall of Tyranny*. London, July 1814. George Cruikshank. MB Satires 12299. British Museum. Museum Number: 1947,1215.3. 70
3.2 Napoleon's Revivification from "Hell-Bay." *The Phenix of Elba Resuscitated by Treason*. London, May 1, 1815. George Cruikshank. BM Satires 12537. British Museum. Museum Number: 1868,0808.8213. 72
5.1 Indonesian Archipelago in the region of the Mt. Tambora eruption. Modified from: Stothers, Richard B. 1984. "The Great Tambora Eruption in 1815 and Its Aftermath." *Science* 224.4654: 1191–1198. 92
5.2 The island of Sumbawa in the Indonesian Archipelago. Redrawn from: Sudradjat, Adjat and Heryadi Rachmat. 2015. *Greetings from Tambora: A Potpourri of the Stories on the Deadliest Volcanic Eruption*. Bandung: Geological Museum. 92
5.3 Extent of the Tambora ash fall in the surrounding islands. Redrawn from: Sudradjat, Adjat and Heryadi Rachmat. 2015. *Greetings from Tambora: A Potpourri of the Stories on the Deadliest Volcanic Eruption*. Bandung: Geological Museum. 93
5.4 Chemical reaction in the stratosphere leading to formation of the reflective sulfate shield as a result of the Tambora eruption. Sulfur dioxide in the stratosphere is converted by an appropriate wavelength of UV light to form sulfuric acid that increases the reflectivity of the atmosphere, reducing the solar energy reaching the earth. 95
7.1 "An Experiment on a Bird in an Air Pump" (1768). Joseph Wright of Derby—National Gallery, London, Public Domain (https://commons.wikimedia.org/w/index.php?curid=3751913). 124
10.1 Bill Morrison, *Spark of Being* (2010), photo courtesy of the artist. 173
10.2 Bill Morrison, *Spark of Being* (2010), photo courtesy of the artist. 178
10.3 Bill Morrison, *Spark of Being* (2010), "Observations of Romantic Love," photo courtesy of the artist. 185

11.1 Alicia Vikander as Ava in Alex Garland's *Ex Machina* (2015), photo courtesy of Universal Studios Licencing LLC. 201

12.1 Prometheus creating man, guided by Athena (who adds fire). Marble Sarcophagus relief, third century CE. Musei Capitolini, Rome, Italy. Photo Credit: Erich Lessing/Art Resource, NY. 209

12.2 Promethene and the creation of the sebex in *Ody-C #2* (January 2015). Excerpted with permission from *ODY-C #2*. *ODY-C* is by Matt Fraction & Christian Ward. © 2018 Milkfed Criminal Masterminds, Inc. & Christian Ward. 221

Introduction: The Modern Prometheus Turns 200

Jesse Weiner, Benjamin Eldon Stevens, and Brett M. Rogers

In late spring and summer 1816, Mary Wollstonecraft Shelley—at that time still Mary Godwin, although already referring to herself as 'Mrs. Shelley' (henceforth MWS)—vacationed near Lake Geneva in Switzerland with her lover and future husband Percy Bysshe Shelley (henceforth PBS), their six-month-old son William, and MWS's stepsister Claire Clairmont, all staying at a small chalet called Montalègre. Some ten days after their arrival they were joined by Claire's former lover, Lord Byron, and his personal physician, John William Polidori, both of whom stayed at the nearby Villa Diodati. To their minor misfortune (and to the great good fortune of literary history), 1816 was the infamous 'Year without a Summer,' featuring historically bad weather caused by the eruption of Mt. Tambora the previous year.[1] Confined indoors by the "incessant rain" of that "wet, ungenial summer," the group passed its time discussing philosophy, science or natural philosophy, and literature. Eventually they read aloud from a recent collection of ghost stories called *Fantasmagoriana* and, charged and terrified, challenged each other to compose their own.[2] PBS seems to have fizzled, although not for lack of feeling: upon hearing Byron read Coleridge's *Christabel*, he had run from the room screaming—we are told by Polidori—in a fit of fantasy.[3] Byron himself produced little more than a squib, a "Fragment of a Novel" eventually appended to his 1819 *Mazeppa*. MWS tells us that these "illustrious poets also, annoyed by the platitude of prose, speedily relinquished their uncongenial task."[4] Polidori did better, that same year publishing his development of similar material, *The Vampyre*, which would exert an influence on Gothic and horror.

And then there's Mary. In January 1818, not two full years later, MWS published her story as *Frankenstein; or, the Modern Prometheus*. It is remarkable that the young woman who described herself as a "devout but nearly silent listener" to conversations between PBS and Byron has gone on to help shape modern literature and culture in ways neither of those male authors matched or, perhaps, could have predicted.[5]

Now, two hundred years later, at the bicentennial of *Frankenstein*'s publication, we find ourselves in a timely moment to devote attention to her novel and to its place in literary, philosophical, mythological, and cultural traditions. *Frankenstein* has continued to provide vivid images for modern experience, images whose power comes in part from their transformations of older materials. If this confluence of old and new seems paradoxical, other studies have shown that it is essential to the novel: there is something peculiarly 'Frankensteinian' to the story itself, as if MWS's 'hideous literary progeny' is formed on the model of Victor's stitched-together Creature—a cutting-edge scientific practice infused by an antiquarian turn toward alchemy—and vice versa. Thus, for example, Jerrold E. Hogle describes *Frankenstein* as "sewn together from different types of previous writing as the creature is fabricated from different portions and classes of older bodies."[6]

The present volume focuses on how *Frankenstein*, some contemporary works that inspired it, and some other works it has gone on to inspire all involve transformations of materials that are not just old but ancient, that is, from ancient Greece and Rome. In other words, *Frankenstein* and its traditions perform 'classical receptions,' transmitting and transmuting material from Greek and Roman antiquity.[7] MWS and her fellow vacationers had variously received and pursued classical educations and were enthusiastic antiquarians; as a general rule they could expect similar knowledge and appreciation in their likely contemporary readers.[8]

Frankenstein signals its engagement with classical materials first of all via its subtitle, *the Modern Prometheus*. The novel thus offers a reimagining of the Titan Prometheus, who in ancient myths shaped humankind from lifeless clay (*plasticator*) and became its greatest champion by stealing fire (*pyrphoros*), a symbol of technology, from the Olympian gods. For that challenge to the order of the cosmos, Prometheus, immortal but not invulnerable, was punished by being chained to a mountaintop where his liver could be pecked out daily by Zeus's eagle. Like Prometheus, Victor Frankenstein suffers repeated torment, while 'Promethean' creation and its consequences are running themes in the novel.[9] In addition to such Prometheism, *Frankenstein* engages with other materials from ancient authors including Lucretius (*De rerum natura*), Ovid (*Metamorphoses*), Seneca (*Hercules furens*), Lucan (*Bellum civile*), Plutarch (*Parallel Lives*), and Apuleius (*Metamorphoses* or *The Golden Ass*). At a more abstract or thematic level, the novel's depiction of monstrosity also has deep roots in classical literature, where monsters, including monstrous hybrids, are made to define 'humankind' by contrast.[10]

This volume is devoted to tracing these and other classical filiations. Although some discussion can be found in scholarship focused on contemporary and literary-historical contexts for the novel and its legacy, to our knowledge the present volume is the first to focus specifically on *Frankenstein*'s classical receptions. As the summary of chapters below should indicate, the volume is not intended to be exhaustive: instead, the chapters all together are intended to help raise the question of '*Frankenstein* and its classics' in ways that are productively different from each other, even divergent, but complementary and, we hope, inviting to scholars, students, and other readers alike. Our highest goal is to help each reader ask for herself how *Frankenstein*, some of its sources, and parts of its subsequent traditions all constitute important sites of classical reception. How do Greek and Roman myth, literature, and philosophy inform *Frankenstein*, and how might *Frankenstein* work to reanimate our modern readings of ancient classics? Given its influential or even foundational status in science fiction (SF), what does *Frankenstein* suggest about relationships between modern SF and ancient classics more generally?[11] If MWS's novel remains important into the future, how might it continue to help shape readers' experience of the classics, even as science and technology continue to change?

Such questions look forward as well as backward, inviting us to consider technoscientific futures hardly imagined by MWS in connection with themes, figures, images, and stories from ancient literature.[12] Other scholarship on *Frankenstein* and its traditions has looked in that direction to a degree by linking SF and Romanticism, occasionally touching on classical receptions. Such scholarship has left the door open for the more focused considerations offered by this volume's chapters.

To illustrate that context here, we note briefly just one very recent prominent collection, *The Cambridge Companion to Frankenstein* (2016; *CCF*). *CCF* includes about a dozen references to ancient materials, most of which are dominated by Prometheus.[13] Indeed, even Prometheus comes in second to the adjective 'Promethean' in reference to various understandings of the theme of 'Romantic overreach.' That theme is, of course, essential to the novel, as it was important to MWS and contemporaries. And yet it seems telling that a figure as important to the novel's Romanticism as Prometheus has no entry in the *CCF* index.

To take a more substantive example from *CCF*, as students of Classics we are positively struck by how an interest in the 'Promethean' appears in the *Companion* in the particular sense of "the use of 'technology' to make life," suggesting Victor's evocation of both of Prometheus's major roles in ancient myth, *pyrphoros* and *plasticator*.[14] This usefully implies the link between *Frankenstein*'s modern

Prometheism—inspired for MWS by contemporary concepts like galvanism—and its theme of theft, not of electricity but of fire from the heavens.[15] But we cannot agree entirely with Morton's further statement, that:

> Hesiod, or Ovid, or Virgil do not have a monopoly on the myths they are telling. Myths are precisely stories that exceed their authors in a profound way. You do not need to quote Ovid to talk about Arachne. You do not need to read the *Theogony* to talk about Prometheus. You do not need to cite *Frankenstein* to refer to 'Frankenfoods.'[16]

Morton is correct insofar as, for example, Philip K. Dick and Ridley Scott, among others working in a *Frankenstein* tradition, are not obligated to cite their (or MWS's) ancient sources in the midst of their own "profoundly allusive meditations on the Promethean theme—the human use of 'technology' to make life—and the theme of what it means to be alive, let alone the theme of what it means to be a person."[17] Other *CCF* chapters make that basic point in different ways, some with direct reference to aspects of ancient myth.[18] And these are brought to bear on crucial elements of MWS's novel: for example, "[i]t would seem natural to assume that the Promethean figure thus indicated is Victor himself, but the creature's own search for (self-)knowledge has also been seen as Promethean," a doubling or ambiguity that has long intrigued scholars and other readers as well as artists working in a *Frankenstein* tradition.[19]

Especially when the stakes are so high, however—when, as other chapters in the *CCF* also suggest, at stake is the very definition of 'personhood' and 'humankind'—scholarship does have an obligation to detailed historical comprehension. This imperative is strengthened by MWS's and other contemporary authors' explicit attention to ancient authors like Hesiod, Ovid, and Virgil. Scholarship like that found in *CCF* therefore points to the opportunity for more detailed attention to *Frankenstein*'s classical receptions. Such research should help clarify and deepen ambiguities like those noted above, which lead to the related question: "Is Victor meant to be presented as a worthy successor to the original Prometheus, or rather as a downgraded equivalent, thus satirizing the whole notion of the Promethean, at least within a modern context?" That question should be crucial to readers of *the Modern Prometheus*. For this volume's purposes, the very last phrase is crucial, too: *Frankenstein*, like others of MWS's and her contemporaries' works, exists not only 'within a modern context' but also in close, purposeful relation to shared cultural knowledge of—and strong personal feelings about—classical antiquity, above all Greek and Roman literature.[20]

We therefore take the present moment—2018, in celebration of the bicentennial of MWS's remarkable novel—as an invitation to think further about our own possible futures in terms of how *Frankenstein* and its traditions develop important images for modern experience in part by performing classical receptions. These transmit and transmute ancient Greek and Roman materials in forms as multiple, powerful, and plural as the 'race of devils' Victor imagined arising from his Creature and its bride. In what follows in this introduction, we aim to suggest some of the richness of this approach: first, we explore the novel's relationship with one ancient source, Plutarch, which has been mostly passed over in modern scholarship; then, we discuss a recent example from SF; and finally, we point to some of the urgent ethical questions that have been raised in response to developments in science and technology. We conclude the introduction by summarizing the volume's chapters.

Frankenstein and Its Classics: The Case of Plutarch

In this section, we consider the second-most prominent example, after Prometheus, of a Greco-Roman influence in *Frankenstein*—and the single most direct classical influence on the Creature himself. As the Creature tells Victor, during his time living near the De Laceys (2.7: 88–89):[21]

> One night ... I found on the ground a leather portmanteau, containing several articles of dress and some books.... Fortunately the books were written in the language the elements of which I had acquired at the cottage [i.e., French]: they consisted of *Paradise Lost*, a volume of *Plutarch's Lives*, and the *Sorrows of Werter*. The possession of these treasures gave me extreme delight; I now continuously studied and exercised my mind upon these histories ... I can hardly describe to you the effect of the books.

We pass by the Creature's confused description of these texts as "histories" and focus on the one that might plausibly be called 'history,' although it is properly 'biography': *Plutarch's Lives* or, more precisely, *Parallel Lives* (Βίοι Παράλληλοι).[22] Composed by the Greek biographer and essayist Plutarch of Chaeronea (before 50 CE to *c.* 120 CE) late in his life during the second century of the Roman empire, *Lives* consists of twenty-three pairs of biographies about Greek and Roman statesmen; for each pair, Plutarch also offers a short comparison of the two figures.[23] Special attention is drawn to the statesmen's moral qualities, making the *Lives* a key document for ideas about virtue and vice during the Roman empire.

Critics of *Frankenstein* afford *Plutarch's Lives*—and MWS's use and transformations of Plutarch—scant attention. This may be due in part to Plutarch's diminished popularity in our time, both in scholarly circles and among wider audiences. However, throughout the seventeenth and eighteenth centuries, the *Lives* were among the most highly regarded Greco-Roman texts.[24] The *Lives* were widely available both in the Creature's native French and, more importantly, in MWS's native English: six English translations were published between 1710 and 1800, in addition to several editions of Plutarch's complete works in Latin translation or the original ancient Greek.[25] Plutarch found special favor among thinkers and political philosophers of this time for "his stress on the virtues of humanity and of calmness in the face of adversity, and his preference for enlightened monarchy."[26] MWS's father, William Godwin, had undoubtedly read him; as Lisa Vargo suggests, MWS likely first encountered the *Lives* in Godwin's library or even in Godwin's own work, such as "Of History and Romance" (1797).[27]

MWS's journals indicate she was reading Plutarch's *Lives* sometime during 1815, presumably in translation; her journals also record that PBS read the *Lives* several times over the course of the next few years: from August 18 to 20, 1816 (in Greek); from November 17 to 19 and 25 to 29, 1816 (including the *Life of Alexander*, relevant below); and on July 9, 1817.[28] It is unclear whether MWS took part in this reading, although the entry for November 19, 1816 may indicate PBS read Plutarch aloud to her.[29] It is also unclear how much of Plutarch MWS had read or we are meant to think the Creature reads. The Creature notes that he was "led to admire peaceable law-givers, Numa, Solon, and Lycurgus, in preference to Romulus and Theseus" (*F* 2.7: 90). Theseus and Romulus make up the first pair in the extant *Lives*, Lycurgus and Numa the second; Solon comes in the third pair with the Roman Poplicola.[30] Thus the Creature is explicitly represented as reading the first five of *Plutarch's Lives*, though not necessarily the entire collection. MWS returns to Plutarch in her later work, including a direct reference in her next novel *The Last Man* (1826), a possible allusion in her last novel *Falkner* (1837), and as a model for the biographies she wrote for Lardner's *Cabinet Cyclopedia* (1829–1846).[31]

Plutarch's *Lives* are relevant to *Frankenstein* in several ways. First, as Macdonald and Scherf observe, "[i]t is appropriate that a being in search of his own origins should find himself reading these stories of the origins of society. It is particularly important that the first words he reads, the introduction to the life of Theseus ... should be a meditation on the difficulty of investigating origins."[32] Macdonald and Scherf go on to focus on the parallel between the Creature and Theseus as individual figures in search of their fathers (although Theseus may be distasteful to the Creature, since he is also a killer of monsters). However, those editors do not take up the further link the Creature himself makes between the *Lives* and his observations of the De Laceys: "The patriarchal lives of my protectors caused these impressions [i.e., what he read in Plutarch] to take a firm hold on my mind" (F 2.7: 90). In the Creature's eyes, the peaceable behavior of the De Laceys proves correct the social theories of Numa, Solon, and Lycurgus as represented in Plutarch: in other words, the Creature sees the De Laceys and these ancient figures as leading parallel lives.[33] Given these parallels, the Creature believes he can extrapolate from the domestic (via the De Laceys) to the political (via Plutarch's statesmen).[34] He subsequently comes to see the importance of membership in a community—a lesson perhaps reinforced through Lycurgus's Sparta—and valorizes the heterosexual, patriarchal family as a model sociopolitical community.[35] However, as Macdonald and Scherf rightly note, the Creature's future actions will mirror not the De Laceys' community-oriented acts but the murders (including patricide) committed by Theseus and Romulus.[36]

The Creature's word "impressions" merits closer attention, as it may allude to a part of Plutarch's *Lives* not included in the Creature's list—the *Life of Alexander*, which, as noted above, PBS was reading in November 1816, possibly aloud to MWS.[37] In the *Life of Alexander*, Plutarch compares his biographical method to portraiture (1.3): he claims to provide the "impression of [the] character" (ἔμφασιν ἤθους; 1.2) of his subject so as to reveal "the signs of [his subject's] soul" (τὰ τῆς ψυχῆς σημεῖα; 1.3).[38] When the Creature speaks, then, of how the De Laceys confirmed "these impressions" in his mind, he demonstrates his careful reading and understanding of Plutarch's intended program in the *Lives*.

The Creature also repeatedly evokes Plutarch's moral language: as Plutarch states in the *Life of Alexander*, he records the deeds of his subjects in service of the "revelation of virtue and vice" (δήλωσις ἀρετῆς καὶ κακίας; 1.2).[39] The Creature recounts to Victor that the *Lives* "taught me high thoughts; [Plutarch] elevated me above the wretched sphere of my own reflections, to admire and love the heroes of past ages . . . I read of men concerned in public affairs governing or massacring their species. I felt the greatest ardour for *virtue* rise within me, and abhorrence for *vice*" (F 2.7: 89–90, emphasis added). The *Lives* thus offer a model of virtue that the Creature wants to choose but feels compelled to reject, first due to his own rejection by the De Laceys (2.7–8), then due to Victor's refusal to make him a female counterpart (3.3). Notably, when the Creature attempts to persuade Victor to make this mate and spells out the consequences of Victor's refusal, he employs Plutarch's moralizing language: "If I have no ties and no affections, hatred and *vice* must be my portion ... My *vices* are the children of a forced solitude that I abhor; and my *virtues* will necessarily arise when I live in communion with an equal" (2.9: 103–104, emphasis added).[40]

The Creature's use of such moralizing language in terms of social relations—"ties," "affections," "solitude," "communion"—points to yet another way Plutarch's

Lives becomes important for *Frankenstein*. The *Lives* are a study not merely in individual virtue, but in virtue as practiced between individuals—that is, as applied to kin, friendship, and alliances. Alexander the Great's ambitions ultimately cause him to turn against his friends.[41] In the *Life of Pompey*, Pompey's kin and friendships both help and harm him: Pompey is virtuous for loyally committing murder on the behalf of the general Sulla, excusable for making political mistakes due to marriage ties, and inexcusably weak in dealings with friends.[42] Cato the Younger's refusal of friendship with Pompey through a marriage alliance leads Pompey to marry Julius Caesar's daughter; Plutarch treats this as the cause of the civil wars that destroy the Roman Republic (*Cato the Younger* 30.2–6).[43] The bonds of kin and friendship thus become crucial to one's ultimate success or failure.

This is reflected in *Frankenstein*. The Creature is driven to vice because he is denied kin and companionship. In contrast, Victor is offered affection and friendship from many—especially his father Alphonse, Elizabeth Lavenza, and Henry Clerval—yet he repeatedly refuses these kin and friends at crucial moments, failing to reply to (or even read) letters from family (1.4: 38–1.5: 43; 3.2: 116), delaying his marriage to Elizabeth (3.1: 108–109), and leaving Clerval behind during their tour of Scotland (3.2: 116–117, which leads to Clerval's death in 3.4: 126–127). Victor tellingly remarks that, during his and Clerval's tour of the Lake District, "some acquaintances … almost contrived to cheat me into happiness" (3.2: 115). For his part, Clerval reveals that he has learned the lessons of Plutarch. Indeed, the novel's first indirect reference to the *Lives* comes when Clerval attempts to console Victor upon the death of William: Clerval says, "Even Cato wept over the dead body of his brother" (1.6: 48), alluding to Cato the Younger's grief upon the death of his (half-)brother Caepio (*Life of Cato the Younger* 11.2–4, 15.4).[44] Victor thus struggles throughout *Frankenstein* to practice the virtue in his personal relationships that Plutarch presents as crucial to success, happiness, and humanity in the *Lives*.

Finally, Plutarch may also serve as one inspiration for MWS's use of three narrators: just as Plutarch presents *pairs* of biographies so that the reader may compare and contrast the lives, so does *Frankenstein* juxtapose its three narrators—Robert Walton, Victor Frankenstein, and the Creature—to invite a comparison of their 'parallel lives.'[45] For example, Walton may share Victor's ambition and thirst for scientific discovery, yet he acts in ways that are not only crucially different from Victor but also introduced prior to Victor's actions: in this way, readers are prepared to recognize Victor's vices. Walton writes to his sister Margaret Saville—another MWS—on a fairly regular basis, despite being on an expedition to the Arctic north (Letters 1–4). He takes great care for the delirious and dying stranger, Victor, a kindness that anticipates Clerval's care for Victor (1.4: 39–43). Even the Creature pointedly describes Walton as "You, who call Frankenstein your friend" (3.7: 160) and declines to harm him, despite such an affiliation. In his final speech, the Creature claims that his suffering is beyond such comparison—"No crime, no mischief, no malignity, no misery, can be found comparable to mine" (ibid.)—but, in making this claim, he invites Walton and readers to seek out such parallels. Thus Plutarch's *Lives* not only shapes the Creature's 'impressions' of political life and moral virtue, but may also provide a template for *Frankenstein*'s larger narrative structure, with repeated comparisons or parallels making possible its various revelations of the 'signs of its characters' souls.'

The *Frankenstein* Tradition: The Case of Scalzi (and Jared)

Frankenstein's engagement with Plutarch's *Lives* raises questions about moral ambiguities, and these questions have remained of interest to the genre arguably founded by MWS's novel: SF. Even as what counts as 'science' has changed, SF has continued to frame ethical questions in response to scientific theory and technological advances, often with reference to materials from classical antiquity.

To take just one example, we consider John Scalzi's 2006 novel, *The Ghost Brigades* (the sequel to *Old Man's War* [2005]). Set in a generically familiar future of interstellar colonization and space-based warfare, *The Ghost Brigades* centers around a genetically and technologically enhanced soldier named Jared Dirac. Like his fellow soldiers, Jared is created in a laboratory from the DNA of deceased humans and born into a fully mature, adult body; however, he has no memories or life-experience. To begin his education, on the first evening of his existence Jared is made to read the revised 1831 edition of MWS's *Frankenstein*. Contemplating his place in humanity, Jared recognizes himself in the Creature (93–94):

> He and all the members of the 8th—all of the Special Forces soldiers—were the spiritual descendants of the pathetic creature Victor Frankenstein had assembled from the bodies of the dead and then jolted back into life. Jared saw how Frankenstein felt pride in creating life, but how he feared and rejected the creature once that life had been given; how the creature lashed out, killing the doctor's family and friends, and how creator and created were finally consumed in a pyre, their fates interlocked. The allusions between the monster and the Special Forces were all too obvious.

Jared is rapt with how the Creature reflects himself and his fellow soldiers. Not satiated with MWS's novel, he "greedily [seeks] out links to the text" (94) and watches every film version he can find. Still not satisfied, Jared broadens the scope of his search to include other SF stories about "created beings," which he understands as reaching back to MWS and forming a *Frankenstein* tradition of which he himself is a part (95):

> Jared tried another tack and sought out stories of other created beings, and was soon acquainted with Friday, R. Deneel Olivaw, Data, HAL, Der Machinen-Mensch, Astro Boy, the various Terminators, Channa Fortuna, Joe the Robot Bastard and all manner of other droids, robots, computers, replicants, clones and genetically-engineered whatsits that were as much the spiritual descendants of Frankenstein's monster as he was.

Jared thus sketches a genealogy of humanistic inquiry into fictional images of artificial life after *Frankenstein*. Next, in a move that resonates with MWS's own work, "Jared moved backward in time from Shelley to find" earlier examples. These include such medieval and early modern figures as "golems, homunculi, [and] clockwork automatons." Most pertinent to this volume's topic, Jared also finds the example of Pygmalion (95): a sculptor from Greco-Roman myth who wrought a statue of a human woman from ivory—which was then brought to life by the goddess Venus, to the delight of its sculptor, who had fallen in love with it (esp. Ovid *Metamorphoses* 10.243–297).[46]

With its main character tracing his 'spiritual descent' to a figure from ancient myth, *The Ghost Brigades* exemplifies how SF in *Frankenstein*'s wake transmits and transmutes classical, Greco-Roman materials. Not only *Frankenstein* itself but also its sources, contemporaries, and subsequent traditions together form rich sites for classical receptions. As we see in both the novel's subtitle and in the quotation found just below—Adam's existential complaint to God from Milton's *Paradise Lost*—*Frankenstein* emphasizes how classical receptions help modern SF raise ethical and moral questions. This begins with Frankenstein's Creature, who educates himself by reading 'classic' texts (*F* 2.7: 88–90)—including not only *Paradise Lost* but also the literal, ancient classic discussed in the previous section, Plutarch's *Lives*.

MWS's Creature thus provides a model or prototype for Scalzi's soldier: not just physical, insofar as Jared is reconstituted from the deceased, but also psychological or even spiritual, as Jared frames his reading of *Frankenstein* as a moral lesson in emulation of the Creature. Both Jared and the Creature—both of these modern SF monsters—provide a suggestive parallel for how we can understand classical receptions in the tradition of *Frankenstein*: from

Frankenstein's Creature on, modern Promethean creatures read ancient classics as such; and so, too, may we, who might think of ourselves as postmodern Promethean creatures, read those classics through the lens of MWS's novel.

This is an exciting aspect of how *Frankenstein* refracts ancient materials into new genres of storytelling. Since *Frankenstein* is a foundational work of modern SF, and since science fictional visions of speculative, futuristic science have virtually become 'the mainstream' of modern popular culture, what we discover about the novel's classical receptions will bear on the roles played by ancient classics in modern culture more generally. To give an impression of that possibility, in the next section we discuss some of the urgent ethical questions raised by modernity, to which answers may be sought in *Frankenstein*'s classical receptions.

Frankenstein's Classical Receptions and Twenty-First-Century Questions

A SF character like Scalzi's Jared represents a version of ourselves; and like Jared, too, we may see ourselves in Frankenstein figures and their ancient antecedents like Pygmalion's statue and Pandora. Indeed, we are invited, in the manner of Plutarch, to look for parallels with other ancient figures like the animated bronze giant Talos (Apollonius of Rhodes *Argonautica* 4.1638–1693), the inventor Daedalus or his sadly more famous son, Icarus (Ovid *Metamorphoses* 8.183–235), or even the hybrid creature Daedalus helped produce, the Minotaur.[47] Mediated by *Frankenstein*, these and other ancient figures might suggest things about humankind and the nature of human being in our modern, technoscientific world. Even if we are not quite the "race of devils" feared by MWS's Victor (*F* 3.3: 119), it could seem right to say that we human beings are still somehow 'Other.' Thus it has been said, with deliberate ambiguity, "we live in a time of monsters."[48]

Frankenstein and its traditions have been important sources for articulating such visions of the modern world. For some, Victor's 'hubris' has been reflected in potentially destructive technoscientific advances. Mainstream press has routinely referred to genetically modified foods (GMO) as 'Frankenfoods.' Scientists are able to clone non-human animals, and stories surface of interest in, if not attempts at, cloning humans. The news brims with reports suggesting that true artificial intelligence is on the verge of fruition. Displaced visions of these ideas appear in fictional narratives in *Frankenstein*'s traditions, especially in SF, along with feelings of excitement and fear. Such technoscientific advances promise ever more intimate connections between organic, biological humans and inorganic machines, which provoke recurrent concerns.[49] As the boundaries that separate the human or natural from the machine or technological grow blurrier, what distinguishes human from monster?

The presence of classical receptions in SF as inaugurated by *Frankenstein* invites us to meditate on these seemingly modern concerns in terms of ancient myths of technology, like Daedalus's waxen wings, Talos's dual nature as human being and bronze statue, and of course—with its apparently endless resonance— Prometheus's theft of fire and creation of humankind. It is partly by 'receiving' such stories—transmitting them in pieces, transmuting them for new purposes, transforming them—that *Frankenstein* retains its prescient power. In other words, part of that power may be found in similarities between how a given work in *Frankenstein*'s traditions recomposes ancient materials and Victor Frankenstein's prototypical reanimation of the patchwork Creature.[50] The results are not always pleasant or regarded positively; indeed, Victor's revulsion upon first seeing his creation, the Creature's antipathy toward his creator, and the Creature's own self-loathing anticipate some current responses to novel technologies and the prospect of artificial creation of new life forms.

To put that more positively, *Frankenstein* and its traditions help us challenge certain ancient stories, by definition pre-industrial, as possibly too complacent in the face of technoscientific change or as too blithely unconcerned about unintended consequences. If ancient classics continue to form part of our 'humanities,' then how might they be read as the definition of 'humanity' undergoes technoscientific change? An example would be Ovid's blissful version of Pygmalion and his statue (*Metamorphoses* 10.243–297). When the Creature chastises Victor for bestowing his "spark of existence" (*F* 2.8: 95), classicists may hear an echo not just of Milton's Adam, as on the novel's frontispiece, but also of a different poem, Lucan's *Bellum civile*: a corpse revived by the witch Erichtho finds its second life a burden, and the narrator calls the act of reanimation 'unholy' (*nefas*; 6.526).[51] With this sort of echo, *Frankenstein* complicates Ovid's version of Pygmalion, whose ending is straightforwardly happy, but whose animated statue seems to have no inner life of her own.[52] That failure of perspective is made up for in modern thought about non-human life, recalling questions raised already in *Frankenstein* about the right to make or take life and the power to include or exclude from society.

In these contexts, Victor's primal, Promethean act of creation evokes concerns about biopower and biopolitics (including sovereign control over biological life), issues with urgent implications for modern society that yet relate to ancient stories.[53] *Frankenstein* may thus be read as interrogating ancient discourses in ways that speak to ongoing concerns about politics and society in the global twenty-first century. For example, the Creature's violent expulsion from the De Laceys' hut after his sole attempt at belonging (*F* 2.7–8: 93–95) and his relegation to solitary locales (e.g., 2.2: 65–70, 2.8: 95–99) articulate themes about the individual and society that look back to classical political thought: we might think of Aristotle ranking political inclusion as essential for a good life (*Politics* 1252b). Similarly, Sophocles' famous "Ode to Man" (*Antigone* 334–383) juxtaposes the sovereign power to grant a position of privileged inclusion (ὑψίπολις; 370) with the power to exclude from the polis (ἄπολις).[54] By echoing such ancient examples, *Frankenstein* anticipates contemporary political thought from authors like Michel Foucault, Giorgio Agamben, and Judith Butler, all of whom consciously reach back to—and also offer critique of—classical antiquity.[55]

Related issues are raised by Victor's initial description of the Creature: his "dull yellow eye ... yellow skin ... hair ... of a lustrous black ... teeth of a pearly whiteness [and] straight black lips" (*F* 1.4: 35). This passage has been linked with "terms ... commonly encountered in colonial depictions of Asian, Indian, and African 'savages.'" The Creature's composite nature, taken to mark him as abject and subhuman, represents the challenge posed by hybridity to monolithic authority.[56] These sorts of discourses, considered colonial or colonizing, recall ancient Greek and Roman ethnography, which frequently categorized 'other' cultures and races as 'barbarian' and 'monstrous' (e.g., Ctesias's and Megasthenes' accounts of India; Pliny's descriptions of monstrous races of men in *Natural History* 7.2).[57] The Creature's struggles for inclusion in society and for identification as human speak to current biopolitical crises, including the Black Lives Matter movement, struggles for LGBTQ protections and rights, the plight of Syrian refugees across Europe, and Islamophobia throughout the West. Although we do not mean to suggest any simple equivalence between ancient ethnographical taxonomies and modern structures of injustice including systemic racisms, nonetheless modern Orientalizing discourses, alive in MWS's context, can be linked to modes of thought inherited from classical antiquity.[58]

In these and other ways, *Frankenstein* accommodates ethical responses to ongoing technoscientific developments in part via classical receptions. The *Frankenstein* traditions thus form part of an intertwining of mythic and scientific discourses that has taken place since antiquity. The marvelous promises of progress and the terrible potential for chaos unleashed by Prometheus's theft of fire are all around us. MWS's *Modern Prometheus* serves as a mediating prism for many issues that were articulated in the ancient world, that were of concern in MWS's time, and that remain of urgent interest today. Not coincidentally these sorts of issues are also of great interest to ancient literature and modern SF alike, both of which probe many of the same fundamental questions of boundaries: between human and monster, between inclusion and exclusion, between licit and illicit knowledge.⁵⁹

These shared ethical concerns are emphasized by shared aesthetic strategies. Ancient literature and modern SF generate cognitive estrangement through their construction of worlds at once familiar and defamiliarizing, whether wondrous or disturbingly uncanny. Ultimately, classical myth and science fiction each offer estranging distance from the known, the normal, and the now (be it temporal, epistemological, or metaphysical), and allows for reflection upon the contemporary world.⁶⁰ For two centuries now, *Frankenstein* has served as an important link between antiquity and modernity, suggesting that ongoing discussions of contemporary issues in science, society, technology, and more will continue to be enriched by ancient materials.

Outline of the Volume

Frankenstein and Its Classics: The Modern Prometheus from Antiquity to Science Fiction is the first volume of essays devoted to classical receptions in *Frankenstein* and its traditions. All together the chapters offer an invitation—for readers of *Frankenstein* and the traditions it has inspired, for viewers of the many film versions and adaptations, and for scholars and students of Classics, SF studies, Romanticism, and more—to explore some of the ancient roots of MWS's paradigmatically 'modern' monster.

The chapters are organized roughly chronologically, emphasizing thematic connections and raising shared questions. The first group of essays, "Promethean Heat," primarily explores *Frankenstein*'s engagement with the past, focusing on events and materials preceding the novel's composition and publication in 1816–1818. The chapters in this section illustrate some of the ways in which MWS's novel transmits and transmutes ancient sources both directly and via the intermediary of other works. This section suggests that MWS drew not only on experiments in electricity and galvanism to give life to her novel, but also drew energy of sorts—call it 'heat'—from Greco-Roman antiquity.

Genevieve Liveley—in "Patchwork Paratexts and Monstrous Metapoetics: 'After tea M reads Ovid'"—examines classical aspects of MWS's Romanticism, especially in *Frankenstein*, by focusing on her engagement with the Roman poet Ovid's great epic, the *Metamorphoses*. Drawing on documentary evidence including MWS's own journals and letters, Liveley shows how *Frankenstein*'s composition may be linked to MWS's complex reading of the *Metamorphoses*, sometimes in the original Latin—indeed, seemingly more often than for many ancient texts—and sometimes in certain modern translations. Liveley thus argues that important aspects of *Frankenstein*, including its complex embedded narrations and collage-like mode of storytelling, are linked historically to MWS's reading of Ovid.

Martin Priestman—in "Prometheus and Dr. Darwin's Vermicelli: Another Stir to the *Frankenstein* Broth"—delves into how *Frankenstein* is informed by multiple versions of the Prometheus myth to be found in the ancient authors Hesiod (*Theogony, Works and Days*), Aeschylus (*Prometheus Bound*), and Ovid (*Metamorphoses*). Priestman connects the Prometheus traditions of classical antiquity, including depictions of the Titan as both 'fire-thief' (*pyrphoros*) and 'creator of humankind' (*plasticator*), with their revival in the scientific milieu of the late eighteenth century. Examining how authors including Benjamin Franklin, Immanuel Kant, and especially Erasmus Darwin make their own references to Prometheus and other ancient figures, Priestman argues that, since their writings influenced MWS and her circle, they provide another category of sources for *Frankenstein*'s classical receptions.

Andrew McClellan turns to MWS's engagement with another contemporary concept in "The Politics of Revivification in Lucan's *Bellum Civile* and Mary Shelley's *Frankenstein*." McClellan suggests that MWS's depiction in *Frankenstein* of the Creature's manner of animation may be rethought through comparison with imagery of 'revivification' in two linked writings: the ancient Roman poet Lucan's epic of the war between Caesar and Pompey, *Bellum civile*, and writing about the French Revolution and Napoleon. By relating the Creature's animation to poetic and documentary images of the grotesqueries of war, McClellan argues for a reinvigorated attention to the contemporary political aspects and allegories of *Frankenstein*'s classical receptions.

Suzanne L. Barnett—in "Romantic Prometheis and the Molding of *Frankenstein*"—develops a complementary image of how *Frankenstein* engages with the figure of Prometheus by focusing on some lesser-known Romantic literary forms taken by the ancient Titan. Barnett examines how *Frankenstein* offers a novel version of Prometheus thanks to MWS drawing on a diverse and sometimes contradictory storehouse of classical allusions in somewhat earlier and contemporary authors including John Frank Newton, William Godwin, Mary Wollstonecraft, and Erasmus Darwin. Emphasizing that PBS's *Prometheus Unbound* (1820) was not even drafted until after the publication of *Frankenstein* (January 1818), Barnett argues that MWS's novel exerts its own great influence on Romantic Prometheism both directly and by proxy of PBS's writings.

David A. Gapp discusses some of the climate science behind *Frankenstein* in "Why the 'Year without a Summer'?" MWS famously began work on what would become her novel in response to a 'ghost story challenge' during the summer of

1816, the so-called 'Year without a Summer,' when she and companions on vacation were beset by "wet" and "uncongenial" weather. Gapp investigates those settings as reported in both contemporary writings and up-to-date scientific work, with a special focus on the effects of the 1815 eruption of Mt. Tambora and its aftermath. Gapp thus offers a rich description of the extra-literary context for *Frankenstein*'s conception and a more detailed explanation for the dreary, 'Promethean' landscapes of the novel.

Revisiting this dreary landscape of *Frankenstein*, Matthew Gumpert—in "The Sublime Monster: *Frankenstein*, or The Modern Pandora"—offers a different way of viewing *Frankenstein*'s monstrosities and dreary landscapes that is intended to complement existing readings of the Creature, especially, as 'monstrous' or, as in MWS's phrase, "hideous." Gumpert argues that the Creature, like his habitual landscapes including the Arctic where he meets his apparent end, receive negative reactions not because of ugliness but rather because of an excess of 'the sublime.' A crucial quality in Romantic ideology derived from ancient literary criticism, the sublime allows Gumpert to suggest that, if Victor is "the modern Prometheus," then the Creature recalls the Titan's counterpart in ancient myth, the synthetic human woman—and sublimely beautiful—Pandora.

The second group of essays, "Hideous Progeny," examines *Frankenstein*'s role in mediating the reception of Greco-Roman myth, literature, and thought in later works of art and literature. Elements that *Frankenstein* brings into popular awareness—iconic scenes, the figure of the 'mad scientist,' the very idea of a synthetic, pseudo-human monster—are inflected with Greek and Roman material. From this perspective, many spaces characteristic of modern culture, especially in SF, are haunted by the "daemons" or "devils" of the ancient world, a "hideous progeny" whose swarming vitality its author could not have foreseen.

Benjamin Eldon Stevens—in "Cupid and Psyche in *Frankenstein*: Mary Shelley's Apuleian Science Fiction?"—continues Part One's focus on MWS's engagement with ancient literature. Stevens considers *Frankenstein*'s climactic 'bedroom tableau' (Victor's discovery that the Creature has killed Elizabeth on their wedding-night) in a tradition of similar scenes originating in the ancient Latin author Apuleius's novel, *Metamorphoses* or the *Golden Ass*. Drawing on documentary evidence including MWS's journals and letters, Stevens argues that MWS repeatedly rewrites Apuleius's story of Cupid and Psyche, originally a happy allegory of the soul's capacity for love and pleasure, to emphasize darker themes of fragmented personhood and frustrated love. Exploring variations on those themes in *Frankenstein* and throughout MWS's works, especially *The Last Man* (1826), Stevens concludes by asking what it would mean to read *Frankenstein* and its traditions as representing an 'Apuleian' kind of SF.

Carl A. Rubino—in "The Pale Student of Unhallowed Arts: Frankenstein, Aristotle, and the Wisdom of Lucretius"—interrogates how *Frankenstein* engages with several ancient Greek and Roman philosophies. Focusing especially on the novel's lasting depiction of scientific inquiry as raising difficult ethical questions, Rubino ranges widely from Aristotelian ethics and Epicurean atomism to modern thermodynamics, chaos theory, and the invention of the mad scientist's assistant in later adaptations of the novel. Ultimately, Rubino suggests that *Frankenstein* incorporates such ancient philosophy into its status as modern template for a cautionary tale, Lucretian at its heart, whose moral is that "there is a Frankenstein in all of us."

This focus on scientific ethics, including public and institutional perceptions of 'cautionary tales,' takes a psychedelic turn in Neşe Devenot's "Timothy Leary and the Psychodynamics of Stealing Fire." Devenot breaks new ground by examining the longstanding connection between *Frankenstein* and scientific ethics through the lens of overt Promethean themes in Timothy Leary's psychedelic research and activism. Devenot explores how Leary frames his contentious interactions with 'establishment' limits on scientific research in terms drawn explicitly from popular understandings of *Frankenstein* as a cautionary tale about scientific hubris. In contexts of public and institutional constraints on research, Leary presents himself as a Prometheus figure offering revolutionary technology—first psychopharmacology, later virtual reality—in parallel to the ancient Titan's theft of fire from Olympian Zeus. Focusing especially on Leary's experimental autobiography, *High Priest* (1968), Devenot argues that Leary draws directly on Victor Frankenstein's creation of the Creature so as to offer a corrective to the pessimism traditionally found in MWS's novel.

Jesse Weiner—in "Frankenfilm: Classical Monstrosity in Bill Morrison's *Spark of Being*"—interrogates ways in which constructions of monstrosity in Frankensteinian film reach back to classical antiquity. Weiner focuses on Bill Morrison's *Spark of Being* (2010), a film adaptation of MWS's novel made entirely from spliced reels of found-footage celluloid film, 'dug up' from cinema archives in a way parallel to how Victor assembled material for his Creature. On Weiner's reading, *Spark of Being* taps into at least two of the classical filiations for 'monstrosity' and 'monsters': one based on the idea of transgression or hybridity, the other based on the etymology of 'showing' and therefore viewing. Weiner thus argues that Morrison, in a self-conscious mode informed by aesthetic statements by the Roman authors Horace and Cicero, creates a fragmentary and allusive film that positions both itself and its viewers as monsters.

Continuing a focus on film, Emma Hammond—in "Alex Garland's *Ex Machina* or The Modern Epimetheus"—explores a recent and celebrated example of *Frankenstein*'s legacy in SF film, Alex Garland's *Ex Machina* (2015). Situating *Ex Machina* in a context of other influential cinematic visions of artificial life, Hammond explores how this tradition continues to raise concerns about the possibility of artificial intelligence. With its main character Ava marked as a dangerous *femme fatale*, special attention is paid to how concerns about artificial intelligence are framed in gendered terms, with a tradition of artificial women that look back to the ancient figure of Pandora. Ultimately, Hammond suggests that, in the sort of shape provided by *Ex Machina*, ancient Pandora and MWS's Creature prefigure the Turing test, raising troubling questions about whether an artificial being can 'pass' as human.

Rounding out Part Two, Brett M. Rogers—in "The Postmodern Prometheus and Posthuman Reproductions in Science Fiction"—examines recent versions of the Greek and Roman mythic figure most central to *Frankenstein*, Prometheus, and his continued role in debates about human reproduction in the context of modern technoscience. Rogers focuses on two examples of SF that raise questions about biotechnological intervention in 'human being' and practice overt classical receptions, Ridley Scott's film *Prometheus* (2012) and Matt Fraction's and Christian Ward's comics series *Ody-C* (2014–). In their own ways, the film and the comics series envision worlds in which biological reproduction is complicated by technoscience, entailing shifts in the boundaries of the 'human.' Ultimately, Rogers argues that visions of ancient Prometheus mediated by *Frankenstein* may lead us to unintended and unimaginable outcomes, "hideous progeny" that reconstitute humanity, human knowledge, and society on fundamental levels.

In the spirit of *Frankenstein*'s endlessly ramifying influence, the volume concludes with "Other Modern Prometheis: Suggestions for Further Reading and Viewing," in which Samuel Cooper offers an annotated list of works in *Frankenstein*'s traditions with special focus on classical receptions.

Notes

1 See Gapp (this volume).
2 *Fantasmagoriana* was published in French in 1812 (anonymously) by Jean-Baptiste Benoît Eyriès, adapting stories from German sources. The title page includes a quotation from classical literature: *falsis terroribus implet*, "he fills [sc. his breast] with terrifying falsehoods" or "imagined fears," attributed to "Horat.", i.e., the first-century BCE Roman poet Horace (*Epistulae* 2.1.212). An abridged English translation of *Fantasmagoriana*, published in 1815 (anonymously) by Sarah Elizabeth Utterson, replaces Horace with Shakespeare: "Graves, at

my command, / Have waked their sleeper; oped, and let them forth / By my so potent art" (*The Tempest* 5.1.48–50); for that speech of Prospero's, Shakespeare draws in turn on another ancient model, the witch Medea in Ovid's *Metamorphoses* (7.192–219). Certain stories from *Fantasmagoriana*, especially "The Family Portraits" and "The Death-Bride," may have exerted an influence on scenes in *Frankenstein*.

3 Reported in Polidori's June 18, 1816 diary entry; Rossetti (1911: 128). This story Polidori also related in a "Letter Prefaced to *The Vampyre* (1819)," in Hunter (2012: 169–170).
4 "Introduction to *Frankenstein*, Third Edition (1831)," in Hunter (2012: 167).
5 Ibid., 168.
6 Hogle (2002: 6).
7 *Frankenstein*'s (henceforth *F*) classical receptions are the focus of Weiner 2015a; some discussion is to be found in Rogers and Stevens (2015: 1–6, 8n11, and 9; after [2012a: 127–130]), Priestman 2007, Liveley 2006, Mellor (1988: 70–88), Small (1973: 48–67), and Pollin (1965: 101–103). On classical receptions and traditions more generally, see, e.g., the chapters in Hardwick and Stray (2008: esp. 13–25), Hardwick (2003: esp. 1–11).
8 See, e.g., Markley 2003, Wallace 1997, McWhir 1990.
9 See further below and the chapters by Barnett, Priestman, and Rogers (this volume).
10 On monsters in antiquity, see, e.g., Liveley 2006, Atherton 1998.
11 On SF and the classics, see Gloyn 2015, Rogers and Stevens (2015: esp. 1–19), Keen 2014, Bost-Fiévet and Provini 2014, Rogers and Stevens 2012a, Brown 2008, Keen 2006, and Fredericks 1980 and 1976. *F*'s foundational status for modern SF was first argued by Aldiss (1976: 38–44).
12 MWS imagines the future in her 1826 *The Last Man*; on its connections with classics, see discussion and sources in Stevens (this volume).
13 Vargo's (2016) chapter mentions Godwin's "account of the story of Prometheus" in *The Pantheon* (1806) and notes that PBS and Byron were "fascinated by the story": PBS "read Aeschylus's *Prometheus Bound* in 1817" (28–29); Vargo also describes the Arctic as like "a Hyperborean paradise" (31) and notes that the Creature's reading of Plutarch invokes "the politics of classical heroism" (34). Discussing Henny M. Milner's stage play *The Man and Monster; or, The Fate of Frankenstein* (1826), Hoeveler (2016: 181) identifies "Frankenstein as Prometheus and the monster as a vulture," while Punter (2016: 209) suggests that "mythologically Deucalion was Prometheus's son, as he was also responsible for the rebirth of mankind after the great flood" (209, discussing a series by horror writer Dean Koontz including a Creature called 'Deucalion' made by one 'Victor Helios').
14 *CCF* 144.
15 On scientific contexts for *F*, see Ziolkowski 1981, Knellwolf and Goodall 2008, Smith 2016c, Vargo (2016: 31–32), and Priestman (this volume).
16 *CCF* 143–144.
17 *CCF* 144.
18 Haggerty (2016: 119): "Queer theory can explain that the Promethean myth that [*F*] embodies does nothing less than explain what it is to be a human being" in terms of "monstrosity"; Mousley (2016: 161–162): "one of literature's most notorious Promethean over-reachers, [Victor] exemplifies the posthuman in the human" and "co-opts the role of a creator-god in a capricious act of individualistic hubris"; Punter (2016: 2015): *F* draws on "age-old myths to do with transgressive knowledge and human aspiration."
19 Punter (2016: 205). Cf. Wright (2016: 106 with n17), quoting Anne Mellor's reading of *F*'s Walton as "another Promethean poet, seeking to create a more perfect humanity by revealing

a new land of fire and light [sc. the Arctic] to man." A recent example of such doubling is the 2011 Royal National Theatre production of Nick Dear's stage play *Frankenstein*, in which actors Benedict Cumberbatch and Jonny Lee Miller alternated playing Victor and the Creature.

20. In a letter of July 1812, PBS expresses his "opinion ... that the evils of acquiring Greek and Latin considerably overbalance the benefit" (Ingpen [1915: 348–350]).
21. Unless otherwise specified, all references to *F* are to the 1818 edition in Hunter 2012.
22. Is MWS implying that the Creature confused these texts for "histories"—that is, for factual accounts of human pasts—or is she pointing to the Creature's native tongue, French, in which *histoire*, 'history,' also means 'fictional story'? Cf. Vargo (2016: 34), who notes that the Creature "does not seem able to separate fiction from reality."
23. In fact twenty-two pairs, one of which compares two pairs of statesmen. A twenty-third pair probably started the collection but does not survive; see Duff (1999: 2 with nn4–5).
24. For a thumbnail sketch of the afterlife of Plutarch's *Lives*, see ibid., 3–5.
25. On English editions of Plutarch, see Howard (1970: esp. 23); on other editions, 16–17.
26. Duff (1999: 4). Craciun (2016: 87) notes that Plutarch was a "favourite" in French revolutionary thought.
27. Vargo (2016: 35). Vargo also asserts that "Plutarch represents one of the key texts in Mary Shelley's own education by her father," but provides no clear evidence for this claim. Cf. Kelly (2000: 158), who links the reference to Plutarch, and such references and allusions in general, to political self-representation in the novels of the Godwin and Shelley coterie.
28. Feldman and Scott-Kilvert (1987: 126, 129, 146–147, 176, 247, 668). The journals also relate that PBS returns to Plutarch in 1819, and MWS (possibly in Greek) in 1824, as she relates in a letter to Thomas Jefferson Hogg (August 30, 1824); for the latter, see Bennett (1980: 446–447).
29. Cf. Vargo (2016: 35).
30. This sequence seems to have been the traditional order, although different editions change the order of later pairs: see Perrin (1959 [1914]: esp. ix–x).
31. Vargo (2016: 35).
32. Macdonald and Scherf (1999: 27).
33. Macdonald and Scherf (1999: 27–28) also speculate about what the Creature might have thought of Numa's use of "religious terrors"—to pacify the Romans—and the Spartan practice of eugenics.
34. See also Brooks (1979: 210) and Macdonald and Scherf (1999: 24).
35. Cf. Macdonald and Scherf (1999: 28): if Lycurgus's educational policies produce law-abiding Spartan citizens, then "Victor's abandonment of the monster is likely to produce a lawless outcast."
36. Macdonald and Scherf (1999: 27), who also point to Leonard Wolf's suggestion that MWS, the daughter of Mary Wollstonecraft, might have found Theseus and Romulus unsatisfactory since "Theseus was a serial rapist and Romulus was a mass rapist."
37. MWS and PBS also read the *Life of Alexander* by Quintus Curtius Rufus several times between July and November 1816; see Feldman and Scott-Kilvert (1987: 669) and Hurst (2006: 59).
38. Duff (1999: 15–17), with additional reference to Plutarch's *Life of Cato the Younger* (24.1). This presumed link between physical appearance and moral virtue is one of the central problems explored in *F*.
39. On moral virtue in Plutarch, see Duff (1999: esp. 13–71). Duff is careful to note the importance Plutarch places not on larger actions but rather on "the smaller matters of everyday life and interaction with others" (15).

40 Even the Creature's final speech is steeped in Plutarch's moralizing language: "Oh, it is not thus—not thus... yet such must be the impression conveyed to you by what appears to be the purport of my actions.... No sympathy may I ever find. When I first sought it, it was the love of virtue, the feelings of happiness and affection with which my whole being overflowed, that I wished to be participated. But now, that virtue has become to me a shadow.... But now vice has degraded me beneath the meanest animal" (*F* 3.7: 159–160).
41 Duff (1999: 85–86).
42 Ibid., 276–277.
43 Ibid., 135.
44 Macdonald and Scherf (1999: 28 with 297–298), who also note that the allusion to Cato is removed from the 1831 edition of *F*.
45 Gilbert and Gubar (1979) similarly observe that *F* "consists of three 'concentric circles' of narration" (224). Cf. Weiner's discussion of *F* and Bill Morrison's film *Spark of Being* (this volume).
46 Like Frankenstein's Creature, Pygmalion's ivory woman—sometimes called Galatea—may be a patchwork assemblage of parts; see Salzman-Mitchell 2008. Beyond *F*, SF versions of Pygmalion's story include, e.g., the film *Weird Science* (John Hughes 1985), whose protagonists are inspired by watching James Whale's 1931 *Frankenstein*, Richard Powers's 1995 novel *Galatea 2.2*, and the *Star Trek: Voyager* episode "Someone to Watch Over Me" (S5E22, Robert Duncan McNeill 1999). Many such versions recall George Cukor's 1964 film version of Lerner's and Lowe's 1956 stage musical *My Fair Lady*, itself based on George Bernard Shaw's 1913 play *Pygmalion*. See James 2011 and Wosk 2015.
47 Talos and Pygmalion are discussed in connection with SF by Raphael (2015: 182–188).
48 Cohen (1996a: vii); cf. Liveley 2006.
49 See Haraway 1991 and Liveley 2006. The timeliness of these questions and the continued relevance of *F* at its bicentennial manifest in the June 25–July 1, 2016 issue of *The Economist*, entitled "March of the machines: A special report on artificial intelligence" and invoking *F* at several points.
50 For such similarities, see esp. Weiner 2015a.
51 See further McClellan (this volume).
52 See further sources cited in n46, above.
53 See esp. Agamben 1998 and Foucault (2003: 243–246).
54 See Weiner 2015c.
55 The biopolitics of Foucault and Agamben are taken up by Butler 2000 and interrogated by Butler and Spivak 2007. MacCormack (2012: 297–303) connects monstrosity to biopolitics with an invocation of "Frankensteinian man-making goals" (299n9).
56 Quoted material Hirsch (1996: 118), who writes that the creature is "terrifying not merely in his physical otherness, but more profoundly in his call for recognition as a humane, if not also human, being." See further Bhabha 1994 and O'Connor 2014.
57 On ancient distinctions between Greek or Roman and 'others' (e.g., 'barbarian' and 'monster'), see esp. Hall 1989, Friedman 2000, and Cartledge 2002. Rossi-Reder 2002 links nineteenth-century racisms and colonial discourses with classical accounts of India and Africa. Williams (1996: 107–108) argues that Isidore (sixth to seventh century CE) drew upon Pliny to propose a taxonomy of monstrosity that 'normalized' the European human body. *F* contains other elements of Orientalism: e.g., Volney's *Ruins of Empires* (1791) has the Creature hearing "of the slothful Asiatics," "the stupendous genius and mental activity of the Grecians," and "the wars and wonderful virtue of the early Romans" (2.5); cf. Weiner 2016.

58 See esp. Said 1978. Said traces Orientalism back to Homer and suggests that, "as early as Aeschylus's play *The Persians*," Orientalizing discourses transformed "far and often threatening Otherness" into reductive, totalizing, and Western-centric symbols (29).
59 On one cautionary SF tale about questioning the boundaries of licit knowledge through the classics, see Weiner 2015b.
60 On cognitive estrangement in classics and SF, see Rogers and Stevens (2015: 11–19), after Suvin (1979).

Part One

Promethean Heat

1

Patchwork Paratexts and Monstrous Metapoetics: "After tea M reads Ovid"

Genevieve Liveley

Mary Shelley's *Frankenstein* is, like its own monster, notoriously made up of disparate literary genres and parts, stitched together into a novel shape at once familiar and strange.[1] Amidst its patchwork of mismatched genres, we find fragments of epic, epistles, snatches of poetry, travelogue, and tragedy, as well as material from scientific, political, and philosophical treatises. Alongside bits and pieces taken from her father's novels, from various European ghost stories, and from Shakespeare, Milton, Goethe, Rousseau, and Locke, we find fresher meat cut from Wordsworth, Coleridge, and Percy Shelley (henceforth PBS), as well as from the latest scientific dissertations (especially on Erasmus Darwin's work and electrical galvanism).[2]

Yet, just as Victor Frankenstein garners the knowledge to animate his monstrous creation from both ancient and modern sources, it is the ancient corpus of the classical tradition that—indirectly and directly—provides Mary Shelley (henceforth MWS) with several of the core body parts for her ghost story. Recognizable bits and pieces are plundered from Aeschylus, Lucretius, Seneca, Lucan, Plutarch, and Ovid—especially Ovid's *Metamorphoses*.[3] What is more, by re-examining the paratexts to *Frankenstein* where MWS meditates upon her own poetics—adopting Genette's heuristic model of a 'paratext' as those materials "whose mere existence, if it is known to the public, makes some commentary on the text and bears on its reception"—we notice that her reading of Ovid in particular is mediated through a secondary patchwork of texts—a monstrous corpus made up of different translations, commentaries, notes, and illustrations.[4]

In this chapter, then, I want to take a closer look at MWS's engagement with Ovid. In particular, I want to propose a fresh evaluation of George Sandys's 1632 *Ouid's Metamorphosis Englished* in terms of the significant influence this key translation and commentary is likely to have had upon the reception of Ovid in *Frankenstein*. Sandys's work represents a crucial paratext that mediates MWS's access to Ovid, and therefore presents an important 'beside-text' for *Frankenstein* in its shaping of MWS's reading and reception of the *Metamorphoses*. Sandys's edition of *Ovid Englished* is also aptly enough, in Genette's terms, "composed of an assorted set of practices and discourses of all sorts and of all ages, ... [a] convergence of effects."[5] Its own patchwork of translation, commentary, quotation, cross-referencing, and illustration has much to contribute to our finer appreciation and understanding of what happens when MWS reads the *Metamorphoses* or—as the Godwin-Shelley journal for spring 1815 puts it—what happens when "M reads Ovid."[6]

Monstrous Metapoets: Ovidian Frankensteins

> My mind compels me to tell of shapes changed into new
> bodies; Gods (for you have inspired these changes too)
> inspire my work and from the first origins of the world
> up to my own times, spin out my continuous song.
>
> In *nova* fert animus mutatas dicere formas
> corpora; di, coeptis (nam vos mutastis et illas)
> adspirate meis primaque ab origine mundi
> ad mea perpetuum deducite tempora carmen.
>
> <div align="right">Ovid, <i>Metamorphoses</i> (<i>Met.</i>) 1.1–4</div>

Ovid's *Metamorphoses* is made up of incongruous literary genres and story parts, epic transformed into a novel shape (*nova*) at once familiar and strange.[7] This is a work which—like *Frankenstein*—repeatedly calls attention to its own veracity and believability, not least of all through its intricate structure of tales within tales, its biased narrators and credulous narratees, its monstrous humans and humanized monsters who demand our sympathy even while they invite our horror. Amidst this poetic patchwork of mismatched genres—again, like *Frankenstein*—we also find epic and epigram, elegy and epistle, travelogue, tragedy, science, politics, and philosophy fused together in a complex narrative form.[8]

Beyond these 'formal' parallels, there are a great many points of correspondence between *Frankenstein* and the *Metamorphoses*. The affinity between MWS and Ovid is perhaps most obviously signalled in the parallels between the central plot of *Frankenstein* and the choice bits of Ovid's *Metamorphoses* in which some human creature is brought to life. There is a remarkable number of such stories in Ovid's poem: Prometheus's creation of humankind from the elemental parts of chaos (1.76–88); Deucalion's and Pyrrha's transformation of hard stones into men and women (1.313–415); Medea's rejuvenation of Aeson (7.159–349); Pygmalion's creation of a woman from pieces of ivory (10.243–297); and Aesclepius's reanimation of the dismembered body parts of Hippolytus (15.479–546). Ovid's versions of these stories are each further remarkable for the dark tones and sombre hues in which they are depicted. Ovid does not focus *any* of these miraculous (re)creation narratives upon a successful dénouement. Instead, Ovid denies a happy ending to each of these characters. He chooses to follow the narrative of each story beyond the point of the miracle moment of (re)-vivification, moving forward in time to show the dreadful repercussions in the aftermath of each of these transformations.

Thus, when Ovid's Prometheus mixes together earth, water, and air to make the first human body, he unwittingly reintroduces conflict and chaos to the fragile equilibrium of the newly formed cosmos.[9] In Ovid's account, an unnamed deity had only recently imposed order and stability upon the primordial chaos by *separating* its hitherto warring elements—earth, water, and air (1.32–31). Prometheus's mistake in bringing them back together in that first human body is confirmed by the references in Ovid's narrative to the new earth (*recens tellus*; 1.80) only recently separated from the air (*seductaque nuper ab alto / aethere*; 80–81), which Prometheus now mixes with water (*mixtam pluvialibus undis*; 82). Prometheus's creature represents the re-embodiment of chaos and, as such, reintroduces conflict and disorder to the new world order.

Deucalion, child of Prometheus, and Pyrrha, child of Prometheus's brother Epimetheus, blindly repeat Prometheus's mistake when the time comes for *them* to recreate the human race—the first Promethean iteration having been wiped out in a cataclysmic flood sent by the gods as punishment for its violence and disorder. In this case, the couple lack Prometheus's technical skill, and the crude creation process they adopt brings to life men and women whose hearts and lives turn out to be as hard as the stones from which they are formed (*Met.* 1.414–415). Indeed, in Ovid's version of this story, Deucalion and Pyrrha are overtly censured for turning to artificial means of reproduction and for their failure to procreate naturally: Deucalion seeks to emulate his parent in this story but, Ovid suggests, might have done better to have simply become a parent himself.

Ovid's account of Medea's preparations for Aeson's rejuvenation emphasizes her dangerously 'Promethean' or Titanic character as her airborne search for magical herbs leads her to eye-up (*perspicit*; 7.226) "Mount Ossa, Mount Pelion, Othrys, Pindus, and higher Olympus" (224–225)—the very mountains that the Titans had once used in their fight to take Olympus from the gods. Medea's magical powers represent an analogous threat to the immortal gods no less than to humans in Ovid's tale: her rejuvenation of Aeson leads to the murder of Pelias (294–349), but her real crime, Ovid intimates, is rooted in her appropriation of powers properly reserved for the gods.

Ovid's Pygmalion story *appears* to offer a happy ending. But, as the story itself warns, appearances can be misleading (10.252). Ovid's narrative ends abruptly at the point of vivification, with the artist's creation opening frightened eyes and seeing for the first time her creator and the sky (10.293–294). A brief epilogue explains that Pygmalion's creature (she is never named in *Met*.) subsequently bears a child, Paphos. But Ovid is uncharacteristically silent on either Pygmalion's or his creature's reaction to her transformation and refrains from offering authorial comment on this. However, Pygmalion's quasi-incestuous desire for his own beautiful creation will lead in the next generation to an incestuous horror that deforms and destroys the lives of his descendants—casting a retrospective shadow and question-mark over the Pygmalion story too.[10]

Ovid's tale of Hippolytus, a strange mash-up of two mythic characters and their stories, offers a similar blend of light and dark. After Hippolytus dies in a tragic chariot crash, the pioneering doctor Aesclepius puts the pieces of his mangled body back together again. Successfully brought back to life by the doctor's arts and powerful herbs, Hippolytus is hidden away and given a new face—it is not clear whether this is to hide his disfigurement or to conceal from others the fact that he has been brought back from the grave—and a new name. He spends the rest of his life as Virbius (the name may suggest 'twice-born man,' *vir bis vivus*), living out of the way and out of sight in the woods (15.479–546), just as Frankenstein's Creature will do. Like that Creature, too, Virbius also blames his father for his cruel fate. As Ovid's *Metamorphoses* makes clear, the creation—or reanimation—of man (or woman) is a dark art, with consistently unpredictable and dangerous results.

Appropriately perhaps, given the dreadful repercussions that Ovid's own poetry would bring him in the form of his exile in 8 CE, these Ovidian creator/re-animator characters can be and have been read as metapoetic figures for the author of the *Metamorphoses* himself.[11] Their stories of re-animation and transformation serve as potent analogies for Ovid's own project to breathe new life into old, inert material or, as Ovid puts it in his programmatic proem, "to tell of forms changed into new bodies" (1.1). Similarly, MWS's creator/animator character has been read as a metapoetic figure for the author of *Frankenstein* too. In the 1818 edition, both Frankenstein and his Creature are represented as storytellers, self-referentially referring to the veracity of their 'narrations.' In her introduction to the revised 1831 edition, MWS retrospectively identifies herself with Victor in referring to the novel as her own "hideous progeny" (xii). What is more, in that same introduction, she refers to her inspiration for the story as "so very hideous an idea" (v); to Frankenstein's Creature as a "hideous phantasm of a man," a "hideous corpse" (x); and to all three as "my hideous phantom" (xi). She thus invites us to conflate the nightmare inspiration for her literary creation both with the text of *Frankenstein* and with Frankenstein's Creature, both of which "terrify the artist" responsible (x). She writes (v–xii, emphases added):

> How [did] I, then a young girl, come to think of, and to dilate upon, *so very hideous an idea*? ... I saw the pale student of unhallowed arts kneeling beside the thing he had put together. I saw *the hideous phantasm of a man* stretched out, and then, on the working of some powerful engine, show signs of life, and stir with an uneasy, half vital motion. Frightful must it be; for supremely frightful would be the effect of any human endeavour to mock the stupendous mechanism of the Creator of the world. *His success would terrify the artist*; he would rush away from his odious handywork, horror-stricken. He would hope that, left to itself, the slight spark of life which he had communicated would fade; that this thing, which had received such imperfect animation, would subside into dead matter; and he might sleep in the belief that the silence of the grave would quench for ever the transient existence of *the hideous corpse* which he had looked upon as the cradle of life.... I could not so easily get rid of my hideous phantom; still it haunted me.... And now, once again, I bid *my hideous progeny* go forth and prosper.

So inextricably connected are the monstrous metapoetics of this commentary that MWS conflates the opening of Victor's narrative of the making of *his* monstrous creation with the original opening of *hers*. MWS tells us that the morning after her horrible dream, she began her story (xi): "with the words, *It was on a dreary night of November*, making only a transcript of the grim terrors of my waking dream." Victor's narrative begins identically: "It was on a dreary night of November that I beheld the accomplishment of my toils" (*F* 1.4: 35). We are invited by such metapoetic allusions in this paratext, therefore, to identify the 1818 novel as a 're-animation' of MWS's dream, and to see the 1831 reworking of the novel too as a kind of 're-animation' of MWS's "hideous progeny"—her 'creature,' *Frankenstein*. At the same time as the new body of the 1818 *Frankenstein* novel is revised and republished by MWS in 1831, so the monster inside it is brought to life anew.[12]

Monstrous Metamorphoses: Matter unform'd and Ovid

> Every thing must have a beginning, ... and that beginning must be linked to something that went before.
>
> Mary Shelley, *Frankenstein*, "Introduction" (1831: ix)

In the paratextual introduction to the 1831 re-animation of her "hideous progeny" from 1818, MWS offers us a detailed metapoetic commentary upon the "beginnings" of her novel, upon both the inspiration and composition of her creature, *Frankenstein*. She writes that "[i]nvention, it must be humbly admitted, does not consist in creating out of void, but out of chaos; the materials must, in the first place, be afforded: it can give form to dark, shapeless substances, but cannot bring into being the substance itself" (ix).

According to MWS's metapoetics, poetic creativity is a process of transformation—all poetry a kind of metapoetry. Literary creation entails giving form to "dark, shapeless substances," giving form to the material of chaos. In this analysis, literary "invention" is explicitly figured as a kind of metamorphosis. And MWS's 'creature,' her *Frankenstein*, is explicitly represented as the product of such metamorphosis—literally fashioned out of a chaos of pre-existing materials, re-formed from the corpses and corpuses of the dead "that went before."

Appropriately, MWS does not herself 'invent' these ideas about invention and inspiration. Behind her allusions to literary beginnings and chaos lies Milton's *Paradise Lost*, in which Chaos consists (im)precisely of such "Matter unform'd and void" (7.233) and represents the raw 'classical' material out of which Milton shapes his poem. Milton even begins his epic with the metapoetic conflation of his (own) and His (God's) creation: "In the Beginning ... the Heav'ns and Earth / Rose out of Chaos" (9–10). And behind the beginning of Milton's epic lies the beginning of Ovid's *Metamorphoses* and its metapoetic cosmogony (1.5–9) where Ovid tells us that:

> Before there was sea and earth and sky to cover all   5
> there was one face of nature in the whole world,
> which is called chaos: a rough and disordered mass,
> nothing but lifeless substance and crowded together
> the turbulent seeds of incompatible elements.
>
> ante mare et terras et quod tegit omnia caelum   5
> unus erat toto naturae uultus in orbe,
> quem dixere chaos: rudis indigestaque moles
> nec quicquam nisi pondus iners congestaque eodem
> non bene iunctarum discordia semina rerum.

Ovid's primordial chaos—a state of continuous change and flux in which "nothing retains its own shape" (*nulli sua forma manebat*; 1.17)—reminds us that this new poem does not emerge from a void but from a pre-existing mass of classical stuff. Just like Ovid's chaos and cosmos, his poem also represents a transformation of the mass of literary material "that went before."[13]

MWS's paratextual comments remind us to value the transformation and the translation no less than the model. They invite us, too, to go in search of the raw materials behind MWS's inspiration and invention in *Frankenstein*—the classical "Matter unform'd and void" from which she shapes her novel. They invite us in particular to look to the wealth of shape-shifting substance afforded her by Ovid, his *Metamorphoses*, and its own paratexts—the translations, commentaries, notes, and illustrations that would have been to hand 'when M read Ovid.'

In fact, the co-authored journals from the Shelley-Godwin household tell us that MWS was reading Ovid's *Metamorphoses* throughout the spring of 1815, as these extracts from the journal show:[14]

April 8 ... read 15 lines of Ovids metamo[r]phosis with Hogg
April 9 Read some lines of Ovid before breakfast ... Read Ovid with Hogg (finish second fable). Shelley reads ... the story of Myrrha in Ovid.
April 10 Mary reads third fable of ovid
April 11 Read fourth and fifth fables of Ovid
April 15 Read Ovid till 3 ... Read Ovid (ninety-five lines)
April 16 draw and read a few lines of Ovid ... Read Ovid (54 lines only)
April 17 Read Ovid ... After tea Read Ovid 83 lines
April 18 [by Percy] Rise late – S. reads Aristo – the Maie [Mary] Ovid – S. & C. go out. C makes S. a present of Seneca. buy Good's Lucretius – Jefferson [Hogg] & the Maie go for bonnets after dinner with Clara. S. reads Ovid – Medea & the description of the Plague – After tea M reads ovid 90 lines ...
April 21 After tea read forty lines of Ovid
April 22 Read a little of Ovid ... After dinner Fanny goes. Read 60 lines of Ovid. [several leaves of journal lost]
Between April 23 and May 4 Construe ovid (117) & read some cantos of Spenser – Shelley reads Seneca
May 5 Read Spenser—construe Ovid ... Shelley reads Seneca
May 10 Construe ovid. After dinner construe Ovid (100 lines)
May 12 Construe Ovid (90 lines) ... read over the ovid to Jefferson [Hogg], and construe about ten lines more.
May 13 Read ovid (60 lines)

MWS encounters Ovid's poem in bits and pieces—on some days reading whole books or episodes ("fables"), and on other days construing the text line by line, parsing and analysing the grammatical parts and syntactical connections of Ovid's Latin. The distinction she draws between reading "fables" and reading "lines" suggests that she is sometimes reading the text in translation, making swift progress, and sometimes construing in Latin, making much slower progress. Together, her progress is such that she includes in her reading list for 1815,

"Ovid's Metamorphoses in Latin."[15] This is a unique entry in her extant reading lists. MWS reads much of her classics in translation and by the page or book chapter rather than by the line. What's more, references to her efforts to "construe" and to reading by "line" appear in the Shelley-Godwin journals in reference to Ovid's *Metamorphoses* alone. Elsewhere in her journals, any numbering she gives explicitly refers to whole book chapters or volumes, pages, and cantos. Thus, in her journal of August 1816 she occasionally records "translate and read" in relation to Italian (Cerceau) and French writers (Izouard and Madame de Genlis), but *not* to any of the classics (Virgil and Quintus Curtius Rufus), which she evidently reads in translation. And in her entry for August 4 that year (PBS's 24th birthday), she records: "go out with Shelley in the boat & read aloud to him the fourth book of Virgil—after dinner we go up to Diodati but return soon—I read Curt. with Shelley and finish the 1st vol."[16]

Something special is happening, then, when "M reads Ovid." And if we can establish a better understanding of what is involved in this reading, we might also gain a better understanding of how MWS's construal of Ovid is mixed in with her construction of *Frankenstein*.

Patchwork Paratexts: "Prometheus mixt"

> That Maker, the best World's originall,
> Either Him framd of seed Caelestiall;
> Or Earth, which late he did from Heauen diuide,   80
> Some sacred seeds retaind, to Heauen allyd:
> Which with the liuing streame *Prometheus* mixt;
>   Sandys, *Ouids Metamorphosis Englished* (1632) 1.78–82

From the paratextual evidence of MWS's journal entries, we can confidently assume that she sometimes reads Ovid in translation and sometimes in the original Latin.[17] Sometimes she has Hogg/Jefferson to help her, sometimes (presumably) she has PBS, and sometimes she will have had a dictionary, a commentary, and a reference translation or 'crib' to help her. There are a number of different possible texts and paratexts that MWS could have had at her disposal to aid her reading of the *Metamorphoses* in Latin. The most recent English-Latin edition in circulation was that of Orger (1811), which aims—and largely fails—to capture the poetry of the original in a literal rendering in English rhyming verse. The translation itself takes centre-stage in this edition, with the corresponding Latin text squeezed onto the bottom of each page in a pica font, making this a largely useless text for readers seriously interested in translating Ovid's Latin for themselves.

Much more helpful to MWS would have been one of the standard English-Latin editions of the *Metamorphoses* popularly used in schools at this time. One such text from 1748 (reprinted in various formats up to 1812) "for the use of schools as well as private gentlemen," edited and translated by Bailey, advertises on its cover: "The Latin text and order of construction on the same page; and critical, historical, geographical, and classical notes, in English, from the best commentators both ancient and modern; with a great number of notes entirely new." On each page it presents ten lines of Latin set alongside a breakdown of the Latin syntax, set on top of a literal translation, and an abbreviated commentary. The commentary notes include relatively little that is actually 'new,' but very clearly represent (as its cover promises) the summary and synthesis of pre-existing commentators—most notably Sandys. For, although Sandys's is a decidedly 'literary' translation and not a 'school' edition *per se*, his detailed notes and commentary accompanying his heavily revised 1628 translation in the 1632 *Ouid's Metamorphosis Englished* continued to be reprinted (in handy duodecimo as well as folio) and to serve as an authority on Ovid's text well into the nineteenth century.[18] Bailey's annotated 'school' edition of the *Metamorphoses* explains that Prometheus was a scientist, a "knowing Prince" skilled in "Agriculture, Physic, and other Sciences," as well as a sculptor. Bailey also notes (again, *pace* Sandys) that Ovid's pagan account of the creation of man mirrors that of God's creation of Adam in *Genesis* (1748: 9–10). The other Latin-English texts of the *Metamorphoses* circulating in this period broadly follow the same line of commentary, and the same format, again typically summarizing and synthesizing key bits of Sandys.[19]

There are plenty of other 'literary' English translations that might have additionally or alternatively mediated and aided MWS's reading of Ovid's *Metamorphoses*. Yet once again, Sandys's facilitating influence as a commentator comes to the fore. Golding's creative translation in thumping fourteeners would have been as little help to a student translating Ovid's Latin in 1815 as it is today, so is an unlikely option. But MWS's journal references to reading Ovid's "fables" might suggest familiarity with Dryden's 1700 *Fables Ancient and Modern*. Admittedly, Dryden's selection of stories in the arrangement—comprising only six of Ovid's "fables"—does not supply anything like that which might be understood as configuring the second and third, or "fourth and fifth fables" that MWS records reading sequentially in her early engagement with the *Metamorphoses*. This makes it highly unlikely that MWS is using Dryden's *Fables* as her 'crib' for translating the whole of Ovid's epic—although it is highly probable that she would have had known this popular collection.

It is also probable that MWS would have consulted the famous multi-authored translation of the whole *Metamorphoses* from 1717, produced under the direction of Samuel Garth and including bits and pieces from Dryden (who translates book one), Pope, Addison, Congreve, and "other eminent hands." Yet, as a 'crib' to aid a student's linguistic understanding and parsing of Ovid's *Metamorphoses* in the Latin, Garth's Augustan translation is far from ideal. Beyond Garth's preface, there is no commentary or annotation, and the translations—albeit exquisitely formed—are, as Garth himself acknowledges in a preface, not "too exact" (1751: xlix). Note the elaboration and deviation from the original in Dryden's translation of Ovid's proem (*Met.* 1.1–4):

Of Bodies chang'd to various Forms, I sing:
Ye Gods, from whom these Miracles did spring,
Inspire my Numbers with Celestial Heat;
'Till I my long laborious Work compleat:
And add perpetual Tenour to my Rhymes,
Deduc'd from Nature's Birth, to *Caesar's* Times.

My mind compels me to tell of shapes changed into new
bodies; Gods (for you have inspired these changes too)
inspire my work and from the first origins of the world
up to my own times, spin out my continuous song.

Garth makes no apologies for this free style of translation, criticizing by comparison Sandys's earlier rendering as too "verbal." He does, though, recommend that readers of his multi-authored translation consult Sandys's work on the *Metamorphoses*: "Mr. Sands [*sic*] has, by a laborious Search among the Mythologists, been very full. He has annex'd his Explanations to the End of each Book, which deserve to be recommended to those, that are Curious in this figurative Learning" (1751: xli–xlii). Even if reading Garth, Dryden, *et al.*, then, MWS will have been directed toward Sandys to illuminate her reading of Ovid.

Whatever Ovidian texts and paratexts MWS consulted during the spring and summer of 1815, it is highly likely that Sandys's 'classic' translation and commentary was among them. Despite Garth's criticisms, Sandys's version was read widely among members of the Romantic circle. This is the translation of the *Metamorphoses* that we know Wordsworth (and in all probability, PBS) read at school, and which Keats also preferred.[20] Byron knew Sandys's translation of the *Metamorphoses* too—reportedly reading it on his wedding day.[21] And among the library sale catalogue lists for MWS's father, William Godwin, we find not one but three editions of Sandys's translation of the *Metamorphoses* (from 1626, 1638, and 1640). Godwin also owned Golding's translation in Seres's 1567 imprint, but the Garth edition is noticeably absent.²² The balance of probability suggests, therefore, that Sandys—in some form—figured prominently among the paratexts supporting MWS's reading of Ovid in 1815. At a bare minimum, this would have been through the reproduction of something based on his commentary and notes in an edition of the Latin text—"Every thing... must be linked to something that went before." But evidence in both *Frankenstein* and in the Shelley-Godwin journals suggests that when MWS reads Ovid, she is also reading Sandys directly.

In the notes to his commentary on each book of the *Metamorphoses*, Sandys draws attention to a host of classical sources treating similar myths and themes or sharing common allusions and phrasing. In his commentary and notes to Book 1, we therefore find references to Homer's *Iliad*, Hesiod's *Theogony*, Horace's *Odes*, and Virgil's *Aeneid* and *Georgics*, alongside cross-references to other parts of the *Metamorphoses* and to other Ovidian works. There are quotations too from Manilius (*Astronomica*) and Pontanus (*Meteorologica*). We also find frequent references to Lucretius, Seneca (especially the tragedies), and Lucan. Sandys quotes from such ancient authors repeatedly and extensively, giving both the original Latin and his own verse translation in each instance. In his notes to the commentary on Book 1, for example, Sandys quotes at length from Lucretius *De rerum natura* 2.600–603, Lucan *Bellum civile* 3.247–248 and 4.74–82, and Seneca *Hippolytus* (as the *Phaedra* was then called) 972–989. Sandys does not mind that Ovid could not have read Seneca or Lucan and that they could not have been influences on Ovid's epic. For Sandys, the *Metamorphoses* is a patchwork poem, its origins and inspirations—along with its generic affiliations and its poetics—an ordered chaos.

Now, it may be simply coincidence that the Shelley-Godwin journals and reading lists for 1815 show PBS reading Lucretius and Seneca at the same time as he and MWS are reading Ovid. And it may be coincidence that, as Jesse Weiner has demonstrated, *Frankenstein* echoes these classical authors in its learned allusions to Senecan philosophy, Lucretian atomism, and Lucanian chaos.²³ But the Sandys connection is certainly suggestive, not least because his references to Lucan help to explain an apparent anomaly in the chain of reading and reception, which has MWS demonstrating her close familiarity with Lucan in the 1818 edition of *Frankenstein* but seeming only to read his *Pharsalia* or *Civil War* in the summer of 1819. The Sandys connection also reminds us that it is not only Seneca's philosophies that PBS is likely to be reading, but also Seneca's tragedies *Oedipus*, *Thyestes*, and *Hippolytus*—those horrifying, gruesome palimpsests infamous for the monstrous poetics of disintegration and amalgamation that they perform.

If we take a closer look at Sandys's translation, notes, and commentary on the Promethean creation story from Book 1 of the *Metamorphoses*, we can map yet more significant parallels between his Ovid and MWS. In Sandys's translation of *Metamorphoses* 1.76–83, we find the Latin translated thus:

> The nobler Creature, with a mind possest,
> Was wanting yet, that should command the rest.
> That Maker, the best World's originall,
> Either Him fram'd of seed Caelestiall;
> Or Earth, which late he did from Heauen diuide,
> Some sacred seeds retain'd, to Heauen ally'd:
> Which with the liuing streame *Prometheus* mixt;
> And in that artificiall structure fixt
> The forme of all th' all-ruling Deities.

> sanctius his animal mentisque capacius altae
> deerat adhuc et quod dominari in cetera posset:
> natus homo est, sive hunc divino semine fecit
> ille opifex rerum, mundi melioris origo,
> sive recens tellus seductaque nuper ab alto   80
> aethere cognati retinebat semina caeli.
> quam satus Iapeto, mixtam pluvialibus undis,
> finxit in effigiem moderantum cuncta deorum.

There is not much of significance to note in Sandys's translation here beyond his close rendering of the Latin, his translation of Ovid's *sanctius animal* as "nobler Creature," and his avoidance of Ovid's epic circumlocution in translating *satus Iapeto* (literally, 'son of Iapetus') as "Prometheus." In his commentary, however, a more interesting picture of Prometheus and his "Creature" emerges that anticipates *Frankenstein*. Maintaining the same ambiguity found in Ovid in respect to who *really* created man, Sandys aligns Prometheus with Ovid's *opifex rerum* ("maker of things"), the all-powerful deity responsible for the original creation of cosmos out of chaos, the "Maker, the best World's originall," he who "raised the heauy, illuminated the obscure, quickned the dead, gaue forme to the deformed, and perfection to the imperfect" (1632: 19).

Sandys takes pains here as throughout his commentary to insist upon the proto-Christian sensibilities of his pagan poet. In his commentary to the birth of Prometheus's "Creature" (1632: 24–25), he stresses the remarkable similarities between Ovid's account of Prometheus's creation of man and that found in the Bible's *Genesis*. In an allegorical reading of the text, Sandys further seeks to explain why Ovid paradoxically attributes the first creation of humankind to a man, figuring Prometheus as an ancient sculptor, philosopher, astronomer, and even as a pioneering natural scientist. Sandys also connects here the myth of *Prometheus plasticator*, creator of humankind, with that of *Prometheus pyrphoros*, 'thief of fire'—an aspect of Prometheus that is absent from this story in the *Metamorphoses*.[24] We can readily see how *this* Prometheus—scientist and philosopher, *plasticator* and *pyrphoros*, with the godlike power to quicken the dead—might inspire MWS and serve as a prototype of Victor Frankenstein.

There are several further striking analogues that potentially link Sandys's Ovidian commentary to MWS's novel. In Sandys's rationalization of Ovid's account of the earth-born giants, we find a hint as to why Frankenstein's earth-born Creature might also be represented as a giant; that size seems somewhat unexpected and unnecessary given that the Creature is made out of human and, possibly, animal body parts appropriated from "the dissecting room and the slaughterhouse" (F 1.3: 33), but it makes sense in terms of his rebellious, destructive character. As Sandys has it (1632: 27):

> It is said that the Earth, inraged with *Iupiter* for the slaughter of the *Titans*, in reuenge produced Gyants of a vast proportion: yet rather so called of their monstrous Mindes. For the statures of Men are now as heretofore: as appears by the embalmed bodies of the *Aegyptians*, and by the ancient Sepulchers in *Iudea*.

Sandys's commentary, as it were, fleshes out the bones of Ovid's narrative and offers a more detailed picture of those key parts of the *Metamorphoses* that appear to have found their way into MWS's imagination and thence into *Frankenstein*. Frankenstein's monster is a 'giant' not only literally, because Victor finds that in building his creature "the minuteness of the [body] parts formed a great hindrance" (F 1.3: 32), but also figuratively, because his mind is monstrous, prone to rebellion and destruction like the "Gyants" of myth. Sandys's connection between giants and Egyptian mummies may also be significant here, given Frankenstein's description of his horror at first seeing his Creature brought to life: "A mummy again endued with animation could not be so hideous as that wretch" (1.4: 36).

Indeed, among the patchwork of paratexts that makes up *Ouid's Metamorphosis Englished*, there are several illustrated plates which make their own important contribution to Sandys's translation and transformation of Ovid—and, in turn, to MWS's reception of Ovid and to her own translation and transformation of the *Metamorphoses* in *Frankenstein*. As a final consideration of the potential impact that such paratexts might have made upon MWS as she read Ovid in 1815, we should therefore consider the images used to illustrate the *Metamorphoses*—and the Prometheus story in particular.

In the editions of Sandys's translation and commentary published from 1632 onwards (including, then, two of the editions in Godwin's library), the opening text of each Book chapter is illustrated with a copperplate engraving by Clein and Savery (Fig. 1.1). Each plate depicts a composite tableau of key scenes from the Book to follow. Thus, in the illustration to Book 1, we see sketched out in the background Syrinx pursued by Pan, Mercury playing his pipes to Argus as he guards Io, and Daphne transformed into laurel, with the slain Python at Apollo's feet. In the centre of the tableau, we see the hooded figures of Deucalion and Pyrrha, the stones behind them taking on human form; to the left we see Lycaon fleeing Jupiter's wrath; and to the right we see the giants piling the mountains of Pelion upon Ossa in their attempt to launch an attack upon the heavens and overthrow the gods. In the foreground, the focal point of the tableau and the scene etched out in the greatest detail and depth—contrasting starkly with the brief thumbnail sketch of 13 lines that Ovid gives the story in the Latin text—we see Prometheus at work on his creature (see the lower right corner of Fig. 1.1). In contrast to his maker, the creature is naked, like the giants fighting atop the mountains behind him. And he is proportionately their size, further reinforcing the implicit connection between them. He is not yet animate, as suggested by both the limp arm that Prometheus holds up and (what appears to be) the fennel stalk that Prometheus holds above the creature's heart: Prometheus, it seems, is pictured at the very point of animating his creature— with stolen fire. The myths of Prometheus *plasticator* and Prometheus *pyrphoros* are here conjoined. But it is an unsettling image. The creature's limbs are in anatomical proportion, its features beautiful, its muscles clearly showing beneath the skin, its hair black and flowing, but its pale face with its dark, hollow eyes suggests death much more than life.[25]

The chances of MWS having encountered this image *somewhere*—in her father's library, in PBS's library, or on her own desk—are high. Indeed, taken together with the host of other Sandian details that are scattered throughout the novel, it is no exaggeration to say that scraps of Sandys's patchwork paratext are to be encountered *everywhere* in *Frankenstein*. Anticipating Victor's character, Sandys's Ovidian Prometheus is first and foremost a pioneering natural scientist, a "knowing Prince" skilled in "Physic, and other Sciences," and is even likened to Pontanus—the fifteenth-century scientist renowned for his theories on the powers of lightning. Prefiguring MWS's own parallels between Frankenstein's Creature and the Bible's Adam, Sandys similarly sees Prometheus's creation of his "nobler Creature" directly mirroring God's creation of Adam—in which vein Sandys's Ovidian Prometheus is likened to the divine "Maker" who "raised the heauy, illuminated the obscure, quickned the dead, gaue forme to the deformed,

Fig. 1.1 Illustration from George Sandys, *Ouid's Metamorphosis Englished*, 1632 folio edition.

and perfection to the imperfect." What is more, the illustrations to Sandys's commentary and translation correspond closely with MWS's descriptions of the giant size and ghastly appearance of the Creature. And Sandys's notes and translated quotations from Lucan and Lucretius even cast new light onto how it is that MWS can display a detailed knowledge of Lucan in the 1818 edition of *Frankenstein* but seem only to read his *Civil War* in the summer of 1819.

Of course, we can never determine with absolute certainty the precise translation or translations that MWS consulted during her own readings of Ovid's *Metamorphoses*. Nor can we determine unequivocally the Latin text and any notes and commentary she used. But it would be incredible if her encounter with Ovid did not in some way bring her into contact with Sandys. Indeed, the balance of probability and the weight of evidence suggest that MWS was familiar with the full patchwork of paratexts that makes up *Ouid's Metamorphosis Englished* and that these materials helped both to inform and to give form to the dark shape of her *Frankenstein*. For nothing is ever created "out of void," and Mary Shelley's *Frankenstein* is—in part—made out of Sandys's Ovid.

Notes

1. The Creature tacitly recognizes his own patchwork composition in correctly interpreting Victor's desire to return him to that state: "You, my creator, would tear me to pieces, and triumph" (*Frankenstein* 2.9: 97); this and all subsequent references to the main text of *Frankenstein* (henceforth *F*) are to the original 1818 edition of the novel. Page numbers relate to those in the 2017 Enhanced Media Publishing text of *Frankenstein: Original 1818 Uncensored Version*. See also Reichardt (1994: 155) and Weiner (2015a: 52): "Frankenstein's monster is a patchwork man, a collage of ill-assorted pre-existing parts, grotesque in the artificiality of their combinations." Thanks to the editors and to *Modern Prometheus* conference participants for feedback on earlier drafts of this chapter. My very grateful thanks also to Tim Saunders, David Hopkins, and Emma Hammond for helping me pull my collage of thoughts on this topic together.
2. See Pollin 1965.
3. Frankenstein is influenced by Cornelius Agrippa, Paracelsus, and Albertus Magnus (*F* 1.1: 23: 30). See also Weiner (2015a: 73).
4. Genette (1991: 265). Genette's 'paratext' describes those bits and pieces of a text that are not part of the main body of work or narrative *per se*, but which do contribute to its interpretation and reading: titles, epigraphs, prefaces and introductions, translations, commentaries, correspondence, notes, reviews, illustrations, etc. Here I treat the 1818 edition of *F* as the core text and the 1831 edition as a 'paratext' offering the potential insights into the composition and poetics of the earlier work. 'Metapoetic' describes an author's self-reflexive treatment of writing (poetry or literature) as a subject for or motif within their own writing.
5. Genette (1991: 262).
6. See Feldman and Scott-Kilvert (1987: 73–79).
7. Italics added for emphasis. All translations are my own unless otherwise attributed, based on Miller's Latin text.
8. On diversity of genres in the *Metamorphoses*, see Solodow (1988: 9–36).
9. See Liveley 2002.
10. See Janan 1988.

11 See Wheeler 1999 and Tissol 1997 on Ovid's self-conscious narration. See Ovid *Tristia* 2.207–252 on the *carmen et error* ("poem and mistake") that led to his exile at Tomis; Ovid describes Tomis as an ice-bound polar outpost at the edge of the world, where the sea is frozen solid for several months of the year, where ships become trapped in the ice, and men must walk on foot across the snowy landscape (2.188–196; cf. 3.10.27–40). Both Ovid and Frankenstein end their days as exiles in the ice and snow at the edge of civilization.

12 Frankenstein's own character and story are proleptically conflated with those of the Creature in Walton's repeated descriptions of Victor as a "creature." (*F* Preface and 1.Letter 1: *passim*) who is "restored . . . to life" (*F* 1.Letter 1: 15), helped by Walton's friendly ministrations through which "a new spirit of life animated the decaying frame of the stranger" on board his ice-bound ship (*F* 1.Letter 1: 15). Indeed, Walton is himself a highly metapoetic character: self-educated, having spent his youth running "wild on a common" (*F* 1.Letter 1: 12), he works through the volumes in his "uncle Thomas's library," he is "passionately fond of reading," and "a poet" influenced by Milton, Shakespeare, and the classics, who "for one year lived in a Paradise of [his] own creation" (*F* 1.Letter 1: 10). He is thus a hybrid of PBS, MWS, Victor, and the Creature. What is more, the sister to whom he narrates his tale via letter (Margaret Walton Saville) shares the same initials as his own creator (Mary Wollstonecraft Shelley).

13 This includes Hesiod *Theogony* 116–125, Apollonius Rhodius 1.496–48, Diodorus Siculus 1.7, Aristophanes *Birds* 693–94, and Lucretius *De rerum natura*.

14 See Feldman and Scott-Kilvert (1987: 73–79). In 1815, MWS was not yet married to Percy Shelley and retained her father's name, Godwin.

15 Ibid., 89.

16 Ibid., 123.

17 See Genette (1991: 267) on the status of diaries and private journals as paratexts.

18 On the various editions of Sandys's Ovid, see Davis 1948.

19 See Clark's 1752 edition of Ovid's text with his own translation ("as literal as possible"), aimed at "Beginners" in Latin, both in and out of school. Clark's preface, on the traditional pedagogical and philological merits of using a literal translation to guide a 'reading' of the original Latin, offers ample testament to this long-standing scholarly habit and confirms the likelihood that this is how MWS too would have 'read' Ovid.

20 See Wu (1993: 161) and Colvin (1917: 171).

21 See Hunt 1828.

22 Godwin did own Dryden's *Fables Ancient and Modern*. See "Texts Godwin Read" (Myers *et al.* 2010).

23 Cf. Weiner (2015a: 46–74). MWS's journal records that she "finishes" Lucan's *Pharsalia* between September 24 and September 29, 1819—that is, *after* writing *Frankenstein*.

24 Sandys also links this 'creation' story to that of Deucalion and Pyrrha by stressing their relationship to Prometheus and Epimetheus.

25 Compare Frankenstein's description of his Creature: "His limbs were in proportion, and I had selected his features as beautiful. Beautiful! Great God! His yellow skin scarcely covered the work of muscles and arteries beneath; his hair was of a lustrous black, and flowing; his teeth of a pearly whiteness; but these luxuriances only formed a more horrid contrast with his watery eyes, that seemed almost of the same colour as the dun-white sockets in which they were set, his shrivelled complexion and straight black lips." (*F* 1.4: 35).

2

Prometheus and Dr. Darwin's Vermicelli: Another Stir to the *Frankenstein* Broth

Martin Priestman

I subtitle this essay "Another Stir to the *Frankenstein* Broth" out of a sense that Mary Shelley's (henceforth MWS) novel has attracted so many critical interpretations already that I am unsure whether much more can be added to the mix. These interpretations include the psychological (is the Creature Victor Frankenstein's repressed id?), the political (is he the violent new proletariat created by industrial science?), the feminist (is he an allegory of a woman in MWS's situation as rejected Other?), the self-reflexive (is the novel itself the monster which convention forbad MWS to create?), the autobiographically anti-Romantic (Victor as Percy Shelley [henceforth PBS], unable to deal with the consequences of his idealized Romantic visions), and the straightforwardly Christian (creation is God's work: attempt it at your peril).[1]

Given this rich mix of well-explored possibilities, I was not sure there was too much to add, but—as this book and the conference it arose from suggest—perhaps a new stir can still be given to the broth of *Frankenstein* commentary through a focus on its classical hinterland. Accordingly, I shall begin this essay by considering a range of possibilities raised by *Frankenstein*'s subtitle, "The Modern Prometheus," and then consider some possible scientific influences on the novel, which draw in a further mixture of classical echoes. As a first way into both topics, I shall take a quick glance at two 'Prometheuses' even more 'modern' than in MWS's 1818 novel: the presentations of Victor's animation of his Creature in two twentieth-century movies.

Galvanic or Organic? Two Films

In the first of my two movies, a scientist and his servant exhume a newly buried corpse, then the servant steals a brain (which turns out to be that of a murderer) from a medical school. Later, the scientist explains to some visitors how he has constructed a large recumbent figure from these and other body parts, and then the draped figure is hoisted up by pulleys to a hole in the roof during a tremendous lightning storm, which electrifies various elaborate pieces of equipment before the recumbent figure is lowered once more and the scientist screams, "It's alive!" Once uncovered, the creature displays the most iconic facial features in horror-film history: clumsily stitched up from parts of other faces, with virtually horizontal mouth and cranium, and with tell-tale electrodes protruding from either side of the neck.

In the second movie, a young man carefully mixes some substances and throws them into a large vat. From it emerges some smoke or steam and then, more gradually, a throbbing, amorphous blob resembling something between a chrysalis and the seed-pod of a plant. Like a plant it develops tendrils, one of which becomes a vigorously jerking right arm while the rest of the blob slowly expands into something resembling a human form. By now the youth's mood has switched from exaltation to horror and, as he rushes from the scene, the tendril-like arm emerges through the doors which were meant to screen this experiment from the rest of the world. Once fully emerged and looming over his creator's swooning body like the incubus in Henry Fuseli's famous painting *The Nightmare*, the creature is still a rather shapeless being, with arms and legs protruding at awkward angles from a flabby central mass.

The first scenario needs no introduction: it is from James Whale's 1931 film version of *Frankenstein*, with Boris Karloff as the Monster (as the Creature is billed in the credits). The less familiar second scenario is from the first-ever film of *Frankenstein*, a ten-minute silent made by Edison Studios in 1910, directed by J. Searle Dawley with the Monster (again so called in a title card) played by Charles Ogle. To simplify the difference between these two versions: Whale's reading of the Creature can be seen as 'dry' and Dawley's as 'wet.' Whale's Creature is essentially made up of discretely separate pieces of other bodies, sewn together but only fully coalesced by the 'fire' of electricity. Dawley's Creature starts as a combination of various substances, organically merged together by the fluids within the cauldron and the warming heat from beneath it.[2]

In the novel itself, the 'body parts' theory is supported only by Frankenstein's statement that, "The dissecting room and the slaughter-house furnished many of my materials"; and the 'electricity' theory only by the statement that, "I collected the instruments of life around me, that I might infuse a spark of being into the lifeless thing which lay at my feet" (*Frankenstein* [F] 1.4: 37–38).[3] But that is all. Apart from an incident in Victor's childhood, there is no specific mention of electricity beyond the word "spark" and, as for stitching human parts together, the "dissecting room" might have been useful but Victor's use of animal parts from the "slaughter-house" confirms other, more explicit statements that it is "the *cause* of generation and life" that he seeks to uncover by exploring the *processes* of life and death whereby "to animate the lifeless clay" (38).

Contrasting the alchemical fluids of Dawley's version with what he calls Whale's "spare-parts, galvano-animated Frankenstein's monster," John Sutherland presents the latter as the iconic source of most people's ideas about *Frankenstein*, although "wholly unfaithful to what Mary Shelley wrote and published in 1818."[4] Relating this iconography specifically to the cinema's new ability to make technology look impressive, Sutherland reminds us of the longer tradition of using alchemical fluids to imply 'science' that lies behind many earlier stage versions of *Frankenstein* as well as Dawley's movie. But Sutherland sees *Frankenstein* as taking this tradition a good step further by bringing in more recent advances in biology and obstetrics, whereby:

> The strong implication is that Victor creates his monster not by surgical manufacture, but by a process analogous to fertilization and *in vitro* culture. The initial work 'of his hands' which Victor refers to is, presumably, masturbatory. The resulting seed is mixed with a tissue, or soup composed of various tissues.... He does not make his monster, as one might manufacture a robot—he gives birth to him, as one might to an unwanted child.[5]

It is true that MWS's 1831 Preface, written long after the novel itself, combines the ideas of electricity and animation of parts in one significant sentence: "Perhaps a corpse would be re-animated; galvanism had given token of such things: perhaps the component parts of a creature might be manufactured, brought together, and endued with vital warmth."[6] But even here the parts are "manufactured" rather than simply collected by the creator before being put together, and the electrical "galvanism" which had seemed to reanimate corpses in certain dramatic demonstrations in MWS's day is only a "token" of various possibilities for inducing "vital warmth."[7] In the rest of this chapter—while not totally excluding the 'body parts' theory—I shall try to shine more of a spotlight on the ideas of "vital warmth," animated "clay," and the "cause of generation and life" noted above, and to connect these to some of the classical allusions lurking just below the surface of *Frankenstein*.

Which Prometheus?

First: what does MWS mean by the subtitle, "The Modern Prometheus"? As Brett M. Rogers and Benjamin Eldon Stevens have pointed out, Immanuel Kant applied the phrase "the Prometheus of modern times" to Benjamin Franklin, whose experiments of harvesting electricity from lightning could be compared to Prometheus's stealing of fire from Zeus.[8] If MWS knew of this reference, it would tally well with the passage in her novel's 1818 edition, when after a lightning storm the fifteen-year-old Victor's enlightened father "constructed a small electrical machine and ... made also a kite, with a wire and string, which drew down that fluid from the clouds," exactly imitating Franklin's famous use of a kite for the same purpose (1.1: 24). This passage plus the similarity of the names "Franklin" and "Frankenstein" suggests a possibly deliberate echo of Kant's "modern Prometheus" on MWS's part.

But there are also earlier uses of the phrase. In his influential enlightenment treatise *The Moralists* (1709), the Third Earl of Shaftesbury had applied the phrase "modern Prometheus" more broadly to Alchemists who try "to make Man, by other means than Nature has provided."[9] Here the reference to Prometheus 'making man' also has possible links to *Frankenstein*, from its Miltonic epigraph onwards: "Did I request thee, Maker, from my clay / To mould me man?"[10]

Whether or not MWS had come across these specific usages by Kant and Shaftesbury is less important than their indication that the phrase 'modern Prometheus' was generally in the air as she wrote. However, they also point to two different aspects of the Prometheus myth, which correspond to the two different filmic Frankensteins we have looked at: is he James Whale's 'dry' fire-stealer (*Prometheus pyrphoros*) or J. Searle Dawley's 'wet' man-creator (*Prometheus plasticator*)?

The two most influential treatments of the fire-stealing myth are by the Greek writers Hesiod and Aeschylus, who offer significant differences of emphasis. In Hesiod's *Theogony* (*Th.*) and *Works and Days* (*WD*), Prometheus is a trickster-figure who sides with (the already extant and emphatically single-sexed) mankind against Zeus by bamboozling the latter into accepting the mere bones and fat as the gods' sacrificial share of an ox, while giving humankind the best meat to cook. In revenge, Zeus deprives man of the fire that will help him enjoy the meat, whereupon Prometheus steals some of the fire back from heaven in a fennel stalk and gives it back to man; for this latter act, Prometheus is punished by being chained to a rock, with his liver being pecked out by an eagle (*Th.* 521–525, 535–560, 613–616; cf. *WD* 47–58). To punish man, Zeus with Hephaestus and Athene creates the beautiful Pandora—source of the "deadly race of women" and hence of most of humankind's subsequent troubles (*Th.* 570–616; *WD* 59–105).

A more heroic and less ambivalent figure, the Prometheus of Aeschylus's tragedy *Prometheus Bound* loyally supports Zeus in his war against the Titans but then prevents him from also destroying mankind in his fury. With no mention of devious tricks involving ox-meat, Aeschylus's Prometheus gives man not only fire but also hope and many arts of civilization, for which Zeus duly punishes him by chaining him to a rock, with the further torment of the liver-pecking eagle added only when Prometheus refuses to clarify a prophecy involving a danger to Zeus from one of his future sexual liaisons (*Th.* 436–506, 609–612, 943–952, 1007–1035).

In great contrast to these two Greek versions, as we move into Roman times we come across the completely un-rebellious Prometheus *plasticator* of Ovid's *Metamorphoses*, who mixes earth with fragments of the sky to create the first humans—which explains why we walk upright with our faces to the sky rather than looking down at the ground like other animals (1.76–88). Though this seems to have been done with his approval, Zeus later becomes disgusted with humans and drowns them all except for Prometheus's son Deucalion and niece Pyrrha (1.348–415), who are then able to recreate the human race from "the bones of their great mother" Earth (1.383).

Other Roman versions of Prometheus resemble Ovid's in making him primarily *Prometheus plasticator*—the creator of the human race out of earth—rather than *Prometheus pyrphoros*, the defiant fire-stealer of the Greek tradition.[11] Thus, as described by MWS's near-contemporary Erasmus Darwin (to whose influence on *F* we shall return): "In the Pamphili palace at Rome there is an elaborate representation of Life and of Death, on an antient sarcophagus.... Prometheus is represented making man, and Minerva is placing a butterfly, or the soul, upon his head."[12] Still to be seen in Rome's Capitoline Museum, the evident collaboration between Prometheus and Minerva shown on this sarcophagus confirms heavyweight Olympian approval of the whole man-creating process.

So which of these Greek or Roman versions of the Prometheus story lies behind MWS's "Modern Prometheus"? As other chapters in this volume demonstrate, the clearest main source is Ovid's *Metamorphoses*, which her journal tells us she was avidly—or doggedly—reading in the original Latin throughout April and May, 1815:

> *Sunday, April 9.* – Rise at 8. Charles Clairmont comes to breakfast at 10. Read some lines of Ovid before breakfast; after, walk with Shelley, Hogg, Clara, and C. C. to pond in Kensington Gardens; return about 2. C. C. goes to Skinner Street. Read Ovid with Hogg (finish second fable).[13]

As we have seen, the Ovidian Prometheus is simply the *plasticator* of mankind from clay and other materials—a special ability later replicated by his son and niece Deucalion and Pyrrha, who, having survived a cataclysmic flood, follow a prophecy to fashion new human beings out of stones. To make a new human being from inanimate matter, as Frankenstein does, is therefore to be the Modern Ovidian Prometheus. End of story, perhaps.

But there is clearly more to it than that. Nowadays, the Prometheus most people first think of is the daring Aeschylean rebel who stole fire from heaven to benefit mankind, and this familiarity owes a fair amount to the approach shared by Byron and PBS, at exactly the time MWS was writing *Frankenstein*. During that same Swiss summer of 1816, Byron wrote his self-projecting poem "Prometheus" about the titan as Byronic rebel, which MWS duly copied out and delivered to the publisher John Murray that August.[14] Meanwhile, as written up in MWS's journal of that year, Aeschylus's tragedy *Prometheus Bound* is the second item in PBS's 1816 reading list: a piece of enthralled reading that would lead directly to his defiantly atheistic *magnum opus* of 1819, *Prometheus Unbound: A Lyrical Drama in Four Acts*.[15]

But clearly, if Victor is supposed to be a hope- and fire-bringing rebel on the Aeschylean model, something has gone very wrong somewhere. Victor's greatest achievement might result from bestowing "the spark of being," yet he cannot face the result of his creation. Likewise, in that creation's hands, the supposedly life-giving fire sometimes becomes a horrifically destructive weapon, as when the Creature first supplies the De Laceys' cottage with firewood and then burns it to the ground (*F* 2.8: 113). In her influential reading, Anne K. Mellor sees *Frankenstein* as a critique of the egotistical, male-centered, *faux*-idealism of PBS, Byron, MWS's father William Godwin, and perhaps the whole 'Romantic ideology' more generally: a critique in which "we must track the crossing paths of fire" throughout the novel for its complex implications of good and evil.[16] In this powerful reading, the deliberate undermining of the fire-stealing rebel-figure in MWS's portrayal of the flawed, child-abandoning, ultimately cruel Victor becomes the ironic main point of the "Modern Prometheus" subtitle.

To extend Mellor's argument, MWS's novel may carry a further ironic echo of Aeschylus's *Prometheus Bound* if we see her Modern Prometheus as a flat, point-by-point reversal of the ancient one. In listing his gifts to the first humans, Aeschylus's protagonist describes how, "In the beginning, though they had eyes and ears they could make nothing out of what they saw and heard" until he gave them knowledge of the seasons and stars, reading and writing, and use of animals and boats for transport (445–471). With the dawn of consciousness, MWS's Creature too "saw, felt, heard, and smelt, at the same time; [it was a long while] before I learned to distinguish between the operations of my various senses" (*F* 2.3: 79–80). Finding summer give way to winter where "I found my feet chilled by the cold damp substance that covered the ground," the Creature holes up in the De Laceys' outhouse, through a crack in whose wall he learns to read and write; and by the time of his later travels he has become adept at handling boats and dog-pulled sledges. So, along with the acquisition of fire, the Creature follows much the same track as the primitive humankind of Aeschylus's play. However, there is a fundamental difference in that the Creature receives no help in acquiring these skills, so the *lack* of a Prometheus-figure—in the shape of Victor or anyone else—forces him to become entirely his own self-creating 'Prometheus.' Thus, in what may be a larger, almost existentialist gesture to the rootless modern condition, MWS may be suggesting that the true Aeschylean 'Modern Prometheus' needs to be a wholly self-shaping being, in the absence of any more benevolent mentor and guide.

Arguably, then, the two main models for the Shelleys' ideas of Prometheus—ancient or modern—are to be found in Ovid and Aeschylus. But apart from Ovid's *plasticator* and Aeschylus's heroic rebel, there is also that other version of Prometheus: Hesiod's trickster, whose theft of fire is directly related to his determination to turn humans into meat-eaters, and to his tricking of Zeus with low-grade ox-bones and fat. This particular Hesiodic emphasis might seem beside the point were it not for the emphatic use PBS had made of this version of Prometheus three years before MWS started *Frankenstein* and, probably, before his own close reading of Aeschylus.

PBS's radical-philosophical poem *Queen Mab* (1813) includes a long note on vegetarianism, which presents Hesiod's account as an allegory of the evils of meat-eating, with the eagle or vulture as an emblem of consequent liver disease:

> Hesiod says that before the time of Prometheus, mankind were exempt from suffering.... How plain a language is spoken by all this. Prometheus (who represents the human race) ... applied fire to culinary purposes; thus inventing an expedient for screening from his disgust the horror of the shambles [i.e. slaughterhouse]. From this moment his vitals were devoured by the vulture of disease.[17]

So, in the works of PBS the confirmed vegetarian, this image of a tricksy, carnivorous Hesiodic Prometheus precedes that of the good, revolutionary Prometheus of Aeschylus's *Prometheus Unbound*. We may remember that the only declared vegetarian in *Frankenstein* is the Creature, who promises that if Frankenstein makes him a partner of the opposite sex:

> I will go to the vast wilds of South America. My food is not that of man; I do not destroy the lamb and the kid to glut my appetite; acorns and berries afford me sufficient nourishment. My companion will be of the same nature as myself and will be content with the same fare.
>
> 2.9: 120

By contrast, in his final long pursuit of the Creature through the Northern wastes, Victor tells us how, "I generally subsisted on the wild animals that crossed my path. I ... gained the friendship of the villagers [with] food that I had killed, which [I] presented to those who had provided me with fire and utensils for cooking" (3.7: 173). There may well be an echo here of PBS's reading of Hesiod's Prometheus as an emblem of meat-cooking, giving mankind the ox's best "meat and the innards, rich with fat" (*Th.* 538–539) before Zeus's removal of fire from earth prompts him to continue his pro-carnivorous campaign by stealing it back again. If so, the recent vegetarian convert MWS may well be hinting that eating and needing cooked meat is one of the many failings which raise questions about Victor's supposed moral superiority over his vegetarian Creature.[18]

In summary, then, the question of which ancient Prometheus was the model for MWS's modern version is not so easy to answer as may first appear. As the maker of man out of inorganic matter, Victor Frankenstein is the *Prometheus plasticator* of Romans such as Ovid; as the Franklin-esque channeller of electrical 'sparks,' he is the *Prometheus pyrphoros* of the Greek tradition; as the parental failure, he is an ironic inversion of the nurturing, progress-bestowing Aeschylean hero; as the inwardly-tormented carnivore who destroys his Creature's hopes of a vegetarian utopia, he is Hesiod's trickster. Although at only eighteen MWS cannot be simply assumed to have had such recondite classical references to hand as she began her novel, there is ample evidence that Hesiod's, Aeschylus's, and Ovid's versions of Prometheus all played active parts in either hers or PBS's current or recent reading in the summer of 1816.

Erasmus Darwin's Giants

Earlier in this chapter I contrasted two images of Frankenstein's Creature: the 'dry' electrified *bricolage* of James Whale's movie, and Dawley's 'wet' self-forming organism. In this section, I turn to some possible classical sources for the latter image of the Creature as a fully functioning biochemical organism. The relevance of these sources emerges most clearly in relation to a contemporary writer whom the Shelleys were reading and discussing at the time and whose scientific influence on *Frankenstein* is undeniable. This was the doctor-scientist-poet Erasmus Darwin, whose most influential works were the medico-evolutionary treatise *Zoonomia* (1794–1796) and the long, densely annotated scientific poems *The Botanic Garden, Parts I and II* (1791) and *The Temple of Nature, or The Origin of Society* (1803).

Erasmus Darwin's significant influence on *Frankenstein* is stressed at the very start of PBS's Preface to the 1818 edition of the novel: "The event upon which this fiction is founded has been supposed, by Dr Darwin and some of the physiological writers of Germany, as not of impossible occurrence" (*F* 3). MWS expands on this cryptic hint in her own Introduction to the 1831 edition:

> Many and long were the conversations between Lord Byron and Shelley, to which I was a devout but nearly silent listener. During one of these, various philosophical doctrines were discussed, and among others the nature of the principle of life, and whether there was any probability of its ever being discovered and communicated. They talked of the experiments of Dr. Darwin, (I speak not of what the Doctor really did, or said that he did, but, as more to my purpose, of what was then spoken of as having been done by him,) who preserved a piece of vermicelli in a glass case, till by some extraordinary means it began to move with voluntary motion.[19]

We shall return to the vermicelli experiment later, but first it will be useful to consider a range of other possible points of contact between Erasmus Darwin's work and *Frankenstein*.

Alongside his wide-ranging scientific speculations, Darwin was a political radical who also had a great interest in classical art and mythology, as seen in his (already mentioned) account of the Roman sarcophagus-depiction of *Prometheus plasticator*. This occurs in the poem *The Botanic Garden, Part One: The Economy of Vegetation*, which also includes a series of very suggestive links between Benjamin Franklin's lightning experiments, a fire-stealing classical deity, and the animation of a recumbent giant who then turns against his former masters in a way that seems to anticipate Frankenstein's Creature. Like the deity, Franklin steals lightning from heaven and enables the principle of freedom it represents to be turned against a range of political tyrants, starting with the British in America and Ireland and then—as "man electrised man" —spreading to the French *ancien régime* of "confessors and kings," whose chains are snapped by the hitherto-recumbent "Giant-form" of the French people, now at last raised to its massive revolutionary feet by "the patriot-flame" of Franklin's lightning-like message of freedom (Part One 1.368, 1.383–398, 2.377–390).[20]

For MWS, this passage could well have clicked together with Kant's description of Franklin as "the Prometheus of modern times." However, sadly for the complete neatness of the *Frankenstein* link, the fire-stealing deity to whom Darwin compares Franklin (in an earlier passage with clear connections to this one) is *not* Prometheus *pyrphoros* but instead the love-god Eros, whose stealing and snapping of Zeus's thunderbolts is touched on in a few rather obscure classical sources.[21]

Furthermore, Darwin had already allotted a far less distinguished role to Prometheus's fire-stealing, as an allegory for addiction to alcohol. In his earlier poem *The Loves of the Plants* (confusingly called *The Botanic Garden, Part Two*, though first published in 1789, two years before *Part One*), Darwin offers a poetic description of Prometheus *pyrphoros* (Part Two 3.371–372, 3.379–380) followed by a footnote, which, anticipating PBS in *Queen Mab*, idiosyncratically focuses on the eagle/vulture as an allegory of human liver-complaints:

> So when PROMETHEUS braved the Thunderer's ire,
> Stole from his blazing throne etherial fire, ...
> The gluttonous bird, exulting in his pangs,
> Tears his swoln liver with remorseless fangs.

As Darwin's note on the passage explains: "The antient story of Prometheus, who concealed in his bosom the fire he had stolen, and afterwards had a vulture perpetually gnawing his liver, affords [an apt] allegory for the effects of drinking spirituous liquors." Whether or not this anti-alcoholic focus on liver-problems helped to sharpen PBS's vegetarian reading of Prometheus, he and (perhaps) MWS were very likely to have encountered the two parts of *The Botanic Garden* in which all of the above passages appear, since it was by far Darwin's most popular work.

Little Worms and Dr. Darwin's Vermicelli

However, it is Darwin's last poem, *The Temple of Nature*, which lies behind the exceptional prominence given to him both in PBS's 1818 Preface and MWS's 1831 Introduction. To quote the latter again,

> [Lord Byron and Shelley] talked of the experiments of Dr. Darwin, (I speak not of what the Doctor really did, or said that he did, but, as more to my purpose, of what was then spoken of as having been done by him,) who preserved a piece of vermicelli in a glass case, till by some extraordinary means it began to move with voluntary motion.[22]

Darwin's works may be scoured in vain for references to vermicelli or any other kind of pasta, but there is one particular passage where the ghost of the absent vermicelli seems particularly to hover. This is the first of the long prose "Additional Notes" attached to *The Temple of Nature* (1803), the long poem in which Darwin strikingly anticipates the evolutionist arguments of his more famous grandson Charles.[23]

As part of his evolutionary argument that organic life must at some point have developed from inorganic matter, Darwin's long note on "Spontaneous Vitality of Microscopic Organisms" refers to several apparent cases of present-day spontaneous generation. In fact, all his so-called evidence is wrong because microscopes were not yet powerful enough to detect the tiny spores from which these organisms actually sprung, but his conclusions were shared by many other scientists of the time. Drawing on their observations, Darwin describes a range of tiny wriggling organisms that seem to have been born from inorganic matter, some "in a sealed glass phial" to prevent access by invisible spores, some resembling eels, some grown in flour-paste, and one group with the suggestive name "vorticella":

> To suppose the eggs of [these] microscopic animals to float in the atmosphere, and pass through the sealed glass phial, is so contrary to apparent nature, as to be totally incredible! ... Some of the microscopic animals are said to remain dead for many days or weeks, when the fluid in which they existed is dried up, and quickly to recover life and motion by the fresh addition of water and warmth. Thus the *chaos redivivum* of Linnæus dwells in vinegar and in bookbinders paste: it revives by water after having been dried for years, and is both oviparous and viviparous.... Thus the *vorticella* ..., though it discovers no sign of life except when in the water, yet it is capable of continuing alive for many months though kept in a dry state.[24]

Noting that "vorticella" means 'little whirlpools' in Latin and "vermicelli" means 'little worms' in Italian, it is easy to imagine how all these types of tiny, wriggling, worm-like creatures in a "sealed glass phial"—especially those found in flour-paste—might have coalesced in Byron's, PBS's, and/or MWS's minds as "vermicelli in a glass case." Like MWS's mysteriously animated pasta, these organisms can be preserved indefinitely in a dry state, but only come back to life in the presence of "water and warmth." The great biologist Linnaeus's name for his flour-paste creature might have rung particular bells for MWS as the novel inspired by this conversation took shape in her mind: *chaos redivivum*, or 'chaos reanimated,' would be quite an apt name for Frankenstein's Creature.

MWS's account of the 'vermicelli' conversation admits it might have been garbled, and we might wonder whether this garbling was more a matter of either her misremembering the terms used, or Byron or PBS deliberately playing word-games with them and with other references that might have sprung to their classically educated minds as well. In that case, another poet of great interest to both Byron and PBS may have also played a part in the mix, which returns us to our special focus on *Frankenstein* and the classics: Lucretius, author of the great anti-religious scientific poem *De rerum natura* (*DRN*), from which Shelley had drawn substantially in his long atheist poem *Queen Mab* (1813) and which he was re-reading in Summer 1816, finishing it on July 29.[25] Lucretius was a great influence on Darwin too and also had theories on the spontaneous generation of 'little worms' with the addition of 'water and warmth.'

Discussing the origins of life, Lucretius says, "[In] sticks and clods [the first signs of life] escape our vision; yet these, when they have become rotten, as it were by rain, bring forth little worms" (*DRN* 2.897–899)—that is, *vermiculos*. In the absence of any discussion of pasta in Darwin's works, it is arguable that MWS's half-remembered "vermicelli" emerged from a combination of his "vorticella" with Lucretius's little worms or *vermiculi* in PBS's and Byron's debates. Be that as it may, for Lucretius the birth of these *vermiculi* after soaking rain partially recapitulates the earlier periods of earth's history when (5.805–810)

> [t]he earth, you see, first gave forth the generations of mortal creatures at that time, for there was great abundance of heat and moisture in the fields. Therefore, whenever a suitable place was found, wombs would grow, holding to the earth by roots; and … in due time the age of the infants broke these, fleeing from the moisture and seeking the air.

Taken together, these two Lucretian accounts of the spontaneous generation of organisms suggest a classical origin for Erasmus Darwin's theory of the evolution of all life from inorganic matter. Darwin often invokes Lucretius in such contexts and, while not referring directly to these specific passages, does so indirectly by placing great emphasis on another classical passage echoing the same ideas.[26]

That passage comes from Ovid's *Metamorphoses*, indeed from the same book as the account of *Prometheus plasticator* considered earlier in this essay. Carrying straight on from the re-creation of human beings by Deucalion and Pyrrha (at 1.416), it describes how animals too were regenerated, just as, says Ovid, they can still be observed today emerging from the mud as the yearly floods of the Nile Delta recede (1.416–437):

> As to the other forms of animal life, the earth spontaneously produced these of divers kinds; after that old moisture remaining from the flood had grown warm from the rays of the sun, the slime of the wet marshes swelled with heat, and the fertile seeds of life, nourished in that life-giving soil, as in a mother's womb, grew and in time took on some special form. So when the seven-mouthed Nile has receded from the drenched fields and has returned again to its former bed, and the fresh slime has been heated by the sun's rays, farmers as they turn over the earth find many animate things.

Though nominally linked to the myth of Deucalion's flood, this passage closely echoes Lucretius in its image of a creation scene in which present-day creatures are conceived and born from earth-rooted "wombs" through the all-important agency of warmth and moisture.

In *The Temple of Nature,* Darwin presents his own version of this same passage from Ovid as an extended simile for the early stages of evolution which he has just described in more up-to-date scientific terms (1.401–417):

> Creative Nile, as taught in ancient song,
> So charm'd to life his animated throng; ...
> Bird, beast, and reptile, spring from sudden birth,   410
> Raise their new forms, half-animal, half-earth; ...
> As Warmth and Moisture blend their magic spells.

Critiquing this same Ovid passage in the long note on spontaneous vitality that suggested MWS's 'vermicelli' reference, Darwin stresses that the idea that "the larger animals had been thus produced, as Ovid supposes after the deluge of Deucalion" is a "misrepresentation," given that "animals and vegetables have been perpetually improving by reproduction; and that spontaneous vitality [is] only to be looked for in the simplest organic beings" ("Additional Notes" 1.1). Nonetheless, it was a passage he clearly regarded highly enough to rework as the climax of his poem's first canto.

So to bring all this back to the Shelleys, I would argue that MWS's garbled recollection of PBS and Byron discussing the "piece of vermicelli" animated by Darwin embraced a swirl of echoes that could well have come into the same conversation: Darwin's *vorticella*, Linnaeus's paste-born "revived chaos," the *vermiculi* of Lucretius's *De rerum natura* (which PBS was currently re-reading), and the spontaneously generated Nile-creatures in Ovid's *Metamorphoses*, which appear soon after the account of Prometheus that probably influenced MWS's subtitle. And whatever Byron and the Shelleys thought about the links between Ovid's, Darwin's, and Lucretius's accounts of spontaneous vitality, two aspects are strongly stressed by all these writers. Darwin's "Warmth and Moisture," Ovid's "moisture ... grown warm," and Lucretius's "abundance of heat and moisture" are both essential to the moment of creation, as well as happening to be just what are needed to turn a collection of dry sticks into a nice steaming bowl of vermicelli.

Magi and Alchemists

Darwin has more to say in *The Temple of Nature* about the Ovid passage just discussed. To justify his poetic reworking of its account of spontaneous creation of large animals—despite his scientific assertions of its literal impossibility—Darwin attaches a different, shorter footnote to the passage itself (note to 1.417):

> This story from Ovid of the production of animals from the mud of the Nile seems to be of Egyptian origin, and is probably a poetical account of the opinions of the magi or priests of that country; showing that the simplest animations were spontaneously produced like chemical combinations.

This note is one of many conveying Darwin's conviction that many truths of modern science were known to the ancient Egyptian priests or magi but then disguised in the form of the stories or 'poetical accounts' passed down to us as Greek myths. These magi actually knew perfectly well that only the "simplest animations" could occur spontaneously, but wrapped this truth in hieroglyphic symbols that later became translated into the classical creation myths.

Such "Hermetic" Egyptian truths also supposedly formed the basis of the Renaissance alchemy of Paracelsus and others, who claimed descent from the Egyptian version of Hermes: Thoth or Hermes Trismegistus. While founding his own science firmly on modern experimental research, Darwin gives frequent nods to this Hermetic tradition, for instance by using Paracelsus's 'Rosicrucian' names for the ethereal spirits of the four elements in his earlier scientific poem, *The Botanic Garden* (Part One vii–viii).[27]

If we bear in mind the young Victor Frankenstein's early immersion in such alchemists as Paracelsus and Cornelius Agrippa, we might compare Darwin's attitude to that of the more sympathetic of Victor's two university instructors, M. Waldman, who (F 1.2: 31):

> smiled at the names of Cornelius Agrippa and Paracelsus, but without the contempt that M. Krempe had exhibited. He said that "These were men to whose indefatigable zeal modern philosophers were indebted for most of the foundations of their knowledge. They had left to us, as an easier task, to give new names and arrange in connected classifications the facts which they in a great degree had been the instruments of bringing to light."

As one source for the plot of *Frankenstein*, Marilyn Butler has pointed to Robert Southey's poem "Cornelius Agrippa" (1799) in which a lodger illicitly uses the alchemist Agrippa's books to summon the Devil, who then tears out his heart.[28]

MWS revisited this tale in her later short story "The Mortal Immortal" (1833), and, in his last published book, *Lives of the Necromancers* (1834), her father William Godwin included a fuller version where the lodger's corpse is reanimated and staggers Monster-like through the market-place.[29] Both Godwin's novel *St. Leon* (1799) and PBS's early novel *St. Irvyne, or The Rosicrucian* (1810) dabble in ideas of hermetic/Rosicrucian alchemy, and Byron's Faustian drama about the overreaching magician, *Manfred* (1817), was under way in the year of *Frankenstein*'s composition. So MWS's somewhat confusing attitude to the young Frankenstein's alchemical dalliances—halfway between respect and fearful rejection—may owe much to the mixed messages circulating within her own largely rationalist circle. In particular, Waldman's half-toleration of alchemy may nod obliquely to the bridges Erasmus Darwin finds between up-to-date studies of microbial spontaneous generation and hermetic-alchemical Egyptian wisdom, as discerned within Ovid's creatures emerging—like Frankenstein's, fully-formed—from the Nile mud.

Conclusion

In Dawley's 1910 film for Edison Studios, the Creature is gradually self-formed while his creator hurls various mysterious substances into a vat of nurturing broth. This image may—almost comically—echo various conventional ideas about what alchemists get up to, but it also gestures toward an organicist reading of the Creature's formation that is supported, I would argue, by some of the classical hints explored in this essay. To somewhat re-adapt the metaphor: from the rich broth of possible *Frankenstein* interpretations already extant, this essay has tried to separate out the idea of a wetly 'earthy' product of Prometheus's labors from that of a pre-formed beneficiary of his gift of fire. And from Mary Shelley's stick of dried vermicelli, it has tried to deduce a train of thoughts involving Erasmus Darwin, Lucretius, Ovid, warmth, moisture, little worms, Egypt and alchemy, which might help to direct inquiries about the Creature's origins a little less toward images of reanimated patchwork and a little more toward ideas of organic growth and spontaneous generation: ideas that form a continuum from classical times to the cutting-edge proto-evolutionary science of MWS's own day.

Notes

1   Many of these arguments are put forth in the essays in Levine and Knoepflmacher 1982. An excellent exploration of how the 'defying God' rather than the 'failed parenting' reading

became dominant is given by St Clair 2000, with reference to *Frankenstein*'s publishing and performing history.
2   The distinction between a 'drily' patchwork and a 'wetly organic' reading of the Creature can also be related to his acquisition of mental powers. Whale bestows these on his Creature through a mechanistic understanding of 'mind' as absolutely equivalent to the physical 'murderer's brain' which we have earlier seen Fritz steal from a laboratory, and which clearly accounts for all of the Creature's subsequent murderous behaviour. By contrast, in Dawley's version, the Creature's mind grows organically with the rest of his body, while a caption suggests that Frankenstein has added 'the evil side' of himself to the mixture—a point strikingly underscored later on, when the Creature repeatedly appears to Frankenstein reflected in a large mirror, from which he at last dramatically cross-fades into his creator on the latter's wedding night, when Frankenstein's 'good side' is at last ascendant.
3   All quotations of *F* are from the 1818 text in Butler 1994.
4   Sutherland (1996: 24).
5   Ibid., 33.
6   In Butler (1994: 195–196).
7   On 'vitalism' and electricity, see Holmes 2008, including the account of the scientist Giovanni Aldini's electrical 'revival' of a corpse (317).
8   On Kant's declaration, see Rogers and Stevens (2012a: 127–128).
9   Quoted in Small (1972: 53).
10 In Butler (1994: 1), quoting Milton *Paradise Lost* 10.743–744.
11 This claim that Prometheus *plasticator* was invented by the Romans is a slight overstatement: an early reference to Prometheus as *plasticator* is made by the Greek Herakleides Ponticus in the fourth century BCE, as is related in Hyginus's *Poetica astronomica*; see Gantz (1993: 166). However, among more famous writers the distinction between Greek *pyrphoros* and Roman *plasticator* holds. On the various ancient depictions of Prometheus, see also Rogers (this volume).
12 Darwin (1791: Part One, "Additional Notes" 59). Now in Rome's Capitoline Museum, this sarcophagus is described in similar terms by Small (1972: 48–49), although Small's claim that Cupid can also be seen bestowing the fire of life is (I think rightly) contradicted by Darwin's view that Cupid is actually extracting the butterfly-soul or 'Psyche' at the human figure's death. Elsewhere on the sarcophagus Cupid and Psyche are seen embracing, perhaps as a sign that Love cares for the soul's immortality after death.
13 In Jones (1947: 43). For MWS and Ovid, see especially Liveley (this volume).
14 See Mellor (1988: 71).
15 In Jones (1947: 73). On Prometheus and the Romantics, see also Barnett (this volume).
16 Mellor (1988: 78).
17 In Hutchinson (1907: 817 = note to lines 8.211–212). PBS also mentions Horace's condemnation of Prometheus's theft of fire in *Odes* 1.3.
18 See Adams (1990: esp. Ch. 6: "Frankenstein's Vegetarian Monster," 108–119).
19 In Butler (1994: 195).
20 Several critics have noted how this passage could arguably support a political reading of *F*, with the Creature as a mentally liberated populace turning against its former oppressors, or in some versions as an industrial proletariat created by a scientific enlightenment which has then morally abandoned it. See Fulford, Lee, and Kitson (2004: 189).
21 For Eros as fire-stealer, see Darwin (1791: 1.383–398). In his note to 1.389, Darwin cites only "an agate in the Great Duke's collection at Florence," as copied in one of his favorite sources for classical imagery, Joseph Spence's *Polymetis*. The agate can be seen in Spence (1755: Plate 7.3).

22 In Butler (1994: 195).
23 Darwin (1803: "Additional Notes" 1.1–11).
24 Ibid., 3, 7.
25 In Jones (1947: 55). See PBS (epigraph and note to *Queen Mab* 5.58) in Hutchinson (1907: 754, 794).
26 See Priestman (2007: 291–292).
27 The poem's four cantos address the respective achievements of the 'Rosicrucian' spirits of the four elements: Salamanders (fire), Gnomes (earth), Nymphs (water), and Sylphs (air).
28 Butler (1994: xxvii–xxviii).
29 Sinatra 1997; Godwin (1834: 202).

3

The Politics of Revivification in Lucan's *Bellum Civile* and Mary Shelley's *Frankenstein*

Andrew M. McClellan

This chapter takes as its point of departure Mary Shelley's (MWS) engagement in *Frankenstein* (*F*) with the Roman poet Lucan's *Bellum civile* (*BC*), a historical epic about the civil war between Pompey the Great and Julius Caesar.[1] In particular, Victor Frankenstein's creation of his Creature is partly modelled on a bizarre scene of 'revivification' in Lucan's poem. In *Frankenstein*, during his scientific studies at the University of Ingolstadt, Victor discovers the spark that generates life; becoming obsessed with the generative process, he stitches together a humanoid figure composed of body parts retrieved from charnel houses, and one fateful night brings his Creature to life only to abandon it and flee in horror. This recalls an extended scene in the *Bellum civile*: on the eve of the military climax at Pharsalus, Pompey's son Sextus, seeking to learn what Fate has in store for that final battle, visits a witch named Erichtho (6.413–830). Erichtho summons a soul from the underworld and 're-fuses' it with its formerly lifeless body: this revivified corpse, she says, will predict the future.

My aim in this chapter is to examine the socio-political and historical implications of these scenes. I argue that Lucan's and MWS's texts directly engage with political discourse that equates internecine upheaval with violence toward metaphorical 'state bodies.' We see such metaphorizing both in literature composed in mid-first-century CE Rome concerning the end of the Republic and during debates in England from the 1790s to the early 1800s in reaction to the violence of the French Revolution. Lucan's historical epic replays the Roman civil wars that destroyed the Republic over a century before his own time; MWS's tale is set against the backdrop of the French Revolution, which took place roughly thirty years before *Frankenstein* was published in 1818. Because both writers set their stories in the past, the metaphorical imagery does not simply end with Rome's Republic or with the *ancien régime* murdered and mutilated. Historical perspective allows each writer to see what has emerged from the tombs of these slaughtered states and to retroject elements of the historical present onto the earlier period. In each case, an allegory for the vicissitudes of states crushed by and reborn out of civil war takes shape in the figure of a reanimated corpse.

The "Galvanic Process": Lucan's and Shelley's Monsters

Much like Erichtho, Victor is a student of the occult.[2] His early alchemical interests inspire dreams of raising "ghosts or devils" through incantation (F 1.1: 69).[3] His excitement for the occult resembles Erichtho's, who is overjoyed at the prospect of helping Sextus through her implementation of nature-defying witchcraft ("The wicked witch of Thessaly delighted in her fame's renown / so widely spread," *inpia laetatur uulgato nomine famae* / *Thessalis*; BC 6.604; cf. 541–542: "she gleefully digs out / the cold eyeballs," *gaudetque gelatos* / *effodisse orbes*).[4] Victor's chemistry professor at the University of Ingolstadt, Professor Waldman, describes modern scientists in what amounts to a virtual translation of Lucan's explication of the powers of Erichtho's witchcraft. Lucan focuses on how Thessalian witches manipulate nature (BC 6.443–506) by soaking everything with rain, blocking the sun with clouds, and causing the heavens to thunder without Jupiter knowing (465–467): "Sometimes they drench / everywhere with rains and muffle burning Phoebus with clouds, / and heaven thunders without Jupiter knowing" (*nunc omnia conplent / imbribus et calido praeducunt nubile Phoebo, / et tonat ignaro caelum Ioue*). MWS's Waldman describes scientists similarly (F 1.2: 76–77):

> philosophers ... [who] have indeed performed miracles. They penetrate into the recesses of nature ... They ascend into the heavens ... They have acquired new and almost unlimited powers; they can command the thunders of heaven, mimic the earthquake, and even mock the invisible world with its own shadows.

Lucan and MWS both describe human agents as usurping the prerogatives of celestial forces.[5] Both descriptions establish the limits of the pseudo-scientific fields that Erichtho and Victor will shatter: Erichtho scoffs at the "piety" of her witchy brood (507–509); Victor, donning Erichtho's necromantic cloak, will solve science's greatest mystery: the principle of life (F 1.3: 79).

During this quest, Victor physically becomes a demonic creature like Erichtho. His figure changes, he becomes emaciated, cheeks pale (F 1.3: 81), matching Erichtho's face, which is emaciated and repulsive with decay and hellish pallor ("The blasphemer's face / is gaunt and loathsome with decay: unknown to cloudless sky / and terrifying, by Stygian pallor it is tainted," *tenet ora profanae* /

foeda situ macies, caeloque ignota sereno / terribilis Stygio facies pallore grauatur; *BC* 6.515–517). Victor and Erichtho each spend their time in seclusion, living among tombs and corpses. Erichtho scorns civil society and inhabits abandoned tombs (510–513).[6] Victor becomes a recluse, engaged completely in his studies, intent on hollowing out a space where he can be completely alone (*F* 1.3: 83–84).[7] Erichtho cannot endure the sun's rays (*BC* 6.516–517), while Victor's "eyes [are] insensible to the charms of nature" (*F* 1.3: 83). All his energy is concentrated on his grand project. Victor observes the decay and corruption of the human body, spending "days and nights in vaults and charnel houses" (80). In the process of this study of death, he discovers the cause of generation and life. Victor's transcendent discovery transgresses nature, in a manner akin to Erichtho's dark arts: out of death, Victor begins to create human life.

Victor's creative process begins, like Erichtho's (*BC* 6.624–641), among the fields of the dead: "I collected bones from charnel houses; and disturbed, with profane fingers, the tremendous secrets of the human frame" (*F* 1.3: 83).[8] Erichtho had brought Hell up to Sextus, creating a space between the worlds above and below; now Victor brings the contents of plundered graves and tombs to his laboratory "cell at the top of the house" (ibid.), similarly distorting both the boundaries of the world and those of life and death.[9]

Erichtho's and Victor's creative processes are also similar in that their methods are both esoteric and elaborately specific (in Victor's case, scientific). Erichtho's witch's brew is highly elaborate but obscure. She combines bizarre ingredients (*BC* 6.667–680), as well as "common" and "named poisons" (681), mixing them all together with cacophonic incantations and invocations (685–718), "unspeakable spells" (682), and unnamed "venoms" of her own contrivance (684). Similarly, Victor details his collecting and assemblage of various limbs and appendages, and his penetration into human corpses and the realm of the dead (i.e., charnel houses, dissecting rooms, and slaughter-houses; *F*. 1.3: 80–81).[10] Even so, little attention is given to the precise "spark" that reanimates the corpse.

MWS's allusive engagement with Lucan is most striking in their treatments of the revivification scenes. When Victor reaches his goal of creating life (*F* 1.4: 85–86):

> It was on a dreary night of November, that I beheld the accomplishment of my toils ... I collected the instruments of life around me, that I might infuse a spark of being into the lifeless thing that lay at my feet. It was already one in the morning ... when, by the glimmer of the half-extinguished light, I saw the dull yellow eye of the creature open; it breathed hard, and a convulsive motion

agitated its limbs ... His yellow skin scarcely covered the work of muscles and arteries beneath; his hair was of a lustrous black, and flowing; his teeth of a pearly whiteness; but these luxuriances only formed a more horrid contrast with his watery eyes, that seemed almost of the same colour as the dun white sockets in which they were set, his shrivelled complexion, and straight black lips.

This description mirrors the prophetic corpse in Lucan at the moment of its reanimation by Erichtho, a passage that likewise focuses on the eyes, the heaving of lungs, and the quaking of limbs (*BC* 6.750–760):

At once the frozen blood grew hot and warmed the blackened	750
wounds and ran into the veins and limbs' extremities.	
At its pulse, the lungs beneath the chill breast quiver,	
and into marrow disaccustomed steals new life,	
mixed with death. Then all his frame pulsates, the muscles	
strained; and the corpse lifts himself up from the ground	755
not gradually, limb by limb, but thrust away from the earth	
and raised erect at one go. Uncovered are his eyes with gaping	
stare: there was in him the look of someone not yet living,	
already dying; the pallor and the stiffness both remain;	
and he is stunned by his arrival in the world.	760

protinus astrictus caluit cruor atraque fouit	750
uulnera et in uenas extremaque membra cucurrit.	
percussae gelido trepidant sub pectore fibrae,	
et noua desuetis subrepens uita medullis	
miscetur morti. tunc omnis palpitat artus,	
tenduntur nerui; nec se tellure cadauer	755
paulatim per membra leuat, terraque repulsum est	
erectumque semel. distento lumina rictu	
nudantur. nondum facies uiuentis in illo,	
iam morientis erat: remanet pallorque rigorque,	
et stupet inlatus mundo.[11]	760

Lucan's and MWS's emphasis on the image of the 'waking dead' is largely the same. Lucan's aphorism that the corpse-soldier exists somewhere between living and dying is equally applicable to Frankenstein's Creature.[12] The Creature, like Erichtho's "stunned" corpse-soldier (*BC* 6.760), will later recall how he slowly began to experience this "new" world, disoriented and seized by a "multiplicity of sensations" (*F* 2.3: 130). Neither creature can speak, initially (*BC* 6.760–761; *F* 1.4: 87), and both are brought to tears (*BC* 6.776; *F* 2.3: 131). It seems clear, then, that MWS had Lucan and Erichtho in mind when she composed her revivification scene.[13]

Lucan on the Corpse of the *Res Publica*

The similarity between these two scenes of revivification raises the question as to *why* MWS would want to draw on Lucan for *Frankenstein*. To answer that question, in this section I offer a reading of Lucan's scene in its own socio-political context; in the next section, I turn back to the socio-political contexts and implications that form the background for MWS's own revivification scene. Here I argue that Lucan utilizes body-of-state imagery in order to make sense of an earlier historical time period whose troubling political events led to the emergence of Lucan's own present, Neronian Rome.

Lucan prominently uses body-of-state imagery in his description of civil war as an attack upon the Roman *res publica*. In Lucan's metaphor, civil war eviscerates its own body (politic), as we learn from the opening image of the poem: "we sing of a mighty people / attacking its own guts with victorious sword-hand" (*canimus populumque potentem / in sua uictrici conuersum uiscera dextra*; BC 1.1-2). Lucan is not so much innovating here as he is repurposing a literary and rhetorical trope from the late Republican period; this trope articulated the end of the Republic as the mutilation or killing of a human body.[14] Lucan's major epic predecessor and model, Virgil, deployed the same imagery in his *Aeneid*, in which the ghost of Anchises in the underworld comments upon the bloody civil war between Caesar and Pompey. Anchises beseeches the shades of the future Pompey and Caesar, without naming them: "No, boys, no! Don't accustom your spirits to such wars, don't use your strength and your vigor to disembowel your country!" (*ne, pueri, ne tanta animis adsuescite bella / neu patriae ualidas in uiscera uertite uiris!*; 6.832-833).[15] Anchises' metaphor functions as the launching-pad for Lucan's entire poetic project.

For example, in Book 7, Lucan stages this extended metaphor in the most elaborate terms to depict the nightmarish battle of Pharsalus.[16] Caesar (and thus 'Caesarism') is shown tearing through the *uiscera* of the Republic's last hope of structural integrity on the real and metaphorical battlefield (esp. 578-581, 721-723): this is "the slaughter of the citizen body, and of citizen's bodies."[17] Despite Pompey's efforts to avoid imposing "wounds" on Rome's body before battle (91-92), Pharsalus is where Rome's Republic dies and where 'Caesars'—a title taken by all Roman emperors—take control of Rome (e.g., 387-399, 432-448, 617-647, 697).[18]

While Lucan presents Pharsalus as a climax for the physical destruction of the Republic, imagery related to this destruction occurs throughout the poem. In Book 2, the bloodthirsty Sulla is described as hacking Rome to pieces like a surgeon cutting too deeply into already rotting limbs (140-143). Cato positions himself as a father mourning the "corpse of Rome" burning on a pyre, and with its death pursuing the "shadow of the name" of *Libertas*, 'Liberty,' to the end (297–303). Concomitant with the loss of the Republic is the loss of "freedom," "liberty" (*libertas*), as Cato makes plain: "and, Liberty, / your name, even an empty shade, I shall follow all the way" (*tuumque / nomen, Libertas, et inanem persequar umbram*; 302–303).

The terms in which Cato describes the loss of *libertas* echo Lucan's portrait of Pompey as a "shadow of a great name" (*magni nominis umbra*; 1.135), tying Pompey to the fleeting vestiges of what he and the Republic had stood for.[19] Pompey's death—his brutal murder, decapitation, and makeshift funeral on the Egyptian shoreline—is synonymous with the death of the Republic, and the death pangs of each are everywhere elaborated. But in Lucan's project, all deaths in civil war are treated as self-inflicted wounds dealt to the state body. These wounds proliferate, leaving the State in a constant state of 'dying' or putrefying. From this perspective, the *Bellum civile* is a funeral parade for Rome, especially the Republic, but its corpse (like Pompey's) is never really allowed to be buried: it just keeps rotting.

Augustan ideology worked to reform this image of Rome's self-evisceration by civil war, claiming that the form of government that followed, the principate, was merely a restoration of the *res publica* and of *libertas*, and that power had been returned to the Senate.[20] If the inherent paradox of claiming continuity with the Republic through the establishment of a new form of government seemed a tough pill to swallow, at least (perhaps) the principate was justified by its ability to counterbalance what must have struck most as an endless cycle of internecine war. For Lucan, at least in *Bellum civile*, Caesarism simply meant that "peace came with a master" (*cum domino pax ista uenit*; BC 1.670); Neronian Romans are 'slaves' to the principate (cf. 1.669–672; 3.112–114 and 145–147; 4.221–227 and 577–579; 7.442–447 and 641–646).[21]

Lucan's poem restages the butchering of the *res publica* because, for the poem's narrator, this was the moment when everything went wrong, the origin of the present state of affairs in Rome. Life under the false paradigm of a *res publica restituta* is a constant reminder of the death of the *real* Republic, where *libertas* was not simply a fictive monarchal slogan (cf. Tacitus *Annales* 1.2, *Historiae* 1.1). Lucan would not live to see it, but Servius Sulpicius Galba (Nero's successor as emperor) and Gaius Julius Vindex championed the return of *libertas* as they built their case for Nero's overthrow in 68 CE, explicitly associating Nero's rule with the imposition of 'slavery.'[22] The absurdity of the idea that Caesarism *revived* the 'free Republic' gives Lucan the opportunity to retroject a perversion of the metaphor of the Republic's corporeality back into his conception of its 'death' in the earlier civil wars. Lucan's whole poem thus metaphorically revivifies the dead Republic in order to replay its death and mutilation over again in grisly detail.[23]

What does Lucan's body-imagery for the fall of the Republic have to do with Erichtho's corpse-soldier (and, ultimately, Victor Frankenstein's Creature)? Charles Tesoriero has suggested that Erichtho's corpse-soldier, like Pompey, also represents the republican body politic, and thus links Erichtho's treatment of the corpse with Caesar's subsequent treatment of the corpses of Pompey's Republican army at Pharsalus. However, since the corpse is never fully revivified but exists only in a liminal state between life and death (BC 6.758–759), Lucan presents a grotesque metaphor for the condition of the 'free Republic' after Pharsalus. Like the corpse-soldier, the Republic "will remain forever a ghastly image of its former self."[24]

This is Rome's civil war past, but also its present—as well as Lucan's. If the Republic has been 'restored' under the Julio-Claudian emperors, then, like Erichtho's corpse-soldier, it is a perversion, half-dead, half-living. For Lucan's narrator, life in this post-Republican wasteland is a world of horror and servility. Like the State itself, with true *libertas* a distant memory, upper-class citizens (including Lucan and his audience) live but are not really *alive*; they persist in a world without hope or a future. The stripping of freedom entails slavery, and slavery is synonymous with death (cf. Ulpian *Digest* 50.17.209: "We generally equate slavery with death," *seruitutem mortalitati fere comparamus*). In the view of Lucan's bilious narrator, Romans subjected to a life without freedom as a product of Caesarism and the disruption of the traditional laws of State were like walking corpses moving through a socio-political space devoid of agency. Citizens clung to traditional titles and positions that were now extrajudicial, robbed of function and influence.

This is Lucan's grim picture of his present, and we know this because he projects the universe of Neronian Rome back onto the framework of the civil war that serves as an etiology for the conditions of his own time.[25] Pharsalus pitted Caesar(ism) not against Pompey, but against *Libertas* ("that pair of rivals always with us, / Liberty and Caesar," *sed par quod semper habemus, / Libertas et Caesar, erit; BC* 7.695–696:). And Caesar won.[26] This is why Caesar and Freedom cannot exist *simultaneously*. Lucan's apostrophic wrath is so palpable because Caesar's tyranny is still alive (638–646):[27]

> From this battle the peoples receive a mightier wound
> than their own time could bear; more was lost than life
> and safety: for all the world's eternity we are prostrated.   640
> Every age which will suffer slavery is conquered by these swords.
> How did the next generation and the next deserve
> to be born into tyranny? Did we wield weapons or shield

our throats in fear and trembling? The punishment of others' fear
sits heavy on our necks. If, Fortune, you intend to give a master   645
to those born after battle, you should have also given us a chance to fight.

maius ab hac acie quam quod sua saecula ferrent
uolnus habent populi; plus est quam uita salusque
quod perit: in totum mundi prosternimur aeuum.   640
uincitur his gladiis omnis quae seruiet aetas.
proxima quid suboles aut quid meruere nepotes
in regnum nasci? pauide num gessimus arma
teximus aut iugulos? alieni poena timoris
in nostra ceruice sedet. post proelia natis   645
si dominum, Fortuna, dabas, et bella dedisses.

In collapsing the temporal distance between himself and his subject universe, Lucan is able to project the image of Imperial Caesars back onto Julius Caesar, as well as project himself and his socio-politically defunct contemporaries back onto their political ancestors. Lucan's present becomes thus a timeless 'deathscape' populated with characters who—like the liminal Erichtho, the corpse-soldier, and the rotting trunk of Pompey casting a shadow of its former efficacy—now occupy a space somewhere between living and dying.

Lucan's obsession is not with death *per se* but with the process of dying and the space separating death from life. Nicola Hömke argues that Lucan emphasizes dying "as an independent phase of human existence" largely for aesthetic purposes.[28] But Lucan's point seems more focused and politicized than merely aesthetic. Lucan's various half-living corpses function as visceral analogs for his vision of an imperial slave-state, which at the same time attacks ideology claiming that monarchy was a revived *res publica libera*.

Shelley and the French Revolution

I turn back now to MWS's own revivification scene in *Frankenstein*, and how both Lucan and MWS use the language of reanimation to comment on their own political climates. Before proceeding into this discussion, I should first address an important caveat. There is no way to know for certain whether MWS saw any of this political symbolism in Lucan's poem. As many scholars have demonstrated, MWS's novel restages much of the metaphorical body-language imagery swirling around the revolutionary debates of the 1790s and early 1800s.[29] Chief among the writers involved is Edmund Burke, whose antirevolutionary *Reflections on the Revolution in France* (1790) depicts the participants in familial and parricidal terms. The revolutionaries, he argues, are sorcerers and parricides who have dismembered the *ancien régime* and revivified the State into something monstrous:

> We should approach to the faults of the state as to the wounds of a father, with pious awe and trembling solicitude. By this wise prejudice we are taught to look with horror on those children of their country who are prompt rashly to hack the aged parent in pieces, and put him in the kettle of magicians, in hopes that by their poisonous weeds, and wild incantations, they may regenerate the paternal constitution, and renovate their father's life.[30]

The language of witchcraft, science, and alchemy converges here with imagery of ghoulish grave-robbing in Burke's descriptions of the distorted revivification of the Body Politic: "out of the tomb of the murdered monarchy in France has arisen a vast, tremendous unformed spectre."[31] What remains is wholly "out of nature," a grotesque "chaos of levity and ferocity," a "monstrous tragi-comic scene" inducing "alternate laughter and tears; alternate scorn and horror."[32] Burke contrasts the violent and chaotic zombie-like monstrosity of revolutionary France with the Glorious Revolution of 1688 and subsequent Revolution Settlement of 1689–1701, where order and reason reigned.

Ironically, Burke's efforts to undermine English sympathies with this revolutionary radicalism had the opposite effect.[33] Burke's vociferous detractors, among them Thomas Paine and MWS's parents, Mary Wollstonecraft and William Godwin, argue that if the French mob are "monsters" (and the new State "monstrous"), that is only a result of their cruel treatment by monstrous parents. Wollstonecraft, for example, counters that "man has been changed into an artificial monster by the station in which he was born."[34] The mob's monstrous revolution is precipitated by the despotism of the aristocratic parent (inverting Burke's imagery of parricidal violence), with mob retaliation tantamount to slave revolt: "A brutal attachment to children has appeared most conspicuous in parents who have treated them like slaves, and demanded due homage for all the property they have transferred to them, during their lives."[35] In this view, the children had fought back and destroyed the tyrannical parent, ushering in a new 'liberated' body politic.

MWS's novel about the creation of a physical monster appears to arise out of this debate over the great monstrosity of the French Revolution. She does not come down strongly on either side of the debate. For our purposes, we might argue that MWS's seeming engagement with Lucan may be mediated through this debate—in particular, through Burke: his metaphorical depiction of the state-as-body is drawn from Cicero and Lucan, both of whom he cites, Lucan being a special favorite.[36] Perhaps the writers of the French Revolution who devoured Lucan as a voice for political freedom from oppression function as mediators.[37] We know from the extensive reading lists preserved in her journals that MWS was well-versed in this literature.[38]

Regardless of her precise source(s), it is striking that both Lucan and MWS use the metaphors of the state-as-body and revivification to comment on the violence of their respective political climates. We might go further still: MWS's political commentary in *Frankenstein* shares with Lucan his interest not only in shattered and revivified state bodies, as well as in issues of freedom and slavery, but also in the role of false or deceptive imperial propaganda. Here let us turn to the influence on MWS of political caricatures of Napoleon by examining two caricatures by George Cruikshank, which bring together all of these themes.

Scholarship has framed discussion of politics in *Frankenstein* around the question of the *origin* of the French Revolution and the political debate spawned from Burke's *Reflections* that persisted in England through the execution of Louis XVI and the Terror: was the Revolution caused by radical *philosophe*, Jacobin, or Illuminatic influences? Or were the uprisings the product of oppressive masters? What position does MWS take in *Frankenstein* on France's revolutionary politics? The French Revolution was indeed the "master theme of the epoch," as Percy Shelley (henceforth PBS) wrote to Byron in 1816, and *Frankenstein* is set firmly in the revolutionary 1790s (the "17—" in Walton's letters to his sister must not fool us).[39] Beyond philosophical and ideological polemics across the Channel, however, there was real, tangible political upheaval in France that, during MWS's formative years, would reshape not only French but European history. MWS retrojects elements of revolutionary and post-revolutionary Europe onto the '(re-)birth' of the Burkean revolutionary monster at the end of the eighteenth century. As was the case with Lucan's similar 'regenerative' retrojection, a malformed alchemical 'state body' is again the symbol of this political tumult.

Like the revolutionary events that transformed the political system in Rome in the first century BCE, France at the end of the eighteenth and early nineteenth centuries experienced a series of seismic structural and political changes. The Revolutionaries themselves—Robespierre, Saint-Just, François-Émile Babeuf, Napoleon, *et al.*—revived and appropriated the language, symbols, and political trappings of Republican and Imperial Rome to validate their claims to authority. Karl Marx, looking back on the Revolutionary period in *The Eighteenth Brumaire of Louis Bonaparte* (1852), wrote that "the Revolution of 1789 to 1814 draped itself alternatively as the Roman republic and the Roman empire" and that, "by conjuring up the dead," the leaders of the Revolution "performed the task of their time in Roman costume and with Roman phrases."[40]

The new French Republic ceded control to Napoleon, who was designated 'consul,' in 1799. By 1802 he was offered the consulship for life, which he refused, claiming that only *le peuple*, 'the people,' could grant this title. Valérie Huet rightly stresses that this refusal mirrors the tactical move made by the Roman general Octavian—the future emperor Augustus—who publicly rejected autocratic powers and nominally 'restored' the *res publica* by handing power back to the people and Senate, but in reality monopolized political offices and powers.[41] In evoking the terminology of the Roman Republic, Napoleon too was able to mask his military dictatorship as if it were a Roman-like French Republic. Napoleon may have idolized Julius Caesar, but he had also learned from his Roman models: it was better to be an Octavian than a Caesar, since kings born out of revolution risked experiencing their own Ides of March.[42] By aping continuity with the new French Republic, Napoleon could claim nothing had really changed. But this was a façade. Napoleon was named, by Roman-style *sénatus-consulte* (Senate vote with the force of law), Consul for Life in July 1802. As had happened with Augustus, Napoleon's birthday (August 15) was made a national holiday; a further plebiscite in May 1804 appointed him Emperor of France, as Napoleon I.

Just as Roman citizens had been forced to come to terms with political change precipitated by Augustus and the legacy of 'Caesarism,' so too did the Romantics in the Shelley-Byron circle, for whom Napoleon functioned as a contradictory figure, straddling the line between liberator and despot, freedom-fighter and continental enslaver. PBS, MWS, Byron, and other proponents of radicalism applauded the French Revolution and its overthrow of the old monarchic system; this, it seemed, would bring an end to tyranny and the dawning of an age of 'liberty.'[43] But soon the bloody revolutionary spirit yielded to another despot and the tyranny of the *ancien régime* was revivified in the singular Napoleon (who had rejected his earlier Jacobin associations in favor of the ideology of the old monarchic system) and his aggressive expansionist neo-Roman Empire. Byron would write five poems about Napoleon (along with the Waterloo material in *Childe Harold*) between 1814 and 1816, in equal measure castigating and praising his idolized "grand creature,"[44] and casting him often, after Napoleon's first abdication in April 1814, as a failed Promethean figure who had turned his back on the revolutionary ideals of liberty in search of individual glory (e.g., *Ode to Napoleon Buonaparte* 136–144).[45] The specter of Napoleon and the European Restoration hovers, too, over PBS's *Prometheus Unbound* (1820), while the association with Prometheus was also made by others, including Goethe,

Beethoven, and Sir Walter Scott.[46] After Napoleon's first abdication, George Cruikshank (*The Modern Prometheus, or: Downfall of Tyranny* [1814]) and Jean Baptiste Gautier (*Le Prometheé de l'isle Ste Hélène* [1815]) also cast Napoleon in political caricatures as Prometheus chained to a rock, complete with ravenous eagle.

MWS was equally fascinated and disturbed by Napoleon and kept copious notes in her journal on his atrocities.[47] Her sympathy for the ideals of the Revolution had been crushed by France's collapse into despotism. It is very likely MWS was inspired by Cruikshank's caricature for her novel's subtitle, and a post-Waterloo audience cannot have missed the 'titanic' allusion in her "Modern Prometheus" to the 'shackled' former French Emperor.[48] Cruikshank's caricatures of Napoleon were enormously popular, both in England and abroad, representing the pinnacle of a genre that was profoundly influential during this time period.[49] As Jonathan Bate argues: "[t]here can be little doubt that, socially and politically, caricature was the most influential art of the 1790s and early 1800s,"[50] and scholarship has demonstrated the genre's impact on the Romantic writers, specifically emphasizing MWS's husband PBS's debts to Cruikshank.[51] That Cruikshank's satirical work pillorying Napoleon as a new Prometheus influenced MWS should not surprise us.

Fig. 3.1 Napoleon as a "Modern Prometheus". *The Modern Prometheus, or: Downfall of Tyranny*. London, July 1814. George Cruikshank. MB Satires 12299. British Museum. Museum Number: 1947,1215.3.

Napoleon haunts *Frankenstein*, both in the figure of the Promethean scientist who unleashes a destructive force across Europe and in his malformed alter-ego Creature who carries out intercontinental violence. In this light, we might read the Creature's bodily composition, formed from an assortment of corpses, as a grotesque symbol for the structural and geographic composition of Napoleon's French Empire, comprised of an assemblage of 'murdered' monarchies across Europe (the "shattered thrones" of Byron's *Manfred* 2.3.62).

Fred Randel notes that, at the novel's outset, the first appearance of Victor's Creature on a "sledge" in retreat across ice-covered Russia (*F* 1.Letter 4: 58) "would recall for readers in 1818 the Napoleonic army's desperate retreat from Moscow by a northern route as a severe early winter began in November 1812." Napoleon is reported to have left his army in Russia, journeying home alone in a single sledge under a false name.[52] The Creature disappears, 'exiling' himself from the human world, into darkness and ice. In effect, *Frankenstein* could be said to trace Napoleon's career from Revolution to (wintery) St. Helena. More could be said along these lines.[53]

Here I want to return to Cruikshank and caricatures of Napoleon from the final years of his reign—caricatures that seem to have directly influenced MWS and whose themes help us see most clearly where Lucan and MWS come together in *Frankenstein*. Napoleon abdicated the throne in April 1814 and entered exile on the island of Elba off the Tuscan coast. Caricaturists immediately depicted Elba as "Hell-Bay" and characterized the expulsion as a 'death-march' for the former leader. In February 1815, Napoleon escaped to southern France with a contingent of troops in an attempt to retake power; by March he was in Paris and in control of France again. This dramatic reversal of fortunes—the "Hundred Days" between his escape and defeat at Waterloo in June 1815—prompted imagery of the 'regeneration' of Napoleon and his power.[54] Thomas Rowlandson's *The Flight of Napoleon from Hell-Bay* (April 7, 1815) portrays Napoleon rising on an orb, sword in hand, from Hell with Satan and his minions watching gleefully. The anonymous *Retour de L'ile d'Elbe, Il Ramene La Liberté* (March 1, 1815) presents Napoleon riding a chimeric beast led by the Devil, followed by Death holding a document that reads: "I'll follow him to Mt. Saint Jean," i.e., Waterloo ("Je vais le suivre au Mont St. Jean"). In Cruikshank's *The Corsican's Last Trip under the Guidance of His Good Angel* (April 16, 1815) and *Escape of Buonaparte from Elba* (March? 1815), Napoleon and the Devil together fly from Hell-Bay across the water to the mainland.

The most powerful image from among the caricatures, however, that depict the parodic yet frightening revivification of Napoleon is Cruikshank's *The Phenix of Elba Resuscitated by Treason* (May 1, 1815). The centerpiece depicts a grotesque necromancy: a pallid, distorted, and menacing witch, half-naked in disheveled robes, with serpentine hair and holding a wand, conjures from a boiling cauldron the spirit of Napoleon, whose head is emblazoned onto the body of a phoenix. The witch's incantation reads: "Rise Spirit that can never rest, Offspring of Treason!—sweet Bloodthirsty soul—come forth!!" The divine personification of Fate hovers over the scene, weighing victory or defeat for the revivified 'monster.' Out of Napoleon's mouth issues a familiar phrase: "Veni Vidi Vici."

Ian Haywood suggests that Cruikshank "seemed to hint at the possibility of [Napoleon's] reincarnation" when he had earlier caricaturized Napoleon in exile as the regenerative "Modern Prometheus" in the piece that likely inspired *Frankenstein*'s subtitle.[55] If we read these two caricature works together in the context of the vicissitudes of Napoleon's career, we have, I suggest, a powerful archetype for MWS's revivified (political) Creature. That Napoleon is here merged with the phoenix—a *hybrid* creature of composite parts—recalls Victor's patchwork Creature in its physical structure.

Perhaps even more striking is the Lucanian imagery of Cruikshank's 'Resuscitation' caricature. In this piece, a necromantic witch bearing remarkable resemblance to Lucan's Erichtho (and not, as in Cruikshank's other pieces, a devil or demon) aids Napoleon in his defiance of death. This witch revivifies Napoleon

Fig. 3.2 Napoleon's Revivification from "Hell-Bay". *The Phenix of Elba Resuscitated by Treason*. London, May 1, 1815. George Cruikshank. BM Satires 12537. British Museum. Museum Number: 1868,0808.8213.

and reconfigures him as a sort of *fantoccino* Julius Caesar—placing the viewer simultaneously in post-Revolutionary France and post-Pharsalian Rome.[56] The blending of this imagery in this caricature offers a microcosmic synthesis of the larger socio-political, historical, artistic, and necromantic contexts and influences that I have argued MWS engages with in her complexly intertextual novel. It is tempting to see in Cruikshank's piece the spark that, in linking Lucanian necromancy with Napoleon's revivification, helped animate MWS's multiform Creature.

That Cruikshank's Napoleon is revivified in the guise of *Julius* Caesar is troubling since it eliminates the Augustan approach to political rule that was so crucial to Napoleon's propaganda machine. In aligning Napoleon with Caesar, the illegitimate 'usurper' of power, Cruikshank underscores the dark internecine side of France's almost genetic Roman political legacy.[57] This is also Lucan's tactic in his characterization of the revivified legacy of 'Caesarism' in Neronian Rome.

In the only reference to Caesar in *Frankenstein*, Victor warns Walton of the dangers of self-serving ambition, of striving to be "greater than [one's] nature will allow" (*F* 1.3: 80), through an allusion to historical tyranny and imperialistic conquest: "If no man allowed any pursuit whatsoever to interfere with the tranquillity of his domestic affections ... Caesar would have spared his country" (82). The context is Victor's creation of his Creature. Viewed within the matrix of Napoleon's 'Caesarean' rise from revolutionary to imperialist despot, this is a damning metaphor for the disruption of the ideals of Revolution dissolved into tyranny.

A month after Cruikshank's caricature was released, Napoleon again abdicated and was exiled to St. Helena (June 1815). The following May, MWS, PBS, and MWS's stepsister Claire Clairmont would leave for Lake Geneva to meet up with Byron and John Polidori for the summer; there MWS would conceive of the seeds of her masterpiece. But the colossal specter of Napoleon was hard to shake. Byron imagined still further Napoleonic regenerations (*Manfred* 2.3.16–23) and MWS at least hints at the possibility in the threat that the Monster carves in a tree: "my reign is not yet over" (*F* 3.7: 205).[58] Just as Erichtho's corpse-soldier climbs his own funeral pyre at the end of the episode (*BC* 6.824–825), Victor's Creature promises: "I shall ascend my funeral pile triumphantly" (*F* 3.7: 221).[59]

Notes

1 Connections between these scenes have been discussed recently in Weiner 2015a; cf. the similar analyses in McClellan 2010. Thanks to Susanna Braund and the volume editors for helpful comments on an earlier draft of this chapter. I wrote most of the Shelley/Révolution

française material at La Ferrière, Lourmarin, France, under much more pleasant circumstances than the subject matter that (often) preoccupied me. Love and thanks to Erica, Scott, Imogen, and Hero.
2. On Victor's youthful scientific endeavors, see Higgins (2008: 30–33).
3. My text of *Frankenstein* (henceforth *F*) is Macdonald and Scherf 2012.
4. See Weiner (2015a: 66 and 68).
5. Higgins (2008: 36) notes the connection of thunder here to Zeus/Jupiter.
6. See Gordon (1987: 239–240) on Erichtho as a "night-witch."
7. Sherwin (1981: 892).
8. Ibid., 895.
9. See Punter (1999: 93). On 'inversions' in the generative scene, see Bates (1999: 136–138).
10. Punter (1999: 92 and 95) comments on Victor's "symbolic descent to the underworld."
11. Lucan translations from Braund 1992. The Latin text is Housman 1927.
12. See Weiner (2015a: 67).
13. On MWS's engagement with Lucan's poem, see ibid., 48–52; see also Luck (2006: 62, 212, 247) and Joyce (1993: 140–141). All three assessments hinge in large part on the influence of PBS, who had read Lucan in the years prior to MWS's writing of *F*.
14. Imagery of the Republican 'body politic' as murdered or dismembered became a popular way of symbolizing the crumbling Roman State. Cicero describes the Republic as "dead" as early as 59 BCE (*tota periit*; *Atticus* 2.21) and a lifeless corpse by 54 BCE (*Atticus* 4.18.2); cf. *Epistulae ad familiares* 4.5.4–5, 5.1, *Atticus* 15.13a.1, *Philippics* 2 (*passim*), *De officiis* 3.83. See also Walters 2011.
15. See Casali (2011: 85–86).
16. See Dinter (2012: 29–37).
17. Tesoriero (2004: 189).
18. Gowing (2005: 92–94).
19. See Henderson (1998: 203) and Thorne (2011: 277).
20. E.g. *Laudatio Turiae* 2.25–26 (= *Corpus Inscriptionum Latinarum* [*CIL*] vi, no. 1527, p. 333, l.25): "with the whole world pacified, the Republic restored"; *Fasti Praenestini* for January 13, 27 BCE (= *CIL* i², p. 231). Cf. *ILS* 81, a dedication to Octavian by *senatus populusque romanus*, 29 BCE; Augustus *Res gestae* 34.1; Velleius Paterculus 2.89.3: "that old, traditional form of the Republic was restored." Cf. Vitruvius *praef.* 1–2; Ovid *Fasti* 1.589; Suetonius *Augustus* 28.1; Dio 53.4.4. See Gowing (2005: 4–7). On the Augustan 'restoration' project, see Galinsky (1996: 42–79).
21. It is not clear whether the narrator's strident 'Republicanism'—his rejection of 'Caesarism' and longing for a pre-imperial political system—reflects the historical Lucan's views; see Martindale (1984) for complexities of voice in Lucan's poem.
22. E.g. Pliny *Naturalis historia* 20.160, describing Vindex as an *adsertor* of freedom ("that restorer [*adsertorem*] of freedom from Nero"), using the legalistic term for a middleman who oversaw the freeing of a slave (*OLD* s.v. *assertor* 1); cf. Suetonius *Galba* 9.2. See Gallia (2012: 12–46).
23. Cf. Walters (2011: 187–198).
24. Tesoriero (2004: 191–192). See Korenjak (1996: 29–30); cf. Arweiler (2006: 54–68).
25. See esp. Leigh (1997: 77–109).
26. See Ahl (1976: 25, 42–45, 55–56), Johnson (1987: 32, 122–123, 131–134), Quint (1993: 150–151), Bartsch (1997: 95), and Thorne (2011: 378).
27. See Quint (1993: 148–151), Leigh (1997: 80–81), Bartsch (2010: 28).
28. Hömke (2010: 103–104). Bartsch (1997: 17–29) has anticipated much of this.

29 On the so-called "Revolution Controversy," see Sterrenburg 1979, Paulson (1981: 545–552), Baldick (1987: 10–29), Mellor (1988: 80–88), Botting (1991: 139–163), and Clemit (1993: 145–150).
30 Hampsher-Monk (2014: 100).
31 Ibid., 256.
32 Ibid., 11.
33 Botting (1991: 144–145).
34 Todd (1999: 9).
35 Ibid., 21.
36 Hampsher-Monk (2014: 70, 98, 247).
37 See, e.g., Tucker 1971.
38 Sterrenburg 1979.
39 See Stock (2010: 102 and 214n7).
40 McLellan (2000: 329–330); cf. Nicolet (2009: 410).
41 Huet (1999: 55).
42 Canfora (2007: xii–xiv and 432), Nicolet (2009: 410–414).
43 See Stock (2010: 39–63) on these themes in reference to the fall of Napoleon and the later Restoration.
44 Byron's phrase, recorded by Lady Blessington from a conversation with Byron in 1823. See Lovell Jr. (1969: 120).
45 Dougherty (2006: 91–115); cf. Paulson (1981: 550), Clemit (1993: 155–157), Randel (2007: 188), and Franklin (2013: 45–46). On Napoleon's rejection of Jacobin associations, see McLynn (1998: 81–82).
46 Franklin (2013: 38). For the caricature work, see Haywood (2013: 74–99).
47 See Franklin (2013: 37).
48 Franklin (2013: 37), Haywood (2013: 86).
49 Patten (1992: 108–117).
50 Bate (1986: 196); cf. Haywood (2013: 7).
51 See Cross (2004: 202n13) for a hefty bibliography on Cruikshank and PBS.
52 Randel (2007: 188); cf. Franklin (2013: 37).
53 See further allusions in Franklin (2013: 37–46).
54 Haywood (2013: 86–91).
55 Ibid., 86. Upon hearing news of Napoleon's escape, Byron wrote to Robert John Wilmot: "As I have not seen you since that happy event I beg to congratulate you upon the resurrection of Bonaparte" (in Marchand [1994: 34]).
56 The quotation is attributed to Caesar after the Battle of Zela (August 2, 47 BCE), a year after Pharsalus (Suetonius *Vita divi Iulii* 37).
57 Attempts to disassociate Napoleon from Caesar's 'usurper' legacy began immediately: see the anonymously penned *Parallèle entre César, Cromwell, Monk et Bonaparte* (1799), with Nicolet (2009: 411–412).
58 *Contra* Randel (2007: 189).
59 Noted by Weiner (2015a: 66–68).

4

Romantic Prometheis and the Molding of *Frankenstein*

Suzanne L. Barnett

Our idea of 'the Romantic Prometheus' has largely been shaped by Percy Shelley's (henceforth PBS) *Prometheus Unbound*, arguably his *magnum opus* and the major work of the Romantic era that presents the Titan as the "champion of heaven's slaves" (1.443). PBS's Prometheus is a noble sufferer who endures Jupiter's wrath with stoic resolution and passively affects the unseating of tyranny via non-violent resistance when he "recalls" and repents his curse on Jupiter. But there is more than one 'Romantic Prometheus' just as there is more than one classical Prometheus, variations on whose tale were told by Hesiod, Aeschylus, Horace, and Ovid, among others. When Mary Shelley (henceforth MWS) attaches the subtitle "the Modern Prometheus" to *Frankenstein* (1818), then, she draws on a long literary and mythic tradition—from Hesiod and Horace to Francis Bacon, John Frank Newton, and Erasmus Darwin; and from Andrew Tooke to William Godwin—that predates PBS's formative depiction of the Titan in *Prometheus Unbound*, which he did not even begin to draft until well after *Frankenstein* was published.[1]

For the younger Romantics of the Shelleys' circle, pagan literature and mythology were not merely markers of traditional erudition or stylistic window-dressing but a fundamental characteristic of their philosophical, political, and aesthetic projects. For these writers, embracing joyous, polytheistic, pre-Christian literature (especially sensual pastorals and less traditional choices from the *Homeric Hymns* and Plato) functioned both as embedded rebellions against the religious and political status quo and as markers of a cultish devotion to communality and pleasure.[2] While the Tory press frequently derided members of the circle as "Satanic" or "Cockney," they preferred to call themselves "Athenians." The second-generation Romantics—a group that includes, to various degrees, both the Shelleys, Leigh Hunt, Thomas Love Peacock, John

Hamilton Reynolds, Barry Cornwall, Horace Smith, Claire Clairmont, Lord Byron, John Keats, and others—all produced works, both translations and original compositions, that invoke and celebrate the pagan classical past (MWS, for example, wrote two classically inspired dramas, *Proserpine* and *Midas*, in 1820).[3] And within this pagan framework, the figure of Prometheus looms large, appearing most prominently in the subtitle to *Frankenstein* (1818), in Percy Shelley's *Queen Mab* (1813) and *Prometheus Unbound* (1820), and in Byron's "Prometheus" (1816), among others.[4]

MWS was certainly familiar with the character of Prometheus from her youth; as the daughter of two philosophers with keen interests in pedagogy but an inveterate distrust of formal schooling, she received an informal but wide-ranging education.[5] She did not learn Greek until she lived with PBS, but her father, William Godwin, started her on Latin when she was an adolescent, and by all accounts she read widely from a young age in his library, which included significant holdings in Greek and Roman history and mythology, as well as classical literature and modern history.[6] She also grew up listening to her parents' friends and colleagues who called regularly, a who's who of philosophers, inventors, politicians, musicians, scientists, and poets that included Charles and Mary Lamb, Maria Edgeworth, Humphrey Davy, William Wordsworth, William Hazlitt, and Aaron Burr, among many others; MWS later recalled hiding under the parlor sofa to hear Coleridge recite "The Rime of the Ancient Mariner"—another Promethean tale of noble suffering—when she was nine years old.[7] Several painters of her parents' acquaintance—including William Blake and her late mother's former paramour Henry Fuseli—also adopted Promethean subjects for their work in this period.[8] Thus from her infancy MWS was surrounded by artists, writers, and philosophers who instilled in her both interest in and access to ancient literature and mythology, a trend that would continue into her adult social circle that was already thoroughly steeped in pagan culture by the time she turned her attention to the creation of her resolutely modern Prometheus story.

My purpose in this essay is neither to provide an exhaustive account of every Romantic allusion to Prometheus—Stuart Curran has already done so with great comprehensiveness—nor to suggest a mechanical chain of direct influences.[9] Neither can I presume to offer here an extensive reading of PBS's notoriously complex *Prometheus Unbound*, which has also been addressed at length and depth elsewhere.[10] Instead, I suggest some ways in which 'the Romantic Prometheus' is actually 'Romantic Prometheis,' plural, a shifting and evolving set of allusions and adoptions that MWS molds and manipulates in her first novel.

Newton's *Return to Nature* and Percy Shelley's *Queen Mab*

One direct influence on the younger Romantics' early reception of Prometheus was John Frank Newton, an acquaintance of PBS's and Peacock's from 1812 who was maniacally devoted to Zoroastrianism, the zodiac, and radical vegetarianism. Newton's *The Return to Nature, or, A Defence of the Vegetable Regimen* (1811) led directly to PBS's first recorded invocation of Prometheus in *Queen Mab*. Newton identifies the Prometheus myth and the Book of Genesis as allegories for "mankind's dereliction of his natural diet" (7) and cites an eccentric version of the myth of Prometheus as creator of humankind—*plasticator*—that seems to have entered English literature from the Roman poet Horace by way of Francis Bacon. In *Carmina* 1.16.13–16, Horace offers a peculiar additional detail to the Ovidian story of Prometheus's molding of humans from clay:

> It is said that Prometheus, compelled to add
> to primordial clay some parts
> from every side, set in our human stomachs   15
> the very violence of the raging lion.[11]
>
> fertur Prometheus addere principi
> limo coactus particulam undique
> desectam et insani leonis   15
> vim stomacho adposuisse nostro.

Unlike, for example, in Book 1 of *Metamorphoses*, where Ovid describes Prometheus as creating man "by mixing new-made earth with fresh rainwater," according to Horace, Prometheus's man was made not only of clay and water but also of parts of various animals.[12] Bacon takes up this detail in "Prometheus, or the State of Man" (from *Of the Wisdom of the Ancients*, 1610), in which he claims that "man was the creation of Prometheus, and made of earth, except inasmuch as Prometheus mixed with the mass certain particles from different animals" (307), a version that seems to follow Horace. This detail certainly recalls to us—or rather prefigures—MWS's description of Victor Frankenstein's piecemeal assemblage of his Creature from various parts, presumably both human and animal (*Frankenstein* [F] 1.4:81). Victor Frankenstein is intentionally circumspect with his interlocutor and ersatz biographer, Robert Walton, about both the "cause of generation and life" and the precise physical composition of the Creature, but his claims that he "collected bones from charnal houses" and that both "the dissecting room *and* the slaughter-house furnished many of [his] materials" (1.4: 81, my emphasis) suggest that MWS's "modern" Prometheus, Victor, also utilized both human and animal materials.¹³

In *The Return to Nature*, Newton runs with this idea from Bacon, claiming that "Prometheus first taught the use of animal food, and of fire with which to render it more digestible and pleasing to the taste" (8). Newton, citing Pliny's *Naturalis historia* (7.57.9), also awards Prometheus the honor (dubious, in this context) of being the first to slaughter an ox: "it was the same man [*sic*], Prometheus, who first preserved fire to human uses, and who likewise set the example of slaughtering an ox; a coincidence on which it will be quite unnecessary to comment" (*Return to Nature* 10). The rest of Newton's discourse is devoted to his strenuous advocacy of nudism and a diet of plants and distilled water, all of which he identifies as humankind's natural and most healthful state, as well as attacks on the enfeebling domestication of animals. So according to Newton's version (via Horace, via Bacon) of the Prometheus myth, humans are *already* made up of animal parts, which makes carnivorism particularly sinister, even cannibalistic. Newton goes on at great length to describe the rotting teeth, pustulent organs, and horrific skin conditions he attributes to human consumption of animals, and it is easy to see why this text would have appealed to PBS, who was always inclined to hypochondria and had already experimented with a "Pythagorean" diet as early as his Oxford days.¹⁴ Newton did, in fact, make an impression on him, and PBS not only befriended the Newton circle in Bracknell and adopted (more or less) their dietary regimen for the rest of his life, but also quoted and borrowed extensively from Newton's *The Return to Nature* in a note to *Queen Mab*.¹⁵

What is pertinent to the present discussion about these dietary discourses is the role played by Prometheus in these early years of PBS's career, roughly the time at which MWS (at that point still Mary Wollstonecraft Godwin) entered his life. Their ongoing experiments with vegetarianism invite us to consider, too, how the Shelleys' lifelong fascination with a vegetable diet figures in *Frankenstein*'s depiction of the creature's bloodless diet of "acorns and berries."¹⁶ *Queen Mab* is the result of what Donald Reiman and Neil Fraistat refer to as PBS's "virtual crash course in the classics and in history" in December 1812.¹⁷ William Godwin had tried to interest his young protégé in the classics when they first began to correspond in early 1812, but PBS was dubious, claiming in a July 1812 letter that "it certainly is my opinion—nor has [Godwin's] last letter sufficed to refute it—that the evils of acquiring Greek and Latin considerably overbalance the benefit."¹⁸ His burgeoning friendship with the resolutely pagan Thomas Love "Greeky Peaky" Peacock, however, inspired him to change his tune by the end of that year, when he placed an enormous order from London bookseller Thomas

"Clio" Rickman toward building a fledgling classical library and wrote to Thomas Hookham that he had become "determined to apply myself to a study that is hateful and disgusting to my very soul," history.[19] PBS's exposure to Peacock's eccentric vision of paganism, a magical and playful world of frolicsome nymphs and joyful conviviality, was to exert considerable influence on the rest of this corpus; after 1812, PBS embarked on a dedicated (if unconventional) study of classical literature that would significantly color not only his work but the work of his entire circle, MWS most emphatically included.

Prometheus would become a central, even characteristic, figure of PBS's distinctive paganism after the publication of *Prometheus Unbound* in 1820, but the Titan makes a brief appearance already in the final note to *Queen Mab*, a note that PBS also published separately, with an apparent nod to MWS's mother Mary Wollstonecraft, as *A Vindication of Natural Diet* in 1813.[20] In Note 17, attached to lines 8.211–212 ("No longer now / He slays the lamb that looks him in the face"), PBS proclaims that "the story of Prometheus is one likewise, which, although universally admitted to be allegorical, has never been satisfactorily explained" (*CPPBS* 296). Closely following Newton, PBS asserts (ibid., 297) that Prometheus,

> who represents the human race [...] applied fire to culinary purposes [...and] from this moment his vitals were devoured by the vulture of disease. It consumed his being in every shape of its loathsome and infinite variety, inducing the soul-quelling sinkings of premature and violent death. All vice arose from the ruin of healthful innocence. Tyranny, superstition, commerce, and inequality, were then first known [...].

Unlike the later Romantic Prometheus of *Prometheus Unbound* who saves humankind from Jupiterian tyranny, in *Queen Mab* Prometheus actually *introduces* "tyranny, superstition, commerce, and inequality" into the world via the fire that cooks flesh. For this Prometheus, the torment inflicted by the eagle that pecks his liver is an allegory for the intestinal distress which, PBS repeatedly maintains, necessarily accompanies an omnivorous diet.

Vindication opens with a Greek epigraph from Hesiod's *Works and Days* (lines 54–58) that Newton also cites. Newton offers the following translation of the passage (*The Return to Nature* 12):

> You rejoice, O crafty son of Iapetus [Prometheus], that you have stolen fire and deceived Jupiter; but great will thence be the evil both to yourself and to your prosperity. To them this gift of fire shall be a gift of woe; in which, while they delight and pride themselves, they shall cherish their own wretchedness.

Newton—and, following his lead, PBS—argue that this "evil" is sickness and mortality; in other words, Prometheus's theft of fire doomed humankind to suffer because it allowed them to consume meat. However, Newton is clearly misreading—or perhaps intentionally misrepresenting—the original text, since Hesiod actually refers in this passage to the first woman, Pandora (though she is not named here), whose creation he describes in the lines directly following these.[21] It is unclear if PBS realized that Newton had misread Hesiod and was willing to play along for the sake of rhetoric, or if PBS simply had not read Hesiod yet and did not realize that Newton had taken these lines out of context.[22] Regardless, what results in Newton's *Return to Nature* and in PBS's *Queen Mab* and *Vindication* is a version of Prometheus that contrasts significantly with the more familiar Romantic portrayal of the Titan as the "savior of mankind."

Two other roughly contemporary writers, Erasmus Darwin and Johann Wolfgang von Goethe, also offer Prometheis that may have influenced PBS's early treatment of the Titan in *Queen Mab*. Though PBS does not explicitly cite Darwin's *The Botanic Garden* (1791), he was certainly familiar with it and might also have recalled Darwin's note identifying the Prometheus myth as:

> an allegory for the effects of drinking spirituous liquors [...] It is remarkable, that all of the diseases from drinking spirituous or fermented liquors are liable to become hereditary, even to the third generation, gradually increasing, if the cause be continued, till the family becomes extinct.[23]

Whereas Newton (and later PBS) argue that Promethean fire doomed humankind to an unnatural diet and, consequently, mortality, Darwin suggests that fire led directly to fermentation ... which then doomed humankind to an unnatural diet and mortality. This aligns with the version of the Titan in Goethe's "Prometheus" (first published in 1789), a *Sturm-und-Drang* antitheistic manifesto that also posits Prometheus as forming humans specifically for them to suffer; the final stanza reads:

> Here I sit, forming humans
> After mine own image,
> A race the same as me
> In sorrowing, in crying,
> In enjoying and in rejoicing,
> And in not heeding yours
> As I don't![24]
>
> Hier sitz ich, forme Menschen
> Nach meinem Bilde,
> Ein Geschlecht, das mir gleich sei,

> Zu leiden, zu weinen,
> Zu geniessen und zu freuen sich,
> Und dein nicht zu achten,
> Wie ich!

Goethe's Prometheus curses Zeus and all who worship him, refuses to honor him, and depicts his own creation of man as a form of nose-thumbing vengeance against an uncaring deity. Humans, created in the Titan's image, are born to sorrow and lament before they enjoy and rejoice but do all of those things while ignoring Zeus. For Goethe, as for Newton, a human is a creature that is made to suffer, and Prometheus, as humankind's creator, is not exactly the hero of any of these creation stories. When in *Queen Mab* PBS follows Newton's version of the Titan, it is clear that, in the infancy of his classical education, PBS had clearly not worked out precisely what Prometheus *means* to the modern world.

Pantheons and Modern Prometheis

Despite PBS's initial resistance to Godwin's endorsement of a classical education, Godwin's *The Pantheon; or Ancient History of the Gods of Greece and Rome* (first published in 1806 under one of Godwin's pseudonyms, "Edward Baldwin, Esq.") certainly informed some of the second-generation Romantics' ideas about the Titan, especially those of one of his youngest, earliest, and most serious readers.[25] Godwin published his *Pantheon* when MWS was around eight years old, making her his precise target audience, and she was exposed to her father's idiosyncratic version of Prometheus as well as the other classically inclined children's literature he authored and distributed during his twenty-year career as a children's publisher, including his *Fables Ancient and Modern* (1805) and *History of Rome* (1809) (though his *History of Greece* was published in 1821, long after MWS had left Godwin's household).[26] In his preface to *History of England* (1806), Godwin remarks that he uses his own children as his test subjects: "I am accustomed to consult my children in this humble species of writing in which I have engaged. I put the two or three first sections of this work into their hands as a specimen" (v).

The Pantheon is, on one level, Godwin's answer to Andrew Tooke's *Pantheon of the Heathen Gods and Illustrious Heroes* (1698), one of the standard school texts on ancient myth; Godwin's fawning dedication of the volume to "Rev. Matthew Raine, D.D., Master of the Charter-House School" appears to be a blatant attempt to court the lucrative textbook market and present his *Pantheon* as an attractive alternative to Tooke's (who was himself an alumnus of Charterhouse and its headmaster from 1728 until 1731). On another level,

Godwin's treatment of classical myth stands in stark contrast to Tooke's overtly moralizing and triumphant Christian attitude toward classical paganism, and Godwin's depiction of Prometheus as a virtuous rebel—both the creator of human suffering and the alleviator of that suffering—sets the tone for the later Romantic Prometheis of PBS and MWS.

Tooke consistently presents figures from classical myth in ways colored by a piously Christian worldview; for example, he quotes 2 Samuel 12:12 ("Thou didst this thing secretly . . .") to pass judgment on Mars's and Venus's affair (83).[27] Tooke begins his *Pantheon* with numerous references to what is, in his view, the superiority of Christianity over pagan "idolatry" and identifies paganism on the first page as a "superstitious folly" that arose from "gross ignorance of the true and only GOD, or through a detestable contempt of him." This pejorative tone continues throughout Tooke's *Pantheon*: Jupiter's exploits are so "lewd and dishonorable" that Mystagogus, the principal narrator, is "almost ashamed to mention them" (14); Bacchus is described as the "captain and emperor of drunkards" (58); and Venus is a "whore" (207) and "impudent strumpet" whose eyes emit "clouds of dark and hellish impurity, and black mists of lust" (129).

Prometheus does not figure prominently in Tooke's exhaustive catalog of mythic figures; a brief outline of the Titan's story takes up only two and a half pages of this 359-page, two-volume text, or, for comparison, roughly one-third of the space Tooke allocates for Hercules and half of that devoted to Theseus. According to Tooke, Prometheus was "the first (as we find in history) that formed a man out of *clay*; which he did with such art and skill that *Minerva* was amazed" (italics in original), and when that goddess offers the titan anything from "heaven" that might be useful to his creation, he notes that he has never been there, so Minerva takes him on a tour. Prometheus observes that "the heat of the sun would be very useful in animating the man which he had formed" and returns to Earth with a stalk he ignited on the wheel of the chariot of the sun. Unlike, for example, Hesiod's version of Prometheus, who intentionally steals back the forbidden fire a vengeful Zeus has withdrawn from humankind, this version of Prometheus apparently acquires fire innocently, with no intention of rebelling; Tooke does not even frame it as a theft. Nevertheless, Jupiter is "displeased" that Prometheus has acquired fire and sends Pandora and her "box that was filled with all sorts of evils" to Prometheus, who, "fearful and suspecting the matter, refuses to accept" the gift; his unwitting brother Epimetheus, however, "was not so cautious" (320).[28] Tooke acknowledges the familiar story that Prometheus is punished by being bound and having his liver consumed by an eagle, then provides a less common explanation for the binding: "Yet some say, that he was not punished, because he stole fire from heaven, but because he had made woman, which, they say, is the most pernicious creature in the world" (321), an interpretation for which Tooke, unusually for him, cites no source. Tooke's *Pantheon* colors classical myth in general (and the Prometheus myth in particular) with double-handed doses of misogyny and religious conservatism that paint 'heathen' myth as both quaint and silly, though necessary to a gentleman's education. Tooke's brief preface refers to the edition's usefulness to "young scholars," and the unwritten implication is that the edition is for young male readers specifically.

Godwin's 1806 *Pantheon*, on the other hand, offers itself to "young persons of both sexes" on its title page and claims in its dedication to "remedy" the "imperfections" of Tooke.[29] Godwin's preface condemns the "dulness" [sic] and "malice" of previous compilations of classical myth for young readers, which have "combined to place Pantheons and Histories of the Heathen Gods among the most repulsive articles of the juvenile library" (3). Godwin pulls no punches from Tooke, whose effort "contains on every page an elaborate calumny upon the Gods"—Godwin always deferentially capitalizes the plural noun—and does so "in the coarsest thoughts and words that rancor could furnish" (v–vi). Godwin then slyly observes that Tooke "seems continually haunted by the fear that his pupil might prefer the religion of Jupiter to the religion of Christ." The utility of his *Pantheon* is, he then claims, threefold: first, to empower young readers "of both sexes" to "understand the system of the poets of former times" and to recognize allusions to them in English literature; second, to collect "the most agreeable fables that ever were invented," stories to awaken young readers' imagination (which is, Godwin claims, "the great engine of morality"). Finally, Godwin claims that the study of ancient myth offers an "instructive lesson on the nature of the human mind" by introducing stories that simultaneously have been made familiar by their repetition but also exotic due to their distance in space and time from nineteenth-century England. His introduction continues this agenda by maintaining that the Greeks were "the finest writers in the world" (1) and "probably the finest race of men that ever existed" (2), claims that are a far cry from Tooke's haughty condescension and derogation of stories he repeatedly dismisses as "ridiculous." Godwin argues throughout the early chapters of the *Pantheon* that "the language of the Greeks was the language of poetry" (8) and that his young readers must understand the mythic before they can hope to grasp the poetic.

While Godwin's treatment of Prometheus in his *Pantheon* is not considerably longer than Tooke's, his version of the Titan certainly appealed more directly to the younger Romantics and shaped their visions of Prometheus as a symbol of noble rebellion. Godwin introduces Prometheus as "an enemy to the progeny of

Saturn" (74–75) and retells Hesiod's version of the sacrifice at Mekone, offering a biting condemnation of Jupiter's reaction to the Titan's trick with the two bulls: "this is an ugly story; and the part assigned in it to Jupiter is wholly unworthy of our idea of a God" (76). From Prometheus's introduction, Godwin presents him as the adversary of Jupiter, or perhaps more appropriately, presents Jupiter as *Prometheus's* adversary: the Titan "surpassed the *whole universe* in mechanical skill and contrivance" (italics added), a category that includes Jupiter himself, and from the moment that Prometheus tricked Jupiter at Mekone, "Jupiter became the bitter enemy of Prometheus" (76). Godwin, like Tooke, includes the plot of Jupiter's creation of Pandora as punishment for Prometheus's acquisition of fire, but Godwin suggests that Jupiter's anger is joined with jealousy over the creature that "creator" Prometheus has endowed with life: "Jupiter became still more exasperated than ever with this new specimen of Prometheus's ability and artifice" (77). Jupiter's binding of Prometheus is then presented as the last resort of a floundering tyrant: "Jupiter thus constantly failing in every indirect attempt of retaliation upon his redoubtable adversary Prometheus, at last proceeded to more open hostility" (78) when he orders Vulcan and Mercury to chain the Titan to the rock. Godwin's final word on Prometheus is to note that the creation of man is not always credited to Prometheus, and many ancient writers deemed it "more decent and just to ascribe this event to the power of Jupiter" (80). This oddly vague and undeveloped claim ends the chapter and section containing what Godwin calls his "account of the superior Gods" (80), with Prometheus occupying the conspicuous final slot.

Whereas Tooke presents Prometheus as a somewhat hapless victim of Jupiter's fickle vengeance, Godwin's retelling of the same source material paints a more nuanced and complimentary portrait of the fundamentally antagonistic Titan. For Tooke, Prometheus is a clever craftsman who unwittingly runs afoul of Jupiter; in Godwin's *Pantheon*, Prometheus begins to take the shape of the Romantic figure we later see in PBS, Byron, and MWS: he is rebellious, the enemy of a brutal oppressor, a "creator" and a savior, and the long-suffering martyr to a petty tyrant's jealousy and rage.[30] Godwin's sly acknowledgement that some writers find it more "decent" to credit "the power of Jupiter" with the creation of humans is undercut by his claim that ancient writers attribute Prometheus and not Jupiter with humankind's creation because, in their view, humankind's creator must *necessarily* be his enemy (78–79):

> the ancients saw to how many evils the human race is exposed, how many years of misery many of them endure, with what a variety of diseases they are afflicted, how the great majority is condemned to perpetual labour, poverty, and ignorance,

and how many vices are contracted by men, in consequence of which they afflict each other with a thousand additional evils [...] the views of the early ancients, in times of savage rudeness, and before the refinements of society were invented, were most melancholy respecting the lot of man than ours have been since: they could not therefore admit that he [humankind] was the creature of Jupiter: they were rather more prone to believe that Jupiter was from the first his enemy: the same views led them to revile and speak evil of the female sex [...] it is impossible not to remark a considerable resemblance between the story of Pandora's box, and that of the apple with which Eve in the bible *tempted* her husband, *and he did eat.*

Several aspects of this passage are remarkable: first, it is rather somber material for children and evidence of Godwin's general disinclination (in the *Pantheon* and the rest of his pseudonymously authored Juvenile Library texts) to talk down to his young readers. Second, as Godwin critiques the essential misogyny of the Pandora story, he draws parallels to the Book of Genesis, simultaneously elevating Hesiod to the level of the Bible and downgrading the Christian Bible to the level of pagan myth.[31] Perhaps most notable, however, is the idea that Jupiter could not have created humans to live in a world of such hardship and torment because that would necessarily make him the "enemy" of humankind. In this claim we find the precursor to a central philosophical quandary of *Frankenstein*: how can a loving creator bring a creature into this world only to watch him struggle and suffer? If Prometheus, not Jupiter, created humankind, then humans can take solace in the idea that the celestial god they worship is not responsible for their pain and torment but instead offers them succor from those pains. But without the Prometheus myth, humans would be confronted directly with the idea that they were created by a maker who molded them from clay of misery. According to Godwin, Prometheus functions as an allegory that allows humans to continue to worship the gods (and Jupiter in particular). Without Prometheus, the ancient Greeks would have had to accept that the god that created them also created their pain.

So when MWS affixes the subtitle "*or, the Modern Prometheus*" to *Frankenstein*, she invites her readers to consider a diverse and sometimes contradictory storehouse of Promethean allusions, both ancient and contemporary. Was Prometheus the creator or humankind, its savior, or its destroyer? Did he craft humans so that they might suffer, or does he endeavor to alleviate their suffering at the hands of a fickle and tyrannical deity who created them? MWS's Promethean invocations and allusions, colored by the sometimes contradictory treatments offered by her family and peers, necessarily color our understanding of the relationship between Victor and the creature, between creator and destroyer.

Notes

1 Famously, MWS dreamt the germ of *Frankenstein* (henceforth *F*) about a month after the ghost-story-writing contest at the Villa Diodati on June 19, 1816 and, according to Charles Robinson (2009: 16), she drafted the "version of her story that then became the basis for the complete Draft of her novel" by August 1816; see further Introduction and Gapp (this volume). From August 1816 until April 1817, she (with, as Robinson notes, some editing and drafting contributions from PBS) drafted the full novel, the Fair Copy of which was completed by May 1817. She corrected the proofs in September and November 1817, and it was published in December 1817, despite "1818" on the title page (Macdonald and Scherf [2012: 34]). Macdonald and Scherf argue that MWS's journal entry on December 30, 1817, "Fran[kens]tein comes," suggests that the first edition was printed on the last day of 1817 and note that the Shelleys had already received their printed copies on January 1 or 2, 1818). PBS began *Prometheus Unbound* in Este in 1818, the first act in October 1818 and Acts II and III between March and May 1819. He added the fourth act in December 1819 and completed the additional poems for the volume in January 1820, and the volume was finally published in August 1820.

2 See, for example, Barnett 2014 and 2017. Peacock is instrumental in inspiring both PBS and MWS to study the classics seriously; this curriculum begins in 1812 and arguably reaches its apogee in Marlow in 1817, when in a two-week frenzy in July PBS translated Aeschylus's *Prometheus Bound* as well as extensive selections from Plato and Sophocles, and he and Peacock together translated some of the *Homeric Hymns*. Due to the Shelleys' longstanding practice of communal reading and writing, MWS was at the very least an observer, if not an active participant, in these activities, which she records in their shared journal.

3 In contradistinction to the "second-generation" or "younger Romantics," the "first-generation" or "older" Romantics included William Wordsworth, Samuel Taylor Coleridge, William Blake, and their peers.

4 Two of these texts—*F* and "Prometheus"—are products of the same "wet" and "ungenial," seemingly apocalyptic summerless summer the Shelleys, Byron, and John Polidori spent in Switzerland. Leigh Hunt mentions in a letter to PBS in July 1819 that he thought of writing a poem called *Prometheus Throned* "in which I intended to have described him as having lately taken possession of Jupiter's seat. But the subject, on every account, is in better hands," i.e., PBS's (Hunt 1862). In 1820, Hartley Coleridge also attempted a *Prometheus*, which he abandoned as a fragment; his editor, his brother Derwent Coleridge, suggests that, since their father Samuel Taylor Coleridge (who delivered his lecture "On the Prometheus of Aeschylus" to the Royal Society in 1825) "saw in the fable of Prometheus, as treated by Aeschylus, a profound and complex *philsopheme*, which the unspehered spirit of Plato might have been taxed to unfold," Hartley was intimidated and abandoned the project as being "foreign to his own genius [...so] the youthful Telemachus shrunk from the attempt to bend his father's bow" (280). Derwent also credits the 1820 publication of "splendid genius" PBS's *Prometheus Unbound* with discouraging Hartley Coleridge's attempts to address the same subject (283).

5 When asked in 1812 if he was educating MWS and Fanny according to Wollstonecraft's educational principles, Godwin responded that, "They are neither of them brought up with an exclusive attention to the system and ideas of their mother" due to Godwin's belief in his "incompetence for the education of daughters" and his and his new wife Mary Jane's lack of time to devote to "reducing novel theories of education to practice" (Paul 1970: ii.213–214).

6   Sunstein (1989: 39–41).
7   See Mellor (1988: 11), Sunstein (1989: 40).
8   Blake's significant engagement with Prometheus is too weighty a subject to do justice to here, but see Lewis 1992. A 2006 exhibition at the Tate Britain, *Gothic Nightmares: Fuseli, Blake and the Romantic Imagination*, featured a room entitled "Perverse Classicism," which contained several Prometheus-themed works by Fuseli, George Romney, Richard Cosway, and John Flaxman dating from the 1770s to 1810, testaments to that mythic figure's cultural circulation in the Romantic era. A guide to the exhibit can be found at: http://www.tate.org.uk/whats-on/tate-britain/exhibition/gothic-nightmares-fuseli-blake-and-romantic-imagination (accessed 3 September 2017).
9   In particular, Curran 1975 and 1986 offer exhaustive and enlightening catalogs of readings of Prometheus in the late eighteenth and early nineteenth centuries.
10 For more comprehensive treatments of *Prometheus Unbound*, see Bloom 1959, Wasserman 1965, Curran 1975, Robinson 1976a, Scrivener 1982.
11 My thanks to the editors and to Chris Washington of Francis Marion University for assisting in this translation.
12 Mandelbaum (1993: 6). Both Shelleys were certainly familiar with Ovid's version of Prometheus *plasticator*; MWS's journal notes that she began working her way through *Metamorphoses* on 8 April 1815: "read 15 lines of Ovids metamo[r]phosis with Hogg" [sic] (73). She also notes that she was reading Ovid again in April and May of 1820, but a text is not specified. See also Pollin 1965 for Ovid as a source for *F*.
13 All citations from *F* are from Macdonald and Scherf 2012. On the Creature's piecemeal nature, see chapters by Weiner and Gumpert (this volume).
14 PBS was certainly familiar with Pythagoras via Ovid's *Metamorphoses* and Diogenes Laertius's *Lives of Eminent Philosophers*; see Male and Notopoulos 1959 for an examination of Shelley's copy of Diogenes Laertius, which he owned by 1814, since MWS notes in her journal entry of 4 December 1814 that "Shelley reads Diogenes Laertius." In his letter to Rickman on 24 December 1812 (while PBS was at work on *Queen Mab*), he requested "Pythagoras," though it is unclear which work he means; see also note 18 below.
15 PBS's roughly vegetarian diet—and MWS's involvement in it—is too complicated a subject to address fully here, but see Morton (1994: esp. 57–80).
16 See also Adams (1990: esp. 95–108).
17 Reiman and Fraistat (2004: 501), henceforth *CPPBS*.
18 Ingpen (1915: 348–350), henceforth *PBSL*.
19 The requested texts included works by Aeschylus, Euripides, Tacitus, Hippocrates, Pythagoras, and Sappho, among many others. See *PBSL* 372 for the complete book order of 24 December 1812. PBS is clearly not yet proficient at reading Greek but is comfortable with Latin, since he tells Hookham that "the Greek classics should have Latin or English versions printed opposite. If not to be attained thus, they must be sent otherwise" (*PBSL* 373–374). Peacock's sobriquet was bestowed upon him by Thomas Taylor (a.k.a. "the pagan Methodist" and "the Platonist") and is often referenced in the correspondence of the circle, which had a penchant for playful nicknames. For example, on December, 17 1824, Leigh Hunt wrote to Thomas Jefferson Hogg and asked "How is 'Peaky with his Greeky?'" (Butler [1979: 20]; Scott [1943: 71–72]).
20 Wollstonecraft released *A Vindication of the Rights of Men, in a Letter to the Right Honourable Edmund Burke; Occasioned by His Reflections on the Revolution in France* in 1790 and *A Vindication of the Rights of Woman: with Strictures on Political and Moral Subjects* in 1792.

PBS's *A Vindication of Natural Diet* was printed in 1813 as a pamphlet; it is, in essence, the pertinent notes from *Queen Mab*, collected separately. Reiman and Fraistat note that "the text of the *QM* notes closely parallels the next of *Natural Diet*, which PBS composed sometime between October 1812 and November 1813, perhaps as early as October or November 1812"; they also note critical disagreement as to which went to print first, the poem or the pamphlet, though they side with the latter (*CPPBS* 652–653). PBS's similar "On the Vegetable System of Diet" (composed 1814–1815) was published posthumously.

21 On Pandora in Hesiod's *Theogony* and *Works and Days*, see also Gumpert (this volume).
22 PBS was likely exposed to Hesiod as a student at Eton or Oxford, but he certainly read him as an adult; Jones 1964 includes Hesiod among the contents of PBS's library, and PBS cites Hesiod in the preface to *Prometheus Unbound*. Interestingly, the editors of the 1884 "new edition" of *Vindication* (London: F. Pitman) published by the Vegetarian Society (the prefatory notice of which claims it as "perhaps the most powerful and eloquent plea ever put forward in favour of the Vegetarian cause") quietly replace the Hesiod epigraph with one from PBS's *Epipsychidion* (1821).
23 Darwin (1799: 156). It is also worth noting that Darwin, following Immanuel Kant, thought of Benjamin Franklin as a "new Prometheus." Charles Robinson (in the 1996 Garland edition of *The* Frankenstein *Notebooks*) and others have suggested that the name 'Frankenstein' intentionally recalls Franklin.
24 I have found no direct evidence that MWS read Goethe's "Prometheus," but since she and her circle were familiar with his work—*The Sorrows of Young Werther* (1774) is the source of the Creature's emotional education in *F*, and Claire Clairmont undertook a translation of Goethe's *Memoirs* for Byron, at PBS's behest, in 1822—it is possible that they knew the poem, which was first published anonymously in 1785 and with Goethe's name attached in 1789. My thanks to Julian Knox of Georgia College and State University for this translation.
25 *The Pantheon* was one of Godwin's most successful titles published by his Juvenile Library, going through at least seven editions between 1806 and 1836. For more on Godwin's children's publishing venture, see my and Katherine Bennett Gustafson's ongoing digital edition of Godwin's ten books for children and our introduction, "The Radical Aesop: William Godwin and the Juvenile Library, 1805–1825," on *Romantic Circles Electronic Editions*.
26 It was, in fact, Godwin's attempts to secure his new acolyte PBS's financial support of the Juvenile Library that led to the latter's elopement with MWS in 1814: PBS and MWS met after Godwin invited his new protégé to his home to discuss potential patronage (St Clair [1989: 176]). Godwin's Juvenile Library was also the home of young Mary's first publication, "Mounseer Nongtongpaw; or, the Discoveries of John Bull in a Trip to Paris" (1808), a thirty-nine quatrain expansion of Charles Dibdin's brief song of 1796. The 1808 edition was illustrated by William Mulready (who was himself the subject of Godwin's 1805 *The Looking-Glass: A True History of the Early Years of an Artist*), and the poem was reissued in 1830 in an edition illustrated by the great caricaturist Robert Cruikshank.
27 Quotations from Tooke are taken from the thirtieth edition of 1798, the one that the younger Romantics might have been familiar with from their own schooldays and with which Godwin's version was in direct competition; all passages are also present in earlier editions.
28 Here Tooke diverges from Hesiod's *Works and Days*, which claims that Zeus sent Pandora to Epimetheus, not to Prometheus.
29 All page numbers from Godwin's *Pantheon* refer to the 1810 edition printed for M. J. Godwin at the Juvenile Library.
30 Cf. McClellan (this volume).

31 Wollstonecraft makes a similar move in *An Historical and Moral View of the French Revolution; and the Effect It Has Produced in Europe* (1794) when she claims that, "We must get entirely clear of all the notions drawn from the wild traditions of original sin: the eating of the apple, the theft of Prometheus, the opening of Pandora's box, and the other fables, too tedious to enumerate, on which priests have erected their tremendous structures of imposition, to persuade us, that we are naturally inclined to evil" (17).

5

Why the 'Year without a Summer'?

David A. Gapp

Introduction

Europe's dismally cold, stormy, and rain-saturated summer of 1816 provided the dramatic atmospheric backdrop for the creation of Mary Shelley's (hereafter MWS) classic horror story. 1816 was variously called 'Poverty Year,' '1800 and Froze to Death,' 'The Summer That Never Was,' or 'The Year the Elements Were All Mixed Up.' The remarkable climatic event known more widely as the 'Year without a Summer' had its antecedent the year before and half a world away. MWS could not have known that a volcano lay behind the dreary weather that confined her and her companions—Percy Shelley (hereafter PBS), Lord Byron, John Polidori, and Claire Clairmont—to the indoors and inspired them to tell and write ghost stories. Nevertheless, the 1815 Tambora eruption and the subsequent 'Year without a Summer' left their mark on *Frankenstein* in the form of cold, wet, and barren landscapes. This essay examines the science of the summer that lies behind those aspects of MWS's science fiction novel.

The Eruption

On the evening of April 5, 1815, Mt. Tambora, a 14,000-foot (about 4,250 m) volcano on the Indonesian island of Sumbawa, erupted violently (Figs. 5.1 and 5.2). The onset of this climate-altering event was ultimately responsible for the exceptionally cold and stormy year in Western Europe and the exceptionally cold and dry year in much of North America in 1816. Tambora's cataclysmic eruption created a volcanic winter that became an exclamation point to the waning years of the **Little Ice Age**.[1]

The Tambora eruption had a **volcanic explosivity index (VEI)** of 7, making it the most powerful volcano in recorded history. In nearly two weeks of

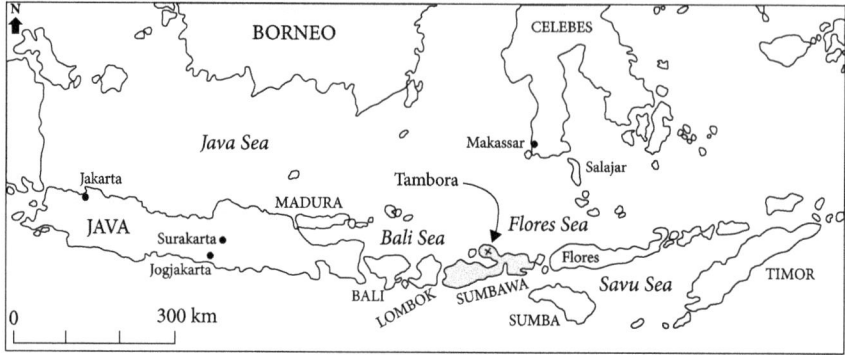

Fig. 5.1 Indonesian Archipelago in the region of the Mt. Tambora eruption. Modified from: Stothers, Richard B. 1984. "The Great Tambora Eruption in 1815 and Its Aftermath." *Science* 224.4654: 1191–1198.

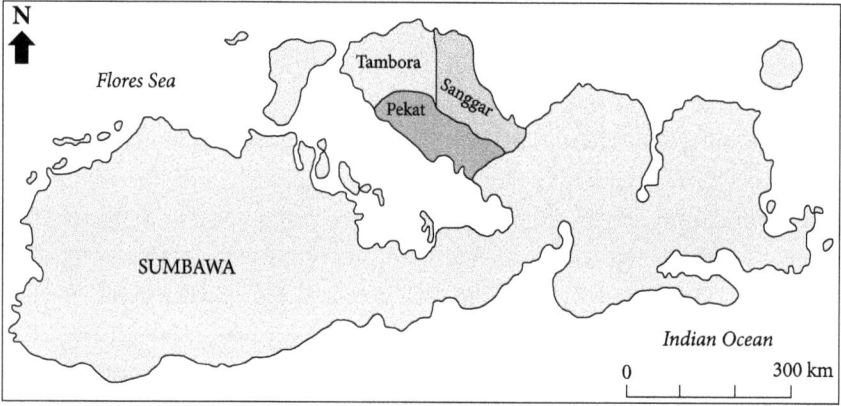

Fig. 5.2 The island of Sumbawa in the Indonesian Archipelago. Redrawn from: Sudradjat, Adjat and Heryadi Rachmat. 2015. *Greetings from Tambora: A Potpourri of the Stories on the Deadliest Volcanic Eruption*. Bandung: Geological Museum.

continuous eruption, Tambora lost one-third of its height while injecting an estimated 100 km³ (about 24 cubic miles) of earth into the atmosphere: more than five times that of Krakatoa (1883), ten times the amount of Pinatubo (1991), and as much as 100 times that of Mt. St. Helens (1980).

Classified as an **ultra-Plinian eruption**, the ejected material reached 25 miles (about 40 km) into the **stratosphere**, and the sounds of the initial and subsequent eruptions were heard up to 1,600 miles (about 2,575 km) away.[2] Sir Stamford Raffles, Lieutenant Governor of Java, heard the eruption from his residence 800 miles (about 1,285 km) away in Java and was concerned that it was distant cannon fire.[3] The greatest devastation would come on April 10, with an exceedingly violent explosion formed from three massive columns of fire that coalesced into a single column and marked the peak of the explosive activity. By April 11, the eruption activity began to subside and by April 17 the eruption was over.[4]

The immediate outcome of the eruption on April 10 was the total destruction of the three kingdoms of Sanggar, Tambora, and Pekat (Fig. 5.2). **Pyroclastic flow** from this eruption killed nearly all 10,000 inhabitants of the peninsula, and with it the unique language and culture of the Tambora Kingdom vanished.[5] It is estimated that 44,000 people were killed outright on Sumbawa and the surrounding islands, and that total casualties swelled upwards of 117,000 human fatalities from the subsequent effects of famine and disease.[6]

A suffocating ash fall of up to 40 inches (about 100 cm) blanketed the peninsula and the nearby islands. Lombok and Bali to the west were covered to the depth of 20 inches (about 50 cm) or more, and the ash fall would spread across the eastern half of Java (Fig. 5.3). The initial ash cloud created pitch darkness that persisted for two days in a 375-mile (600 km) radius from Tambora.[7] This ash cloud subsequently expanded to cover an area approximately the size of the United States. Pyroclastic flows racing down Tambora and traveling at upwards of 450 miles per hour (724 km/hour), created a whirlwind that induced a 13 foot (4 m) tsunami on April 11 reaching East Java 310 miles (about 500 km) away.[8]

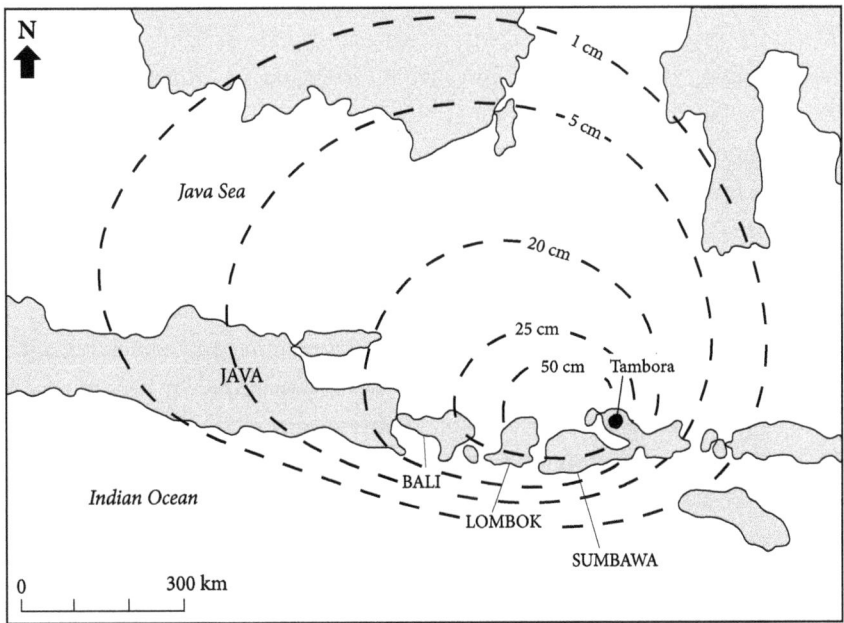

Fig. 5.3 Extent of the Tambora ash fall in the surrounding islands. Redrawn from: Sudradjat, Adjat and Heryadi Rachmat. 2015. *Greetings from Tambora: A Potpourri of the Stories on the Deadliest Volcanic Eruption*. Bandung: Geological Museum.

The magnitude of the eruption was evident months later and over 2,000 miles (about 3,220 km) away from Sumbawa when the East India Company ships *Fairlie* and *James Shibbald* sailed through a massive **pumice raft** from October 1 to October 3, 1815 while *en route* to Calcutta.[9] Unaware of Tambora's eruption, the captain believed this volcanic material originated from an underwater volcano known to be in the general vicinity of his ships.[10]

The Aftermath

Chemical composition of the **ejecta** had a particular impact both locally and worldwide. A significant hydrofluoric acid content in Tambora's ejecta added to the lethality of the eruption, as the acidity killed animal and plant life directly and acidified the landscape for months to come. However, it would be the sulfur dioxide deposited in the stratosphere that persisted for two to three years that would have the widest effect on the world's climate. The estimated 55 million metric tons of sulfur dioxide deposited in the stratosphere was converted into 100 million tons of sulfuric acid by ultraviolet light (Fig. 5.4). The resulting sulfate particles created a reflective shield that further reduced the amount of energy reaching the earth. In 1816, total solar energy was reduced by 0.5 percent through a combination of aerosol particulate absorption of light and increased light reflection. Analyses of ice cores from Greenland and Antarctica suggest that the sulfate screen formed in the stratosphere persisted for two to three years post-eruption, leading to colder than normal years beyond 1816.[11] The outcome would be several years of persistent crop loss and famine.

Tambora's eruption occurred in the waning years of the Little Ice Age. Moreover, the 1810s was an especially cold decade in many parts of the world. Some climatologists consider this decade to have been the coldest in 500 years.[12] Increased volcanic activity prior to the Tambora eruption and coinciding with the **Dalton Minimum** (1790–1820), a period characterized by a diminished solar output, compounded the climatic vagaries concomitant with the Little Ice Age and the 1810s. Contributory to these cold years were five large eruptions of VEI 4 or greater leading up to the Tambora eruption:

- an unknown South American volcano (1809)
- La Soufrière on St. Vincent in the Caribbean (1812)
- Awu in the Sangihe Islands of Indonesia (1812)
- Suwanosejima in the Ryukyu Islands of Japan (1813)
- Mayon in the Philippines (1814)

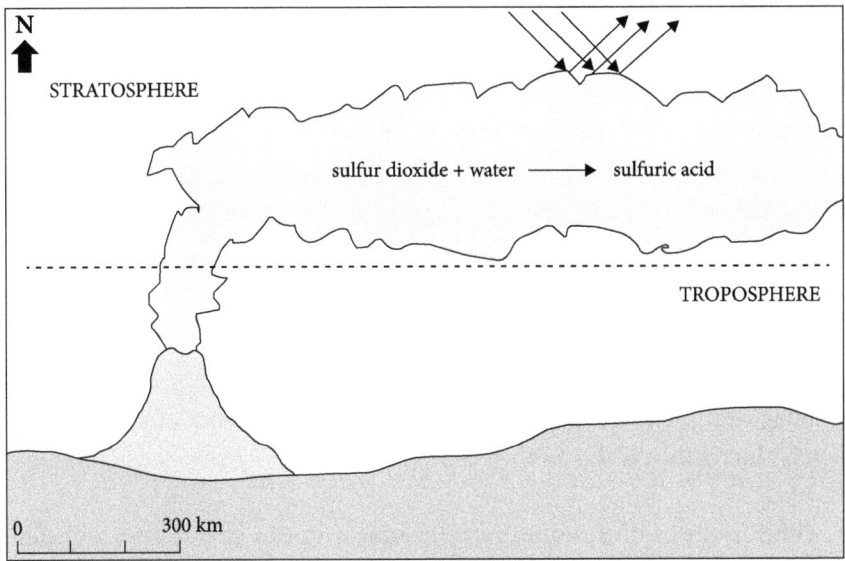

Fig. 5.4 Chemical reaction in the stratosphere leading to formation of the reflective sulfate shield as a result of the Tambora eruption. Sulfur dioxide in the stratosphere is converted by an appropriate wavelength of UV light to form sulfuric acid that increases the reflectivity of the atmosphere, reducing the solar energy reaching the earth.

Thus, the atmosphere in 1815 was already charged with particulates when Tambora erupted and further loaded the atmosphere with light-absorbing and light-reflecting dust. In some places, the cold summer of 1816 may have been just another cold year in a string of unusually cold years. But, for most, 1816 was devastatingly cold, beyond what had been experienced in living memory.

To many people, the cause of such aberrant weather in 1816 was simple: God's wrath. In a posting from Paris dated July 18, later reported in the *Dedham Gazette* (Dedham, Massachusetts) on September 13, 1816, after a most trying spring and early summer: "The grand vicars of the diocese of Paris have just issued an order for public prayers of 40 hours, with exposition of the Holy Sacrament, to entreat the Almighty for weather more favorable to the fruits of the earth" (p. 1). In a proclamation to the Commonwealth in the following year (March 4, 1817), John Brooks, the Governor of Massachusetts, spoke to the presumed displeasure that Providence visited upon them the year before:

> That while we devoutly beseech Him to shed upon us the blessings of His providence the present year, in granting us a favorable seed time and a plentiful harvest, we may submissively acknowledge the justness of any tokens of His displeasure with which, in the course of the last year we have been visited. That we may be preserved from desolating sickness, from drought and tempests; and that the year may be crowned with his goodness.[13]

In contrast, scientists of the period postulated a number of underlying causes. One of the more obvious observations coinciding with the aberrant weather was the increased sunspots, such as that re-reported in the *Otsego Herald* (Cooperstown, NY) on June 20, 1816 (in vol. XXII, no. 1108, p. 2):

> Philadelphia, June 6
> Another Spot on the Sun,
> Has made its appearance about the centre of its surface. It is about the size of the former large spot, but more round, and is of a jet black color. It is at least worthy of remark, that these phenomena have, each time, been preceded by an extraordinary change of the weather. Fr. Jour.

Coming near the end of the Dalton Minimum, the frequency of sunspots had notably increased and was an obvious phenomenon to ascribe to the unfavorable weather.

Other postulated causes included alteration in the atmosphere, a change in solar output, and descent of polar ice. Shipping logs in 1816 reported a notable increase in the number of ice floes in the North Atlantic, and it was suggested that these ice floes were responsible for the much colder weather.[14] Moreover, the later disappearance of ice in the Great Lakes during the spring prompted some to speculate a cooling effect on North America arising from this phenomenon.[15]

Benjamin Franklin's experiments with lightning rods were suspected by many to have caused the aberrant weather.[16] Relatedly, there was also suspicion that the electric fluid of the atmosphere had been damaged. To that end, some believers resorted to unusual actions. As the *Washington City Weekly Gazette* reported on September 21, 1816, "The inhabitants of Zurich, in Switzerland, have recently destroyed the lightning rods on many houses, on the account, as they have been taught by a weak pamphleteer, that the cold and wet weather is occasioned by their extracting too great a quantity of [caloric] from the air."[17]

Did the rest of the world know about the Tambora eruption? They did. The following article appeared in the *Albany Advertiser* of March 6, 1816, as well as in a number of other newspapers around the world:

> DREADFUL VOLCANIC ERUPTION
> From the Java Government Gazette, May 20, 1815
>
> We are at length enabled to give the public a full and interesting account of the Volcanic eruption that has recently taken place on the Island of Sumbawa, which has been furnished to us from the most respectable authority, and which may be received as an historical fact of undoubted authority.

While the news of Tambora's eruption had spread slowly around the world, the connection of this event with the massive climate alteration was not made. However, Benjamin Franklin had previously posited a role for volcanism and atmospheric effects.[18] In 1784, while in France, Franklin wrote a brief "speculation" that the unseasonably cold weather of the 1783–1784 winter in North America could be attributable to volcanic activity in Iceland. Indeed, one of the deadliest volcanoes on record, Lakagígar (Laki), a volcanic fissure in southern Iceland, erupted over an eight-month period between 1783 and 1784 with catastrophic effects for Iceland and Europe. It would be nearly two centuries before Franklin's ignored theory would be supported.

We know, of course, that the presence of the energy-absorbing, light-reflecting atmospheric veil formed from the Tambora eruption significantly reduced the energy reaching earth in 1816. Reconstruction of the weather patterns of the year provides explanation for the difference in the weather extremes between North America and Europe. The jet stream during the summer of 1816 dramatically altered the normal storm tracks affecting North America and Western Europe. The 1816 track brought cold dry Arctic air to northeastern North America, producing late springs, cool/cold summers, early fall frosts, and drought. The track then turned northeast to cross the Atlantic, picked up moisture as it headed to the Arctic, and turned south again to deliver a steady stream of cold storms to Western Europe.

Temperatures in Western Europe averaged as much as 3–4°C below normal, and precipitation increased by as much as 200 percent in some areas. American newspapers documented the abnormal weather developing in Europe. As early as December 1815, some remarkable changes in the weather were noted, such as the following in the *Otsego Herald* (May 23, 1816):

> Under the head of Terramo, in Italy, 31st December, we read: There has fallen, during six hours, in our city, and in its environs, a greater quantity of snow than has been known in the memory of man. To this phenomenon there is added another, even more astonishing, which is, that this snow is red and yellow.

An early season report from England, published in the *Vermont Gazette* (July 30, 1816), stated:

> There was a heavy fall of SNOW in Derbyshire on the twenty-seventh of May, in places near Buxton, the road was nearly impassable from its drifting. The sheep in that neighborhood suffered severely, and many perished.

And as the growing season progressed, the prospects for an abundant harvest seemed quite remote, as seen in this report from the *Ulster Plebian* (September 17, 1816):

> So late as July, the crops in Europe were very unpromising. In the north of Germany, and upon the borders of the Baltic, one half of the winter grain was ploughed up, and the residue promised but half a crop. In the Low Countries, the heavy rains had destroyed the best hopes of the husbandman. In England, the agricultural report of July 1, mentions the extreme changeableness of the weather, and that every flattering prospect of genial warmth had been succeeded throughout the spring with a reverse of chilling and searching spring with a reverse of a chilling and searching damp atmosphere. The pastures were bare, and the meadows in a backward state, with very indifferent prospect of a crop of hay.

Higher than normal precipitation exacerbated abnormally low temperatures. In Ireland, cold rain fell for 142 out of the 153 days during the summer. Across Europe, continuous rains and periodic torrential rains led to saturated or flooded fields with rivers, streams, and canals breaking their banks, as can be seen in the following reports from the *Otsego Herald* (September 12, 1816) and *New Hampshire Patriot* (September 10, 1816):

> Arnheim, July 5.
>
> The torrents of rain which have fallen, accompanied by water-spouts and storms, in Germany and Switzerland, together with the continued rain we have had in this district, have produced such and effect upon the Rhine, that the water has risen in the river at this city to the almost, at this season, unparalleled height of 15 feet and 7 inches.
>
> In England, the prospect as to the harvest was very gloomy. Agriculture had been extremely injured by excessive rains. In several parts of Europe the same afflictive effect has proceeded from the same course. The waters of the Rhine and Necker have been raised from 9 to 11 feet above their usual level—and have inundated the plantations on their banks. The waters of the Seine were 8 feet higher than usual.

Coming on the heels of the Napoleonic wars, the 'Year without a Summer' was characterized by continued population displacements, trade disruption, floods, crop failures, food riots, famine, and multiple outbreaks of typhus.[19]

Conclusion: Mary Shelley in 1816

Switzerland was hit especially hard by the extreme weather. Maximum decrease in summer temperature relative to neighboring decades was 3.8°C in Geneva. The country experienced 130 days of rain between April and September, severely reducing agricultural output and leading to widespread flooding, including Lake Geneva. The outcome was extensive crop losses of an estimated 10–40 percent, attributable to impaired planting, germination, and growth of the crops. Those crops that managed to reach maturity would rot in the field due to the never-ending rain and cold.

The Swiss were reduced to eating their cats, grass, and **reindeer moss**.[20] Any hopes of importing food were compromised by the flooded rivers and by interception of grain deliveries coming from the Mediterranean countries from the south. One quote stated that famine diet was "the most loathsome and unnatural foods—carcasses of dead animals, cattle fodder, leaves of nettles, swine food."[21]

MWS and her circle of British Romantics joined company in Switzerland during that 'Year without a Summer.' The coterie sought refuge from this "wet, ungenial summer" in the Villa Diodati on the shores of Lake Geneva in June 1816, "and incessant rain often confined [them] for days to the house."[22] The journals of MWS testify to this experience. In a fragment written in the hand of PBS during the Geneva trip of 1816, MWS's journal reports "a violent wind & intervals of rain, which prevents the possibility of departure" and a day with only one "interval of sunshine" suitable for travel.[23] "Today is rainy therefore we cannot go to Col du Baume," writes MWS on July 24, 1816. While "about ten the weather appears to clear up ... it began to rain almost as soon as we left our inn." MWS reports that "a dense white mist covered the vale." "The rain continued in torrents—we were wetted to the skin so that ... we resolved to turn back."[24] On July 26, 1816, MWS repeats her frustration, as "we determine to return today as it rained and we could not possibly go to Col de Balme as we intended."[25]

With the weather raging outside and the countryside awash in famine-plagued, displaced, and diseased humanity, the companions settled in to reading *Fantasmagoriana*, discussing Erasmus Darwin's theories, and speculating on the potential of galvanism as the life-giving principle.[26] The outcome of the great Tambora eruption thus provided the time and circumstances for the creation of *Frankenstein; or, the Modern Prometheus*.

Glossary

Dalton Minimum: a period (1790–1820) of low sunspot activity near the end of the Little Ice Age.
Ejecta: general term for material ejected during a volcanic eruption.
Little Ice Age: a period of global cooling and erratic seasons that lasted from approximately 1300 until 1850. Characteristically, the winters were significantly colder and the summers were shorter and less predictable, making for crop shortfall and losses and famine. The period was characterized by three distinct

sunspot minima: the Spörer Minimum (1450–1550), Maunder Minimum (1645–1715), and Dalton Minimum (1790–1820). Additionally, the Little Ice Age coincides with a period of increased worldwide volcanic activity. The sunspot minima and volcanic eruptions are thought to have contributed to this widespread global cooling and were part of a complex and poorly understood climate change involving changes in oceanic currents, weather patterns, and perhaps variations in the earth's orbit or axial tilt. (For further reading, see Fagan 2000.)

Pumice raft: a light form of volcanic glass characterized by extensive porosity attributable to gas bubbles trapped during ejection. Because of its highly porous nature, pumice floats and will form oceanic rafts from volcanic eruptions.

Pyroclastic flow: a fast-moving (up to 435 miles/hour (about 700 km/hour)) current of hot gas (up to 1000°C) and volcanic particulate formed during eruption. Differentiated from lava, which is molten rock flowing from the volcano after the explosive part of the eruption.

Reindeer moss: not a true moss but a lichen, *Cladonia rangiferina*, a slow-growing, cold-tolerant lichen found in alpine habitats. Also known as reindeer lichen or caribou moss.

Stratosphere: the second major layer of the atmosphere; lying above the troposphere, it begins approximately 3.75–6.2 miles (about 6–10 km) above the earth's surface

Ultra-Plinian eruption: the most extreme form of the Plinian eruption category of volcanic eruption. A Plinian (or Vesuvian) eruption is the largest and most violent class of volcanic eruptions; the term 'Plinian' takes its name from the younger Pliny's eyewitness account of the Vesuvius eruption that famously buried Pompeii in AD 79 (Pliny *Letters* 6.16 and 6.20). A Plinian eruption is characterized by a VEI of 4 to 6 and by the ash plume reaching up to 35 miles (about 50 km). An ultra-Plinian eruption has an explosivity index of 6 to 8 and a column extending to at least least 25 miles (about 45 km). The volume of ejected material may be from 2 to 200 cubic miles (about 10 to 1,000 km^3). The Tambora eruption was an ultra-Plinian eruption and represents the largest explosion in recorded history.

Volcanic explosivity index (VEI): a logarithmic scale from 0 to 8 that takes into account the volume of eruption material, the height of ejection, and several qualitative factors.

Notes

1 Technical terms in boldface are defined in the Glossary at the end of the chapter.
2 Wood (2014: 22).
3 Klingaman and Klingaman (2013: 1).
4 Mt. Tambora's most recent eruption was in 1967.

5   Sudradjat and Rachmat (2015: 60).
6   Brönnimann and Krämer 2016.
7   Wood (2014: 22).
8   Stothers 1984.
9   According to the *Otsego Herald* (Cooperstown, NY) on July 18, 1816 (p. 2), the position of the ships was as follows: on October 1, Lat: 13 35 South, Long: 84 00 East; on October 3, Lat 10 9 South, Long 84 20 East.
10 Ibid.
11 Cole-Dai *et al.* 2009.
12 Ibid.
13 From "By His Excellency John Brooks, Governor of the Commonwealth of Massachusetts, A Proclamation, For a Day of Public Thanksgiving and Prayer."
14 Chenoweth 1996. *The Reporter* (Brattleboro, Vermont), July 17, 1816, p. 3.
15 Skeen 1981.
16 Ibid.
17 Caloric is a nineteenth-century concept of energy/heat in the atmosphere.
18 Franklin presented a lecture, "Meteorological Imaginations and Conjectures," on December 22, 1784 in Manchester, England; the lecture was later published in 1789.
19 In North America, impact of the climate change was felt primarily in eastern Canada and the northeast United States (New England, New York, and the mid-Atlantic states south to Virginia). In this case, the cold temperatures were combined with widespread drought, wreaking havoc with many crops but especially hay and corn. As Thomas Jefferson wrote to his friend and former Secretary of the Treasury, Albert Gallatin, on September 8, 1816: "We have had the most extraordinary year of drought and cold ever known in the history of America. In June, instead of 3 ¾ inches, our average of rain for that month, we only had ⅓ of an inch; in August, instead of 9 ⅙ inches, our average, we had only ⁸/₁₀ of an inch; and still it continues. The summer, too, has been as cold as a moderate winter. In every State north of this there has been frost in every month of the year; in this State we had none in June and July, but those of August killed much corn over the mountains." Similar reports could be found in the northeast, especially in New York state. The severity of damage to the corn crop, for example, can be seen in a February 1817 letter from Daniel Tompkins, Governor of New York, in which he requested the state Assembly to provide relief for the St. Regis, Oneida, Onondaga, and Seneca tribes, whose corn crops had been devastated during the summer of 1816.
20 Fagan (2000: 174).
21 Post (1977: 128), citing Knapton (1939: 170)
22 *Romantic Circles*, Mary Shelley's Introduction to the 1831 Edition of Frankenstein, https://www.re.umd.edu/print/editions/frankenstein/1831v1/intro (accessed September 13, 2016).
23 Feldman and Scott-Kilvert (1987: 111).
24 Ibid., 117–118. Col du Baume refers to Col de Balme. Here and elsewhere I do not correct spellings in MWS's journals, but I do excise crossed-out errata.
25 Ibid., 119.
26 See Butler (2008: 195–196).

6

The Sublime Monster: *Frankenstein*, or The Modern Pandora

Matthew Gumpert

Introduction

Frankenstein (*F*) is traditionally read as a fable on the hubris of science, which, wresting the creative impulse from the divine, opens a Pandora's box from which springs the monstrous.[1] I suggest another reading, one that makes good on Victor Frankenstein's Promethean credentials: if Frankenstein is "the modern Prometheus," then his Creature is a modern Pandora. My argument refers to the Hesiodic myth of Pandora (*Theogony* [*Th.*] 512-514, 570-593; *Works and Days* [*WD*] 57-99) as a parable of perfect beauty as *synthetic*: she is a superlative artifact made of disparate parts selected and combined to form a complex structure. This method of artistic creation puts Pandora into the category of the 'sublime,' a category we find in various *loci classici*, such as Cicero's *On Invention* (*De inventione*), and given its fullest expression by Longinus in *On Sublimity* (*Peri hupsous*). Thus when Victor as 'creator' responds to his own synthetic, patchwork Creature with simultaneous horror and fascination, we are presented with an aesthetic judgment in the Kantian sense—namely, the appraisal of an object deemed *sublime*.[2]

The sublime has long been regarded as central to, even equated wholesale with, Romantic literature.[3] Yet critics have been unable to see the Creature, the 'Monster' (as Frankenstein's Creature is also called), as the sublime itself—perhaps because the sublime, at least since Immanuel Kant, has been equated with the unseeable.[4] But what if we could see the unseeable? What would it look like, and likewise what would be the true form of the 'Monster'? Thus I return to the myth of Pandora in order to read the 'Monster' in its etymological sense, from Latin *monstrare*, 'to show or indicate.' In fashioning a 'monster,' Victor 'shows' us what is supposed to remain invisible: art in its purest, most pitiless state—and the terrible truth that we may all be 'monsters,' products of an unintelligible art.⁵ But like all objects deemed sublime, the monstrous Creature cannot *truly* be seen, remaining a blank: if the Creature is represented by way of numerous empirical elements, his viewers fail to comprehend them as a unified entity; the result is a kind of cognitive *whiteout* that produces terror in the viewer and echoes the Arctic or the Alps, quintessentially Romantic landscapes labeled sublime and the Creature's preferred milieu.⁶ Here is the setting for *Frankenstein*'s beginning, end, and vast middle; it is, perhaps, to attain this privileged realm that this novel by Mary Shelley (MWS) is designed. The Creature is our shepherd, leading us to the promised land of the sublime, a place where MWS's narrative can claim to be a kind of 'writing degree zero.'⁷

There is another landscape only intermittently perceptible in *Frankenstein* but just as sublime as Mont Blanc: the territory of desire. Is the repulsion Victor feels toward the Creature a hysterical defense against its antithesis, desire? Desire has figured in the technique of the sublime since at least Longinus, who draws his textbook lesson from Sappho 31, an anatomy of *eros*. The equation with Pandora lends support to critics who have viewed Victor's aversion to the Creature in erotic terms.⁸ It helps explain the Creature's imperious demand for a partner and Victor's unwillingness or inability to satisfy it, as well as the long deferral of Victor's union with Elizabeth and its tragic consummation, when the Creature substitutes himself for the bride-to-be.⁹ This romance is not an explicit part of the mythological tradition; it follows logically, rather, from Pandora's mythic-erotic status. There is, however, an old tradition wedding Pandora to Epimetheus (Apollodorus 1.7.2; Hyginus *Fabulae* 142)—and thus *Frankenstein* is Epimetheus's story as much as Prometheus's.¹⁰

Ars poetica: Hesiod's Pandora

Like Frankenstein's Creature, Hesiod's Pandora is a superlative, superhuman, *synthetic* artifact. Pandora is neither born nor summoned into being but *manufactured*, a product of *tekhnē* ('art' or 'skill') rather than *phusis* ('nature') or *theophania* ('divine appearance'). Pandora is also manufactured piecemeal, an assemblage. In *Works and Days*, Hesiod states (60–82):

> [Zeus] commanded renowned Hephaestus to *mix* earth and water ... to *put* the voice and strength of a human into it, and *to make* a beautiful, lovely form [*kalon eidos*] of a maiden *similar* in her face to the immortal goddesses. He told Athena to teach her crafts ... golden Aphrodite to shed grace and painful desire ... around her head ... Hermes ... to put a dog's mind ... into her ... Immediately the famous Lame One *fabricated* out of earth a likeness [*ikelon*] of a modest

maiden ... Athena gave her a girdle and ornaments; the goddesses Graces and queenly Persuasion *placed* golden jewelry all around on her body ... Athena *fitted* the whole ornamentation to her body. Then into her breast ... [Hermes] set lies ... and ... *placed* a voice in her and named this woman Pandora (All-Gift), since all those who have their mansions on Olympus *had given* her a gift.[11]

The Hesiodic myth is often viewed (like *Frankenstein*) as a fable on the triumph of an Olympian order, a gloss on the old proverb that no good deed goes unpunished (unless the deed is Zeus's). Prometheus's gift of fire, after all, is repeated and reversed in Zeus's gift of Pandora: a "beautiful evil thing [*kalon kakon*] in exchange for that good one [*ant' agathoīo*]" (*Th.* 585).[12] But the scene of Pandora's production, reminiscent of the assembly-line—with its succession of verbs (italicized above) denoting the manufacturing process and the division of labor—suggests that Hesiod's tale is a lesson not on the *sin of technology* but rather on the *technology of sin* (*fire* meets *femme fatale*). In other words, the tale is neither an *apologia* (a 'justification') nor a *theodicy* (a meditation on 'divine justice') but an *ars poetica*—that is, a discourse on a 'work of art,' the Creature, whose very status as art or creation is complicated by the fact that it, he, is also a living, human being.[13] Already in Hesiod, Prometheus *pyrphoros*, 'Prometheus the Fire-Stealer' and source of technology, including art, is implicated in Prometheus *plasticator*, 'Prometheus the Creator of Humankind.'[14] *Art = creation = theft* is an insistent principle, we will see, in Hesiod and MWS alike.[15]

That Pandora is a work of art is underscored by the extent to which her production is depicted as *mimesis*: the fabrication of a 'beautiful form' (*kalon eidos*), the "likeness [*ikelon*] of a maiden, similar in her face to the immortal goddesses."[16] This suggests why Zeus chooses Pandora as his instrument of revenge: Pandora as *mimesis* is already endowed with all the virtues and vices Plato ascribes to the work of art—that delightful deception, seductive supplement, "beautiful evil thing in exchange for the good."[17] The same ontological uncertainty—Is she a copy or original? Artificial or natural?—helps explain the disquiet and disgust Frankenstein's Creature engenders. Like Pandora, the Creature is the Platonic nightmare come true—the representation of the unrepresentable.

The essential principles of this divine/diabolical *ars poetica* are threefold: (1) previously disconnected elements are selected; (2) such elements are combined into a unified structure; (3) and the elements selected must be superlative in nature and combined in superlative fashion so that the resulting artifact is always greater than the sum of its parts—so that the artifact is, in short, superlative.[18] Horace's ideal work of art in the *Ars poetica*, on the other hand, is neither more nor less than the sum of its constituent elements: Horace omits (3), while (1) and (2) are subsumed under a very different principle—namely, the adherence to convention or usage. But the Pandoric product is beautiful in an absolute sense: it has the force of a revelation, as if the unseeable were made seeable.

How to Make a Monster

All three 'Pandoric' principles are evident in the creation of Victor's Monster, a "great object," a "being of a gigantic stature," comprised of "parts" distinguished, nonetheless, by their "minuteness," assembled from the "collecting and arranging" of "materials," "selected ... as beautiful" (F 1.3–4: 32–35). The species of object envisioned here, i.e., "man" (33), "with all of its intricacies of fibres, muscles, and veins" (32), is already superlative and composite: an "animal" both "complex and wonderful" (33) (as opposed to "one of simpler organization"; 32), descriptions that point to the Creature's signature hybridity and size. (Even Victor's plan, prior to its execution, is distinguished by its "magnitude and complexity"; 33.) But the individual specimen is not man but superman: "I resolved, contrary to my first intention, to make the being of a gigantic stature; that is to say, about eight feet in height, and proportionably large" (ibid.)—not a mere object but a "great object" (34). Victor's departure from his first intention follows from the quality of the Creature's constituent elements: "the minuteness of the parts formed a great hindrance to my speed"; "I had," Victor recalls, "selected his features as beautiful" (35). But if the Creature is "proportionably large," one is struck by the disproportion between its "gigantic stature" and the "minuteness" of its component parts (33): a sign, surely, of the vertiginous geometries that inhabit it, and the prodigious feat of synthesizing that brought them into being.[19]

At every stage of the process (design, execution, electrification/animation), synthesis or super-synthesis is the crucial act: the selection and combination of disparate elements distinguished by their beauty. Design: "After having formed this determination" (to create a superhuman being), "and having spent some months in successfully collecting and arranging my materials, I began" (F 1.3: 33). Execution: "I pursued nature to her hiding places" (33); "I collected bones from charnel houses"; "[t]he dissecting room and the slaughter-house furnished many of my materials" (34). Electrification/animation: "I collected the instruments of life around me, that I might infuse a spark of being into the lifeless thing" (35). The animation of the inanimate is where Victor's method remains most impenetrable; an imprecision that, we will see, is an integral feature of the sublime.

The Creature is fashioned according to the same *ars* as Pandora. That Victor's *modus operandi* in constructing his creation mirrors MWS's in constructing hers is a critical commonplace, originating in her description of *Frankenstein* in the 1831 introduction as "my hideous progeny."[20] In that same text, MWS recounts her efforts to contribute to the famous ghost-story contest proposed by Byron: "Invention ... does not consist in creating out of void, but out of chaos; the materials must, in the first place, be afforded: it can give form to dark, shapeless substances, but cannot bring into being the substance itself."[21] The fabrication of the Creature becomes a new creation myth, visible at every stage in the production of MWS's (monstrous) creation (as idea, genre, narrative, edition, object of critical analysis): a hybrid, heretical entity.[22]

Victor's project has been misread as onto-theological failure, a failure of creation due to violation of divine law, instead of read as aesthetic success. The reanimation of inanimate matter is viewed as both cheap fraud and usurpation of the divine prerogative. That prerogative depends, traditionally, on the conciliation of ontologically distinct elements: the "discordant elements" (1.7) and "fractious parts" (1.36) of Ovid's *Metamorphoses*; the light and darkness, earth and seas, of Genesis. Victor, however, is a pseudo-Creator, his Creature a pseudo-Creation: neither this thing nor that thing but no-thing, or too many things, an unhappy, unstable, unnatural contradiction. MWS's Creature, in this line of thinking, is the direct descendant of Lucretius's Centaurs, "of double nature and twofold body" (*duplici natura et corpore bino*; *De rerum natura* [*DRN*] 5.879), creatures that never were and never can be (878–879).[23] The Creature is descendant, too, of the monster inaugurating Horace's *Ars poetica*, a chimera fusing human, horse, bird and fish (1–4), but failing to evince that unity which is the *sine qua non* of the work of art.[24] Yet unity for Horace is neither an onto-theological nor an aesthetic property but a rhetorical one, based entirely on the dictates of 'usage' (*usus*; 72). The chimera is a monster not because it violates the laws of nature (or poetry) but the expectations of its audience (who laughs). And it is because usage or 'tradition' (*fama*) dominates the *Ars poetica* with the force of an arbitrary law that hybridity is as blasphemous for Horace as it is for Lucretius.

But what if the Creature is not a blasphemous object, but a miraculous one? What if Victor's story is not that of a failed god, but of an artist who succeeds all too well? What if, finally, we took Victor's role as Prometheus *plasticator* seriously? A new genealogy might emerge better suited to appraise the Creature (not as ontological anomaly, but artistic triumph), beginning not with Lucretius's centaurs, Horace's chimera, or Hesiod's Echidna, Chimaera, or Typhoeus, but with Hesiod's Pandora. For what defines the Creature, finally, is not an irreducible Lucretian antinomy between "incompatible [*discordia*] members" (*DRN* 5.894), ontologically incompatible elements, but a conjoining of distinct elements resulting in a formal unity. The Creature is not a binary but a synthetic being.[25] Made of many parts, its borrowed status is proof that Prometheus *plasticator* and *pyrphoros* are the same, art inseparable from theft.[26]

Victor's *ars*—if we can even call it that, since his method remains shrouded in mystery—depends on the same strategies of selection and combination applied to objects of superlative status: it conforms neatly to the Pandoric paradigm.[27] But in the case of the Creature the result seems to be the antithesis of the beautiful (*F* 1.4: 35):

> His limbs were in proportion, and I had selected his features as beautiful. Beautiful!—Great God! His yellow skin scarcely covered the work of muscles and arteries beneath; his hair was of a lustrous black, and flowing; his teeth of a pearly whiteness; but these luxuriances only formed a more horrid contrast with the watery eyes, that seemed almost of the same colour as the dun white sockets in which they were set, his shrivelled complexion, and straight black lips.

The question remains, then: what went wrong?[28]

Technology of the Sublime: Hesiod

My answer: nothing. Indeed, it has gone all too well. This scene has been misconstrued: the true antithesis of the beautiful is not the ugly but the sublime.[29] Victor's portrait is a *blason* (not an *anti-blason*): an inventory of elements, each beautiful in its own right, but *beyond* (not beneath) beautiful when conjoined. The Creature is greater, not less than, the sum of its parts.[30] The oath Victor utters, then, would not be an admission of abject failure but too much success: the epiphany of absolute beauty.

Compare Victor's response to the Creature with that of the gods to Pandora, a product taken fresh from the assembly line, presented to her prospective investors/consumers: "[Hephaestus] led her out to where the other gods and the human beings were... and *wonder* [*thauma*] gripped the immortal gods and the mortal human beings when they saw the steep deception" (*Th.* 586–589). Like Pandora, Victor's Creature is a superlative object that spellbinds its beholder. To gaze upon the Creature, as upon Pandora, is to be transfixed by *thauma*: terror of the transcendent order. I would compare it to the terror of the Trojan elders before Helen in the *Iliad* (3.154–160).[31] Such terror has been part and parcel of the sublime since Edmund Burke.[32]

As one might expect in an aesthetic judgment, the visual register is dominant in Victor's response: "I beheld the wretch—the miserable monster I had created" (*F* 1.4: 36); "I had gazed on him while unfinished" (ibid.); the Creature is a "sight tremendous and abhorred" (2.2: 67); his "countenance ... almost too horrible for human eyes"; "Begone! ... relieve me from the sight of your destested form" (69).[33] But Victor fails to appreciate the Creature as a work of art. In the *Critique of Judgment*, Kant distinguishes the satisfaction determining judgments of 'taste' (devoid of interest) from that associated with the 'agreeable' and the 'good' (mingled with interest; sections 2–4: 90–94).[34] Victor judges the Creature according to the last two categories, not the first: his revulsion at the sight of the Creature is not that of an object that is not beautiful, but rather neither agreeable nor good. Disinterest has been an integral feature of aesthetic appreciation since Aristotle's *Poetics*: "we enjoy contemplating the most precise images [*tas eikonas*] of things whose actual sight is painful to us, such as the forms of the vilest animals and of corpses" (1448b10–12).[35] But Aristotle pleads his case for mimesis by demonstrating the transformation it effects in the very objects one might have thought most recalcitrant: objects we would call 'monstrous.'

We are now in a better position to understand Victor's aversion: he 'mistakes' the Creature for a *thing* instead of an *image*—a work of art, not nature. This ontological error is manifest in Victor's revulsion at the *sight* of the Creature during their encounter at Montanvert, for it is precisely when Victor looks instead of listens—when he regards him as a mere object—that disgust overtakes sympathy: "His words had a strange effect on me. I compassionated him ... but when I looked upon him, when I saw the filthy *mass* that moved and talked, my heart sickened, and my feelings were altered to those of horror and hatred" (2.7: 92; my italics).[36] In this respect, the Creature appears a better judge of his nature than Victor: "I had sagacity enough to discover," he recalls, "that the *unnatural* hideousness of my person was the chief object of horror with those who had formerly beheld me" (92; my italics). The Creature's insight makes far more sense when *unnatural* is stressed, rather than *hideousness*.

Now, in the moment of the sublime, for Kant, reason (in its capacity to think the boundless) triumphs over the inadequacies of the senses (incapable of apprehending the boundless). Why does such a triumph elude Victor? The answer is clear: his judgment of the Creature is not properly aesthetic but is compromised by interest—that is, ethics (the Creature is pronounced evil, etc.).[37] The aesthetic judgment is always *pure*: "A pure judgment on the sublime ... must have no end of the object as its determining ground if it is to be aesthetic" (section 26).[38]

Victor's response to the sight of the Creature is never that of mere repulsion: it is repulsion on a superlative scale. The Creature is not ugly, he is *transcendently* ugly. Such transcendence demands veneration: the "unearthly ugliness" of his countenance "rendered it almost too horrible for human eyes" (*F* 2.2: 67)—*almost*, but one looks. Indeed, the judgment Victor renders in his first encounter with the Creature explicitly rejects the category of the ugly as inadequate: "Oh! No mortal could support the horror of that countenance ... I had gazed on him while unfinished; he was ugly then, but when those muscles and joints were rendered capable of motion, it became a thing such as even Dante could not have conceived" (1.4: 36). Not just repulsion: terror. Such terror, we know, is an essential feature of the sublime.

Deformity and/as the Kantian Sublime

"A thing such as even Dante could not have conceived"—something offered to the senses, but resistant to the understanding—is the aesthetic object in Kant's *Critique of Judgment*. Both the beautiful and the sublime "please for themselves" (section 23), depending neither on a "sensation" (as in the case of the agreeable) nor on a "determinate concept" (as in that of the good).[39]

There are, however, crucial distinctions for Kant between the beautiful and the sublime regarding the nature of the object from which they originate: "The beautiful ... concerns the form of the object, which consists in limitation; the sublime, by contrast, is to be found in a formless object insofar as limitlessness is represented in it" (ibid.). It is in the formal properties of the object deemed beautiful that its purposiveness inheres: beauty "is the form of the purposiveness of an object, insofar as it is perceived in it without representation of an end" (section 17).[40] But the form of the sublime (the form of the formless) elicits no such perception; on the contrary, the sublime appears "contrapurposive for our power of judgment, unsuitable for our faculty of representation" (section 23).[41] Hence the ambivalence of the Kantian sublime: "since the mind is not merely attracted by the object, but is also reciprocally repelled by it, the satisfaction in the sublime ... deserves to be called negative pleasure" (ibid.). The *thauma* experienced by the gods before Pandora is a type of this 'negative pleasure' constitutive of the sublime.

The role played by form (or its lack thereof) in the sublime suggests another way the Creature has been misconstrued. The universal revulsion engendered by the Creature, it is assumed, is an effect of his 'deformity.' The novel seems very clear on this point; no predicate appears more frequently or more damningly as an indictment of the Creature's aspect. Victor refers to "its gigantic stature, and the deformity of its aspect" (*F* 1.6: 50); it is the Creature's favorite term for describing himself, lamenting "the deformity of my figure" (2.4: 78), his "miserable deformity" (79), his "figure hideously deformed and loathsome," "deformed and horrible" (2.8: 101). What has not been sufficiently examined is the nature of 'deformity' itself. For to equate deformity with ugliness is to deform deformity, which refers, more precisely—from Latin *deformis*, where the prefix *de-* functions as a preposition meaning *from, away from, down from*, or *out of*— to 'that from which form itself has been removed.' The *deformis* is the 'misshapen' or 'deformed' because it is 'that which has no (visible, apparent, recognizable) form.' In this sense, the Creature is indeed de-formed and, therefore, sublime.

The Creature's size is inseparable from his formlessness; I invoke here Aristotle's injunctions in the *Poetics* on the optimum length or 'magnitude' (*megethos*) for a tragedy. It is true that by *megethos* Aristotle refers to extension in time, not space. But in the analogy he employs, the specter of the monster again looms: "beauty consists in magnitude and order, which is why there could not be a beautiful animal which was either miniscule ... or gigantic ... say an animal a thousand miles long" (1450b36–1451a2). Recall here Kant's distinction between the 'sublime' and the 'monstrous': "An object is *monstrous* if by its magnitude it annihilates the end which its concept constitutes" (section 26).[42] Victor, who insists on ascribing ends to that which lacks them, regards as 'monstrous' what is in fact 'sublime'; he mistakes the mimesis of a human being for a human being *tout court*.[43]

Not that any object, *per se*, is sublime. It is rather the case that, as Kant puts it, "the object serves for the presentation of a sublimity that can be found in the mind" (section 23).[44] (Is not the gods' stupefaction at the sight of Pandora tied to their knowledge that she is *their* creation?) Victor's repulsion/fascination is part and parcel with the knowledge that the Creature is *his* creation, a form of self-loathing projected on to the object—a transference Kant sees as symptomatic of the sublime (section 26), which is indeed in the eye of the beholder.[45] Longinus agrees: "the true sublime naturally elevates us ... we are filled with joy and pride, as if we had ourselves produced the very thing we heard" (7.2).[46] This transference is perhaps not unrelated to the common misattribution of Frankenstein's name to the nameless Creature.

A critic sympathetic to psychoanalysis might suggest there is an element of *disavowal* in Victor's rejection of the Creature. As understood by Freud, disavowal is a defense mechanism wherein the ego refuses to acknowledge the reality of a perception due to its traumatic associations.[47] Might it not be the case that what Victor sees in the Creature is the specter of mimesis itself, a specter too terrible to acknowledge, for it offers proof of what we always suspected: that we are all mimetic beings, works of art, creatures/creations made in the image of our God?[48]

Technology of the Sublime: Longinus

For the most influential text on the *technology* of the sublime, we turn to Longinus's *On the Sublime*.[49] The very existence of Longinus's treatise is an argument for the role of *tekhnē*, 'art' or 'skill', in the production of the high style: 'nature' or *phusis* is necessary but not sufficient (1.2). Of the five "most productive" (*gonimōtatai*) sources of the sublime, the last but not least is "elevated *word-arrangement*" (*sunthesis*; 8.1).[50] This emphasis on form seems at odds with Kant's insistence on the formlessness of the sublime object. But, as we will see, *arrangement* in Longinus remains recalcitrant and recondite: a formless form.

By *synthesis* Longinus refers to two distinct (and ostensibly Horatian) operations: the selection of previously scattered elements and their judicious combination.[51] "We shall find one factor of sublimity in a consistently happy *choice* [*eklegein*] of these constituent elements, and in the power of *combining them* [*episunthesei*] together as it were into *an organic whole* [*sōma*]" (10.1). Longinus's diagnostic of the sublime, like his case study (the equally diagnostic Sappho 31), insists on, without explaining, the *organic* nature of the artifact that results. The sublime object is a *sōma*: a (living) *body*.[52] (It is only when the inert components of Victor's Creature are joined that they are endowed with motility.) This insistence on the organic suggests a subtle but salient departure from the Horatian model. Despite Pandora's synthetic origins, her primary ingredients are earth and water (*WD* 61). Pandora's monstrousness is inseparable from her organicism, signaled yet suppressed in the uncanny art of her golden headband: "terrible monsters ... similar to living animals endowed with speech [*zōoisin eoikota phōnēesin*]" (*Th.* 582–584). The monstrous subject suggests the monstrous skill capable of bringing it to life.

The organic body anatomized in Sappho 31 is a body under the spell of *eros*. This body in love is for Longinus a sublime body, simultaneously integrated and disintegrated: "she displays not a single emotion, but a whole congeries of emotions. Lovers show all such symptoms, but what gives supreme merit to her art is, as I said, the skill with which she takes up the most striking and combined them into a single whole" (10.3).[53] The definitive statement of this nascent bio-aestheticism is at 40.1:

> Nothing is of greater service in giving grandeur to what is said than the organization of the various *members* [*melōn*]. It is the same with the *human body* [*sōmata*]. None of the members has any value by itself apart from the others, yet one with another they all constitute a perfect system. Similarly, if these effects of grandeur are separated, the sublimity is scattered with them; but if they are *united into a single whole* [*sōmatopoioumena*, 'given bodily existence'] ... then they *gain a living voice* [*phōnēenta*, 'are endowed with voice'].

Longinus's reading is facilitated by the partitive *melos*, referring both to a physical *limb* and a musical *phrase*. Compare the order visible in Sappho's poem, founded on the organization of constituent 'members' (*melōn*), with the (psycho)somatic disorder it serves to represent (reminiscent of Lucretius's *discordia membra*; *DRN* 5.894).[54] This bio-aesthetics is fated to remain incomplete. The Longinian sublime proves resistant to analysis; the sublime is a technique, finally, without a *tekhnē*. The superlative predicate—the third indispensable, tautological principle of the sublime—serves to evoke its indeterminacy. Of Sappho 31, Longinus asks: "wherein does she show her *excellence*? In the skill with which she selects and combines the *most striking* [*akra*, 'highest'] and intense of those symptoms" (10.1). But the nature of that selection and combination, like the skill which presides over them, remains indefinite. This helps explain why MWS's novel disappoints readers looking for the science in her science fiction—just as Horace's *Ars poetica* disappoints those seeking explicit directives on how to write poetry.[55] For Victor is not a scientist but an artist, and *Frankenstein* not a parable on science gone wrong but art gone (too) right. Nor is this art in the age of mechanical reproduction; MWS's is not, I have suggested, a fable on the sin of technology, but the technology of sin. Since Plato, at least, art is creation as blasphemy. Envisioned thus, art remains shrouded in mystery, animated by electricity, which is not, in fact, a technology at all in *Frankenstein* but a miraculous force, an updated version of the "Promethean spark"—inspiration, we might say, *au courant*.[56]

Another classical *ars* where selection and combination conspire, mysteriously, to produce a 'living' body endowed with super-erotic value is Cicero's tale of Zeuxis in *On Invention*. Zeuxis's portrait of Helen is a composite of Croton's most beautiful girls (2.1.3):

> the citizens of Croton . . . assembled the girls in one place and allowed the painter to *choose* [*eligendi*] whom he wished. He *selected* [*delegit*] five . . . because they were appointed by the judgment of him who must have been the supreme judge of beauty. He chose five because he did not think all the qualities which he sought to combine in a portrayal of beauty could be found in one person.[57]

Zeuxis's portrait of Helen is a parable on art's superiority to nature: artist, subject, and model alike are superlative. In Cicero's parable, the portrait is pronounced "silent and lifeless" but able to "embody the surpassing beauty of womanhood" (2.1.1). In such 'embodiment' looms that revelatory principle inseparable from the sublime: to embody surpassing beauty is to render 'visible what cannot be seen.'

Or to animate the inanimate. Cicero leaves open the possibility that the lifeless object may come to life: "true beauty may be *transferred from the living model* [*transferatur ex animali exemplo*] to *the mute likeness* [*mutum in simulacrum*]"

(2.1.2–3). Much as MWS's recipe for her novel suggests Victor's method for manufacturing monsters, Zeuxis's procedure is the model for *On Invention* itself: "In a similar fashion when the inclination arose in my mind to write a text-book of rhetoric I did not set before myself some one *model* [*exemplum*] ... but after *collecting all the works on the subject* [*sed omnibus unum in locum coactis scriptoribus*] I *excerpted* what seemed the most suitable precepts from each, and so *culled* the flower of many minds" (2.2.4).

Is the Promethean spark the flame of *eros*? The product known as Pandora suggests it is. What is she, according to Hesiod, but a weaponized woman, a *dolon* (*Th.* 589; *WD* 83), a 'device' or 'trick' that we might understand as 'bait,' expressly engineered to lure men, "an evil in which they may all take pleasure" (*WD* 58)? The mechanics of this eroticism are further elaborated in the *Theogony*, where Pandora wears a 'veil' and a wreath of flowers said to be 'arousing desire' (*Th.* 573–577).

Longinus's Sappho, Cicero's Helen, Hesiod's Pandora: all shed light on a shadowy eroticism dimly visible in MWS's novel.[58] Is Victor's revulsion at the sight of the Creature ... love? And if Kant is right that sublimity is located in the beholder, not the beheld, then might the true sublime body belong not to Creature but Creator? There is support for such a reading in the chiastic sequence that attends Creature's birth and Creator's response. Upon the animation of the still-inert Creature, "a convulsive motion agitated its limbs" (*F* 1.4: 35); the agitated and articulated aspect of these birth-throes is uncannily mirrored in Victor's reaction, a seizure in which "every limb became convulsed" (36). Following his "fit" (39), Victor is "lifeless": it is now the Creator's turn to return to the state of the inanimate. Could this strange fit be the sublime ecstasy of *eros* itself?[59]

Conclusions: The Creature as *Genius loci* of the Sublime Landscape

On the reading advanced above, *Frankenstein* looks like a love story, its narrative driven by the imperious demands and reversible dynamics of desire: first Creature seeking out Creator, then vice versa.[60] Our first sight of the Creature is in a chase scene set in the Arctic circle, a figure making "rapid progress" along the "vast and irregular plains of ice, which seemed to have no end," with another figure in pursuit (*F* 1.Letter 4: 13). Victor's first real encounter with the Creature occurs, similarly, upon "a sea of ice" in the shadow of Mont Blanc, when he "[beholds] the figure of a man ... advancing with superhuman speed" (2.2: 67).

It is time, then, to account not just for the structure of *eros* in this novel but its geography—time to put the Creature back in his place.

The Creature seems an anomaly in these inhospitable landscapes. But what if he is their embodiment, their *genius loci*, their 'symbol'? I use the last term in the sense Coleridge intends in *The Statesman's Manual*: an organic entity that speaks for the order of which it is a part; opposed to allegory, a mere artificial device with no place in that order.[61] The Kantian sublime, as adapted by Romantic authors from Schiller to MWS and PBS alike, is championed as a force for bridging the gap between the ideal and the empirical. Toward this end, the symbol is the minimal unit of the sublime. One is tempted to see in the Creature the terrible triumph of this Coleridgean idea. Is he not at once mere man-made mechanical contrivance, and man himself? Is he not an idea come to life?

Critics have tended to view MWS's glacial settings allegorically: didactic landscapes that suggest a compass, moral or otherwise, gone wrong.[62] But once MWS's novel is viewed as a tale of aesthetics, not ethics, it is hard to think of these as anything but sublime landscapes. Kant favors a number of such *sublime-scapes* in the *Critique of Judgment*: "threatening cliffs, thunder clouds towering up into the heavens … hurricanes with the devastation they leave behind, the boundless ocean set into a rage" (section 28), "shapeless mountain masses towering above one another in wild disorder with their pyramids of ice" (26).[63] What these landscapes share is the same essential geometry, that of *disproportion*: they are too big to scale, to see, to solve.[64] Disproportion, of course, has its moral implications: these landscapes are malevolent.[65]

MWS's sublime-scapes largely hew to the Kantian canon: her sublime is of the Alpine order. Hence the significance of Victor's perambulations through the Alps, a set-piece for which, one might argue, the entire novel serves as frame. It is a landscape repeatedly labeled sublime *as opposed to* beautiful: the ravine of the Arve is "a scene of singular beauty. But it was augmented and rendered sublime by the mighty Alps" (2.1: 64); the valley of Chamounix "is more wonderful and sublime, but not so beautiful and picturesque as that of Servox" (ibid.).

But the Alps' sublimity lies not just in their topography but their temperature: here, to vary Barthes's theme, is a 'degree zero-' or 'sub-zero-sublime,' a sublimity of snow, of polysemically *polar* opposites.[66] Could all of *Frankenstein* be thus a gloss on PBS's "Mont Blanc: Lines Written in the Vale of Chamouni," published only two years before?[67] It makes sense, if we equate the sub-zero-sublime with the 'blank (*blanc*) sublime': the epistemological whiteout that, in the Kantian experience of the sublime, heralds the resurgence of reason, the triumph of mind over nature—or writer over blank page.[68] The 'blanc sublime' returns, in MWS's introduction, as the terrain from which *Frankenstein* itself emerges: "I thought and pondered—vainly. I felt that blank incapability of invention which is the greatest misery of authorship."[69] MWS's writer's block is a cynical version of the 'blanc sublime,' just as her *blank incapability* is a negative of Keats's *negative capability*. But the story that finally emerges from this struggle returns to the blankness from which it springs.

Notes

1. Critics, e.g., Baldick [1987] in Hunter (2012: 177–178), note Mary Wollstonecraft's influence on *F*'s image of innovation's promises and perils. Wollstonecraft writes that man is "a lawless planet darting from its orbit to steal the celestial fire of reason; and the vengeance of Heaven, lurking in the subtile flame, like Pandora's pent-up mischiefs, sufficiently punished his temerity, by introducing evil into the world"; see Macdonald and Scherf (1997: 1.119).
2. In the *Critique of Judgment*, the sublime is the limit or absolute case of aesthetic judgment, elicited by an object which exceeds the capacity of the imagination (the faculty of intuition): in effect presenting the unpresentable, the sublime can be apprehended but not comprehended (section 26: 135).
3. See Ferguson 1992, Leighton 1984, Weiskel 1976, Abrams 1973, and Monk 1960.
4. Kant (section 23, trans. Guyer and Matthews): "what is properly sublime cannot be contained in any sensible form"; see Guyer and Matthews (2000: 129). All unattributed translations are my own.
5. Latin definitions from Lewis and Short 1879; Greek, from Liddell and Scott 1996. Following Cicero in *De divinatione*, Weiner (2015a: 70) notes that "Monsters are not only things to *be shown*, but also things that *show*."
6. "These sublime and magnificent scenes," Victor recalls, "elevated me from all littleness of feeling" (*F* 2.2: 65); all references to *F* are to the 1818 text in Hunter 2012. Compare the Alps in MWS's journals; see Feldman and Scott-Kilvert (1987: 199–202). The Apennines are another privileged sublime-scape for the Shelleys, as we learn from Percy Shelley (henceforth PBS) in his "The Passage of the Apennines" (May 4, 1818); see Hutchinson (1907: 548–549). In a letter to Thomas Love Peacock (November 15, 1818), PBS compares Alps to Apennines: "The glaciers of Montanvert and the sources of the Arveiron is the grandest spectacle I ever saw," the cataract of the Velino "the second" (letter 14, in Brett-Smith [1909: 150]); its "scenery is . . . the loveliest and most sublime that can be conceived" (151).
7. Barthes (1967b: 11) uses this phrase to describe the utopian dream haunting modern literature: an absolute, supremely revelatory writing. Thus PBS in the *Defence* dreams of a poetry that "lifts the veil from the hidden beauty of the world"; see Leitch (2001: 700).
8. For Gilbert and Gubar, Victor's curiosity recalls that of Eve or Pandora (1979: 234).
9. Despite Whale's *Bride of Frankenstein* (1935), the Creature already occupies that position.
10. See Hammond (this volume).
11. All translations of Hesiod's *WD* and *Th.* are from Most 2006.
12. See Vernant 1990 on the Prometheus myth as a sequence of gifts/thefts (meat, fire, woman).
13. *F*'s account of the Creature's birth is thus *both* a pseudo-divine creation myth *and* a prescription for poetry or art. Victor mistakenly views the Creature solely as art, forgetting he is also a human being. In this way, *F* troubles a classical distinction between the narrow, literary sense of *poesis* (i.e., poetry) and the term's broader meanings (making, producing).

14 The Romantics do associate Promethean fire with spark of life; e.g., the "Promethean spark" in Byron's *Manfred* 1.1: 154–157.
15 Although Hesiod's Prometheus does not fashion the first woman, his actions prompt Zeus to create her. On Prometheus *pyrphoros/plasticator* in *F*, see Mellor (1988: 70–88).
16 Ovid's Prometheus *plasticator* stresses mimesis: man is made "in the image of the gods" (*in effigiem . . . deorum*; *Metamorphoses* [*Met.*] 1.83).
17 In *Republic* 10, Plato links imitation's ontological deficiencies to its corrosion of ethical faculties (605a–b; trans. Grube, rev. Reeve, in Cooper 1997). On Pandora as Platonic imitation, see Zeitlin 1995: "she is both an imitation and an original" (71).
18 Principle (2) recalls the necessary conditions in structuralist theory for the production of discourse—e.g., Jakobson's selection/combination (1990: 77), Saussure's associative/syntagmatic relations (1986: 121–125), and Barthes's systematic/syntagmatic planes (1967a: 58–88). Discourse proceeds from the selection of elements of a system and their concatenation into a syntactical chain.
19 One might call this synthesis 'sublime' in a Lucretian sense, evoking the atomism of *De rerum natura* (*DRN*); see Porter 2007: "Atomism lends itself particularly well to the sublime" in "the collision and confusion of the . . . micro- and macro-levels" (168). For the application of this to *F*, see Weiner (2015a).
20 In Hunter (2012: 169).
21 In Hunter (2012: 167). See also Baldick in Hunter (2012: 175). 'Invention' here retains its classical sense (*inventio* as the discovery of rhetorical arguments). MWS's is a pseudo-Horatian *ars*, echoed in PBS's 1818 preface: "I have thus endeavoured to preserve the truth of the elementary principles of human nature, while I have not scrupled to innovate upon their combinations" (*F* 5).
22 Many of this volume's contributors emphasize this "patchwork poetics" (Liveley [this volume]; the novel, Rogers succinctly put it in his conference talk, is "built out of pieces"; gathering allusions, they inevitably reproduce the monster they seek. Generically, *F* is a monster: a collage of forms (epic, lyric, epistle, etc.) stitched into a *novel* shape. Liveley's attempt to tie the novel's complex gestation to MWS's eclectic reading reminds us of Barthes's reader as "the space on which all the quotations that make up a writing are inscribed" (2001: 1469). But MWS is not the only reader: Victor's wide-ranging readings prefigure the Creature's heterogeneity: an *éducation sentimentale* and *synthétique* (a 'sentimental and synthetic education'). For Robinson in Hunter (2012), Victor's "assembling of disparate body parts" is replayed in Walton's "assembling his disparate notes about Victor into a narrative" (199), repeated in the novel's *récit* as a relay of "editorial" interventions by characters-*cum*-narrators: "Victor's story as edited by Walton edited by Victor edited by Walton" (200–201). The fruit of that process is, we are to imagine, a manuscript received by Walton's sister, Margaret Walton Saville, MWS's "surrogate reader" (201)—a genealogy that is repeated in *F*'s editorial saga, amended by MWS, PBS, her father William Godwin, a host of publishers' readers, printers and scholars.
23 Translations of Lucretius are from Rouse (1924).
24 "[L]et it . . . be *simple* [*simplex*] and *uniform* [*unum*]" (*Ars poetica* 23; trans. Fairclough 1929).
25 In its synthetic being, the Creature is a 'cyborg': cyborgian readings treat *F* as a jeremiad against miscegenation. The cyborg is but the latest incarnation of the centaur, a hybrid being marked by ontological duality/dissonance; so Liveley (2006: 278), drawing on Haraway (1991: 150): "By the late twentieth century . . . we are all chimeras . . . hybrids of machine and organism." The Cylons of the television remake *Battlestar Galactica* (2004–2009) are cyborgs

in this sense (cf. Gumpert 2008), but are unlike MWS's Creature, whose agonies are rooted not in dualism but in desertion. What happens, MWS asks, when Creation is abandoned by Creator?

26 See Richardson (1988: 30–51) on the Murder Act (prescribing dissection as post-mortem punishment) and the Anatomy Act of 1832 (authorizing the autopsy of bodies); see below, n38. Such measures put a stop to graverobbing, while authorizing state-sanctioned bodysnatching. What is the sublime *ars* but such bodysnatching, based on the recycling of preexisting poetic corpora?

27 Other, Ovidian genealogies are cited—e.g., the fables of Pygmalion (*Met.* 10.243–297) and Hippolytus (15.490–546). Pygmalion, whose sculpture possesses supernatural 'beauty' (*forma*; 10.248–249), suggests an artist of Frankensteinian caliber; see Pollin (1965: 100–101). Pygmalion is also a fable on art as product of and defense against *eros*: like the Creature, Pygmalion's ivory woman is a substitute for the real. Missing is a method based in selection and combination (or any method): "with wondrous art he ... carves a figure out of ... ivory" (10.247–248; trans. Miller 1916); *pace* Salzman-Mitchell 2008, who argues: "*Ars* is for Ovid not carving a solid piece of marble, but joining pieces together ... concealing the process with great art" (307)—converting the absence of such art into its presence, a strategy that depends on the etymology (notoriously pliable, like ivory) of words such as *ars*, and the practical limitations of ivory (the parallels among Zeuxis's Helen, Victor's Frankenstein, and Ovid's *Metamorphoses*, the poem, itself—stitched together out of discrete tales—are then inevitable). Victor's Creature is closer to figures such as Dionysus Zagreus, dismembered by the Titans, reconstituted by Rhea; see Henrichs 2011.

28 Baldick in Hunter (2012: 173): "why should a creature constructed from parts which Victor selects as perfect ... turn out to be hideously repulsive?" Positing Milton's *Paradise Lost* as the novel's central intertext, Baldick reads Victor's creation as a usurpation of the divine prerogative. Baldick nevertheless helps situate the Horatian problem posed by *F*—"the relation of parts to wholes"—in the context of Romantic Idealism's championing of the organic over the mechanistic: e.g., for Coleridge, argues Baldick, "any living 'whole' ... was always more than a mere aggregation of its constituent parts" (ibid.).

29 Croker's appraisal of the Creature in the *Quarterly Review* (1818) already typifies the standard (mis)reading: "by some mistake ... the intended beauty turned out the ugliest monster that ever deformed the day"; see Croker in Hunter (2012: 215). Note that such (mis)readings nonetheless reflect the superlative nature of the object ("ugliest"). The 1824 review in *Knight's Quarterly* takes issue precisely with the Creature's "extreme ugliness," viewing it as illogical, not inevitable; see Hunter (2012: 239).

30 In this surfeit born of synthesis, one sees the extent to which Victor's *ars* adheres to Longinus rather than Horace, suggesting the (grotesque) fulfillment of Coleridge's dream of the organic triumphant over the mechanical.

31 "[T]hese, as they saw Helen along the tower approaching ... were saying 'Terrible is the likeness of her face to immortal goddesses'" (trans. Richmond Lattimore 1951). On Helen as monster, see Gumpert 2001.

32 From *A Philosophical Enquiry*, part 2, section 2: "terror is in all cases ... the ruling principle of the sublime"; see Womersley (1998: 102).

33 Likewise Pandora, or Helen, is *almost too beautiful* for human eyes. In the Creature we confront the *almost too X* (too wondrous, too terrible) *to be seen*.

34 Kant is cited by section numbers, with page numbers—after the colon—from Guyer and Matthews 2000 (including translation).

35 Trans. Halliwell 1995.

36 Victor's revulsion is rooted in the confusion of a copy with its orginal, leading not to the cyborg but the *android* (*andro-* 'male' + *eidês* 'like,' hence 'like a man'; cf. *Oxford English Dictionary* s.v. 'android'). To the extent the android is a machine designed to resemble a human being—the cyborg suggesting the integration of the human in a hybrid being—the Creature is an android, kin to other fantastic robots in nineteenth-century literature, such as Edison's Hadaly in Villiers de l'Isle-Adam's *L'Ève future* (1886 [1992]). It is because the android threatens the distinction between machine and human that it disquiets—hence the Turing test, based on the premise that a machine the behavior of which is indistinguishable from a human being *is* a human being. In this sense, Victor's Creature is a human being: he passes the Turing test.

37 Weiner 2015a shrewdly hypothesizes that after the 1752 Murder Act the bodies available to Victor would be those of executed murderers; the Creature, it follows, is morally compromised on an ontological level (or, as Weiner argues in Lucretian terms, an atomistic one; 58). But note that this raw material originates not just from the "dissecting room" but the "slaughter-house" (*F* 1.3: 34); the Creature is a product of allografts, xenografts, and zoografts. These exotic derivations confirm Weiner's suspicions, no doubt: the Creature is part animal in his very constitution. But again, what MWS stresses is not the Creature's duality but his heterogeneity.

38 In Guyer and Matthews (2000: 136–137). Kant focuses on the sublime in nature (section 26 in ibid., 136), but the distinction proves irrelevant: it is only to the extent that it follows the laws of nature that art succeeds (section 45 in ibid., 185).

39 Ibid., 128.

40 Ibid., 120.

41 Ibid., 129. Cf. PBS, *The Defence*, in Leitch (2001: 700): "Poetry enlarges the circumference of the imagination." Kant's point is that there are things that remain stubbornly outside that circumference. See Longinus 35.3: "our ideas often pass beyond the limits that confine us"—recalling, argues Porter (2007: 174), Epicurus's mind passing beyond the "flaming walls of the world" (*DRN* 1.73).

42 In Guyer and Matthews (2000: 136).

43 To see the Creature as a Monster is, in Kantian terms, an error, based on the insistence of ascribing ends to an entity which, in fact, lacks them. For Kant, only an object that is without discernible ends can be deemed sublime; the monstrous, on the other hand, is an object whose ends are defeated by its magnitude (26: 136).

44 Ibid., 129. Compare Keats's "egotistical sublime" (October 27, 1818, letter to Woodhouse) in Rollins (1958: 387).

45 In Guyer and Matthews (2000: 139). Cf. Weiner (2015a: 70–71): "the monstrous qualities of Victor ... are what the monster must make public and show."

46 Trans. Fyfe 1995 (rev. Russell).

47 E.g., Freud 1953–1974.

48 Humankind discovering, or worrying, that it is a robot or android is a recurrent nightmare haunting science fiction from Richard Matheson's "Deus Ex Machina" to Philip K. Dick's *Do Androids Dream of Electric Sheep?* and Alex Garland's *Ex Machina* (2015); on the last, see Hammond (this volume). Victor's revulsion is a discovery of this order.

49 Discussion of the sublime in Longinus and in classical antiquity is indebted to Porter 2010, 2015b, and above all 2016. Porter establishes the genealogy of the sublime as "an aesthetic category ... as old as Greek literature itself" (2015b: 399).

50 "[G]rand conceptions" and "vehement emotion" are deemed "*congenital [authigeneis]*"; "proper construction of figures," "nobility of language," and "word-arrangement" "come partly *from art [dia tekhnēs]*." Porter's emphasis on the natural and cosmological sublime as pre-Longinian traditions, however, cannot account for Longinus's sublimity as a methodically staged effect, or method *tout court*; on which see Gumpert (2012: 79–101). Porter comes close: "the art of the sublime is forever staged *as though it were* an effect of nature" (2015b: 397). But Porter fails to capitalize on the implications that staging the sublime means *synthesizing* it, and that such synthesizing remains more *mystery* than *method*.

51 Echoed in the accounts of *F*'s genesis in the 1831 introduction and the 1818 preface.

52 On Sappho's 'diagnostic,' see Page: "Sappho describes the physical symptoms of the passion which possesses her ... as dispassionately as if she were an interested bystander" (1955: 26).

53 Longinus's reading of Sappho 31 is absent from Porter 2015b, which investigates the cosmological, natural, and theological sublime but not the erotic.

54 "There is certainly no lack of control in the expression," Page concedes, "whatever there may have been in the experience" (1955: 27).

55 As Haweis writes in 1886: "The manufacture of the human monster ... is slurred over in a few hasty but ghastly paragraphs"; see Hunter (2012: 241). Cf. Rieger (1974: xxvii): "she skips the science." I argue this slurring or skipping over is not bad science but good art and a constitutive feature of the sublime. The lack of directives in the *Ars poetica* has long been noted. Scaliger called it "an Art written without art," cited by Innes (1989: 266); see Zerba (1988: 186).

56 On the Romantic take on electricity as quasi-magical transformative force, see Goodall 2008. Priestly's or Franklin's experiments in electricity are often viewed by eighteenth-century authors in sublime terms: e.g., see Godwin on Franklin's "sublime conjectures" in Kramnick (1976: 759).

57 Trans. Hubbell 1949.

58 'He who loosens the limbs' (*lusimelēs*) is one of *eros*'s traditional epithets; e.g., *eros ... lusimelēs* (*Th.* 910–911), or Alcman's 'desire which loosens the limbs' (*lusimelēs pothos*; 3.61 in Page 1962). The epithet is applied in Homer to sleep (*Odyssey* 20.56–57, 23.342–343) and death (*Iliad* 4.469), articulating the dis-articulation the body suffers in these states. See Calame (1999: 36) and Zeitlin (1996: 226).

59 Sappho 31: "A cold sweat covers me, and a trembling seizes me all over ... I seem to be not far short of death."

60 Sappho 1: "if she flees, she shall soon pursue"—a commonplace in classical lyric.

61 The symbol "partakes of the Reality which it renders intelligible; and while it enunciates the whole, abides itself as a living part in that Unity, of which it is the representative"; see Coleridge in Halmi *et al.* (2004: 351).

62 Rieger views them as "a photographic negative" of Milton's Hell: "[t]heir frozen brilliance renders exactly the snow-blinded rationalism and the moral paralysis of Frankenstein" (1974: xxxii). The whiteness of MWS's Alpine/Arctic landscapes (xxxi) is like that of Melville's *Moby-Dick*, "a colorless all-color of atheism from which we shrink" (1967: 169).

63 In Guyer and Matthews (2000: 144, 139). A catalogue of similar landscapes in *DRN* suggests Kant's debt to Lucretius; see Porter (2007: 172).

64 Porter 2015a draws attention to *Iliad* 18.145–148 where, their colloquy with Achilles concluded, Thetis and the Nereids part ways, the former to the heights of Olympus, the latter to the depths of Ocean. The effect of this passage lies in the logic of disproportion, in the inconceivable interval (physical and ontological) uniting and dividing ocean floor and mountain peak: "the parting of the goddesses ... marks out a sublime gap, a vertical axis" (196).

65 Note that the advent of Pandora marks the birth of a new, morally treacherous landscape: "men used to live upon the earth entirely apart from evils" (*WD* 90-91) but today "the earth is full of evils, and the sea is full" (101).
66 The polar sublime plays a significant role in Gothic horror, e.g., Edgar Allen Poe's *The Narrative of Arthur Gordon Pym of Nantucket* (1838). The influence of these polar fantasies upon modern horror is evident from H. P. Lovecraft's *At the Mountains of Madness* (1936) to John Carpenter's film *The Thing* (1982).
67 See Leighton (1984: 158-172). Note PBS's July 25, 1817 entry in *History of a Six Weeks' Tour* extolling "the glacier of Montanvert, or as it is called, The Sea of Ice, a scene in truth of dizzying wonder" in Hunter (2012: 299). In the view of Rieger (1974: xxiii), the 1831 *F* "virtually plagiarizes" "Mont Blanc," which owes much to Coleridge's 1802 "Hymn before Sunrise, in the Vale of Chamouny" (apostrophizing Mont Blanc as sublime object, "O sovran BLANC"), which in turn borrows shamelessly from Brun's 1791 "Chamounix beym Sonnenaufgange." Can one see in this history of (mis)appropriations that same annexing of authorship symptomatic of the sublime, wherein we 'mistake' what we see or hear for our own invention—the same 'mistake' motivating the old misconception that "Frankenstein" is the Creature's name, not the creator's?
68 In Book 6 of Wordsworth's *Prelude* (1805), the "Vale of Chamouny," dominated by Mont Blanc, is the purgatory of the empirical through which Wordsworth must pass (524-592) in order to attain his sublime epiphany (592-640), which will "break through" (597) after the crossing of the Alps. The sequence helps to establish the archetypal Romantic landscape of the sublime; see Monk (1960: 227-232). The suspension of the imagination at Simplon Pass has generated much critical debate; see Miall 1998. Here it suffices to note how closely it syncs with the "momentary inhibition of the vital powers" prior to their "more powerful outpouring" (section 23) that signals the advent of the Kantian sublime.
69 In Hunter (2012: 225).

Part Two

Hideous Progeny

7

Cupid and Psyche in *Frankenstein*: Mary Shelley's Apuleian Science Fiction?

Benjamin Eldon Stevens

Introduction

It is a moonlit night. Into a darkened bedchamber comes someone carrying a weapon and a light. In the bed lies a beloved partner, asleep or seeming to be. Through the waking partner, a third party works toward nefarious goals: the sleeper is harmed or killed, and the waking partner is held—or holds himself—responsible. The third party may now appear and take its grim or grinning satisfaction.

*

Readers of Mary Wollstonecraft Shelley's (henceforth MWS) *Frankenstein* will recognize this summary as applying to a climactic scene late in the novel (3.6: 140–141).[1] Entering Elizabeth's bedchamber on their wedding-night, Victor finds that the Creature has preceded him and killed her. Having rejected the Creature at first sight and having later destroyed its would-be 'bride,' Victor believes himself responsible. As if confirming judgment, the Creature appears at the window, grinning. Victor fires his pistol but misses, alerting the household to Elizabeth's death. Nobody else sees the Creature, but all must feel that darkness abounds.

With an eye on its painterly quality—a nightmarish still life, whose most vital element is the unnaturally animated Creature—I refer to this scene as a 'bedroom tableau.'[2] Victor, the Creature, and Elizabeth are brought together in a mockery of a wedding's joy—and a travesty of the wedding-night's traditional consummation. The climax of the Creature's revenge, the scene emphasizes many of the novel's themes, including love, hatred, envy, and revulsion; life and death; and fears about sexual reproduction gone wrong. The structure is something of a trope in the novel, appearing in at least two other scenes: first when, the night after bringing the Creature to life, Victor dreams that Elizabeth becomes his mother's corpse—and upon waking sees the Creature at his moonlit

Fig. 7.1 "An Experiment on a Bird in an Air Pump" (1768). Joseph Wright of Derby—National Gallery, London, Public Domain (https://commons.wikimedia.org/w/index.php?curid=3751913).

window (1.4: 36); and second when, on another moonlit night, Victor destroys the 'bride,' prompting the Creature's fatal promise: "I shall be with you on your wedding-night" (3.3: 121). A third scene may offer a variation on the theme, when the Creature frames Justine Moritz for his murder of William Frankenstein (2.8: 100–101). Similar tableaux appear elsewhere in Gothic and—thanks in part to *Frankenstein*'s great influence—in related genres like horror and science fiction (SF).[3] Whatever we discover about *Frankenstein*'s tableaux should thus deepen our understanding of other works.

In this chapter, I argue that *Frankenstein*'s bedroom tableaux form part of a tradition reaching back to classical antiquity, representing receptions of the story of 'Cupid and Psyche' as told by Apuleius in his second-century CE Latin novel *Metamorphoses* or the *Golden Ass* (henceforth *GA*).[4] *GA* centers on a young man, Lucius, who is transformed into an ass due to immoderate curiosity and incompetent experimentation with magic, and who can be changed back only if he accepts religion, symbolized by eating roses associated with the goddess Isis. Lucius's story frames others, including 'Cupid and Psyche,' which occupies the novel's center (books 4.28–6.24 out of eleven) and reflects its central themes.[5] Psyche, a young woman, is so beautiful that the goddess Venus feels threatened; Venus seeks to punish her by having Cupid marry her to a horrible man; but Cupid falls in love with and marries Psyche himself, concealing his identity by visiting only at night and prohibiting her from viewing him. Psyche, spurred by her envious sisters, discovers that her husband is Cupid, loses him for breaking the prohibition, and is reconciled to him after a series of arduous tasks. The story thus reflects the novel's theme of curiosity and anticipates Lucius's own happy ending.[6]

'Cupid and Psyche' features a bedroom tableau that is archetypal thanks to GA's history of reception.[7] Works that draw on Apuleius's novel range from Capella's *De nuptiis Mercurii et Philologiae* (c. 410 CE) and Fulgentius's *Mythologies* (c. early sixth century CE); through the anonymous *Partonopeu Blois* (c. 1170–1196) and Boccaccio's *Ameto* (1341/42); to Spenser's *The Faerie Queene* (3.6.50–52; 1590) and many works by Shakespeare, including *A Midsummer Night's Dream* (c. 1597); to modern works like Pushkin's *Eugene Onegin* (1825) and contemporary work including C. S. Lewis's *Till We Have Faces* (1956) and Salman Rushdie's *Travels with a Golden Ass* (1985).[8] This sampling ignores whole categories including visual arts.[9] It is worth noting, too, that the story has exerted perhaps its greatest influence in the form of 'Beauty and the Beast'; thus 'Cupid and Psyche' has been called "the first literary fairytale" and "an essential Taproot Text for fantasy."[10]

I argue that MWS's *Frankenstein* belongs in this tradition of Apuleian receptions, offering meaningful transformations of 'Cupid and Psyche' in its own bedroom tableaux. Although scholars have examined other aspects of MWS's Apuleian receptions, to my knowledge this link has gone undiscussed.[11] Less overt than *Frankenstein*'s inclusion of Plutarch (2.7: 89–90) or its interest in Prometheus, the link is yet significant. It fits into an explosion of interest in 'Cupid and Psyche' in British literature in the nineteenth century, including contemporary works like Blake's *A Vision of the Last Judgment* (1808), *Rhododaphne* by Percy Bysshe Shelley's (PBS) friend Thomas Love Peacock (1818), Keats's "Ode to Psyche" (1819), and Byron's *Don Juan* (1818–1824), as well as works by later authors like Walter Pater (*Marius the Epicurean*, 1885), William Morris (*The Earthly Paradise*, 1868–1870), and Wordsworth (two poems "To a Butterfly," 1888).[12] MWS's knowledge of some of these and other works allows a case to be made for her indirect awareness of Apuleius's story.[13] More importantly, paratextual evidence shows that MWS was directly interested in the story throughout her life. Her interest seems first to have crystallized while she was finishing *Frankenstein* in May 1817, and in November 1817 she translated part of Apuleius's story from the Latin. Allusions to it appear in other works, including "To the Death" (1839), (possibly) "The Death of Love"

(1831) and "Stanzas" (1832), and her other SF novel, *The Last Man* (1826; henceforth *LM*).

Frankenstein's bedroom tableaux thus represent variations on ancient themes and look ahead to changes in MWS's Apuleian receptions over time. Apuleius's Cupid and Psyche are warmly living beings who take 'pleasure' in each other and indeed produce a child of that name (Lat. *Voluptas*; 6.24.4), allegorizing the soul's communion with divine love. In MWS's work, by contrast, they are eventually reduced to inanimate statues, "unconceiving marble" that 'mocks' mortality (*LM* 3.10: 338).[14] Such frigid figures suggest dissatisfaction with the prospect of 'survival' via the metaphorical progeny of art. MWS's most famous novel thus achieves part of its power by recomposing materials from Apuleius: just as Victor fashions the Creature out of once-living matter, *Frankenstein* incorporates parts of *GA*, transforming them into symbols of the impossibility of even ordinary reproduction, much less idealized Romantic love.

In what follows, I first summarize evidence for MWS's knowledge of Apuleius, establishing the possibility that *Frankenstein* draws on *GA* deliberately. I then discuss each tableau, emphasizing formal similarities and thematic variations. Next, I trace MWS's image of 'Cupid and Psyche' after *Frankenstein*, especially in *LM*. I conclude by suggesting how *Frankenstein*'s influence on modern popular culture means that understanding MWS's Apuleian receptions could help shape further research. What future readings might be prompted by ancient Apuleian elements in Mary Shelley's immortal 'Modern Prometheus'? Is there—has there always been, could there be, and what would it mean for us to read—'Apuleian science fiction'?

Historical Connections via Paratextual Evidence

'Cupid and Psyche' was significant to many nineteenth-century authors, including MWS and members of her immediate and extended circles. Here are relevant dates:

Dates Relevant to MWS's Interest in 'Cupid and Psyche'

Early Context
1795 – Thomas Taylor's translation of 'Cupid and Psyche'
1805 – Mary Tighe's *Psyche, or The Legend of Love*
1806 – William Godwin's *The Pantheon*

In Context of *Frankenstein*'s Composition and Publication
September 29, 1816, etc. – PBS reads ps.-Lucian, 'Lucius, or the Ass'
October 6, 1816 – MWS jokes about a metamorphic, rose-eating cat
December 2, 5–7, 1816 – MWS reads ps.-Lucian, 'Lucius, or the Ass'
April 18, 1817 – MWS starts fair copy of *Frankenstein*
May 8, 1817 – PBS writes about Apuleius to Hogg
May 9, 1817 – PBS reads Apuleius
May 10–13, 1817 – MWS finishes fair copy of *Frankenstein*
May 14, 1817 – MWS finishes *Frankenstein*
May 20 & 21, 1817 – MWS reads Apuleius
by October 13, 1817 – receipt of proofs for *Frankenstein* vol. I
by October 23, 1817 – receipt of proofs for *Frankenstein* vol. II
(October 23, 1817 – MWS "translate[s Apuleius]"?)[15]
November 3–16, 1817 – MWS translates 'Cupid and Psyche'
by November 22, 1817 – receipt of proofs for *Frankenstein* vol. III

MWS's Lifelong Interest
1820 – *Matilda*, comparison to Psyche
1826 – *LM*, statues of Cupid and Psyche
1831 – "The Death of Love," comparison to Psyche?
1832 – "Stanzas," comparison to Psyche?
1836 – *Lives* mentions Boiardo's version of Apuleius
1839 – "To the Death," comparison to Psyche

Thomas Taylor published his translation of 'Cupid and Psyche' in 1795, two years before MWS was born; in 1822 he translated all of *GA*. Mary Tighe privately printed her *Psyche, or The Legend of Love* as early as 1805 (published 1811); incidentally, a cousin of Tighe's had a daughter, Laura, who "was Mary's friend to the last."[16] Of potentially greater significance is William Godwin's 1806 *The Pantheon: or, Ancient History of the Gods of Greece and Rome*.[17] This could have provided MWS's first exposure to Apuleius's story, since MWS's "earliest education [was] received directly from Godwin."[18]

More concretely, MWS's 'Reading List' for 1817 includes "Story of Phsyche [*sic*] in Apuleius."[19] The timing is suggestive. In a May 8 letter to Thomas Hogg, PBS praises the story's "miraculous interest and beauty," saying it surpasses "any imagination ever clothed in the language of men."[20] On May 9, MWS notes that PBS "writes and reads Apuleius." Over the next three days she prepared the fair copy of *Frankenstein*, and on May 14 PBS "corrects F" and "write[s its] Preface—Finis."[21] There is thus reason for wondering about connections between *Frankenstein* and *GA*.

MWS's Knowledge of Apuleius

A week after completing *Frankenstein*, on May 20 and 21, 1817, MWS is "Read[ing] Apuleius."[22] Six months later, between November 3 and 16—before *Frankenstein* was published January 1, 1818 and during correction of proofs (from no later than October 13, 1817 to no later than November 22, 1817)—she translated about half of 'Cupid and Psyche.'[23] To de Palacio, the translation shows delicacy, toning down what Walter Pater calls Apuleius's "almost insane preoccupation with the materialities of our mouldering flesh."[24] Thus de Palacio finds that MWS "shrank from that sort of naturalism that did not mince matters," omitting material she considered "over-realistic and offensive."[25] Although the translation "peters out soon after the announcement of Psyche's child-bearing," Apuleius's 'material naturalism' might seem suited to MWS's theme of reproduction, while "materialities of our mouldering flesh" would resonate with the contemporaneous *Frankenstein*.[26] At any rate, the translation shows MWS's interest in 'Cupid and Psyche.'

That interest appears elsewhere. The narrator of *Matilda* (written 1819–1820) says: "Like Psyche I lived for awhile in an enchanted palace, amidst odours, and music, and every luxurious delight; when suddenly I was left on a barren rock" (3).[27] The titular *Last Man* (1826) encounters statues of Cupid and Psyche (3.10, discussed below). The 1836 *Lives* mentions Boiardo's 1518 version of *GA* (1.182). And in "To the Death" (1839), MWS echoes Matilda, comparing herself to Psyche when invoking her deceased husband: "'Twas' thus, as ancient fables tell, / Love visited a Grecian maid, / Till she disturbed the sacred spell, / And woke to find her hopes betrayed. // But gentle sleep shall veil my sight, / And Psyche's lamp shall darkling be, / When, in the visions of the night, / Thou dost renew thy vows to me."[28] de Palacio suggests that "[i]n later years, the story must have more than ever impressed her as the symbol of soon fled happiness": "[t]he Apuleian episode, which had seemed at first the mere occasion for a school-girl's Latin exercise, had become woven into the drama of her life."[29] Well it might: MWS had suffered "the deaths of Percy Shelley, of three of her four children, and of Byron."[30]

Such negative feelings mark a change from MWS's earliest expressions of delighted interest in Apuleian tales. While composing *Frankenstein* but before reading *GA*, MWS heard of and then read a story traditionally attributed to the second-century CE Greek author Lucian of Samosata that had provided a model for Apuleius: "Lucius, or the Ass," describing a man changed into an ass who changes back by eating roses.[31] MWS's journal for October 6, 1816 records (in PBS's hand) that "Mary put her head thro the door & said—Come & look, here's a cat eating roses—she'll turn into a woman. when beasts eat [these] roses they turn into men & women."³² The joke requires both MWS and PBS knowing a story in which eating roses causes return to human form. As Bowen has shown, since MWS reads Lucian not until two months later, on December 2 and 5–7, 1816, and Apuleius aside from 'Cupid and Psyche' not until May 1817, she must have heard the story from PBS.³³ Since PBS himself does not read Apuleius until May 1817, in the fall of 1816 he must have found the story in Lucian, whom he read as early as September 29 and again in October and November.³⁴ Suggestively, MWS drafted the manuscript for *Frankenstein* volume I "most likely by mid-September and no later than mid-October."³⁵ As Bowen concludes, then, Lucian's story "engaged Mary Shelley's imagination … during the composition of *Frankenstein*," his Apuleian theme of transformation surely factoring in.³⁶ MWS would go on to read Lucian again May 9–15, 1818.³⁷ All of this is a far cry from—and helps clarify—the darkness of MWS's later Apuleian receptions.³⁸

Such paratextual evidence strengthens the possibility that Apuleius's *GA* played a role in MWS's *Frankenstein*. Mentions of Apuleius are contemporaneous with the writing of *Frankenstein*, including overlapping with final composition by a matter of days. MWS's translation of 'Cupid and Psyche' and her *re*-reading of Lucian's story come later, but the former yet during receipt and correction of *Frankenstein*'s proofs.³⁹ Sharing in PBS's enthusiasm for the story for some time, MWS may have been aware of it earlier, from childhood reading. There is thus historical justification for considering *Frankenstein* in connection with at least the central, inset story in *GA*.

Cupid and Psyche in *Frankenstein*: Forms and Themes

Frankenstein's climactic bedroom tableau (3.6: 140–141) brings Victor, Elizabeth, and the Creature together in transformed Apuleian fashion: it is night; the bedchamber is lit by lamp and moon; Victor discovers that Elizabeth has been killed; he fires his pistol but misses; and the Creature escapes, enjoying his revenge. The scene emphasizes Victor's responsibility and failure. Any light serves only to illuminate moral darkness, and the weapon likewise does a sort of psychological harm to its wielder—having produced an unnatural creation, Victor cannot stop it from spreading (further) destruction.⁴⁰ Traditional consummation with its promise of life in natural, beloved children is replaced by death caused by an unnatural 'child,' instinctively hated.

Found across *Frankenstein*'s several tableaux, these themes may be emphasized by comparison with *GA* (5.22–23). The formal similarities may be diagrammed as in Table 1.

Table 7.1 Comparison of 'bedroom tableaux' in the *Golden Ass* (*GA*) and *Frankenstein* (*F*)

	GA 5.22–23	F 1.4	F 2.8	F 3.3	F 3.6
awake	Psyche	Victor/Creature	William/Creature	Victor	Victor
asleep	Cupid	Elizabeth/Victor	Creature/Justine	'bride'	Elizabeth
third party	sisters	Creature?	Creature	Creature	Creature
light	lamp	moonlight	sunset	moonlight	lamp?
weapon	blade	—	locket?	hands	pistol

In *GA*, the players are Psyche, Cupid, and—'off-stage'—Psyche's sisters. Persuaded by her sisters that her husband is a monster, Psyche enters the bedchamber carrying a lamp and a blade. The lamp reveals Cupid, and the blade refuses to harm him. Accidentally pricking her thumb on one of his arrows, Psyche 'falls in love with Love' (5.23.3). The lamp too 'falls for Cupid,' dripping hot oil on his shoulder. Startled awake, Cupid upbraids Psyche for breaking the prohibition against viewing him and then flees. Psyche, distraught, attempts suicide, but the blade now refuses to harm *her*. After a series of tasks, Psyche is reconciled to Cupid and they have a child, Voluptas. The story allegorizes how 'the soul' (Greek *psyche*), if it avoids untoward curiosity, may achieve communion with divine 'love' (embodied in Cupid) and find true 'pleasure' (Lat. *Voluptas*; *GA* 6.24.4).[41] This anticipates a happy ending for Lucius, if he abandons magic and embraces religion. In a coda, Cupid's assistant winds, which otherwise ferry visitors to his palace, let Psyche's sisters fall to their deaths.

Apuleius's story helps clarify *Frankenstein*'s climactic tableau. Psyche, Cupid, and the sisters are matched by Victor, Elizabeth, and the Creature. Victor's search for principles of life recalls Psyche's curiosity about her husband (symbolizing love, a generative principle) and Lucius's search for transformative magic: each pursues experimentation involving bodies, with—at least temporarily—destructive results.[42] But Victor is irredeemable, and the other two pairs of characters emphasize the despair in MWS's version. Apuleius's sleeping Cupid, vulnerable but immortal, becomes MWS's Elizabeth, already dead. Whereas Psyche and Cupid have had a happy—if secret—marriage including pleasurable sex, Victor and Elizabeth are married only a short time before she is killed and have not had sex. Their relationship is also darker in a way characteristic of Gothic, suggesting incest: they are first cousins and, after Elizabeth's mother's death, adoptive siblings (1.1: 20).[43] Similarly, whereas Psyche's sisters are stock, malevolent folk-tale characters who envy her unprompted, the Creature is provoked: Victor is doomed to find Elizabeth killed once he has destroyed the 'bride'—and even earlier, upon rejecting the Creature at first sight.[44]

This sort of *lex Talionis*—'a bride for a bride'?—operative in *Frankenstein* represents a significant departure from *GA*. Psyche and Cupid join together to produce Voluptas. Victor is truly paired not with Elizabeth but with the Creature, whom he has produced alone: solipsistically or onanistically Victor creates his own double or *Doppelgänger*, with whom he has his most intimate and consequential relationship.[45] These themes are reflected in the objects. Psyche's lamp and blade, both lightly anthropomorphized, show that her husband is not a monster to be harmed but a god to be loved, while Psyche herself should go unharmed. By contrast, Victor's light reveals the latest violence resulting from his failure, and his pistol only calls attention to it.

Frankenstein's first bedroom tableau (1.4): a dream

MWS continues to draw on and depart from Apuleius in *Frankenstein*'s other tableaux. In the first (1.4: 36), the night after bringing the Creature to life, Victor

> slept indeed, but I was disturbed by the wildest dreams. I thought I saw Elizabeth, in the bloom of health.... Delighted and surprised, I embraced her; but as I imprinted the first kiss on her lips, they became livid with the hue of death; her features appeared to change, and I thought that I held the corpse of my dead mother in my arms; a shroud enveloped her form, and I saw the grave-worms crawling in the folds of the flannel.

This dream has been read as showing "each psyche's pre-conscious drives towards an erotic re-union with the mother and death."[46] Such psychoanalytical reading invites consideration of how other 'dead' matter is incorporated into the story—that is, earlier text, including Apuleius. On one level, Victor is Psyche discovering that his beloved is a monster, exchanging living for dead (recalling his work) and sister-lover for mother-lover. Anticipating the Gothic problematic mentioned above, domestic space and interpersonal relationships conceal here what they should not contain, with necrophilia a further distorted version of a love-relationship between family-members.[47]

Such boundary-crossings are reflected in confusion among roles. On another level, Victor is Cupid, intruded upon in sleep by dangerous 'psychic' forces. This Victor-Cupid, too, is revealed to be monstrous, waking "with horror" and discovered by the Creature as Psyche (1.4: 36):

> by the dim and yellow light of the moon, as it forced its way through the window-shutters, I beheld the wretch—the miserable monster whom I had created. He held up the curtain of the bed; and his eyes, if eyes they may be called, were fixed on me. His jaws opened, and he muttered some inarticulate sounds, while a grin wrinkled his cheeks. He might have spoken, but I did not hear; one hand was stretched out, seemingly to detain me, but I escaped, and rushed down stairs.

Real in a way the dream was not, the Creature's arrival seems staged to confirm the dream's underlying truth. In vitality, the Creature outstrips Elizabeth, only dreamt—and dreamt dead.

This first tableau emphasizes MWS's departures from Apuleius. The Creature's arrival takes the place of the discovery that ancient Psyche does *not* make: there *is* a monster in the bedchamber, since the Creature as Psyche reflects the monstrous in its creator, Victor as Cupid. Victor, *also* a Psyche, is thus linked more closely to a *Doppelgänger*—two versions of the (same) 'soul'—than to Elizabeth, who remains a mortal Cupid. The Creature also serves as third party, a satisfied "grin wrinkl[ing] his cheeks" (as in the second [3.3] and climactic [3.6] tableaux). As Apuleian relationships are perverted, even light becomes a kind of interloper, moonlight "forc[ing] its way" in.

Frankenstein's second bedroom tableau (3.3): the 'bride'

Similar departures from Apuleius are found in the second tableau, when Victor destroys the Creature's would-be 'bride' (3.3: 119):

> I trembled, and my heart failed within me; when, on looking up, I saw, by the light of the moon, the daemon at the casement. A ghastly grin wrinkled his lips as he gazed on me. . . . I thought with a sensation of madness on my promise of creating another like to him, and, trembling with passion, tore to pieces the thing on which I was engaged. The wretch saw me destroy the creature on whose future existence he depended for happiness, and, with a howl of devilish despair and revenge, withdrew.

Here Victor is Psyche, the 'bride' is Cupid, and the Creature the third party. The third party is noticed looking on—as if picking up where the preceding tableau left off—and only then does the Psyche-figure seek to kill its Cupid. This Psyche succeeds where Apuleius's did not, destroying the 'bride' with his bare hands. Such 'successful' violence emphasizes how *Frankenstein*'s versions of 'Cupid and Psyche' end in failure. The Cupid-'bride' is monstrous in Victor-Psyche's eyes—but is that a factual identification or a projection of feeling? Like the Creature, the 'bride' is composed of dead parts and could be called "hideous"—but she also recalls Victor's dream-bride Elizabeth transforming into his dead mother. Victor also resembles Psyche's sisters, fearful and envious of the life he imagines the Creature and its 'bride' would enjoy: "a race of devils would be propagated upon the earth ... at the price perhaps of the existence of the whole human race."[48]

Finally, the third party's satisfaction is spoiled ... or perhaps deferred. Having returned to his apartment, Victor stands by the moonlit window (3.3: 119), and then the Creature comes to his bedroom door (120), eventually saying "I shall be with you on your wedding-night" (121). In these decaying echoes of the preceding tableau, the Creature is Psyche, certain of Victor-Cupid's monstrosity and anticipating the killing that ancient Psyche could not achieve—but which Victor-*Psyche* modeled only hours before.[49] The Creature will repeat Victor's gesture by killing Elizabeth with his bare hands: a vengeful third party learns by watching violent Psyche and so becomes Psyche in turn. With this coda, the second tableau emphasizes how in *Frankenstein* there is to be no reconciliation of (any) Psyche to (any) Cupid, only endless refractions of souls that would rather be rid of each other—or a single, fractured soul that cannot be freed from itself.[50] In their like solitude, recalling and repeating the violence underpinning the original creation, Victor and the Creature embody the *un*creation to be fulfilled in the climactic tableau. Before returning to that climax, we turn to a third possible echo of Apuleius's archetypal scene.

A third possible tableau in *Frankenstein* (2.8: 100–101): William and Justine

Here, Apuleian material is staged in shifting pieces over two linked scenes. The first scene anticipates the second tableau's 'successful' killing. By way of building up to his request for a 'bride', the Creature has been telling the story of wanderings subsequent to his rejection by the De Laceys. Having reached "the environs of Geneva" (2.8: 99) on a certain evening ("sunset"; 100), he is awoken from "a slight sleep" by "the approach of a beautiful child," William Frankenstein. If the Creature is thus briefly sleeping Cupid, William as unwitting Psyche considers him a "monster! ugly wretch! ... an ogre." Learning William's identity, the Creature makes him his "first victim": "I grasped his throat to silence him, and in a moment he lay dead at my feet. I gazed on my victim, and my heart swelled with exultation and hellish triumph" (100). From a sleeping Cupid considered 'monstrous,' the Creature becomes *both* a murderous Psyche, 'succeeding' at violence like Victor, *and* a terribly—erotically?—satisfied third party, taking pleasure in "gaz[ing] on the victim." William, a substitute for Victor, becomes a proxy slaughtered Cupid as well.

Another potential Cupid awaits in the second, linked scene. "[S]eeking a more secluded hiding-place" after killing William, the Creature encounters a "woman passing near," Justine Moritz (101). The Creature "approached her unperceived, and placed [a] portrait" of Elizabeth, taken from dead William, "securely in one of the folds of her dress" (perhaps recalling the location of the "grave-worms" in "the folds of the flannel" shrouding Victor's mother in his necrophilic dream [1.4: 36]). This planted evidence leads to Justine's trial (1.7: 53–57) and execution ('off-stage' between volumes I and II) for William's murder. Thus both William and Justine play shifting roles: William starts as Psyche discovering a 'monstrous' Cupid but becomes a proxy Cupid himself, killed in place of Victor by Creature-Psyche; and Justine, starting as innocent passerby, also is killed—by the court, with the Creature as contriving third party. These shifts anticipate the freighted doublings when the Creature is denied its 'bride' and when Victor in turn is denied his own 'beautiful' wife and (any) child.[51]

A textual variant emphasizes Apuleian resonance here and attests to MWS's lasting interest in 'Cupid and Psyche.' Perhaps recognizing implausibility in the Creature going unnoticed by the passing Justine, in 1831 MWS has him discover her sleeping. Still "seeking a more secluded hiding-place," in 1831 the Creature "entered a barn which had appeared ... to be empty. A woman was sleeping on some straw"; "blooming in the loveliness of youth and health," Justine seems to the Creature like "one of those whose joy-imparting smiles are bestowed on all but me." Bending over her like Psyche over Cupid, he "whispered: 'Awake, fairest, thy lover is near—he who would give his life but to obtain one look of affection from thine eyes: my beloved, awake!'" Alarmed by her stirring, the Creature "bent over her" again "and placed the portrait securely in one of the folds of her dress."[52] 1831 resembles Apuleius even more closely, with the Creature as Psyche discovering—indeed, fashioning—a sleeping Cupid in Justine, contriving to make her seem a 'monster' that must be killed.

Frankenstein in light of the *Golden Ass*

Especially in 1831, the episode just discussed emphasizes *Frankenstein*'s perversions of Apuleian themes. Already in 1818, even a dream of ordinary joy is compromised by suggestions of incest and necrophilia, while the promise of consummation—with its prospect of reproduction—is broken by killing.[53] Thus *Frankenstein*'s tableaux form a series of *un*creations, as one after another desired being or 'beautiful' Cupid is discovered and destroyed by 'monstrous' Psyches. In *GA*, Psyche is kept from Cupid only temporarily and does no lasting harm. In *Frankenstein*, each Psyche-figure harms its Cupid directly or by proxy.

Considering how MWS's characters play such ancient roles also helps specify further how *Frankenstein*'s tableaux reflect the novel's 'primal scene,' when Victor rejects the Creature at first sight. Thereafter reflecting each other, creator and Creature form a single, doubled Psyche-figure seeking to destroy images of its own 'soul'—and so deepening the impossibility of Romantic love.

Whereas Apuleius's Psyche and Cupid reproduce in the form of Voluptas, a 'joyful' addition, in MWS Victor and the Creature endlessly circle each other, a limited life of sterility and negation.[54] Merely misleading curiosity in Apuleius (Psyche's, Lucius's) has become in *Frankenstein* macabre experimentation, a self-fulfilling prophecy of failure to reproduce: Victor and Elizabeth do not have sex; Victor substitutes solitary activity—hardly interrupted by homosocial friendship and protestations of heterosexual love—for time with spouse or other family. The result is the Creature: likewise solitary, it is also solipsistic, reflecting Victor's failures in his own frustrated and perverted search for love. The abandoned De Laceys, the aborted 'bride,' Justine framed for a child's murder (and, in 1831, addressed by the Creature as "lover"): in all of this, the Creature recalls Victor as Psyche. Absent a truly beautiful, loving Cupid, this bipartite Frankensteinian 'soul' births only the opposite of pleasure—namely, disgust and horror at a series of violent killings of proxy Cupids, each 'monstrous' mainly insofar as s/he is a projection of Psyche's own monstrosity.

In this way, MWS's recomposition of Apuleius's story echoes Victor's original act of creation, a transformation of once-living matter into something animated but not precisely—not (re)productively—alive. There is thus failure of the most basic biological imperative—a dehumanizing failure that is the more appalling for replacing what, in Apuleius, was loving communion with the divine. Elsewhere in MWS, the same ancient story is pressed further to suggest dissatisfaction with the possibility of 'surviving' in memory via the metaphorical 'progeny' that is art. To that development of her Apuleian receptions we now turn.

Cupid and Psyche at the End of Human History: *The Last Man*

Modern popular culture is replete with *Frankenstein*'s descendants, a "race of devils ... propagated upon the earth" (3.3: 119) in a wide range of media over the past two hundred years.[55] Reception started quickly, with Richard Brinsley Peake's 1823 play *Presumption; or, the Fate of Frankenstein*. In the audience the second night was MWS herself. Indeed, from among the many people who have produced receptions of *Frankenstein*, MWS stands out. Most famously she revised the text for the 1831 edition.[56] And aspects of the novel appear in her later work. A recurrent part of her "hideous progeny"—a recycled part of its fungible literary body—was 'Cupid and Psyche,' as changed already in *Frankenstein*.

We see this especially in MWS's other SF novel, *LM* (1826), composed starting in 1824, not long after her first experiences with *Frankenstein*'s receptions.[57] Articulating fears we have seen voiced in *Frankenstein* (3.3: 119), *LM* envisions human extinction due to global plague.[58] An Apuleian connection between the two novels is clear from a near-final scene (*LM* 3.10: 338).[59] The last man himself, Lionel Verney

> haunted the Vatican, and stood surrounded by marble forms of divine beauty. Each stone deity was possessed by sacred gladness, and the eternal fruition of love. They looked on me with unsympathizing complacency, and often in wild accents I reproached them for their supreme indifference ... often, half in bitter mockery, half in self-delusion, I clasped their icy proportions, and, coming between Cupid and his Psyche's lips, pressed the unconceiving marble.

Cupid and Psyche are present but as "stone deities" instead of living beings. They are "possessed by ... the eternal fruition of love," a vision of perfection from which Verney—embodying all of humankind—is excluded: "sacred gladness" means their "unsympathetic complacency" in divine pleasure and a "supreme indifference" to human suffering.[60] Verney thus plays the role of Apuleian third party, envying and intruding upon the lovers' relationship. By physically "coming between" them at the moment of their reconciliation, seeking to share in physical aspects of their love, Verney emphasizes his isolation.[61] His self-awareness—"mockery," "self-delusion"—links him to Victor: his isolation seems a literal, physical form of Victor's more figurative experience—and a version too of the Creature's sexual and biological solitude.[62] Intensifying *Frankenstein*'s onanism and solipsism, *LM* replaces the climax of Apuleius's story with an endless deferral, and thus a practical failure, of the soul's loving communion with the divine.

'The last man' is thus also a Psyche, discovering that Cupid is 'monstrous'—that love or "gladness" is distributed unfairly. As if recalling the imagined beginning of post-human life in *Frankenstein*, at the end of human history MWS depicts the biological imperative made vain. Whereas Victor variously reenacted Apuleius's bedroom tableau, Verney merely regards literal art, able to see depicted but not to reach the highest point of the mystical ascent described by neo-Platonists. He is a former potential Psyche, written out of his own story, with no prospect of any child or 'joy'. This is not meaningfully changed by interaction with imagined readers, who may as well be "the illustrious dead" (*LM* 3.10: 339). *LM*'s final line emphasizes that only "the spirits of the dead, and the ever-open eye of the Supreme" (342), recalling the statues' "supreme indifference" (338), "will behold the tiny bark, freighted with Verney—*The Last Man*" (342). Possibly the world will be "re-peopled" by "the children of a saved pair of lovers," but this would be cold—"icy"—comfort.[63]

The same dissatisfying possibility frames the novel, which opens with a self-conscious supernaturalism that can lead us back to Apuleius through one of his sources, whom MWS also read, the first-century BCE Roman poet Virgil.[64] *LM* claims to be the attempt of a nameless editor to give "form and substance to the frail and attenuated Leaves of the Sibyl" ('Author's Introduction' 4). Meant here is the Cumaean Sibyl, a priestess of Apollo whose prophecies were important in ancient Rome and who guides the hero of Virgil's *Aeneid* on his Underworld journey (book 6).[65] Virgil's Aeneas hopes the Sibyl will answer him in speech, lest any leaves scatter in the wind (*Aen.* 6.74–76); *LM*'s editor avers that "[d]oubtless the leaves ... have suffered distortion and diminution of interest and excellence in my hands," although already "they were unintelligible in their pristine condition" ('Author's Introduction' 4). Making the allusion plain, the editor says the Leaves were discovered December 8, 1818 in "the Sibyl's Cave," which is "not indeed exactly as Virgil describes it" (meaning *Aen.* 6.9–44).[66] MWS's modern story about the future is thus framed as an adaptation of ancient prophecy via classical Latin poetry: "the main substance rests on the truths contained in these poetic rhapsodies, and the divine intuition which the Cumaean damsel [i.e., the Sibyl] obtained from heaven" ('Author's Introduction' 4).[67] Readers of *GA* may be struck by similarities to its own complex narrative structure, including purposeful confusions among author, narrator, and main character.[68]

Adding to this is the fact that *LM*'s 'editor' must be MWS herself. On December 8, 1818, she, PBS, and Claire Clairmont visited "Avernus," which in the *Aeneid* is the entrance to the Underworld, and "The Elysian fields," traditional abode of the fortunate dead.[69] MWS thus parallels Apuleius exactly: both are authors, narrators, and models for their main characters. Some years later, MWS writes that she "must go back" to Italy to honor the deceased PBS: otherwise his "poor utterly lost Mary will never dare think herself worthy to visit [him] beyond the grave." This anticipation of MWS's own death—or Underworld journey?—appears in her journal entry for May 14, 1824, when she is on the verge of composing *LM*.[70] The same entry deepens MWS's identification with Verney: "*The Last Man*! Yes I may well describe that solitary being's feelings, feeling myself as the last relic of a beloved race, my companions, extinct before me."[71]

Linking such Apuleian narrative strategy to Virgilian underworldliness, in *LM* Verney suggests that any future readers—already identified as the dead—could only encounter his story in a way that recalls the editor's discovery of the Leaves: in a "cave, deep embowered in earth's dark entrails, where no light will penetrate, save that which struggles, red and flickering, through a single fissure, staining thy page with grimmest livery of death" (3.10: 339).[72] Beyond strengthening the resemblance to *GA*'s framings, this further invokes Apuleius insofar as his Lucius and Psyche also take Underworld journeys (symbolic and real, respectively).[73] As if to emphasize all these echoes, in a letter begun January 28, 1826, MWS refers to *LM*—published January 23—as "my Sibylline leaves."[74]

In *LM*, then, MWS's reception of 'Cupid and Psyche' reaches its ultimate development, as those formerly vital, productive beings are reduced to static images attended by—and described only to—the (future) dead. *LM* empties Apuleius's story of positive, neo-Platonic allegory, filling it with thanatology and death.[75] That all of this is Apuleian is emphasized, finally, by how the statuary scene looks back to a different part of *GA*. Lucius, visiting his aunt's house in Hypata, finds its entryway decorated with statuary: "Parian marble chiselled into the likeness of Diana," and "[i]n the middle of the marble foliage a statue of Actaeon was visible, fashioned in marble" (2.4).[76] This is paralleled in *LM*: the protagonist (Lucius, Verney) has reached a city (Hypata, Rome), where a building (aunt's house, the Vatican) includes statuary depicting an episode from mythology (Diana and Actaeon, Cupid and Psyche). Traditionally, the statuary in *GA* is understood as "a warning to Lucius about the dangers of curiosity, which he disregards"—a theme found, darkened, in *Frankenstein*.[77] *LM* thus fits squarely into a *Frankenstein* tradition not least because of how, like MWS's first novel, it includes receptions of Apuleius's *GA*.

Conclusions: The Future of *Frankenstein*'s Classical Receptions; or, Mary Shelley's Apuleian Science Fiction?

The Last Man is only one of many works in *Frankenstein* traditions that would repay further reading for Apuleian—and other classical—receptions. To my knowledge, this chapter is the first study of *Frankenstein*'s receptions of 'Cupid and Psyche.' As such, the preceding readings are provisional and raise further questions. Does *Frankenstein* truly have no analogue for Psyche's reconciliation to Cupid? If so, is the 'soul' in MWS's view beyond saving, condemned like Victor to confront its *Doppelgänger* forever, or doomed like Verney to live without human contact, much less divine communion? Beyond the sculpture of Diana and Actaeon, how do MWS's works draw on yet other parts of Apuleius's *Golden Ass* or on other classical texts?[78] As the chapters in this volume show, any 'conclusions' should be by way of keeping such questions open.

A general question must be how *Frankenstein*'s influence on SF—like its importance in popular culture more generally—means that its classical receptions are to be found, transmitted and transmuted, *mutatis mutandis*, in other later works. A foundational scholar of SF, Darko Suvin, invited us to think about the genre as being 'metamorphic' in ways he described with reference to antiquity: contrasting 'Ovidian' (spiritual, supernatural) with 'Lucretian' (material, natural) metamorphoses, Suvin preferred the Lucretian, considering it better suited to what he believed should be counted as SF.[79] In light of the present study, we may wonder whether Suvin's binary opposition should be complicated by a third term: the Apuleian. What would it mean to read SF for its Apuleian— metamorphic, Lucianic, Cupid-and-Psychic—modes?

We might think of stories in which 'magic' or 'superstition' gives way to 'religion' and in which physical change and travel are symbols for spiritual journey, like Mary Doria Russell's *The Sparrow* (1996) and *Children of God* (1998) or Michel Faber's *The Book of Strange New Things* (2014). Related are stories in which 'science' itself becomes considered a kind of superstition—even expressly disavowed, as in Victor's injunction to Walton in *Frankenstein* (3.7: 151)—or analogous to irrational 'myth,' as in Isaac Asimov's *Foundation* series (1942–1993), Walter Miller, Jr.'s *A Canticle for Leibowitz* (1960), and Ian Tregillis's 'Alchemy Wars' trilogy (2015–2016). Further in that direction are stories that premise an alternate cosmology, like C. S. Lewis's 'Space' or 'Cosmic Trilogy' (1938–1945), developing the 'discarded image' of the Medieval heavens; Verner Vinge's *A Fire upon the Deep* (1992) and *A Deepness in the Sky* (1999), with 'knowledge' and 'technology' spread unevenly across space; or Richard Garfinkle's *Celestial Matters* (1996), juxtaposing Ptolemaic astronomy and Aristotelian physics with classical Chinese visions of reality.[80]

Such SF could also be considered Apuleian insofar as it approaches (re-) imagining the world in the spirit of thought-experiment, or even—in the case of stories like Philip José Farmer's "Sail On! Sail On!" (1952)—outright play, echoing Apuleius's ludic temper.[81] Looking for Apuleian receptions in these and other similar examples of SF could thus be a way of seeing more clearly how the genre envisions transformations of knowledge, calling into question the premises of modern science and the very rationality ascribed to inquiry.[82] Reversing the equation, we may continue to ask: What might it mean to consider ancient stories as being somehow science fictional or even specifically 'Frankensteinian'?

Do ancient authors—Apuleius himself, predecessors and models like Ovid, Virgil, and others—include Frankenstein figures, whether monomaniacal creators, their monstrous creations, or afflicted bystanders? Considering that possibility lets us ask, again: Is there—has there always been, could there be, and what would it mean for us to read—'Apuleian science fiction'?

Notes

1. References to *Frankenstein* (henceforth *F* in notes) are to the 1818 text in Hunter 2012. A first version of this chapter was presented at 'The Modern Prometheus; or, *Frankenstein*' conference at Hamilton College, April 9, 2016. I am deeply grateful to my conference co-organizers and volume co-editors, Jesse Weiner and Brett M. Rogers, for sharing that work and for their generous help with this chapter. The chapter is dedicated to every student who has asked if I, too, was assembled in a lab.
2. MWS may have seen Joseph Wright's 1768 painting "An Experiment on a Bird in the Air Pump" (Fig. 7.1); for a comparison, see Boucherie 2017.
3. Horror: e.g., *Dracula*'s Harker is attacked by vampire women (Chapter 3 = Auberbach and Skal [1997: 39–44]). For receptions of *Dracula*, see Klinger (2008: 529–536, 547–568) and Auerbach and Skal (1997: 371–407). SF: e.g., *Ex Machina* (Alex Garland 2015), with Hammond (this volume); on *F* and SF, see, e.g., Freedman 2002.
4. On *F*'s intertexts, see Mellor 2003, Morton (2002: 7–33), and Bronfen 1994; on classical receptions, see Weiner 2015a. On *GA*, see, e.g., Schlam (1992: esp. 82–98), Tatum 1979, and Walsh (1970: 141–189). I use inverted commas to distinguish the story of 'Cupid and Psyche' from the characters themselves.
5. See Zimmerman *et al.* 2004, Finkelpearl 1999, Kenney (1990: 12–28), Winkler (1985: 89–93, 55–56), Tatum (1979: 49–68), Schlam 1976, and Walsh (1970: 190–223).
6. See Walsh (1994: xxv, xxxix–xliii), after (1970: 190–223).
7. For Apuleian receptions, see Carver 2012 and 2007, Kingsley-Smith 2010, Gaisser 2008, Accardo 2002, Wright and Holloway (2000; esp. Wright), Walsh (1994: xliii–xlviii) and (1970: 224–243, esp. 232–233), Krabbe 1989, Tobin 1984, and Haight 1963.
8. On Shakespeare, see Kingsley-Smith (2010: esp. 112–116), Carver (2007: 429–445), Holloway 2000, Tobin (1984: 32–40), and Starnes 1945. On Lewis, see Folch 2017.
9. See Cavicchioli 2002, Reid (1993: 1.391–421, 2.939–955), and Haight (1963: 161–181), with *Lexicon Iconographicum Mythologiae Classicae* [*LIMC*] VII (1994: 576–585, plates 436–461), plus supplement 439–440 (Noëlle Icard-Gianolio).
10. Clute and Grant (1997: 51 s.v. 'Apuleius'; Clute); 'Cupid and Psyche' "a distant underlier" (241; David Langford); cf. Accardo (2002: 68–87) and Fehling (1977: 60–65). For classics and fantasy, see Rogers and Stevens (2017: esp. 1–14).
11. Markley (2003: 130) mentions "similarities" insofar as "many of [MWS's] works ... involve the fantastic or the supernatural." Carver notes MWS's translation of 'Cupid and Psyche' (2007: 448n7). Jancovich (2016: 200) refers to "allegory relating the Frankenstein myth to ... 'Beauty and the Beast,'" but does not mention Apuleius as 'taproot.'
12. For the time-period, see Vance and Wallace 2015, Vance 1997, and Turner 1989. Many other works symbolize change via the—Psychean—butterfly, e.g., A. S. Byatt's 1994 *Angels & Insects*; cf. *LIMC* VII (1994: esp. 583).

13 E.g., Shakespeare's *Othello* (tableau esp. 5.2.1–22), linked to *GA* (Tobin [1984: 87–92, esp. 91–92, with 173–179]); cf. Walsh (1994: xlvi). See below, n52.
14 References to *LM* are to Luke 1965.
15 See below, n23.
16 Markley (2003: 566).
17 Ibid., 124–125; cf. McWhir (2001: 160) for Godwin on Pandora. Godwin refers to Apuleius in *Lives of the Necromancers* (1834).
18 Mellor (1988: 8–12, quotation 9); cf. McWhir 1990.
19 Feldman and Scott-Kilvert (1987: 99) [henceforth *Journals*].
20 Jones (1964: 1.542 and n) [henceforth *Letters*]. Hogg writes about Apuleius in 1823 (*Liberal* 3.151.176); de Palacio (1964: 566). On 'Cupid and Psyche' in PBS's works, see Hagstrum (1977: 535–540); on his classicism, see Wallace (1997: esp. 19–52) and (2015: 428–440, plus 255–258 for MWS's feelings on PBS and classics).
21 *Journals* 169. For PBS's work on *F*, see Robinson 1996, Crook 1996, Mellor (1988: 57–69; summarized in [2003: 14–16, with 16–17 on 1818 vs. 1831]), and Hogle (2016: 42).
22 *Journals* 170.
23 On the proofs, see Robinson (2016: 18–19). MWS may have translated Apuleius earlier (*Journals* 169n4 and 182–184): October 15, 1817, meaning October 23 (182n3), records "translate F.", but "'F.'... is probably... mistake for 'S.' [Spinoza] or 'A.' [Apuleius]" (n4). The translation is in the PBS Notebook, Library of Congress, Manuscript Division, access #13, 290, pp. 40–70; the Bodleian has a fragment in Shelley adds. e. 2; see Markley (2003: 126–128), Clemit and Markley (2002: 4.lxii–lxv), de Palacio 1964, and Jones 1948. MWS also translated Virgil *Aeneid* (*Aen.*) 1.1–30; for Virgilian receptions, see below, nn64–66 and text there.
24 de Palacio (1964: 569); the passage is Levey (1985 [1885]: 70).
25 de Palacio (1964: 569 and 570).
26 Ibid., 568.
27 In Todd (1992: 163).
28 Composed December 15, 1834, published 1839, *The Keepsake* 201. Two other poems are similar. "The Death of Love" (November 19, 1831; in Bennett [1997: 72–74]): "darkling air" (16), "laid him[self] down to sleep, / Seeking in balmy dreams for a release" (17–18), and "o'er my dreams thou may'st extend thy power, / Gilding the visions of my sleep:closed eyes!" (31–32). "Stanzas" (*The Keepsake* 1832; in Bennett [1997: 73]): the speaker "love[s] in solitude and mystery... see[ing] a dark gulph... between myself and my selected shrine": "Love... comes in such sweet guise," "using but the weapon of a smile," and speaker "to his worship dedicate[s her] soul."
29 de Palacio (1964: 571), citing "To the Death." Cf. Wallace (2011: 419–422) and Lokke (2003: 117).
30 Mellor (2003: 16). For 'biographical elements,' see Bennett 2001 and Bronfen 1994.
31 The surviving version abridges a lost original: see Walsh (1994: xx–xxxix) after (1970: 144–189); cf. Mason 1999. Apuleius introduced but did not invent 'Cupid and Psyche' (Walsh [1994: xli–xlii]); cf. (1970: 196–197), Schlam (1976: esp. 4–8), and Cavicchioli (2002: 41–56).
32 *Journals* 139.
33 Ibid., 148 and 149.
34 September: ibid., 138; October 21 and 22: 141–142; and November 10–14, 1816: 145–146; alongside *Gulliver's Travels*, a week of fantastical reading if the Lucian included *True History*.
35 Robinson (2016: 14). Manuscript volume II was begun early December 1816, finished April 1817.
36 Bowen (1996: 18); cf. 16: MWS "worked on the novel the very day after the [rose-eating cat] entry was made," and on December 5, 1816, "three days after her first documented reading of

Lucian, and a day on which she read Lucian aloud," she finished the *F* chapter in which Victor animates the creature.

37 *Journals* 209–210.
38 Cf. how MWS describes *F* as "the offspring of happy days, when death and grief were but words" (Hunter [2012: 169]).
39 Aside from the poems, all this evidence precedes *F*'s 1831 edition; see below on *F* 2.8.
40 Elizabeth's killing is preceded by William's (2.8: 100, discussed below) and Clerval's (alluded to 3.3: 125, revealed 3.4: 127).
41 On allegories, see, e.g., Walsh (1994: xxix–xliii, esp. xli), after (1970: esp. 182, 215, 220–221); Kenney (1990: 27–28) and (16) on Apuleius's "neo-Platonic … implications"; Heine (1978: 32–33); Hooker 1955; and Gaisser (2008: s.v., 'Psyche, allegory of'); with *LIMC* suppl. 438–439 (Icard-Gianolio).
42 For 'curiosity' in *GA*, cf. 11.15.1; see also DeFilippo 1999, Walsh (1994: xxxii–xxxiii), Walsh (1970: 176–180), and Schlam 1968. Cf. Plutarch *Moralia* 515b–523b. For love as generative principle, see, e.g., Lucretius *De rerum natura* 1.1–5, 19–23.
43 Mellor (1988: 74, 196–200) and Gilbert and Gubar (1979: 28–29), with Hughes *et al.* (2013: s.v. 'incest,' esp. 342–343 and 692; 'family,' esp. 184–187, 225–227); and Perry 1998. In 1831, Elizabeth is a foundling (Hindle [1992: 34]) but still Victor's "more than sister," "mine only" (35).
44 On *GA*'s folk-tale aspects, see Walsh (1994: xl–xli), Fehling (1977: 29–78), Schlam (1976: 31–40).
45 The Creature says Victor is "bound" to him "by ties only dissoluble by the annihilation of one of us" (2.2: 68). In 1831, Victor says that human beings are "but half made up, if one wiser, better, dearer than ourselves … do not lend his aid to perfectionate our weak and faulty natures" (Letter 4 in Hindle [1992: 27–28]); Robinson (2016: 21) identifies this as an "allusion to Aristophanes' myth of the circular and then divided primal human beings in Plato's *Symposium*" (189c2–193d5).
46 Hogle (2016: 44–45), observing that it "has never been duplicated in any adaptation of *F*" and comparing PBS's "Alastor" (151ff.). Cf. Haggerty (2016: 121).
47 Apuleius's tableau recalls Ovid's story of Myrrha having sex with her father (*Metamorphoses* [*Met.*] 10.471–474; see Kenney [1990: 168 ad 5.22.2]). Myrrha "fascinate[d] Mary for many years" (*Journals* 74n2); in September 1818, "Mary was planning a translation of [Vittorio] Alfieri's [1786] tragedy, *Myrrha*," but "no translation has yet been found" (226n4, after *Letters* 2.39).
48 Cf. Harker's fear that Dracula "might … create [an] ever-widening circle of semi-demons" (Chapter 4 = Auerbach and Skal [1997: 53–54]), and adaptations where the vampire women seek to reproduce, with R. Thomas 2000. For the bride's afterlives, see Hawley 2015; cf. Wosk 2015 and James 2011, with Gilbert and Gubar (1979: esp. 221–247).
49 Would Elizabeth have lived, had Victor delivered the 'bride'? Cf. Mellor (1988: 115–126, esp. 121).
50 Cf. Kenney (1990: 200) on *GA* 6.8.5, when "Psyche gives herself up."
51 Justine held responsible for a child's killing might recall Medea: *Journals* notes PBS reading Medea's story in Ovid *Met.* (7.1–424) April 18, 1815 (75) and in Euripides March 26, 1819 (255); cf. *Lodore* (1835) with Hopkins 2002.
52 All preceding quotations from 1831 are from Hindle (1992: 139). *F*'s tableaux may thus evoke the "'threat of the black male' raping white women" (Brantlinger [2016: 130], quoting Malchow [1996: 23]). Cf. *Othello* 5.2; *Journals* reports *Othello* read aloud by PBS August 29, 1817 (179) and by MWS April 3, 1819 (256).

53 On such joyless unions, see Weiner (this volume, n56). The Justine episode, as Hogle (2016) suggests, exemplifies *F*'s theme of "women [as] fundamentally to blame for the ills of fallen humanity" (49); cf. ibid. 43, comparing Marion in Rousseau's *Confessions* (Scholar [2000: 78–85]). Cf. Gilbert and Guber (1979: 213–247).
54 This is literalized in Victor's pursuit of the Creature into the north, uninhabited and barren.
55 See Horton (2014: 97–112), Hitchcock 2012, Clayton 2003, Schor 2003, Morton (2002: 58–79), Heffernan 1997, Baldick 1987, and Cooper (this volume); cf. Kucich and Sadoff (2000: ix–xxx) with postscript by Armstrong (311–326).
56 Sources in n21, above. A second edition appeared in 1822.
57 See Lokke 2003, Johnson 1993, de Palacio 1968, with Carney 2014 on classical historians and McWhir (1996: xxxii–xxxvi) on intertextuality generally.
58 See Fisch (1993: 279), Eberle-Sinatra (2000: 107–108), and Paley 1993.
59 McWhir (2001: 168–173, esp. 169–170); cf. Wallace (2011: 425–426).
60 Cf. Luke (1965: esp. xviii, xvii).
61 Cf. Wallace (2011: 425): Verney "is not … 'coming between'; he is coming last." See also Markley (2003: 130–131) and McWhir (2001: 170).
62 When the Creature is expelled from the De Laceys' cottage, he feels that "all joy was but a mockery" and he "was not made for the enjoyment of pleasure" (*F* 2.8: 99).
63 A "pair of lovers" could recall not just Cupid and Psyche—or the Creature and his 'bride'?—but Adam and Eve, Noah and his wife, or perhaps Deucalion and Pyrrha, whom MWS would have encountered in Ovid *Met.* 1.313–415. *F* and Noah elements combine in *Alien: Covenant* (Ridley Scott 2017); see Rogers (this volume).
64 MWS and PBS read Virgil as early as 1815 (*Journals* 90) and returned to him for the rest of their lives; December 15, 1818 they visited his tomb (243 with n4; cf. *Letters* 2.76). Examples from MWS's letters: January 22, 1819, the *Georgics* are, "in many respects, the most beautiful poem I ever read" (Bennett [1980: 85]); August 30, 1824, "Virgil is a great favourite of mine" (447); February 3, 1835, partial quotation of *Aen.* 3.57 apparently from memory (Bennett [1983: 219]).
65 On the Sibyl, see Orlin (2002: 76–115) and Parke 1988. On *Aen.* 6, consult Horsfall 2013 and Austin 1986, with Solmsen 1990 and Williams 1990. *Journals* mentions *Aen.* as early as August 4, 1816 (book 4; 123); book 6 on January 6 and 24, 1818 (189, 191), books 1–4 and 7 intervening; "Virgil" July 4 (217) and "half the 9th book" October 9, 1818 (229); and a (nearly) complete rereading of *Aen.* March 26 to June 26, 1820 (313–324).
66 *LM*'s "Diorama of ages" (3.10: 336) recalls *Aen.*'s pageant of Roman history (6.752–892); cf. S. Thomas (2000: 31). *Aen.* 4.642–705 might be recalled in "Dido's pyre" in "The Death of Love" (1831: 5). For Virgil in other SF and fantasy, see, e.g., Rea 2017 and 2010, Stevens 2017 and 2015.
67 See esp. S. Thomas 2000, Eberle-Sinatra 2000, and Goldsmith (1993: 275–294); with Wallace (2011: 423––426), Allen (2008: 96–99), and Gilbert and Gubar (1979: 93–104). Lokke likens *LM*'s "sibylline" voice to "a Cassandra that we ignore at our peril" (2003: 133); cf. S. Thomas (2000: 36), Franci 1985, and the Cassandra-like Beatrice in *Valperga* (1823, with O'Sullivan [1993]).
68 E.g., Walsh (1994: 241).
69 *Journals* 242. MWS (ibid., n4) and PBS (*Letters* 2.61–62) were disappointed by Elysium; see Wallace (2011: 423–424), Paley (1993: 110–111), and Spark (1951: 195).
70 *Journals* 477–478 records Byron's death; cf. Allen (2008: 93–94) and *Valperga* (5.170): "the observant eye of grief … forms omens for its own immortality from combinations more

unsubstantial than the Sibylline leaves" (with Lokke 1998). For classical allusions in MWS's grief over PBS, see Wallace (2011: 419–422) and (2015: 256, 275n60).

71 *Journals* 476–477. Compare McWhir (2001: 164): MWS's "account of her own experience, like several passages in" *LM*, "sees the living woman turned to marble"; cf. A. S. Byatt's 1993 "Medusa's Ankles" and 2003 "A Stone Woman." See also Eberle-Sinatra 2000.

72 For *LM*'s ambivalence about death, e.g., 3.7: 300–301. Verney seems to die of plague after "three days and nights" but comes back to life heralded by a "cock crow[ing] at three o'clock" (3.3: 249), evoking Jesus; further details link him to *F*'s Creature (250).

73 Lucius: *GA* 11.21.6–7 and 23.7. Psyche: 6.16–6.20.5 (and cf. 6.2.5), "virtually a mosaic of ... Aeneas' journey" (Walsh [1970: 215, 56–57]); cf. Kenney (1990: 15, sources in n67).

74 Bennett (1980: 508, with 512n8 for *LM*'s publication according to Godwin's journal).

75 Lokke (2003: 119) and Kingsley-Smith (2010: 60–93).

76 Trans. Walsh (1994: 20). Latin: *lapis Parius in Dianam factus* (2.4.3) and *inter medias frondes lapidis Actaeon simulacrum ... visitur* (2.4.10).

77 Walsh (1994: 244); cf. (1970: 178). Apuleius recalls Ovid's story of Diana and Actaeon (*Met.* 3.138–252). MWS read *Met.* at least April 8 through May 12, 1815 (*Journals* 73–79) and then April 26 and May 4, 1820 (315 and 317), overlapping with composition of *Proserpine* and *Midas*; see Pascoe 2003, Richardson 1993. On MWS's Ovidian receptions, see Liveley (this volume).

78 E.g., "Valerius: The Reanimated Roman" (Robinson [1976b: 332–344]) combines a classical setting with *F* themes.

79 Suvin (1979: xv), with Csicsery-Ronay (2008: 47–75) and Freedman (2000: 16–23); in connection with classics, Rogers and Stevens (2015: 15–19, with nn25–26).

80 'Discarded image': Lewis 1964. On his fictional cosmologies, see Ward 2008; cf. Kears and Paz (2016: 4–27) and Consolmagno 2016.

81 See Riess 2008.

82 Cf., e.g., Priestman 2006 on crime fiction.

8

The Pale Student of Unhallowed Arts: Frankenstein, Aristotle, and the Wisdom of Lucretius

Carl A. Rubino

We picture the future as a reflection of the present projected into an empty space, whereas it is the result, often almost immediate, of causes that for the most part escape our notice.

Marcel Proust

1815 and the years that followed were unsettling times indeed![1]

On the one hand, life in Europe appeared to regain some form of stability. In February 1815, Napoleon Bonaparte escaped from exile on the Mediterranean island of Elba and returned to France. He prevailed for only a hundred days after that, until his decisive defeat at Waterloo, after which he was exiled once again, this time to St. Helena, a far more remote island in the Atlantic. There he spent the rest of his life, dying in 1821 at the age of 51.

More important for my purposes in this chapter, however, the other side of the world was witness to a spectacular example of instability. On April 5, 1815, Mount Tambora, a volcano on the island of Sumbawa in Indonesia—then known as the Dutch East Indies—erupted. The eruption, which reached its peak on April 10, was one of the most powerful and enormously destructive in recorded history, taking some 71,000 lives. The years following the Tambora eruption saw unusual and severe climatic aberrations in areas far away. The greatest such effects occurred in New England, in eastern Canada, and especially in parts of Western Europe. The summers of 1816 and 1817 were, for example, extremely cold in southwestern Switzerland, so much so that an ice dam formed below the Giétro Glacier in the Valais, high in the Val de Bagnes, leading to a catastrophic flood in 1818. Thus Europeans and Americans have long referred to 1816—even without knowing why—as the 'Year without a Summer.'[2]

The future Mary Shelley (henceforth MWS) and Percy Shelley (PBS), who had run off together two years earlier when PBS had left his wife, spent that summer-that-was-not on the shores of Lake Geneva, where their neighbors included Lord Byron and his physician John Polidori.[3] Although it is extremely unlikely that they were aware of the cause, the members of this extraordinary group of British travelers were all, as Gillen Wood notes, "keen eyewitnesses to the alarming glaciation of the Tambora period," as readers of PBS's "Mont Blanc," Byron's "Darkness"—both written in July and August 1816—and MWS's journal entries from the same period can attest.[4]

The weather was, of course, miserable: cold, dark, and rainy. Thus, as MWS tells us in her introduction to the 1831 edition of *Frankenstein*, they spent a good deal of their time indoors, reading and talking about ghost stories. One evening, at Byron's instigation, four of them—PBS, MWS, Polidori, and Byron himself—agreed to write a ghost story.[5] MWS reports that she busied herself "*to think of a story*—a story to rival those which had excited us to this task."[6] This caused her a great deal of anxiety. But one night, after an evening listening to PBS and Byron talk about what constituted life and whether it could be discovered and transmitted—a discussion that ranged as far as Galvani's beliefs about "animal electricity"—she had a vision that would become the heart of the novel it made possible: "I saw—with shut eyes but acute mental vision—I saw the pale student of unhallowed arts kneeling beside the thing he had put together."[7] "Frightful must it be," she goes on to tell us, "for supremely frightful would be the effect of any human endeavor to mock the stupendous mechanism of the Creator of the world."[8]

That "pale student of unhallowed arts" is, of course, Victor Frankenstein, the eighteenth-century hero of MWS's novel and its seemingly endless progeny—the long line of books, films, and the rest, continuing to this day, to which it has given birth.[9] From his youngest days Victor was obsessed by the power of what he calls "natural philosophy"—that is, classical physics, what we now call classical or Newtonian mechanics. While others were content to observe "the magnificent appearances of things," he wanted "to investigate their causes." Note here that with the exception of the notion of final cause (what is it, for example, that makes a little acorn become a noble oak tree?), to which Victor gives no attention, causal explanations attempt to define the present—and the future—in terms of the past. "The world," Victor tells us, "was a secret which I desired to divine" (*F* 1.2: 38). Unlike his sympathetic friend Henry Clerval, Victor remains stubbornly uninterested in "the structure of languages," "the code of governments," or "the politics of various states"—what we might now call the liberal arts. Instead, it was the physical "secrets of heaven and earth" that he desired to learn (*F* 1.2: 39).

The great discoveries of Isaac Newton had led many people to believe that this was indeed possible. Upon Newton's death in 1727 (or perhaps 1726), he was eulogized as a "new Moses," a being sent to lead us out of the darkness of superstition into the light of reason. As Alexander Pope's proposed epitaph puts it, "Nature and Nature's laws lay hid in night / God said, 'Let Newton be!' and all was light."[10] Newton's devoted followers went a good deal farther, imagining a closed and transparent world in which every single detail could be explained in terms of universal, general laws. According to Roger Hausheer's introduction to the work of Isaiah Berlin:

> They sought all-embracing schemas, universal unifying frameworks, within which everything that exists could be shown to be systematically—i.e. logically and causally—interconnected, vast structures in which there should be no gaps left open for spontaneous, unattended developments, where everything that occurs should be, at least in principle, wholly explicable in terms of immutable general laws.[11]

The dream of omniscience reached new heights in 1814, two years before the composition of *Frankenstein*, when Pierre Simon de Laplace imagined what to him would be the ultimate scientific intelligence. Laplace's demon, a being of supreme intelligence, would be able to comprehend the exact position at any time of every particle in the universe and of all the forces acting upon it. For such an intelligence, Laplace says, nothing would be uncertain, and both the future and the past would be present to it.[12] Note that well into the twentieth century, Einstein, writing on the occasion of a friend's death, says that for those "who believe in physics, the separation between past, present, and future is only an illusion, however tenacious."[13] If time is an illusion, then change, novelty, and surprise are rendered impossible. If there is no difference between past, present, and future, everything is simply a given, a mere function of the present.

When pushed to its limits, this view of the universe, it can be argued, is the same one that Voltaire parodies so savagely in *Candide*. We live, says Dr. Pangloss, Candide's tutor—a thinly veiled parody of Leibniz—in "the best of all possible worlds," a world governed by the all-encompassing Principle of Sufficient Reason, where nothing is without a reason and there is no effect without a cause. Voltaire, who was an admirer of Newton, though not of the so-called Newtonian synthesis, goes out of his way to demonstrate that, contrary to the noble but misguided notions of Pangloss, as well as the dreams of Victor Frankenstein, we do not live in an idealized and transparent universe of stability and order. On the contrary, our world remains the scene of disorder and chaos.[14]

Compounding Victor's quest for deciphering the hidden secrets of the universe was his dedication to alchemy, the forerunner of chemistry—and one of the "unhallowed arts" of MWS's description. Going far beyond the vulgar attempt to convert base metals into gold, alchemy was an entire way of thought based on the attempt to transform matter. Victor tells us that when he was only thirteen he stumbled on a volume by the learned occult writer Cornelius Agrippa. Despite his father's discouragement, Victor became a convert, going on to procure the complete works of Agrippa and then taking up Paracelsus and Albertus Magnus (*F* 1.2: 40–42).[15] Alchemy, of course, is held in very low regard today, but we should remember that it was not always so. Newton himself was dedicated to alchemy and the occult. When his hair was examined after his death, it was found to contain mercury, which was most likely the result of his alchemical pursuits. Mercury poisoning, some think, explains Newton's eccentric behavior at the end of his life.

And so, armed with his obsession with the unveiling of nature's secrets, his devotion to alchemy, and his belief in galvanism and the mysterious powers of electricity, Victor Frankenstein sets off on the course that ends up destroying his life and the lives of those dearest to him. Joined to his thirst for forbidden knowledge and his seduction by the Siren song of certainty is the Promethean desire to create—and he proceeds to create the being that undoes him. What Victor lacks, of course, is Newton's modesty. He says, repeating something that is well known, "Sir Isaac Newton is said to have avowed that he felt like a child picking up shells beside the great and unexplored ocean of truth" (*F* 1.2: 41). I am reminded of my late collaborator and mentor, Ilya Prigogine, the Belgian physicist who was awarded the 1977 Nobel Prize in chemistry. He used to say that the science of physics, for all of its accomplishments and marvelous discoveries, has hardly scratched the surface.[16] Not so with Victor who, under that Siren song, imagines himself assuming the role of the omniscient creator.

But let us back up a bit. All this brings to mind some prophetic words of Aristotle, speaking in this case about ethics, which he defines as a branch of "political science" (*Ethics* 1094b11–27):

> Our account of this science will be adequate if it achieves such clarity as the subject-matter allows; for the same degree of precision is not to be expected in all discussions . . . it is the mark of a trained mind never to expect more precision in the treatment of any subject than the nature of that subject permits; for demanding logical demonstrations from a teacher of rhetoric is clearly about as reasonable as accepting mere plausibility from a mathematician.[17]

Ethics, Aristotle says, involves choices whose consequences extend into an uncertain future—thus it cannot yield certainty.

In 1893, the great French mathematician and physicist Henri Poincaré wrote an essay arguing that the "new science" of thermodynamics reveals a complex universe in which the time-honored laws of mechanics no longer apply universally.[18] We have not, Poincaré concludes, managed to resolve the enormous difficulties involved in reconciling mechanics and thermodynamics, and it is unlikely that we ever will. Thus the science of thermodynamics shows that the laws of mechanics no longer apply universally, suggesting that Aristotle's words about ethics might be extended to the world of natural science.[19] The bottom line here is that certainty is available to us only in limited situations, not in all of them, as Victor and his ilk imagine. Uncertainty, unpredictability, and surprise are qualities built into the very structure of Nature. It is foolish, as Aristotle notes, to pretend otherwise. Nature, we might say, does not even know its own secrets. How, then, could we?[20]

All of this brings us to the matter of Frankenstein's assistant, a character who does not appear in MWS's novel. A servant, who is named Fritz, first appeared in 1823 as a character in *Presumption: or the Fate of Frankenstein*, a stage play by Richard Brinsley Peake. Over a hundred years later, in 1931, Fritz, played by the actor Dwight Frey, appears in James Whale's classic film version of *Frankenstein*, where the Creature is played by Boris Karloff. Thereafter, in *Son of Frankenstein* (1939) and *The Ghost of Frankenstein* (1942), the assistant is played by the great Bela Lugosi, with his name changed to Ygor. And so, played by Marty Feldman in Mel Brooks's 1974 film *Young Frankenstein*, he becomes Igor, the name by which he is perhaps best known today.[21]

The figure of the assistant—whether he be Fritz, Ygor, or Igor—provides a 'rational explanation' for what happens in the story. In the 1931 film, Fritz, who steals a brain for the still lifeless monster from Professor Waldman's classroom, drops and breaks the jar containing a "normal brain" and ends up delivering an "abnormal," criminal brain in its place. The implication is that, if Fritz had delivered a normal brain, the creature would have been 'normal' as well—and Frankenstein's experiment would have worked. MWS's point, however, is that Victor's attempt to play God was by its very nature doomed to failure. My point is that the attempt was doomed because, where life is concerned, the future is supremely and irreducibly unpredictable, something that Victor could not fathom until it was too late.[22]

And so, at last, we come to Lucretius, the Epicurean poet and author of *De rerum natura* (*On the Nature of Things*), who lived in the first century BCE—and whom, MWS tells us, PBS was reading in July 1816, after she had begun work on *Frankenstein*.[23] Michel Serres, the French historian of science, locates the true birth of physics not in the Newtonian synthesis but in the work of Lucretius, underlining the significance of the *clinamen*, the 'swerve' that interrupts the regular motion of atoms at indeterminate times and places, thereby making our universe possible.[24] Here is Lucretius (2.216–224):

> In this connection there is another fact that I want you to grasp.
> *When the atoms are travelling straight down through empty space by their own weight, at quite indeterminate times and places they swerve ever so little from their course,* just so much that you can call it a change of direction. If it were not for this swerve, everything would fall downwards like rain-drops through the abyss of space. No collision would take place and no impact of atom upon atom would be created. Thus nature would never have created anything.[25]

> illud in his quoque te rebus cognoscere avemus
> corpora cum deorsum rectum per inane feruntur
> ponderibus propriis, incerto tempore ferme
> incertisque locis spatio depellere paulum,
> tantum quod momen mutatum dicere possis.   220
> quod nisi declinare solerent, omnia deorsum
> imbris uti guttae caderent per inane profundum
> nec foret offensus natus nec plaga creata
> principiis; ita nihil umquam natura creasset.

Were it not for the swerve, Lucretius says, there would be no collisions: no impact of atom on atom would occur. His conclusion bears repeating: without the swerve, without this fundamental indeterminacy, "nature would never have created anything." Lucretius asks us to understand and respect the truth about our mutable world, which is not the perfect universe imagined by Victor Frankenstein and his alchemical cohorts. Lucretius exhorts us to abandon the quest for certainty, settling instead for the unmistakable virtues of the human and mutable.

Victor, I think we can all agree, would have been better off listening to him. And so would we all. I, along with many others, am intrigued by the fact that so many people consider 'Frankenstein' to be the Creature, or rather the Monster, and not his creator. In the popular imagination, Boris Karloff, who played the Monster in the 1931 film, and his successors have assumed the name of the creator. Who, then, is 'Frankenstein'? I would like to give that question a different twist by asserting that there is a Frankenstein in all of us. We have become overly attached to the notion that the world is stable and therefore predictable. But, as Ilya Prigogine and others have shown, the future is no longer a given, and the classical ideal of omniscience is no longer viable. "At the dawn of the Western world," Prigogine argues, "Aristotle introduced a basic distinction between the divine and immutable world of heaven and the changing and unpredictable sublunar world to which our earth belongs."²⁶ Classical science, Prigogine says, brought Aristotle's description of heaven to earth. But we are now witnessing a reversal of that move: we are now bringing earth to heaven. We have come to the end of certitude—to the beginning of "a period of multiple experimentation, of an increased awareness of both the incertitude and the great possibilities implied by our human condition."²⁷ MWS's novel is but one more warning that we should take this message to heart.

Notes

1 This essay was inspired by a chapter by Jesse Weiner on Lucretius, Lucan, and *Frankenstein* (2015a). I wish to express my gratitude to my Hamilton colleague, one of the editors of this volume and an organizer of the conference that led to its publication. The epigraph, suggested to me by my colleague Peter Rabinowitz, is from Proust (1992–1993: 5.430); I have altered the spelling of "reflexion" to "reflection" and changed "which" to "that."
2 See Gapp (this volume). See also the book-length studies of Wood 2014 and Klingaman and Klingaman 2013.
3 At the time, MWS was still named Mary Godwin, since PBS's first wife, Harriet, was still alive; MWS and PBS were not able to marry until December 30, 1816, twenty days after Harriet committed suicide.
4 Wood (2014: 151); on PBS and MWS, see 151–157; on Byron, 66–69. See also MWS's journal for July and August 1816 in Feldman and Scott-Kilvert (1987: 1.110–132; henceforth *MWS J.*).
5 Shelley in Hindle (2007: 6–7); all citations from *F* are from this edition of the 1831 text. MWS's stepsister—and Byron's lover—Claire Clairmont was also a member of the Shelley group in Switzerland but she appears not to have been party to the agreement.
6 Hindle (2007: 7), emphasis in the original.
7 On Galvani, see Hindle (2007: 267n8). For a full treatment of the debate around 'vitalism' and electricity, see Holmes (2008: 305–336); I am grateful to my colleague Benjamin Haller for calling my attention to this book.
8 Both preceding quotations from MWS are Hindle (2007: 9).
9 For a list of films, see Wolfe (2004: 338–345), taking us up to 1994; there have been additions since then, culminating with Paul McGuigan's *Victor Frankenstein* and Bernard Rose's *Frankenstein*, both released in 2015. See further Cooper (this volume).
10 See Prigogine and Stengers (1984: 27–40); cf. Rubino 1994a.
11 Hausheer (1980: xxvi).
12 See Koyré 1957.
13 Einstein (1972: 539); translation from Bernstein (1991: 165).
14 See Rubino 1994b.
15 See also Hindle (2007: 268nn6–7).
16 A far cry from the notions advanced in such books as Lederman 1993 and Weinberg 1992.
17 Trans. J. A. K. Thomson 1976, revised by Hugh Tredennick.
18 Poincaré 1893; translated (with the assistance of Laurence Lemaire) as "Mechanism and Experiment" in Juarrero and Rubino (2008: 57–59).
19 See Juarrero and Rubino (2008: 7–8).

20 Ibid., 1–19.
21 In McGuigan's 2015 film *Victor Frankenstein*, for example, the story is told from Igor's point of view.
22 See Rubino (2007: 244–245).
23 See *MWS J.*: on 121 she notes that PBS was reading Lucretius on July 28, finishing the book on July 29; while 188 confirms that MWS was writing her "story" on July 24. The editors note that, "Shelley [i.e., PBS] had bought Good's 1805 translation of Lucretius on April 18, 1815." See the journal entry, written in his own hand, for April 18 of that year (75).
24 Serres 1977. Lucretius achieved a certain measure of notoriety with the publication of Greenblatt 2011, which won both a Pulitzer Prize and the National Book Award; for recent classical scholarship, see Holmes and Shearin 2012, Gale 2007, Gillespie and Hardie 2007, Kennedy 2002, Johnson 2000.
25 Translation by E. R. Latham; emphasis is that of the translator. I have altered the spelling of "connexion" to "connection."
26 Prigogine (1980: 7).
27 Ibid.; cf. Prigogine 1997.

9

Timothy Leary and the Psychodynamics of Stealing Fire

Neşe Devenot

On January 21, 1970, psychedelic activist Timothy Leary received a ten-year prison sentence for the possession of a minuscule amount of marijuana. Richard Nixon had allegedly described Leary as "the most dangerous man in America" around this time, and the draconian sentence was widely seen as reflecting Leary's status as a political prisoner.[1] Supporters immediately organized fundraisers on his behalf, including a series of performances of Aeschylus's *Prometheus Bound* with the lead actor playing Leary in the place of the Titan Prometheus. Even Leary identified himself as a Promethean figure, characterizing the prison sentence as a punishment for attempting to spread psychedelic 'technologies' to the masses in order to free them from psychological subservience to established powers of Church and State. Scholars have acknowledged Leary's historical importance for the cultural revolutions of the 1960s; however, little scholarship has considered the literary significance of his extensive creative writing, much less his prominent use of the figure of Prometheus.[2] This chapter focuses on Leary's experimental autobiography *High Priest* (1968), where Leary portrays his life story in mythological terms—including self-identifying as that Titan—as a rhetorical strategy to intervene in contemporary culture wars.

As institutional and cultural forces sought to reinforce the status quo and turned against his psychedelic research program in the early 1960s, Leary drew on Greek myth to dramatize and communicate the stakes of this ideological impasse. *High Priest* represents Leary's research in positive terms by reframing it via a narrative revisioning of mythic archetypes. In particular, Leary fashioned himself as a modern-day Prometheus, seeking to establish moral superiority over his adversaries within psychiatry and the government, who—in his view— sought to consolidate their power at the expense of open inquiry and experimentation. Leary thus presents himself as a Titanic figure battling against these Olympian forces of hegemony and inertia, disseminating a mind-altering technology to humanity for the democratic purpose of restoring individual agency and self-determination.

To emphasize his positive spin on the Prometheus myth, Leary distances his modernization from the negative portrayal in Mary Shelley's (henceforth MWS) *Frankenstein* (1818). More than a simple foil, *Frankenstein* serves as the locus of influential popular myths, for which *High Priest* represents an explicit corrective. *Frankenstein* was—and is—popularly understood as a sort of "shorthand … illustrat[ing] the dangers of 'playing God,' the moral sin of humankind daring to reach beyond our natural limitations"; the story serves as "a cautionary tale warning that science divorced from ethics will produce monsters," resulting in unforeseen outcomes replete with tragedy and remorse.[3] Leary believed that such readings of *Frankenstein*'s rehearsal of the Prometheus myth reflected and reinforced cultural tendencies to ignorance and inaction, affirming prejudices against radical change and transformation. In this sense, Leary conceptualized the cultural circulation of myths in terms analogous to Richard Dawkins's notion of viral 'memes'—collections of cultural ideas that influence individuals' experiences of reality.[4] To Leary, *Frankenstein* and derivative stories thus function as a meme, propagating resistance to novelty and hence impeding his psychedelic research. In *Change Your Brain*, Leary blamed the 'Frankenstein myth' for reinforcing a resistance to novel experimentation within the wider culture:

> [T]he ultimate in superstitious, Ayatollah-type future-fear is the Frankenstein myth—a scientist of the primitive 19th century who created life! And now the name of Frankenstein, to the easily-spooked natives of America, is synonymous with "monster." The historic origin of this hatred of the creative, this phobic taboo against change is, of course, the Prometheus myth. She who has the confidence and heroic daring to seize the future for humanity is punished by paranoid, jealous, frightened Gods.[5]

As he would describe later, Leary saw himself as engineering new "communicable memes" capable of replacing outmoded cultural assumptions.[6] I argue that *High Priest* represents Leary's attempt to 'reprogram' the Frankenstein mythos—in other words, hacking its meme—by modeling his own experimentation with psychedelics on Victor's creation of the Creature. Leary ultimately rejects the fearful reaction that Victor displays toward his experimental subject, implying that Victor's downfall is due to an excess of conservatism—the projection of past associations and fears onto the present moment—which prevents him from relating responsibly to his Creature. Rather than emphasizing novelty as the source of Victor's problems, this reinterpretation implies that Victor's reaction to novelty was always distorted by his attachments to past conditionings.

By using the medium of literature to model an ethical approach to the dissemination of experimental technology, Leary hoped his take on the Prometheus myth would contribute to a culture more hospitable to his vision of a future science.

Literary Activism, or Hacking the Promethean Myth

High Priest represents Leary's self-mythologization along the lines of a classic 'hero's journey.' Joseph Campbell describes the general contours of this "monomyth" in *The Hero with a Thousand Faces* (1949): "A hero ventures forth from the world of common day into a region of supernatural wonder (x): fabulous forces are there encountered and a decisive victory is won (y): the hero comes back from this mysterious adventure with the power to bestow boons on his fellow man (z)."[7] Leary championed the pragmatic function of myths to serve as navigational tools in the process of individuation. In place of the expectations and narrative 'games' traditionally imposed on individuals by established authorities, Leary advocated adopting various cultural mythologies to help direct autonomous self-development. As he advised in *Start Your Own Religion*: "You will do well to have an explicit connection to a mythic figure.... You select a myth to guide you when you drop out of the narrow confines of the fake-prop studio set."[8] Leary's self-identification with Prometheus served to dramatize both the importance of his psychedelic experimentation and resistance to his work on the part of conservative authorities.

Leary identified with Prometheus throughout his lifetime, advocating a shifting constellation of new technologies with the aim of promoting self-determination and freedom of thought. Leary describes his take on different versions of the myth in *Chaos & Cyber Culture*:

> Every stage of history has produced names and heroic legends for the strong, stubborn, creative individuals who explore some future frontier, collect and bring back new information, and offer to guide the human gene pool to the next stage.... The classical Olde Westworld model for the cyberpunk is Prometheus, a technological genius who "stole" fire from the Gods and gave it to humanity. Prometheus also taught his gene pool many useful arts and sciences. According to the official version of the legend, he/she was exiled from the gene pool and sentenced to the ultimate torture for these unauthorized transmissions of classified information. In another version of the myth (unauthorized), Prometheus (*aka* the Pied Piper) uses his/her skills to escape the sinking kinship, taking with him/her the cream of the gene pool.[9]

In his anachronistic reading of the Prometheus myth, Leary replaces Zeus and the other Greek gods with the political and cultural establishment of his time. As Leary's interests evolved from psychedelics to personal computers, a recurrent theme remained the effort to democratize technologies once monopolized by a privileged elite bent on maintaining control. As he explained in an interview:

> [A] few of us saw what was happening and we wrestled the power of LSD away from the CIA, and now the power of computers away from IBM, just as we rescued psychology away from the doctors and analysts. In every generation I've been part of a group of people who, like Prometheus, have wrestled with the power in order to hand it back to the individual.[10]

Leary thus cast himself as a heroic underdog, removing humanity's fetters by sharing forbidden knowledge as Prometheus did, and as similarly persecuted by established powers for daring to shake up the status quo.

Leary's identification with Prometheus was already apparent in his handling of public relations in the aftermath of his dismissal from Harvard in 1963. Leary used elements from the myth of Prometheus to frame himself as a persecuted hero in a bid to popularize his controversial views. While it is popularly thought that Leary and his associates were fired from Harvard University due to the controversial nature of their psychedelic research, the reality is more complicated.[11] Officially, Richard Alpert was dismissed for providing LSD to undergraduate students against university policy, Leary for neglecting his academic duties after failing to attend an honors committee meeting. Leary was quick to mobilize this change in fortune for his own rhetorical purposes, co-authoring with Alpert a declaration for the *Harvard Review* in which they characterized the university as an "intellectual ministry of defense" operating as "the Establishment's apparatus for training consciousness contractors."[12] As the first Harvard faculty members to be fired during the twentieth century, the collaborators took advantage of widespread national media coverage to promote their interpretation of events, including Leary's own Promethean narrative.

Leary characterized Harvard's censure as a predictable backlash against his Promethean efforts to destabilize the political order: his efforts, in other words, to provide a technology—psychedelics—he believed capable of freeing popular consciousness from its benighted state. In his preface to *High Priest*, Beat poet Allen Ginsberg echoes this view of Leary as a "hero of American consciousness" whose advocacy of psychedelics represented a threat to "our whole 'establishment' of civilization that defends us from knowledge of our own unconscious by means of policemen's clubs, and would resist the liberation of our minds and bodies by any brutish means available."[13] From this perspective, Leary aligns with the heroic archetype he associated with Aeschylus's *Prometheus Bound*, in which an omnipotent Zeus is driven by "lascivious self-interest" and the pursuit of power at the expense of humankind.[14] Leary identified with the compassion of Aeschylus's Prometheus, who bestows fire—technology, knowledge, and tools—upon humanity "out of pity for their ignorance and helplessness."[15]

Like Prometheus, whose gift of foresight provided knowledge of the consequences of his decision to help humanity, Leary and Alpert viewed themselves—from a projected future vantage point—as operating on the 'right side' of history. Describing his dismissal from Harvard to a reporter, Alpert stated confidently: "Some day it will be quite humorous ... that a professor was fired for supplying a student with 'the most profound educational experience in [his] life.' That's what [the student] told the Dean it was."[16] Leary evinces a similar certainty in *Flashbacks*: "We saw ourselves as anthropologists from the twenty-first century inhabiting a time module set somewhere in the Dark Ages of the 1960s."[17] With psychedelics 'out of the bag' and available to the public, they believed that it was only a matter of time before popular consciousness caught up with their minority perspective.

Timothy Leary; or, the Modern Victor Frankenstein

Like Victor Frankenstein at the precipice of his creation, Leary felt sure of his unique significance within the history of science. As Michael Horowitz explains, Leary "felt certain his work ... was of a momentous time in history that was going to change everything": the discovery of LSD seemed to be one of the most important events of the twentieth century, alongside "the fissioning of the atom and the discovery of DNA."[18] Based on his first experience with psilocybin in 1960, Leary was convinced that psychedelics represented a paradigm shift for the fields of psychology and psychiatry. He insisted that he had "learned more about ... [his] brain and its possibilities ... [and] more about psychology in the five hours after taking these mushrooms than ... [he] had in the preceding fifteen years of studying [and] doing research in psychology."[19] This conviction parallels Victor's discovery of the principle of life, which he immediately views as a scientific revolution set to transform long-held assumptions about biology.[20]

Indeed, throughout *High Priest*, Leary establishes himself as a Victor-like mad scientist; but unlike Victor, Leary works past his initial fears toward his experimental subject, changing the story's outcome. There are several indications that Leary had the story of *Frankenstein* in mind as he established the Harvard Psilocybin Project. Robert Greenfield discusses correspondence in which Leary characterized Concord Prison's physical appearance as looking like "Frankenstein made it."[21] Leary himself would later describe his *Psychedelic Prayers* as an attempt to experiment with human consciousness, with implications as far-reaching as Victor's attempts to create life:

> *Psychedelic Prayers* ... [was] the first book ever specifically designed to reimprint human brains during the "critical periods" of neural vulnerability.... The insidious aim of this Dr. Frankenstein gambit was to prepare young people taking large doses of LSD to absorb a new reality-view.... *Psychedelic Prayers* has been reprinted over 20 times and has probably bent over 200,000 young brains.[22]

Leary characterized himself as 'creating life,' but in a more figurative sense than Victor. According to Leary's working theory, psychedelics impacted the mind by loosening habitual patterns of thought and behavior. Leary adapted the language of 'imprinting' from Konrad Lorenz, who had used the term to describe how newly hatched goslings develop by mimicking the first moving object they encounter in their environment. In Leary's view, humans develop similarly, organizing their mental lives according to abstract concepts derived from early life experiences.

These abstractions form a static mental picture of the world that constricts perception, limiting one's attention based on predictions and priorities from the past. Leary describes this as a 'dead' symbolic system, since it occludes any nuanced comprehension of the real, living universe outside the narrow lens of conceptual expectations:

> Man's mind imposes upon the variegated flow of energy one static model—years out of date, kept current only by the slow process of conditioning and association.... What happens outside or inside, we perceive in terms of our mental imprinting system. We live in a dead world—cut off from the flow of life and energy.[23]

Although the respite from such habits provided by psychedelics was temporary, Leary believed they offer a window of opportunity in which new patterns of thought and behavior could be introduced. He thought of this process according to the metaphor of 'ego death'—the dissolution of existing personality structures—and a subsequent 'rebirth' or creation of new life: "During the psychedelic session the nervous system returns to that state of flux and unity-chaos of infancy.... As the session ends, one is reborn.... In scientific papers we described this as the process of re-imprinting. A rewiring of the nervous system."[24] In other words, what is achieved is a surrender from attachment to one's expectations: when cognition is no longer constrained by preconceptions, ideas once inconceivable may be contemplated. Although the end result is positive, the moniker 'ego *death*' alludes to the fact that the process is emotionally fraught—sometimes to the point of existential terror.

Leary's account of ego death offers an explanation for Victor's first reaction to his Creature. While Victor's aspirations to create life are ultimately successful, he describes the accomplishment of his single-minded toils as a "catastrophe," which appears paradoxical (F 1.4: 83). Victor insists that his revulsion is the natural result of a discrepancy between his expectations and reality, noting that "the beauty of the dream vanished, and breathless horror and disgust filled my heart" (84). Rather than providing indications of veridicality, however, Victor's assertions remain colored by his own emotional projections: instead of a natural and inevitable reaction to circumstances, Victor's panic represents a failure to release emotional attachments to his ideas about himself and his place within society.

Thus, although Victor succeeded in 'creating life' in a literal sense, his reaction reflects an aborted opportunity to undergo ego death as described by Leary—a failure to be 'reborn.' Essentially, Victor was traumatized by a 'bad trip' due to his unwillingness to confront repressed aspects of his self-image. This reading is supported by other scholarship on this scene. For instance, Denise Gigante attributes Victor's reaction to the Creature's fleshly corporeality, which challenges his own carefully curated sense of societal significance. Gigante argues that Victor's self-image depends upon the repression of aspects of reality that conflict with that socially constructed identity—aspects which the Creature embodies:

> Victor's description takes the form of what might be called an "anti-blazon," whereby individual features, such as the Creature's hair "of a lustrous black, and flowing" and "his teeth of a pearly whiteness," are sutured together with other unsightly features (his "work of muscles and arteries," his "straight black lips") that radically disrupt aesthetic representation. As cracks and fissures emerge in the representation, the visceral reality of the Creature leaks through to destroy all fantasy.[25]

The specific nature of Victor's 'fantasies' is multiform, relating to an inflated sense of his importance and to unrealistic accounts of his family relationships. Indeed, he is a "famously unreliable narrator," whose descriptions of relationships are suspiciously insistent on near-paradisiacal perfection.[26] Thus Victor characterizes his childhood as a period of unprecedented, superlative domestic bliss: "No creature could have more tender parents than mine.... No youth could have passed more happily than mine" (1.1: 65–67). This idyllic portrait is difficult to reconcile with Victor's own statements later, while at university, including a new admission of restlessness at home: "I had often ... thought it hard to remain during my youth cooped up in one place, and had longed to enter the world, and take my station among other human beings" (1.2: 74).

Such discrepancies point to Victor's inflated sense of importance, including a desire for adoring, everlasting fame. The implicit prospect of becoming immortalized as a great man of science helps account for Victor's total absorption in his work.[27] The same desire extends to his fantasies about creating life, as he imagines being worshipped by his creation: "A new species would bless me as its creator and source; many happy and excellent natures would owe their being to me. No father could claim the gratitude of his child so completely as I should deserve theirs" (1.3: 80–81). Victor's imagined future as 'parent' to a new form of life is profoundly colored by the unrealistic fantasy of domestic bliss associated with his own childhood.

Victor's example provides insight into the emotional upheavals associated with ego death, during which one must not only give up personal fantasies, but also confront how they have been used to justify selfish and harmful behaviors. Victor's narcissistic self-absorption serves to justify an indefensible neglect of family: although his father had urged him to remain in communication with his family back in Geneva, Victor remained out of contact for years. This avoidance is the more troubling considering that Victor's mother—the family matriarch—had recently died, and that Victor's fiancée Elizabeth was last seen in misery over his departure. Victor explains this silence as a side effect of his obsession with work (1.3: 82):

> I could not tear my thoughts from my employment ... which had taken an irresistible hold of my imagination. I wished, as it were, to procrastinate all that related to my feelings of affection until the great object, which swallowed up every habit of my nature, should be completed.

This rare moment of self-awareness, explicitly acknowledging Victor's repression of his emotional life, remains superficial insofar as he refuses to confront the origins of those emotions in relation to his personal fantasies.

The fact that Victor's emotional life remains unconscious is expressed in the compulsive nature of his work. His scientific pursuits were immoderate even by his own account, becoming "nearly [his] sole occupation" (1.3: 77). To underscore the point, Victor repeats variations of this claim several times in the first paragraphs of chapter 3.[28] The obsessive quality of his work is fueled by "an almost supernatural enthusiasm," such that tedious tasks and sustained sleep deprivation were embraced enthusiastically (1.3: 78). Victor downplays his agency in creating the Creature by describing the work in terms of compulsion or even addiction: he was *unable* to focus on anything else. This inability to acknowledge personal responsibility accords with Victor's reliance on 'fate' to describe his tragic downfall. In his view, Victor is never fully accountable for his life circumstances, with free will and personal agency subordinate to fate or destiny. Even though he is presented with opportunities to make alternate decisions, Victor describes the progression of events as a foregone conclusion, presenting himself in the role of victim.[29]

High Priest calls Victor's fatalistic presentation of his tragic downfall into question by dramatizing Carl Jung's notion of fate: "Until you make the unconscious conscious, it will direct your life and you will call it fate."[30] In other words, what remains unconscious plays out as a 'fate' that only *appears* to be inevitable. *High Priest* presents an 'alternate ending' to MWS's story by introducing the element of choice into the mad scientist's confrontation with his creation. While Leary initially mirrors Victor's reaction of mortal terror, their paths diverge as Leary recognizes the perceived 'threat' as merely an externalization of his own conditioned biases. Leary thus implies that *Frankenstein* is indeed a cautionary tale—but rather than warning about the dangers of departing from the past, it warns about the dangers of being controlled by it.

Unmasking the Monster: Magic Mushrooms and the Neuropolitics of Empathy

Leary discovers the possibility of an alternative ending to *Frankenstein* through his first steps along Campbell's 'hero's journey.' Leary arrives at this insight by listening to his emotions rather than repressing them. Like Victor, Leary initially buys into abstract cultural definitions of professional success, but he differs in altering habitual behaviors that contribute to his malcontent. By his own account, Leary was conventionally successful but emotionally unfulfilled during the years before he began work at Harvard. Even before discovering psychedelic mushrooms, Leary was already beginning to question inherited 'truths' about his profession and society at large:

> I ... awoke to the consciousness that I was trapped in a dark room, in a hastily constructed, thin-walled stage-prop home in Berkeley.... I was a rootless city-dweller. An anonymous institutional employee who drove to work each morning in a long line of commuter cars, and drove home each night and drank martinis and looked like and thought like and acted like several million middle-class liberal intellectual robots.[31]

In the manner of mid-life crisis, Leary intuited that he had been living on autopilot, humming along on the motor of culturally sanctioned expectations. Faced with this inauthenticity, he decided to quit his plush job as Director of Psychological Research for the Kaiser Foundation Hospital and travel abroad, giving up privileges including his "staff of statisticians and clerks and rooms of calculators and computers" in order to write and crunch data on his own.[32]

Leary's disaffection was only beginning, as his research forced him to question the very institutions and academic disciplines to which he had devoted his life:

> Each laborious calculation was proving that psychology was just a mind-game, an eccentric head trip on the part of psychologists, and that psychotherapy was an arduous, expensive, ineffective, unimaginative attempt to impose the mind of the doctor on the mind of the patient.[33]

Leary concluded that modern psychology was premised on unexamined assumptions and limiting metaphors about the human mind, which emphasized prediction and control over collaboration and improvisation.[34] Rather than focusing on detached observation of external behaviors, Leary began advocating for a new emphasis on the patient's subjective experiences, with the therapist in a collaborative—rather than authoritative—role.[35] More than a slight shift in emphasis, Leary's suggestions aimed to counteract the narcotizing effects of projecting past assumptions onto the present moment, a projection he identified as the root cause of both his dissatisfaction with society and the inefficiencies of his profession.

As he began researching psilocybin at Harvard, these cumulative insights provided Leary with the tools to navigate his own ego death experience, revealing a possibility that Victor had overlooked in his traumatic encounter with his creation. In psilocybin, Leary believed he had discovered a technology that reproducibly exposes conditioned habits of mind—that is, a means of transmuting obsolete cognitive attachments underlying individual and societal suffering. Rather than seeking—as Victor did—personal self-aggrandizement, Leary undertook Promethean efforts in popularizing psychedelics so as to free humanity from its benighted cultural hypnosis.

Recognizing that this project undermined the power claims of institutional authorities, Leary approached his Harvard research strategically. Although personal testimonies about changed perspectives and deep insights from psychedelics abounded, such introspective narratives were unlikely to sway the quantitative behaviorists at the discipline's center. As an alternative to this 'imprecision,' Leary reasoned that a measurable variable for quantifying the impact of behavioral changes could be found in recidivism among freed prisoners:

> Prisoner rehabilitation offers the most objective check for someone who claims he can bring about change in behavior.... Seven out of every ten men who leave prison, return. If you develop a new and surefire way of changing man's mind, the prison presents the toughest and cleanest test of your effectiveness. Can you keep him out of jail?[36]

Leary began his research at Concord Prison in 1961. Insisting on a non-hierarchical relationship between the prisoners and the researchers, Leary insisted on educating the prisoners about the effects of psilocybin so that—as autonomous subjects—they could give informed consent. As a further departure from conventional psychiatry, Leary determined that researchers would take psilocybin *alongside* the prisoners during the dosing sessions. He surmised that the shared experience would reaffirm their mutual equality, instead of reasserting the conventional power imbalance associated with the doctor–patient relationship.

The first dosing session took place on March 27, 1961. On par with Victor bringing his creation to life, this was when Leary's psychedelic research ambitions were actualized. Ever since taking psilocybin mushrooms in Mexico the previous year, Leary had been gripped by a single-minded obsession with achieving this unprecedented and revolutionary work. As in Victor's case, the precise moment of the project's fruition is greeted with animus rather than the expected feeling of triumphant success. Leary's discomfort likewise marks the beginning stages of an 'ego death' confrontation with attachments to preconceptions. Leary specifically describes the first effects of psilocybin as a "loosening of symbolic reality," noting: "I could feel the effect coming up ... the feeling of humming pressure and space voyage inside my head, the sharp, brutal intensification of all the senses."[37] Although his previous psilocybin experiences had begun positively and often mirthfully, his reaction on that date was decidedly negative: "I felt terrible. What a place to be on a gray morning! In a dingy room in a grim penitentiary, out of my mind."[38]

In this state of disaffection and heightened sensitivity, Leary's gaze falls upon a prisoner named John, whose visceral physicality comes to dominate Leary's attention in language that recalls Victor's description upon first beholding his awakened Creature:

> I could see him so clearly. I could see every pore in his face, every blemish, the hairs in his nose, the incredible green-yellow enamel of the decay in his teeth, the wet glistening of his frightened eyes. I could see every hair in his head, as though each was as big as an oak tree. What a confrontation! What am I doing here, out of my mind, with this strange mosaic-celled animal, prisoner, criminal?[39]

Leary portrays John with—to use Gigante's term—an 'anti-blazon' similar to the one provided by Victor, focusing on isolated, 'unsightly' features rather than a synthetic gestalt of his total form and subjecthood. The fractured nature of Leary's perceptions is reinforced by the word "mosaic," which implies a collection of individual, isolated features. At root, Leary's gaze is one of objectification, at odds with his intellectual commitment to respecting and upholding the subjectivity of study participants.

Gigante's discussion of Victor helps us comprehend the significance of the physiological features singled out in Leary's account. Highlighting differences between Victor's descriptions of the Creature's eyes and Elizabeth's eyes, Gigante notes: "Unlike the 'dull yellow' or 'dead grey' eye, the beautiful eye diverts attention from the [horrific] substance of the eye itself."[40] Whereas Victor focuses on the physical components of the Creature's body, his descriptions of Elizabeth in the 1831 edition seek to transcend (or repress) the physical: "Her brow was clear ... her blue eyes cloudless ... none could behold her without looking on her as of a distinct species, a being heaven-sent, and bearing a celestial stamp in all her features."[41] As Gigante explains:

> While a smooth skin provides an imaginary screen for the subject to project his or her fantasy of the transcendent human being inside the object of perception, the "shrivelled complexion" of Frankenstein's Creature radically disrupts any effort to elevate him above the "filthy mass" ... of his flesh.[42]

Victor's perceptions of Elizabeth's beauty allow him to "etherealize" her as a subject that is "unencumbered" by the messiness of bodily functions. By contrast, his microscopic focus on the Creature's textured body parts objectifies the Creature and prevents Victor from relating to him as an independent subject.

Leary's initial description of John places a similar emphasis on the messy materiality of the prisoner's body. Instead of projecting a dynamic personality on a screen of smooth skin, Leary fixates on John's textured pores, hairs, and blemishes, and emphasizes the physical substance of the eye in describing it as "wet" and "glistening." Further descriptions maintain this focus on unsightly physicality:

> John drew back his purple-pink lips, showed his green-yellow teeth in a sickly grin. ... I looked with my two microscopic retina lenses into his eyes. I could see every line, yellow spider webs, red networks of veins gleaming out at me. ... I could look into his mouth, swollen red tissues, gums, tongue, throat. I was prepared to be swallowed.[43]

Leary uses 'grin' here to describe an abhorrent display of John's fleshly composition, which is emphasized most explicitly in his "swollen red tissues."

John's lips—which would usually present some variety of red coloring on a healthy Caucasian male—are described as a sickly "purple-pink," hinting at disease or even death and recalling the "straight black lips" of Victor's Creature. Leary's attention also returns to the physical substance of the eye, with its intricate "networks of veins" mirroring the chaotic structure of the Creature's "work of muscles and arteries" (F 1.4: 83)—a confusing jumble that resists simple conceptualization.

These passages in *High Priest* and *Frankenstein* are also linked by each narrator's explicit assumption of a mortal threat. Victor beholds his creation upon waking from a disturbing nightmare and he watches in horror as the Creature moves toward him and lifts the curtains of his bed. Victor's emotional response is unambiguously steeped in terror, as indicated by his comment that "He might have spoken, but I did not hear" (1.4: 84): his feelings of fear and revulsion have warped his experience of the encounter, and thus his recollection of it. This point is important when evaluating Victor's claim that "one hand was stretched out, seemingly to detain me" (ibid.): rather than representing an accurate description of the Creature's malicious intent, this seems more likely to be a fear-based projection resulting from Victor's panic. From the Creature's own account of this period described later, the Creature possessed the cognitive capacities of a newborn, without the ability for conscious 'intent': "A strange multiplicity of sensations seized me, and I saw, felt, heard, and smelt, at the same time; and it was, indeed, a long time before I learned to distinguish between the operations of my various senses" (2.3: 120–121). This infantile orientation recasts the encounter as one of innocent exploration, as supported by Victor's own recollection that the Creature "muttered some inarticulate sounds, while a grin wrinkled his cheeks," much as a newborn might act (1.4: 84).

Leary's "confrontation" with John is colored by a comparable feeling of irrational panic. The "networks of veins" are imbued with an inhuman, monstrous agency, "gleam[ing] *out at me*," implying a threat directed toward Leary in particular. That implicit threat becomes more explicit in Leary's description of John's throat. Just as Victor fears that the creature seeks to detain him, Leary projects that John's fleshly innards are set to *swallow* and contain him. He feels himself to be at the mercy of a diabolical force that is eager to overpower him, which threatens his sense of identity and his socially mediated subject position.

It is as this point, however, that Leary is able to reject *Frankenstein*'s legacy of "suspicious ... future-fear" by resuscitating the Prometheus myth. Leary begins by openly expressing his feelings to John, admitting that "I feel lousy.... I'm afraid of you."[44] Their subsequent conversation reveals that this fear is mutual:

> Then I heard him say, Well that's funny, Doc, 'cause I'm afraid of you.... Doc, he said, why are you afraid of me? I said, I'm afraid of you, John, because you're a criminal. He nodded. I said, John, why are you afraid of me? He said, I'm afraid of you, Doc, because you're a mad scientist.[45]

Through this shared experience of fear, Leary becomes aware that he had been projecting assumptions about John based on the reductive, abstract concept of "criminal." He recognizes, in other words, that his fear arose from his own psychological preconceptions rather than being genuinely warranted by the circumstances.

As with Victor in *Frankenstein*, this fear in turn warped and filtered Leary's perception of sensory details from the surrounding environment, such that his description of John's body seemed to corroborate the notion of an external threat where no threat actually existed. As Leary's collaborator Aldous Huxley would describe the effects of paranoia in *The Doors of Perception*, "If you started in the wrong way ... everything that happened would be a proof of the conspiracy against you. It would all be self-validating.... If one began with fear and hate as the major premise, one would have to go on to the conclusion."[46] Although Leary had sutured together details that seemed to confirm a sinister intent, he comes to recognize his role in manufacturing this chain of circumstances rather than seeing his response as 'natural' or 'fated.'

Ultimately, then, instead of following Victor's lead and succumbing to the impulse to flee from his responsibilities, Leary is able to form an empathetic connection with John based on their mutual fear-based projections:

> Then our retinas locked and I slid down into the tunnel of his eyes, and I could feel him walking around in my skull and we both began to laugh. And there it was, that dark moment of fear and distrust, which could have changed in a second to become hatred and terror. But we made the love connection. The flicker in the dark. Suddenly, the sun came out in the room and I felt great and I knew he did too.[47]

Leary recognizes that he could have gone the way of Victor and rejected the fruits of his experiment, but that such a reaction was only one option among many. It certainly was not a foregone conclusion or a matter of 'fate,' as Victor invokes so frequently. By becoming aware of his conditioned reflexes, Leary demonstrates in practice what his theories promote in principle: suffering provides information about the psyche and often indicates the presence of unconscious attachments and expectations. From this perspective, psychedelics are precision tools for eradicating malignant preconceptions such as those that ultimately destroyed Victor.

Reanimating Leary's Legacy

In adapting the Prometheus myth for consciousness-altering technologies, Leary established a precedent that would outlive the controversies surrounding his research at Harvard. In 2017, Steven Kotler and Jamie Wheal published *Stealing Fire*, which relies on a Promethean trope to describe how industry leaders in Silicon Valley and beyond are harnessing altered states of mind to enhance performance and creativity. Although this book supports Leary's claims about the potential of psychedelics, it ultimately avoids the political urgency of Leary's original message. While Kotler and Wheal celebrate the benefits of ecstatic experiences within the limited context of capitalism and entrepreneurship, cultural taboos continue to constrain the democratic adoption of these tools in ways that could challenge or undermine established society.

Like a meme hack that alters an existing packet of cultural information in order to express an opposite viewpoint, *High Priest* recodes the virulent 'Frankenstein mythos' in order to reverse the polarity of its warning—in other words, hacking the pathogen to deliver the antigen. To Leary, the Frankenstein myth encoded and propagated cultural fears against departing from convention, representing the nucleus of popular resistance to his psychedelic research at Harvard. While the horrors of *Frankenstein* are commonly attributed to the sin of reaching beyond convention, Leary's literary 'remix' of Mary Shelley's text inverts this message, linking Victor's self-destruction to his conditioned inability to move beyond convention—like a moth drawn to fire. Where the original myth impeded Leary's research by framing psychedelics—like other revolutionary technology—as a threat to established society, Leary's revised myth recasts psychedelics as the *solution* to the actual problem. Just as Percy Shelley described poetry's power to emancipate perception from dead abstractions, Leary suggests that psychedelics reveal the extent to which our behaviors are controlled by abstract patterns, unconscious projections, and manipulative propaganda.[48] By applying this principle to reading *Frankenstein* without its abstract cultural 'mythos,' Leary's explicit conclusion articulates the implicit message of Shelley's original. Since Mary Shelley left so many textual clues that Victor orchestrated his own downfall, the 'Frankenstein mythos' is itself a cultural abstraction that distracts unscrupulous readers from connecting those clues. By contrast, *High Priest* emphasizes those connections, suggesting *Frankenstein* could have ended differently had Victor only taken magic mushrooms.

Notes

1. Siff (2015: 115).
2. To my knowledge, this chapter is the first published scholarship on Leary in relation to Prometheus and *Frankenstein* (henceforth *F*). Leary's descriptions of psychedelic experiences were heavily informed by his close friendship with Beat poet Allen Ginsberg: as Conners observes (2010: 50), "Ginsberg's hip poetic slang gave Leary a language—aside from the rigid, confining language of his profession—in which he could discuss his psychedelic experiences."
3. Chan (2009: 398) and Caldwell (2004: 29).
4. Dawkins 1976.
5. Leary (2000: 27–28).
6. Leary (1994: 71).
7. Campbell (2008: 23).
8. Leary (1967: 10).
9. Leary (1994: 62–63).
10. Ibid., vii.
11. Michael A. Martin, for instance, writes that "Harvard fired Leary and his colleagues in 1963 because of ethical concerns over these controversial experiments" (2015: 429).
12. Lee and Shlain (1992: 88).
13. Leary (1995: xviii and xx).
14. Farley (1990: 28)
15. Ibid.
16. Lee and Shlain (1992: 88).
17. Leary (1990: 190).
18. Rein and Horowitz (2015). Owing to a sense of his work's revolutionary nature, Leary preserved all of his papers and correspondence, the majority of which has since been acquired by the New York Public Library. The same sense of importance also informed his multiple autobiographies, including *High Priest* (1968) and *Flashbacks* (1983).
19. Roberts (2012: 77).
20. Although generations of learned men had sought to uncover the principle of life, Victor notes that he alone had succeeded at this discovery: "while I became dizzy with the immensity of the prospect which [the discovery] illustrated, I was surprised that among so many men of genius, who had directed their inquiries towards the same science, that I alone should be reserved to discover so astonishing a secret" (*F* 1.3: 78–79). All references to *F* are to the 1818 text in Macdonald and Scherf 2012.
21. Greenfield (2006: 145).
22. Leary (2001: 71).
23. Leary (2014: 277).
24. Leary (1995: 192).
25. Gigante (2000: 570).
26. Carlson (2007: 101).
27. In his introductory lecture, Waldman describes the history of natural philosophy by romanticizing the contributions of individual men of genius. Victor is enchanted as his professor "pronounces with fervour the names of the most distinguished discoverers," which contributes to Victor's desire to be canonized similarly (1.2: 75).
28. "That application ... became so ardent and eager, that the stars often disappeared in the light of morning whilst I was yet engaged in my laboratory. ... I ... was engaged, heart and soul, in

the pursuit of some discoveries, which I hoped to make.... I ... continually sought the attainment of one object of pursuit, and was solely wrapt up in this" (1.3: 77–78).
29 For instance, when describing Waldman's encouragement to study the various branches of natural philosophy, Victor insists that "it decided my future destiny" (1.2: 77).
30 Although this is the most frequently cited 'meme version' of Jung's idea, the official translation from his *Collected Works* reads thus: "The psychological rule says that when an inner situation is not made conscious, it happens outside, as fate" (1979: 71).
31 Leary (1995: 3–4).
32 Ibid., 4.
33 Ibid., 6.
34 In 1970, Leary summarized the repressive preoccupations of mainstream psychology thus (2014: 42): "The outmoded philosophies to which I refer are the impersonal, abstract, static, externalized, control-oriented conceptions of nineteenth-century physics which led men to classify the elements and processes of a depersonalized subject matter and to determine the general laws which governed these elements and processes."
35 According to *Flashbacks*, the manuscript that Leary began writing at this time served as a significant factor in his subsequent job offer from Harvard. From Leary's recollections, David McClelland—the Director of the Harvard Center for Research in Personality—remarked (1990: 18): "There is no question that what you're advocating is going to be the future of American psychology.... You're spelling out the frontline tactics. You're just what we need to shake things up at Harvard."
36 Leary (1995: 177).
37 Ibid., 183.
38 Ibid.
39 Ibid., 184.
40 Gigante (2000: 572).
41 Ibid.
42 Ibid., 573.
43 Leary (1995: 184).
44 Ibid.
45 Ibid.
46 Huxley (2009: 57).
47 Leary (1995: 184).
48 Percy Shelley describes the importance of poetry for defamiliarizing language in "A Defence of Poetry" (1840): "Their [poets'] language is vitally metaphorical; that is, it marks the before unapprehended relations of things and perpetuates their apprehension, until the words which represent them, become, through time, signs for portions or classes of thoughts instead of pictures of integral thoughts; and then if no new poets should arise to create afresh the associations which have been thus disorganized, language will be dead to all the nobler purposes of human intercourse." For an analysis of Shelley's passage along these lines, see Keach (1993: 116).

10

Frankenfilm: Classical Monstrosity in Bill Morrison's *Spark of Being*

Jesse Weiner

Was I, then, a monster, a blot upon the earth, from which all men fled and whom all men disowned?

Mary Shelley, *Frankenstein* 2.5: 123[1]

Introduction

What makes a monster a monster remains a vexing question, and one particularly germane to *Frankenstein* (*F*) and its traditions. Monsters are Linnaean nightmares:[2] ontologically liminal, they "refuse to participate in the classificatory order of things."[3] Monsters are markers of radicalized difference, Others who transgress culturally specific norms of biology, gender, sexuality, race, ethics, and aesthetics. Because these boundaries have been ever-present, even if ever-shifting, the taxonomical uncertainty of monsters reaches back to classical antiquity, frustrating the epistemological systems of Aristotle, Pliny, Augustine, and Isidore.[4] For the late antique Isidore, who grounds his own theories of monstrosity in classical traditions, epistemic uncertainty is the very marker of monstrosity: "Varro said that portents are things which seem to have been born contrary to nature: but they are not contrary to nature … Therefore, a portent does not come into being contrary to nature, but against what nature is understood to be" (*Portenta esse Varro ait quae contra naturam nata videntur: sed non sunt contra naturam … portentum ergo fit non contra naturam, sed contra quam est nota natura*; *Etymologiae* [*Etym.*] 11.3.1–2).[5]

As Abigail Lee Six and Hannah Thompson note, "*Frankenstein* has influenced ideas on monstrosity to an extent that can hardly be overestimated, but it did not come out of a literary vacuum."[6] Is Mary Shelley's (henceforth MWS) Creature truly a 'monster' and, if so, why? How have the answers to this question varied throughout *Frankenstein*'s traditions? Certainly, Boris Karloff's iconic, lumbering Creature is at some level a much different beast than MWS's articulate, athletic creation.[7] This essay investigates one recent interpretation of *Frankenstein* and traces its constructions of monstrosity back to roots in classical antiquity. As MWS herself wrote of writing the novel, perhaps channeling Lucretius and Ovid, "Everything must have a beginning.... Invention ... does not consist in creating out of void, but out of chaos; the materials must be in the first place afforded."[8]

Frankenstein is an Ovidian tale of 'forms changed into new bodies' (*in nova fert animus mutatas dicere formas / corpora*; *Metamorphoses* [*Met.*] 1.1–2) and the same is true of Bill Morrison's *Spark of Being* (*Spark*).[9] MWS's novel finds its premise in the experimentation of its Modern Prometheus, and *Spark* emulates its subject as one of the more experimental of the dozens of *Frankensteins* adapted to the silver screen. Released in 2010 (coincidentally or not, at the centennial of the first *Frankenstein* film), Morrison's film harks back to cinema's silent origins.[10] Morrison splices together frames from rare archival footage to follow MWS's novel, setting its images against an originally composed score. *Spark* thus combines new music and avant-garde cinematography while reaching back to the past with its old, dated material. This turn toward cinematic antiquity for material emulates Victor's experimental science in *Frankenstein* and mirrors the antiquarianism of both Victor and MWS's novel at large.

In MWS's novel, "Frankenstein's creature has impeccable credentials for a monster."[11] To take Isidore's categorization of monstrosity (*Etym.* 11.3.7–1) as a starting point, *Frankenstein*'s Creature fits as many as five of Isidore's twelve types of monsters: (1) hypertrophy, (2) composite makeup, (3) disturbed growth (he is born into a mature adult body), (4) mixture of human and animal parts, and (5) monstrous race.[12] To these physiological conceptions of monstrosity we might add aesthetic and ethical ones. The Creature is visually hideous and self-identifies as such.[13] While Victor is a "morally monstrous villain" in the Gothic mode, the Creature's turn toward violence makes him a "malevolent, vindictive, indeed murderous" monster, "the forerunner of innumerable evil creatures in fantasy and science fiction texts."[14]

MWS refers to her novel as her "hideous progeny," and, in its metaliterary reflections on literature and art, *Frankenstein* engages with at least two approaches to monstrosity that go on to be prevalent in its later traditions, both of which find geneses in classical antiquity. First, if a monster is a creature of mixed parts, then Morrison's film itself becomes the monster. Like MWS's patchwork man, *Spark* is a discordant assemblage of parts, which self-consciously embraces its own aesthetic disunity. This approach to monstrosity reaches back to Empedocles and Lucretius, while Horace's *Ars poetica* (*AP*) stigmatizes such hybrid monstrosity as aesthetically displeasing. And if the film is monster, then its maker, Bill Morrison, is cast as its "pale student of unhallowed arts." Morrison's choice to use archived material channels both Victor's antiquarianism and his desire to raise the dead.

In addition to its ludic mimesis of the Creature's hybridity, *Spark* plays with a second classically inspired definition of monstrosity. As Cicero observes of its Latin etymology from *monstrare* (discussed below), a 'monster' is something that displays or is displayed. *Spark* is primarily shot (more properly spliced, since Morrison recycles old film reels) from the Creature's eyes. Rather than see the Creature, the viewer is put in the position of the Creature, and it is only the revulsion of others' gazes that signals the Creature's monstrosity.

Antiquarianism, Recombination, and Reanimation in *Spark of Being*

MWS's Victor Frankenstein "was led to examine the cause and progress of decay, and forced to spend days and nights in vaults and charnel-houses" (*F* 1.4: 52–53). Similarly, Morrison has made a career of delving into the archival tombs of lost, forgotten, and decayed footage and breathing new life into this 'dead' matter by combining and "recontextualizing earlier imagery."[15] Since his early filmmaking career, Morrison has taken keen interest in correlations between "what's happening in the story and what's happening materially to the frames" of the film itself.[16] Material decay has played a central role in Morrison's films ever since he began working with found footage suffering from severe emulsion deterioration uncovered at the Moving Image Research Collections archive. Beginning with *Decasia* (2002), Morrison's work has confronted "the inevitable decay of celluloid cinema and its transformation of the imagery recorded on the filmstrip, and, by implication, the specter of decay and demise that all of us face."[17] Victor's Creature is a discordant assemblage of parts that combine to form a sublime whole—at once beautiful and ugly, wondrous and terrifying— and the same is generally true of Morrison's cinematic *corpus*.[18] Morrison combines "the montage approach … with the alterations of found images over time through chemical transformation."[19] In his films, Morrison pairs this visual montage of found, often decayed, images with original scores written by collaborating composers. Thus, as Scott MacDonald observes, "Morrison's films involve at least two collaborators: whichever musician/composer he's working with and Time itself."[20]

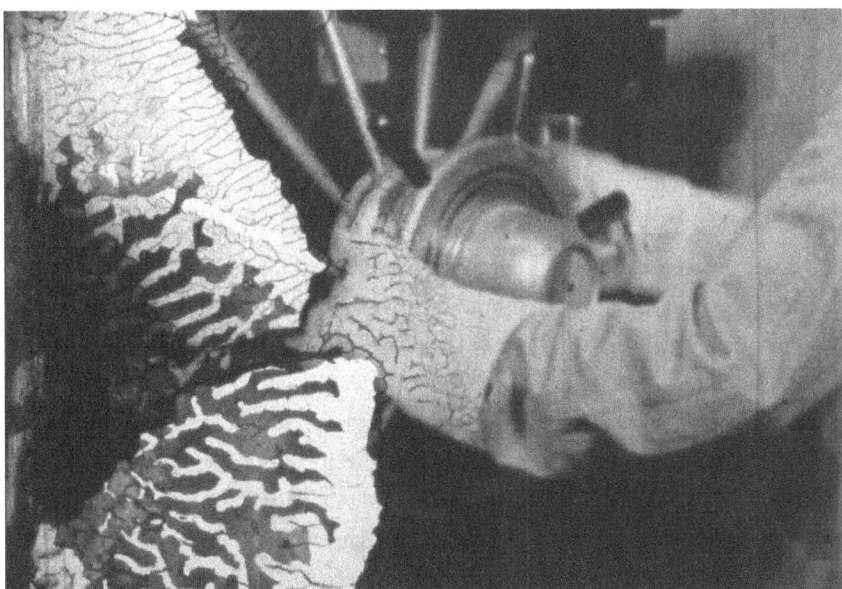

Fig. 10.1 Bill Morrison, *Spark of Being* (2010), photo courtesy of the artist.

Morrison's artistic techniques and thematic interest in decay mirror Victor's, and the same is true of *Spark*'s turn toward antiquity and classical pasts. Victor's science and artistry are inspired by a dated, antiquarian interest in the Medieval and Renaissance alchemists Cornelius Agrippa, Paracelsus, and Albertus Magnus (*F* 1.2: 40–41). Likewise, Morrison's antiquarianism is marked not only by his attraction to turning ancient (by film standards) footage into new art but also by use of original scores set against otherwise soundless films, which reaches back to the early days of cinema. As MacDonald astutely suggests in terms that recall MWS's Victor, "Morrison can be understood as a cine-alchemist who transforms trash into cinematic gold, or as a mad scientist who creates new beings from the shards of past cinematic 'bodies,' or as a magician who reverses the process of decay, bringing what looked to be dead back to momentary life."[21] As Genevieve Liveley notes, Victor is not only a modern Prometheus but also a modern Pygmalion, Medea, and Asclepius.[22] These Ovidian filiations reach forward to include Bill Morrison.

MWS's *Frankenstein*, then, serves as a programmatic myth for Morrison's filmmaking. As Morrison recounts of *Spark*'s nascence, he "re-read *Frankenstein*, and ... started thinking about a film made out of found-footage-spare-parts, like the monster is made out of 'found' body parts."[23] *Spark* thus reaches back to MWS's novel, and Morrison largely privileges MWS's text over its cinematic traditions in its construction of monstrosity:

It was interesting to realize how much of what we associate with the monster—a grunting awkward, slow-moving beast—did not come from the book, but through the James Whale films. In the book the creature is a superman—super-athletic, super-smart, a much quicker learner than his creator. And he's articulate.[24]

Morrison breathes new meanings into his archival material and, with them, new life.[25] Morrison thus develops one construction of monstrosity, present in MWS, of a 'monster' as a hybrid creature of mixed parts.

This approach to monstrosity reaches back through MWS to origins in classical antiquity. Lucretius—whose radical materialism, atomistic physics, and Epicurean ethics seem to have been important sources for MWS—makes hybridity the primary defining characteristic of monsters.[26] At *De rerum natura* 5.878–924, Lucretius offers reasons why Nature forbids the existence of mythic monsters. These creatures are collectively designated as "beings bound together with a double nature and twin body and mixed limbs" (*duplici natura et corpore bino / ex alienigenis membris compacta*; 5.879–880), and each of Lucretius's monstrous exempla are hybrids: centaurs (half-human, half-horse), Scylla (fish mixed with dogs), and chimaeras (lion/goat/serpent).[27] Lucretius's hybrid-as-monster draws upon Empedocles, who earlier suggested that Nature first generated individual limbs and organs, which then came together into wild and randomly mixed creations (B57–61), such as "man-headed ox-creatures" (βουγενῆ ἀνδρόπρῳρα; B61.2) and "ox-headed man-creatures" (ἀνδροφυῆ βούκρανα; B61.3). Examples include:[28]

> There sprouted many neckless heads, arms wandered naked, bereft of shoulders, and eyes wandered, lacking foreheads.
>
> ἧι πολλαὶ μὲν κόρσαι ἀναύχενες ἐβλάστησαν,
> γυμνοὶ δ' ἐπλάζοντο βραχίονες εὔνιδες ὤμων,
> ὄμματά τ' οἶ(α) ἐπλανᾶτο πενητεύοντα μετώπων.
>
> B57
>
> Single limbs wandered, cut off by Strife in isolation, seeking union with each other.
>
> μουνομελῆ ἔτι τὰ γυῖα ἀπὸ τῆς τοῦ Νείκους διακρίσεως ὄντα ἐπλανᾶτο τῆς πρὸς ἄλληλα μίξεως ἐφιέμενα.
>
> B58
>
> But then daemon mixed with daemon, and these disparate parts fell together.
>
> αὐτὰρ ἐπεὶ κατὰ μεῖζον ἐμίσγετο δαίμονι δαίμων,
> ταῦτά τε συμπίπτεσκον.
>
> B59

Many were born two-faced, and two-chested, man-headed cow-creatures sprang up along with cow-headed man-creatures.

πολλὰ μὲν ἀμφιπρόσωπα καὶ ἀμφίστερνα φύεσθαι,
βουγενῆ ἀνδρόπρῳρα, τὰ δ' ἔμπαλιν ἐξανατέλλειν
ἀνδροφυῆ βούκρανα.

B61

Even the Creature's superlative attributes (giant stature, superhuman strength and speed) are suggestive of genetic "human/god hybrids—that is, demigods or *heroes* (in the Greek sense of the term)," to whom Hesiod refers as "demigods" (ἡμίθεοι; *Works and Days* 160).[29]

Biological hybridity in these terms has long provoked ambivalent reactions. "While Darwin praised the process of cross-pollination," as Vanessa Guignery observes, both Empedocles and Lucretius point "to the risk of degeneration."[30] Such positions subscribe to a particular heterosexist reproductive politics. As Donna Haraway points out, Victor assumes the Creature's hybridity could lead to a "race of devils" if he were to create a female mate (*F* 3.3: 170).[31] Perhaps surprisingly, neither Victor nor the Creature consider the possibility that the Creature might not be able to reproduce; after all, many zoological hybrids are sterile. Applied metaphorically, the hybrid-as-monster has supplied fodder in modernity for racist and colonialist myths of purity.[32] In addition to prompting such major questions concerning the boundaries between the human and non-human, the monster-as-hybrid also points toward aesthetic questions concerning the unity of art. What, for example, do we make of multimedia art and works of mixed genres? Can a mashup attain the status of high or fine art?[33]

Exempla of hybrid monsters pervade classical myth, literature, and art, ranging from centaurs and griffins to the Sphinx and Pegasus. As the folklorist Vladimir Propp observes, such combinations reflect upon the fantastic imagination and also find their way into the production of art and linguistic development.[34] Horace, himself heavily influenced by Lucretius, develops these monstrous aesthetics at the outset of the *Ars poetica*, a poem whose influence upon *Frankenstein* may have been direct, mediated through Percy Shelley (henceforth PBS) and Lord Byron, and/or received indirectly through the cultural matrix.[35] Byron translated the *Ars* (*Hints from Horace*, published posthumously in 1831). PBS was classically educated from a young age and engaged with Horace well before he began his affair with MWS. In a letter to MWS's father, William Godwin (dated July 29, 1812), in which he considers the value of a classical education, PBS directly quotes Horace's introduction to the second book of the *Epistles*, which is dedicated to the topic of aesthetics.[36] MWS would almost certainly have been exposed to Horace through PBS and Byron.[37] Whatever the mechanics of transmission, the influence of Horatian aesthetics can be felt throughout *Frankenstein*.

The *Ars* opens with the image of a hypothetical painting, depicting what sounds very much like what could be a mythological monster (1–5):

> If a painter wished to join the neck of a horse to a human head, and to put multicolored feathers everywhere on collected limbs so that a lovely woman up top ends repulsively in the tail of a black fish: admitted to a viewing, friends, could you stifle a laugh?

> humano capiti cervicem pictor equinam
> iungere si velit, et varias inducere plumas,
> undique conlatis membris, ut turpiter atrum
> desinat in piscem mulier formosa superne,
> spectatum admissi risum teneatis, amici? 5

The monster-as-hybrid is given aesthetic expression and extends his analogy beyond the visual arts to literature (6–13):

> Believe me, Pisos, a book would be like that picture, whose idle forms, like the dreams of a sick man, are fashioned such that neither foot nor head can be assigned a unified form. "But painters and poets have always shared the right to dare whatever they want." I know this, and I seek this license and grant it in turn; but not so the wild should mate with the tame, not so serpents should couple with birds, or sheep with tigers.

> credite, Pisones, isti tabulae fore librum
> persimilem, cuius, velut aegri somnia, vanae
> fingentur species, ut nec pes nec caput uni
> reddatur formae. "pictoribus atque poetis
> quidlibet audendi semper fuit aequa potestas." 10
> scimus, et hanc veniam petimusque damusque vicissim;
> sed non ut placidis coeant inmitia, non ut
> serpentes avibus geminentur, tigribus agni.

Daring artistic innovation, then, has its boundaries. The Horatian artist must exhibit an awareness of generic norms, should employ "diction, metre and subject ... appropriate to the genre chosen," and mind the gap between 'high' and 'low' genres.[38] Horace insists upon the "unity and coherence" of artistic form.[39]

In his essay *In Defence of Poetry* (1821, published posthumously in 1840), PBS follows Horace when he insists upon unity as an aesthetic ideal. PBS's celebration of Athenian tragedy, which "disciplined" each artistic element into "a beautiful proportion and unity" at once channels Horace and suggests Victor's failed attempt to achieve the same beauty through proportion and unity.[40] *Frankenstein* and *Spark* both channel and challenge the Horatian aesthetic of formal unity.

Victor's Creature is ontologically monstrous as a creature of mixed parts, some of them potentially non-human in origin—Victor confesses that not only human graveyards but also "the dissecting room and the slaughter-house furnished many of my materials" (F 1.4: 55). His monstrosity is aesthetic as well.[41] As artist, Victor composes his Creature with an eye toward unity, beauty, and proportion (1.5: 58):

> His limbs were in proportion, and I had selected his features as beautiful. Beautiful!–Great God! His yellow skin scarcely covered the work of muscles and arteries beneath; his hair was a lustrous black, and flowing; his teeth of pearly whiteness...

Nevertheless, the artificial combination cannot help but result in hideous aesthetic disunity: "but these luxuriances only formed a more horrid contrast with his watery eyes, that seemed almost of the same colour as the dun-white sockets in which they were set, his shriveled complexion and straight black lips" (ibid.). The Creature's hybridity renders it monstrous both ontologically and aesthetically, and its creator, filled with "breathless horror and disgust," cannot "endure the aspect of the being" (ibid.).

Horatian aesthetics inform MWS's *Frankenstein*, and they are at the very core of Morrison's *Spark*, which is, essentially, a mashup. Visually, the film's frames range from the nearly pristinely preserved to the badly decayed to the intentionally manipulated. Likewise, the spliced reels span 16mm footage shot by members of the Shackleton expedition while stranded in Antarctica, old education films, 1970s soft-core pornography, Fox Movietone footage of a Bavarian wedding, etc.[42] Dave Douglas's score to the film similarly blends jazz with electronic elements, ranging in style from industrial to ambient.[43] Moreover, as Annaëlle Winand observes, *Spark* stages "an aesthetic of ruins: The monster wanders in spaces surrounded by antiques or industrial ruins, all while the film itself is seen decomposing or suffering from fading or damages. In another scene, the creation of the monster is paradoxically staged with decomposing and dying, nitrate footage."[44]

Decay looms over the monstrous, material bodies of both the Creature and the film; the sublime prospect—at once beautiful and terrifying—of corporeal disintegration immerses the viewer in a landscape of ruination. Hybridity is the marker of creation even as it hints at impending degradation. The effect is unsettling; the body monstrous, stitched and spliced together, teeters on the

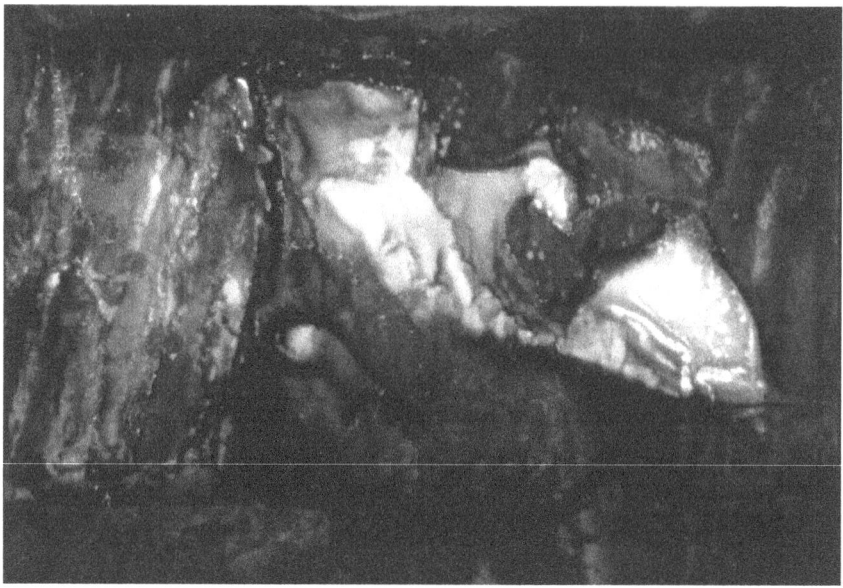

Fig. 10.2 Bill Morrison, *Spark of Being* (2010), photo courtesy of the artist.

brink of dissolution and fragmentation. As Morrison describes his own interest in MWS's novel, "with *Frankenstein* there was this opportunity to merge the text and the form."[45] With each deteriorated frame, *Spark* undermines its own unity of form, so essential to Horace (*uni formae*; *AP* 8–9), and raises the question: can this patchwork film hold together?

Spark's monstrous aesthetics mirror not only those of Victor's Creature but also those of the novel itself, MWS's "hideous progeny." As Liveley points out, "The narrative of Mary Shelley's *Frankenstein* is, like its own monster, notoriously made up of disparate literary genres and parts, stitched together into a novel shape at once familiar and strange."[46] Liveley's extensive list of literary "parts" and "mismatched genres" conjures PBS's preface to the 1818 first edition of *Frankenstein* (which purported to be written by the then-anonymous author). This preface similarly describes the activity of writing as a process of alchemy and amalgamation:

> I have thus endeavored to preserve the truth of the elementary principles of human nature, while I have not scrupled to innovate upon their combinations. The *Iliad*, the tragic poetry of Greece,—Shakespeare in *The Tempest* and *Midsummer Night's Dream*,—and most especially Milton, in *Paradise Lost*, conform to this rule; and the most humble novelist, who seeks to confer or receive amusement from his labours, may, without presumption, apply to prose fictions a licence, or rather a rule, from the adoption of which so many exquisite combinations of human feeling have resulted in the highest specimens of poetry.[47]

Through their daring combinations, both MWS's *Frankenstein* and Morrison's *Spark* stand as challenges to Horace's guidelines for art—which, importantly, remained very influential in MWS's day and in her literary circle.[48] As perhaps mismatched assemblages of parts, each puts Horatian aesthetics to the test by asking its audience either to find unity and harmony in its patchwork assemblage of parts or to find this aesthetic pleasure despite the disunity of the whole—in essence, to find beauty in the monstrous.

In the wake of Modernist movements, *Spark* can perhaps claim its place in avant-garde aesthetic traditions, which explicitly disavow Aristotelian and Horatian formalism and emphasis on aesthetic unity.[49] By emulating its source material and its aesthetic strategies, *Spark* highlights all the more the daring innovation of MWS's *Frankenstein*. *Frankenstein*'s "monstrous metapoetics" (to borrow Liveley's phrase) transgresses the aesthetic theory of its age, which still very much privileged Horace. This aesthetic context perhaps helps account for William Beckford's unfavorable early reception of *Frankenstein*: "This is, perhaps, the foulest Toadstool that has yet sprung up from the reeking dunghill of present times."[50] Ultimately, both MWS's *Frankenstein* and its own hideous progeny, *Spark*, are themselves monsters in the classical tradition.

Monsters in the Mirror, Monsters on the Screen

"Are you a monster?" the little girl asked, suddenly.

Sorvalh cocked her head and considered the question. "I don't think I am" Sorvalh said. "But maybe that depends on what you think a monster is."

"A monster fights and wrecks things," the little girl said.

"Well, I try to avoid doing that," Sorvalh said. "So maybe I'm not a monster after all."

"But you *look* like a monster," the girl said.

John Scalzi, *The Human Division*, 486

In John Scalzi's *The Human Division* (2013, the fifth book of the *Old Man's War* series), Hafte Sorvalh is an alien of distinctly non-human appearance. In the above exchange, Sorvalh's child interlocutor elides two definitions of monstrosity, both of which are present in MWS's *Frankenstein*. First, the girl suggests a behavioral approach: a monster is something or someone whose actions violate the normative ethics of a community. Victor's Creature violates codes of conduct once he turns toward vengeance, yet the Creature comes to self-identify as 'monster' well before he experiences the faintest inkling toward violent behavior. The girl's second charge of monstrosity against Sorvalh is strictly based upon visual appearance, and this seems to map more neatly onto MWS's narrative. First from the revulsion of humans, then through seeing his own reflection for the first time, the Creature's monstrosity is marked by his physical, visual appearance. Victor demands that the Creature "not be seen, as if visuality were the sole source of the monster's accusation."[51] Whereas the cottagers "behold only a detestable monster" (*F* 2.7: 136), De Lacey is the one character in the novel who does not treat the Creature as a monster, and, importantly, this tolerance is joined to the old man's blindness.[52] In his anti-Narcissan moment before a reflective pool, the Creature becomes the monster in the mirror (2.4: 116–117):

> I had admired the perfect forms of my cottagers—their grace, beauty and delicate complexions: but how was I terrified, when I viewed myself in a transparent pool! At first I started back, unable to believe that it was indeed I who was reflected in the mirror; and when I became fully convinced that I was in reality the monster that I am, I was filled with the bitterest sensations of despondence and mortification.

Spark's construction of monstrosity privileges such a vision-based monstrosity over a behavior-based alternative. Morrison notes that just as "Shelley glossed over how the creature was created, *I* glossed over the damage he does. I focused on his loneliness, his isolation."[53] In so doing, Morrison departs from previous film versions of *Frankenstein*, many of which make the Creature's violence a central emphasis.

Morrison does not cultivate the Creature's sense of social isolation through dialogue, nor does he construct the Creature's visual difference through any grotesque appearance. Instead, much of *Spark* is focalized through the Creature. Just as MWS's *Frankenstein* allows the Creature to give his own autobiographical account of his early life and education, Morrison presents many of the film's episodes through the Creature's eyes. "The Creature's Education," "Observations of Familial Love," and "Observations of Romantic Love" each effect the Creature's estrangement through his voyeurism. "Observations of Familial Love," "Observations of Romantic Love," and especially "The Doctor's Wedding" are consecutive lengthy scenes, which segue into "The Creature in Society." Having gazed upon different forms of companionship and bonding, the Creature's venture into society is met with marginalization. The scene is by far the shortest in the film, which emphasizes the Creature's isolation; his attempt at social integration is short-lived. As Morrison has said of the film, his Creature commits "no visible murder or mayhem." Instead, *Spark* presents "a story of alienation" because the Creature "can't participate in, can't have love."[54]

Morrison's technique for establishing the Creature's monstrosity does reach back to MWS's mechanics of ethical monstrosity. MWS's Creature is not inherently evil. Rather, "it was the cruelty which [the creature] encountered that turned [him] from noble-spirited to malevolent."[55] In *Spark*, the cruelty of the outside world—represented by ugly, hateful stares into the camera—functions as the speculum, the gaze into the reflecting pool, which marks and determines the Creature as monstrous. The malevolent gaze of the public is depicted with the very first frames of the film, and these stares into the camera form the entirety of "The Creature in Society," which reiterates their importance.

If our first approach to monsters—hybridity—positions the filmmaker as a Victor Frankenstein, our second definition of *monstrosity*—based upon vision and reflection—places the viewer in the position of the monster. Through the point-of-view technique of the Creature's education and observation, we, the audience, experience the Creature's isolation, looking as outsiders upon scenes of a couple in love, dancing at a Bavarian wedding, and floods people crowding urban streets.[56] Whenever our gaze is returned, the suspicious, disgusted, even hateful faces of others confirm our abjection; we are degraded, demoralized, and pressed to shrink from view. We become the monster in the mirror.

This visual conception of monstrosity reaches back, through Foucault, to origins in Cicero and Latin etymologies. In *Madness and Civilization*, Foucault's discussion of the public exhibition of the insane by early modern European asylums draws upon the Latin *monstrare* ("to demonstrate") as the etymological root of "monster."[57] Cicero twice explains *monstra* from *monstrare* as things that "show" or "are shown":

> For because they show, portend, demonstrate, and predict, they are called signs, portents, monstra, and prodigies.
>
> quia enim ostendunt, portendunt, monstrant, praedicunt, ostenta, portenta, monstra, prodigia dicuntur.
>
> De Divinatione 1.93

> Again, predictions and presentiments of things to come declare nothing else to men except those things which may be shown, demonstrated, portended, and predicted—from which they are called signs, *monstra*, portents, and prodigies.
>
> Praedictiones vero et praesensiones rerum futurarum quid aliud declarant nisi hominibus ea quae sint ostendi monstrari portendi praedici, ex quo illa ostenta monstra portenta prodigia dicuntur.
>
> De Natura Deorum 2.7

This reciprocal nature of monstrosity pervades *Frankenstein*. That pivotal moment in which the Creature gazes into a reflecting pool is emblematic of a broader process by which the *monstrans* (actively 'showing') monster and the *monstrum* (taken by Cicero to mean passively 'shown') become difficult to separate. Victor and his Creature resemble one another in numerous respects, each exhibiting the faults of the other. For example, drawing upon Lacan's theory of the gaze, Dean Franco argues that "when the monster awakens" Victor experiences a "sudden sense of self-sight."[58] Barbara Johnson notes of all three of *Frankenstein*'s narrators (Captain Walton, Victor, and the Creature), that "Frankenstein recognizes in Walton an image of himself, and rejects in the monster a resemblance he does not wish to acknowledge. The teller is in each case speaking into a mirror of his own transgression."[59]

Spark effects this monstrous mirroring in several ways. First, the titles of many of the episodes suggest that certain of these chapters be viewed in tandem. For example, "The Captain's Story" and "The Traveler's Story" place Captain Walton and Victor in mirrored juxtaposition. Pairing episodes such as "A Promising Student" and "The Creature's Education," "Observations of Romantic Love" and "The Doctor's Wedding," and "The Doctor Flees" and "The Creature's Pursuit," also present parallel lives. This conjures Plutarch's *Lives*, with which the Creature educates himself in MWS's novel. Second, the Doctor and the Creature cannot be visually distinguished. The very nature of Morrison's found-footage montage technique means that neither character has a singular visual appearance, nor does the Creature appear phenotypically monstrous. (This conjures the hybrid-as-monster, too, since the characters within the film, as well as the film itself, are composite; no single actor or image represents either the Doctor or Creature.) In an interview with Scott MacDonald (SM), Morrison (BM) reflects upon the extent to which monster and maker collapse into one another and *show* the other's isolation:

> **SM:** As in most of the *Frankenstein* films, you're more interested in the creature than in Dr. Frankenstein.
>
> **BM:** Well in my mind they sort of become the same guy. While I was making *Spark of Being*, I was reading *The Casebook of Victor Frankenstein* [Peter Ackroyd, 2009]—in which the monster is collapsed into the doctor: the doctor is insane, schizophrenic.
>
> **SM:** Sounds like *The Cabinet of Dr. Caligari* [1921].
>
> **BM:** Or *Dr. Jekyll and Mr. Hyde*. But it is also the same plot device that J. Searle Dawley introduced to Shelley's characters, in the very first film version of Frankenstein (Edison, 1910).

To my mind *Spark of Being* can be thought of as a loop. You have these three men—the ship's captain, the doctor, and the creature—and they change roles. The captain of the ship welcomes the passenger who starts telling the story that the captain then relays. The passenger is a doctor, who tells how he created a living creature with his own hands. The story is then told from the perspective of this creature, who describes his education and his ultimately fruitless quest for love. The creature ultimately confronts his creator, and, in my twist on the original story, the doctor flees the monster, ultimately captaining a boat to the polar region seen at the beginning of the film. The film returns full circle with creator and creation in reversed roles. In *Spark of Being* the *film* is in fact the "creature," and the point of view of the creature is often just the decay of the film.

At one point a man comes walking up the road and you see him looking into the camera and this is perhaps the point at which their roles are first inverted...

SM: The viewer doesn't know whether the man is the doctor or the creature, though if for you the *film* is looking at that man, he must be the doctor.

BM: Let's just say I've conflated the two roles.[60]

The Creature is a monstrous reflection of Victor, and he is, more generally, determined and conditioned by the humans he observes. After all, how could the Creature self-identify as hideous, had his conception of beauty and phenotypical normativity not been conditioned by his observations of humans? In *Frankenstein*, the Creature is a *tabula rasa* of sorts, educated through the observation and imitation of the cottagers, the De Laceys. Visual and behavioral monstrosity become conjoined. For example, the Creature learns both language and values through the speech and (often classical/classicizing) literature of his cottagers. This literature includes Volney's *Ruins of Empires*, Plutarch's *Lives*, Milton's *Paradise Lost*, and Goethe's *Sorrows of Werter*. Anticipating his later behavior, the Creature learns from these texts and discussions that humans are "at once so powerful, so virtuous, and magnificent, yet so vicious and base" (*F* 2.5: 122). At first, the Creature's education is largely benevolent. He reports that in his reading of Plutarch, he "was led to admire peaceable lawgivers, Numa, Solon, and Lycurgus, in preference to Romulus and Theseus" (2.7: 132). However, if his "first introduction to humanity had been made by a young soldier, burning for glory and slaughter," the creature "should have been imbued with different sensations."

The Creature's education in humanity, however, is not uniformly peaceful. He learns of the "hapless fate" of Native Americans, becomes educated in classical ideals that promoted racist and Islamophobic discourses, and, eventually, is initiated into violence when he is beaten by De Lacey. To the extent that the Creature descends into monstrous behavior, it is as a direct result of being *shown* the worst of humanity, which he then imitates and shows back to Victor in a Ciceronian, Foucauldian sense. As Darko Suvin writes generally of science fiction:

> the aliens—utopians, monsters, or simply differing strangers—are a mirror to man just as the differing country is a mirror for his world. But the mirror is not only a reflecting one, it is also a transforming one, virgin womb and alchemical dynamo: the mirror is a crucible.[61]

Although *Spark* never does *show* its monster misbehaving, I suggest that Morrison captures the Creature's miseducation in MWS and suggests the possibility that the Creature's mimesis of humanity might show our own worst features back to us. We, the audience, are made to confront our own distrusting, isolating gazes. Moreover, Morrison devotes several chapters of the film to the nascent Creature's observations of the world. Viewing our own cultural materials through the eyes of the Creature, we are challenged—at the least invited, I think—to contemplate how we might behave in love if our only romantic education came through viewing pornography ("Observations of Romantic Love"). Were our introductions to our communities and early attempts at social integration met with hostile rebuttal, what forms might our maladjustments take? The monster becomes a mirror that reflects far and wide. In the words of Morrison, "we are all products of these images, as much as they are products of us."[62]

Conclusion

In parallel to how the definition of 'monster' has long been contested, nomenclature remains a controversial issue in *Frankenstein* studies. MWS's novel vacillates between "monster," "creature," and "daemon," and what, if anything, makes the 'monster' (and Victor) monstrous invites both debate and divergent interpretations. These range from Boris Karloff's portrayal in film to the Royal National Theatre stage production, in which the actors alternated roles to effect a mirroring of Victor and the Creature, to Morrison's *Spark*, in which creator and created collapse into one another, and filmmaker, film, and audience each become cast, metatheatrically, as characters. That *Frankenstein* invites such widely disparate visions of monstrosity is only natural; in Roman antiquity,

Fig. 10.3 Bill Morrison, *Spark of Being* (2010), "Observations of Romantic Love," photo courtesy of the artist.

Varro and Isidore each define monsters as beings that challenge our epistemologies of nature.

MWS's *Modern Prometheus* cannot help but place Bill Morrison in conversation with antiquity and its various monsters and theories of monstrosity. In a sense, Morrison and all adaptors of *Frankenstein* become like the Prometheus credited with creating humankind, modern Prometheis *plasticatores*, molders of their own monsters and hideous progeny. This is especially true of Morrison, who makes the film itself the monster and so casts himself in the role of Victor. Reaching back to Empedocles and Lucretius through MWS, *Spark*'s hybridity puts its Creature into conversation with Scylla, chimaeras, centaurs, Pegasus, and many other monsters of mythology and the classical imagination. Aesthetically, the film's composite nature rejects Horace's guidelines for art—so influential among the British Romantics—and serves to highlight the avant-garde, patchwork nature of its source text. Viewed differently through the activity of *showing*, which is, etymologically, the root of our word 'monster,' *Spark*'s Creature becomes, like MWS's creation, a being made monstrous through viewing and being viewed by humanity. Through his point-of-view technique, Morrison positions us, the viewing audience, as the monster in the mirror.

Notes

1. I presented portions of this essay at the 2016 Northeast Popular Culture Association in Keene, NH and at Hobart and William Smith Colleges in November 2016, and I am grateful for the helpful comments I received on each occasion. Thanks are also due to my co-editors of this volume, Brett M. Rogers and Benjamin Eldon Stevens, as well as to Bill Morrison, who kindly read a draft of this essay and provided images from his film. Finally, I am indebted to my colleague at Hamilton College, Scott MacDonald, who first brought *Spark of Being* to my attention, screened the film for me, generously provided me with transcripts of his interviews with Bill Morrison (2016a and 2016b), and commented on a draft of this essay. For the text of *Frankenstein* (henceforth *F*), I use the 1831 standard edition printed in Hindle 2007.
2. Carl Linnaeus (1707–1778) formalized the modern system of naming organisms and so is a foundational figure of modern taxonomy. I borrow the phrase "Linnaean nightmare" from Greenberg (1991: 90), who uses these words to describe the monstrous alien in Ridley Scott's *Alien* (1979). See also Cohen (1996b: 6). On the *Alien* franchise's (especially *Alien Resurrection*, 1997) engagement with classical traditions, see Rogers 2015 (which anticipates my discussion of hybridity below) as well as Rogers in this volume.
3. Cohen (1996b: 6).
4. Ibid.
5. Isidore uses 'portent' and 'monster' interchangeably: "Portents are also called 'signs,' 'monsters,' and 'prodigies'" (*portenta autem et ostenta, monstra atque prodigia ideo nuncupantur*; *Etym.* 11.3.2). All translations of Greek and Latin are my own.
6. Six and Thompson (2012: 238).
7. Forry (1990: x) notes that from its earliest receptions on stage and in popular culture, interpreters "heightened the demoniacal aspects of the Creature."
8. These words are drawn from MWS's authorial introduction to the 1831 standard edition of *F*; Hindle (2007: 8). While Britton (2015: 3) finds these first materials in MWS's psyche and subconscious, I suggest a turn toward the literary past and the thought of antiquity for the origins of her monster; see Weiner 2015a. As Baldick (1987: 35) observes of this quote from MWS, "what we too often call literary 'creation' is really a process of assembling and combining pre-existing elements."
9. *Spark of Being* (dir. Bill Morrison, 2010) won The Douglas Edwards Experimental/Independent Film/Video Award at the 2011 Los Angeles Film Critics Association Awards. The film's original score is written by the composer and trumpeter, Dave Douglas. On MWS's relation to Ovid, see especially Liveley (this volume).
10. *Frankenstein* (dir. J. Searle Dawley, 1910). For overviews of *Frankenstein*'s film traditions, see Jancovich (2016), Friedman and Kavey (2016), and Schor (2003).
11. Six and Thompson (2012: 239).
12. I use the organization of Isidore's constitution of monstrous forms given by Williams (1996: 107). Although the Creature appears human in form, Victor admits that he experimented with animal as well as human bodies, suggesting that the Creature's pillaged parts might not be fully human in origin: "The dissecting room and the slaughter-house furnished many of my materials" (*F* 1.4: 55). As Six and Thompson (2012: 239) note, after reading *Paradise Lost*, the Creature situates himself as an abnormal species: "Like Adam, I was apparently united by no link to any other being in existence; but his state was far different from in in every other respect" (*F* 2.7: 132). Victor considers the Creature to be of its own species and who might, given a female companion, propagate "a race of devils" (3.3: 170).

13 As Andrea Rossi-Reder (2002: 53-54) notes of nineteenth-century racisms (reaching back to ancient discourses on monstrous races), this human standard of beauty is best qualified as white-European in its formulation. See also Brantlinger 2016.
14 Six and Thompson (2012: 238-239). As they also note (240), the causal relationship between physical monstrosity and moral monstrosity can be traced to Francis Bacon's essay "Of Deformity." In her introduction to the *Essays*, Scott (1908: xxi) notes that "Bacon was 'drenched' in classicism."
15 MacDonald (2016b: 116). MacDonald's title, "Orpheus of Nitrate," connects Morrison with the classical figure of Orpheus, an artist who sought to raise the dead from the Underworld.
16 MacDonald (2016a: 57).
17 Ibid. These themes, too, pervade Morrison's more recent *Dawson City: Frozen Time* (2016).
18 Mellor (1988: 132) writes that "[t]he creature himself embodies the human sublime."
19 MacDonald (2016b: 116).
20 Ibid., 117.
21 Ibid.
22 Lively (this volume). Pygmalion, Medea, and Asclepius all feature in Ovid's *Metamorphoses*. Pollin (1965: 98-102) notes that MWS would have engaged with Madame de Genlis's play, *Pygmalion et Galatée*. See also Nielson (2015: 73). MWS reports reading Genlis in Switzerland during the summer of 1816 while she began work on *F*, finishing her reading on August 23. See Feldman and Scott-Kilvert (1987: 130).
23 MacDonald (2016a: 58).
24 Ibid.
25 Winand (2016: 7).
26 On Lucretius and MWS, see Weiner 2015a and Priestman 2007. In privileging MWS's novel as its source text, Morrison's *Spark* is unusual among the many film adaptations of *F*; see Jancovich (2016: 191).
27 Cf. 2.700-717 and 4.732-748. Like Isidore, Lucretius uses *portenta* and *monstra* interchangeably, for example at 5.845. In addition to mythological creatures of mixed parts, Lucretius's conception of monstrosity includes hermaphrodites (839) and creatures born either with extra body parts or missing body parts whose genetic mutations rendered them evolutionary dead ends (840-854).
28 See Garani (2007: 15).
29 See Rogers (2015: 237-238). Hes. *WD* 159-160: "a godlike race of heroic men, who are called demigods" (ἀνδρῶν ἡρώων θεῖον γένος, οἳ καλέονται / ἡμίθεοι). Lively 2006 also connects the Creature's hybridity in *F* with ancient Greek and Roman monsters.
30 Guignery (2011: 2).
31 See Haraway (1991: 151). Haraway suggests that hybrids, divorced from heterosexual logic, emphasize replication over reproduction (161-162).
32 Ibid. See also, e.g., Brantlinger 2016, Prabhu 2007, Nussbaum 2003, Pieterse (2001: 228), and Pieterse 1989. As this volume's introduction discusses, the physical description of Victor's Creature has been situated in these discourses, and, in fantastic literature, we might also think of the slur, "mudblood," in the *Harry Potter* series.
33 These questions have bearing, I think, also on texts composed in creole languages (for example, the plays of Luis Alfaro, which intermix English, Spanish, and Spanglish in Chicano retellings of Greek tragedy). See also Rogers and Stevens (2017: 6-7).
34 Propp (1983: 78-79). Propp's observations on hybridity remain valuable even if we dismiss the teleological historicism upon which they are founded. This line of argument and my ensuing discussion of Horace's *Ars poetica* builds upon Baldick (1987: 13-15).

35 As Jane Stabler (1994: 47) observes, "Horace's literary criticism had been accepted in England ...from the Renaissance onward" and in the Romantic period "the *Ars poetica* was a source of authoritative maxims and instruction." Cf. McGann (2007: 305): "One of the constants in reception of Horace had been, and would long continue to be, the importance of the *Ars*, which during the sixteenth century was joined as canonical text by Aristotle's *Poetics*." See also Hopkins (2010: 39).

36 Ingpen (1909: 348): "But '*in publica commoda peccem / si longo sermone morer tua tempora*' says Horace at the commencement of his longest letter." PBS's internal quote is Hor. *Epistles* 2.1.3–4 ("I would sin against the public good, if I wasted your time with protracted chatter"). PBS also reports that his first wife, Harriet, worked on her Latin by reading Horace. See Ingpen (1909: 374, 377). In a letter to Thomas Hookam, dated December 17, 1812, PBS wrote that "Mrs. Shelley is attacking Latin with considerable resolution, and she can already read many odes in Horace." On January 2, 1813, PBS again wrote to Hookam and made mention of Harriet's ongoing study of Horace.

37 MWS's journals record that she read some of Horace's *Odes* in 1816 but does not profess to have returned to Horace until shortly after *F*'s initial publication. She read the first two books of the *Odes* beginning on April 26, 1818 and continuing through the summer. She reports reading *Odes* 1–3 in 1819. The journals show that MWS read the *Epistles* with PBS in 1820–1821. See Feldman and Scott-Kilvert (1987: 652) and the journal entries for September 9, 1820, January 1, 1821, and March 3, 1821.

38 Rutherford (2007: 250–251). In ancient poetry, epic and tragedy were 'high' genres, while satire and elegy were considered 'low' genres.

39 Laird (2007: 134). As Laird notes, Horace here appears to reach back to Philodemus and Neoptolemus of Parium.

40 Shelley (1845: 5). See also Posey (1971: 107–108).

41 The film *Victor Frankenstein* (dir. Paul McGuigan, 2015) resuscitates this reading. See also Barnett and Gumpert (this volume).

42 MacDonald (2016a: 58–59).

43 Dave Douglas acknowledges that his techniques of incorporating elements like electronic music and DJs into his art partially generated his interest in *F* and, in some respects, mirror Morrison's montage approach to the film's visual material. See Walker Art Center 2010b.

44 Winand (2016: 6). Winand notes that Morrison's narratives are motivated by "the clash created by the mixing of diverse images."

45 Walker Art Center 2010a.

46 Lively (this volume). Forry (1990: x) suggests that MWS's novel "combined the techniques of romance and realism in one virtually self-destructing narrative."

47 Hindle (2007: 11).

48 See Bevilacqua (1976: 12).

49 See Adorno (1984: 338) and Weiner (2017: 42).

50 I quote Beckford's note, handwritten in his 1818 first edition of *F*, reprinted in Gotlieb (1960: 61) and Forry (1990: ix).

51 Cohen (2012: 462).

52 See Mellor (1988: 129) on De Lacey's blindness and her surrounding discussion of vision and perception more generally.

53 MacDonald (2016a: 58). See also Walker Art Center 2010b, in which Dave Douglas reports that he, too, drew his inspiration from MWS's novel rather than *F*'s film traditions, and so composed the score in sympathy with the Creature's isolation.

54 Walker Art Center 2010a.
55 Six and Thompson (2012: 251–252).
56 Stevens (this volume) observes of Shelley's novel that "the traditional job of a wedding ... is travestied" esp. at 3.6. The same is true of "The Doctor's Wedding," which is a lengthy, drab scene, especially when contrasted with the preceding "Observations of Romantic Love." One of the most colorful scenes in the film gives way to drab, black and white footage. When asked about "The Doctor's Wedding," Morrison (MacDonald 2016a: 59) responded: "[laughter] What a drag, right? ... A very bizarre and somehow unjoyous occasion." Understood thusly, the scene might add to the monstrous doubling of the Doctor and the Creature, for which I argue below; neither is able to experience social joy.
57 See Foucault (1988: 68–70). This line of argument has previously been connected with *F* by Baldick (1987: 10) and Weiner 2015a. See also Troshynski and Weiner 2016.
58 Franco (1998: 80).
59 Johnson (1982: 3). See also Thornburg (1987: 9) and González and Calvo (1997: 17).
60 MacDonald (2016a: 59), punctuated as in original. In this sense, *Spark* prefigures the 2011 Royal National Theatre stage adaptation (dir. Danny Boyle), in which Benedict Cumberbatch and Jonny Lee Miller swapped roles each performance, alternating who played Victor and who the Creature. In this production, Victor and the Creature reconcile and their fates are coterminous. See Smith (2016b: 9).
61 Suvin (1972: 374).
62 Walker Art Center 2010a.

11

Alex Garland's *Ex Machina* or The Modern Epimetheus

Emma Hammond

Once upon a time there was a cyborg, a fully 'living machine,' imbued with beauty, knowledge, grace and charm—she was "a wonder to behold" (*thauma idesthai*).[1] Yet deep within her core programming she was a liar, full of deceit, and designed to bring death and destruction to mankind (a gendered term for the species that this chapter preserves to reflect its gendering in ancient and modern sources). The name of that cyborg was Pandora, and she is, as this chapter will argue, the ghost in the machine who haunts 'creature'-creation narratives in the Western canon, including Mary Shelley's (hereafter MWS) *Frankenstein* and Alex Garland's science-fiction film, *Ex Machina* (2015).

Parallels were drawn between MWS's creation myth and Garland's *Ex Machina* from the moment of the film's release. Robbie Collin noted that "*Ex Machina* whips up the same kind of existential terror MWS harnessed almost exactly 200 years ago in *Frankenstein*, but for a time in which the flow of information holds the same world-conquering potential that the flow of electricity once did."[2] Guy Lodge described the film as:

> A worthy companion piece to "Under the Skin" and "Her" in its examination of what constitutes human and feminine identity—and whether those two concepts need always overlap—Garland's long-anticipated directorial debut synthesizes a dizzy range of the writer's philosophical preoccupations into a sleek, spare chamber piece: Mary Shelley's "Frankenstein" redreamed as a 21st-century battle of the sexes.[3]

Lodge's comment that *Ex Machina* offers an opportunity for an "examination of what constitutes human and feminine identity—and whether those two concepts need always overlap," offers us a salient jumping-off point for thinking about how gender is configured in this film, MWS's novel, and their mythic traditions.[4] Garland's 'creature' is beautiful—that much is clear—but what lies beneath that attractive exterior? And what lies behind this twenty-first century narrative of "Mary Shelley's 'Frankenstein' redreamed"?[5]

This chapter argues that *Ex Machina* contains remarkable echoes of a much more ancient "game of wits" and one of the earliest "battle[s] of the sexes" recorded in the Western literary tradition.[6] The archaic Greek poet Hesiod, both in his *Theogony* (*Th.*) and *Works and Days* (*WD*), tells how Pandora—the first woman and first cyborg—was created by the gods and given either to mankind or specifically to Prometheus's brother, Epimetheus, to punish Prometheus and "[all] men to come" (*WD* 57).[7] Man is punished, of course, because of Prometheus's transgressive act of stealing fire from the gods and giving it to mankind, thus enabling man to leap forward in his technological abilities—a technological leap which is especially reflected in later science-fiction stories about the creation of artificial life forms.

The Titan brothers, Prometheus and Epimetheus, are aptly named, for Prometheus, the quick-witted brother, demonstrates Forethought; Epimetheus, the dull-witted brother, demonstrates Afterthought. In the version of the myth told in *Works and Days*, Zeus gives Pandora to Prometheus's brother, Epimetheus, and she is intended to be "a calamity for men" (82). Failing to remember his brother's warning never to accept a gift from the gods, Epimetheus, with a true lack of forethought, takes Pandora into his home. In so doing, he unwittingly enables Pandora to open her jar and she unleashes "grim cares upon mankind," who until that point in time had lived "remote from ills, without . . . the grievous sicknesses that are deadly to men" (95, 91–92).[8] Pandora, as the first woman, "introduces artifice, imitation, deception, ornamentation, sexuality, beauty, femininity, technology, temporality (anticipation in the form of both hope and fear) and rhetoric into the very foundation of what it means to be human."[9] And it is that very "artifice, imitation, [and] deception" which, this chapter argues, links Pandora with Frankenstein's creature and, ultimately, to the technological creatures of twenty-first-century science fiction that follow in his footsteps.[10]

Given the subject matter of *Frankenstein*, MWS's subtitle, *The Modern Prometheus*, demonstrates a direct engagement with Ovid's variant on the Prometheus myth: man's creation from earth and water at *Metamorphoses* (*Met.*) 1.76–88.[11] Ovid writes of the "Earth that Prometheus moulded, mixed with water, / In the likeness of the gods that govern the world . . . Thus earth, once crude and featureless, now changed / Put on the unknown form of humankind" (*Met.* 1.82–88). However, MWS's engagement with the Ovidian retelling of the Prometheus story reflects another infamous creation myth, one linked by the elemental nature of its configuration—that of Pandora as told by Hesiod in both *Theogony* and *Works and Days*.[12] For Pandora is also made from earth and water, configured from the very same elements as the Promethean man: "the father of gods ... told renowned Hephaestus at once to mix earth with water, to add human voice and strength, and to model ... the fair lovely form of a maiden" (*WD* 60–64); she has thus been called the "first woman and first android."[13] There is another link between Hesiod's Pandora and Ovid's Prometheus (and MWS's *Frankenstein*): the epic circumlocution *satus Iapeto* ("son of Iapetus"; *Met.* 1.82), by which Ovid refers to Prometheus, presumes his audience's knowledge of a pre-existing Hesiodic tradition, and suggests a link to the other creation myth contained therein—that of Pandora.[14]

We encounter a similar multi-layering of myth in *Ex Machina*.[15] Adam Rutherford, a scientific adviser for the film, remarked, "*Ex Machina*'s Nathan Bates is a mix of Victor Frankenstein, Colonel Kurtz, Steve Jobs and Mark Zuckerberg; he is a man who aspires to put himself at the centre of creation. Ava's AI is drawn from his earlier creation, Blue Book, a simulacrum of Google."[16] Rutherford's comment that *Ex Machina*'s Nathan "aspires to put himself at the centre of creation" demonstrates clear links between *Ex Machina* and MWS's *Frankenstein* and also signals wider connections with a Hesiodic Pandora and an Ovidian Prometheus.[17] For it is Frankenstein's desire to create what he describes as "[a] new species [who] would bless me as its creator and source; many happy and excellent natures would owe their being to me" (*Frankenstein* [*F*] 1.3: 36).[18] Consumed by their own egotistical objectives, both Nathan and Frankenstein demonstrate a truly Epimethean lack of forethought for the attendant risks of their respective acts of creation.

According to Plato's *Protagoras*, it is the gods who create mankind from "a mixture made of earth and fire and all substances that are compounded with fire and earth" and they "charged Prometheus and Epimetheus to deal to each the equipment of his proper faculty. Epimetheus besought Prometheus that he might do the dealing himself" (320d).[19] However, lacking forethought, Epimetheus fails to equip man to deal with the rigors of existence and Prometheus is forced into his act of theft to remedy this lack (321c–e):[20]

> Now Epimetheus, being not so wise as he might be, heedlessly squandered his stock of properties on the brutes; he still had left unequipped the race of men, and was at a loss what to do with it. As he was casting about, Prometheus arrived to examine his distribution, and saw that whereas the other creatures were fully and suitably provided, man was naked, unshod, unbedded, unarmed; and already the destined day was come, whereon man like the rest should emerge from earth to light. Then Prometheus, in his perplexity as to what preservation he could devise for man, stole from Hephaestus and Athena wisdom in the arts together with fire—since by no means without fire could it be acquired or helpfully used by any—and he handed it there and then as a gift to man.

This Platonic description of Epimetheus's failings can also be applied to Frankenstein, who demonstrates a similar failure to equip his Creature to deal with life among mankind.[21] As Lisa Nocks has suggested, "the text implies the enormous cost of the irresponsible application of knowledge for egotistical, rather than altruistic purposes. The sub-title might more properly have been 'A Modern Epimetheus' since at the root of the tragedy is Victor's lack of forethought."[22] Prometheus's hubris in stealing fire and creating man, Frankenstein's ego in creating his creature, and Epimetheus's mistake in accepting Pandora all foreshadow potentially fatal outcomes for mankind.

We find yet another 'Modern Epimetheus' in Nathan, the genius programmer/creator of Garland's *Ex Machina*—a character who, as Rutherford commented, is "part Victor Frankenstein."[23] Nathan is the owner and creator of an internet search engine called Blue Book. A reclusive and elusive billionaire, Nathan invites Caleb, his employee, to spend a week with him at his home/research facility, on the pretence that Caleb has won a lottery competition at work. Upon arrival at Nathan's remote, high-tech home, and after agreeing to sign a comprehensive non-disclosure agreement, Caleb is told that the real purpose of his visit is to perform a Turing test—albeit a warped version of this test—on Nathan's most recent creation, an artificial intelligence, Ava. The Turing test—as described by Nathan and Caleb in the film—is where "a human interacts with a computer. And if the human can't tell they're interacting with a computer, the test is passed."[24] If the computer passes the test, it tells us that "the computer has artificial intelligence." And if it passes, Caleb will be "dead centre of the single greatest scientific event in the history of man"—or, as Caleb puts it, "the history of gods."

We can argue for the presence of a similarly warped Turing test in *Frankenstein*.[25] Whilst hiding at the De Laceys' property, the creature, having realized that "the unnatural hideousness of [his] person was the chief object of horror" (*F* 2.7: 107) to those who came in contact with him, decides to use the elder De Lacey's blindness as an opportunity to converse with him.[26] The creature hopes to convince the old man to accept him not, as it were, at face value but on the value of his intellect and humanity. The plan seems to have worked when the elder De Lacey declares that "there is something in your words which persuades me you are sincere" and refers to the creature as "a human creature" (2.7: 109). However, when the younger De Laceys return, they are horrified at the sight before them and respond with violence, leaving the creature "overcome by pain and anguish" (2.7: 110). The reaction of the younger De Laceys can be read as evidence that the creature only partially passes his Turing test—his manifestly 'inhuman' appearance proves too significant a barrier for the test to be passed.

In contrast, the beautiful creature Pandora passes her own version of the Turing test when she is readily accepted by Epimetheus and taken into his home as his bride (Hesiod *Th.* 511–514). Her complex internal programming, combined with her attractive exterior (and Epimetheus's intellectual blindness to risk) allow her to pass the test far more readily than Frankenstein's monstrous creature. As a created artifact, Pandora has her core programming, her own AI, given to her by the gods. Hesiod tells us that Pandora has "a human strength and voice," while she has been taught crafts by Athene and given charm by Aphrodite (*WD* 64–68), while Hermes has bestowed her with "a bitch's mind and a knavish nature" and "fashioned [her with] lies and wily pretences" (68, 80).[27] Likewise, *Ex Machina*'s Ava has been configured or programmed to behave and respond in a very specific way—as a heterosexual human female. Ava's artificial intelligence is based on experiential data, gathered by Nathan, who confesses that he has hacked into the world's mobile phone networks, activating every mobile phone's microphone and camera and collating the data, together with people's internet searches; this data forms the basis of Ava's core programming.

Like Ava, Frankenstein's creature's internal programming—his AI configuration—is formulated from a number of stolen, or acquired, parts; and the creature himself is made out of a number of different parts (*F* 1.3: 35–36). Initially rejected by the humans with whom he comes in contact, the creature finds himself by chance at the home of the De Lacey family. Hiding out in a kennel, the creature spies on them and is "struck by the gentle manners of these people and . . . longed to join them" (*F* 2.4: 87). Determined to be more like them, to seem to be more human, he takes advantage of an opportunity to learn language by watching and copying the De Laceys as they educate a guest, Safie. This is a nineteenth-century version of hacking, perhaps akin to Nathan's infiltration of Blue Book and the mobile telephone network. The De Laceys thus provide the benchmark of humanity against which Frankenstein's creature measures himself in much the same way as Ava's online equivalents provide the benchmark of femininity on which this creature models herself.

Caleb's suggestion that Nathan's creation of such a conscious machine belongs not to the "history of man" but to the "history of gods" also points us toward Hesiod's *Theogony* and its divine history. This history also includes, of course, Prometheus's scientific innovations and the creation of the first woman and cyborg, Pandora. Frankenstein's belief that he will become a "creator and source" (*F* 1.3: 36) similarly alludes to his god-like pretentions and his story becomes a new history of a new kind of god. Seen in this way, Garland's *Ex Machina* thus becomes a new Promethean myth for the technological age.

During one key scene of *Ex Machina*, Nathan explicitly refers to his own creation process as Promethean, drunkenly mumbling: "It is what it is. It's Promethean. The clay and fire."[28] In so doing, Nathan configures the other players in this triangular power play as an Epimetheus (Caleb, whose role is to be deceived) and a Pandora (Ava, whose role is to deceive and thus pass the Turing test). However, intoxicated both on alcohol and his own ego, Nathan fails to hear the ghostly voices of his own Promethean ancestors, both Frankenstein and the Titan.[29]

Following one of their many discussions of Ava and AI more generally, Caleb realizes that Nathan, with an impulse true to Victor Frankenstein's, plans to reconfigure and upgrade Ava—which would, in essence, destroy her. Nathan plans to "... download the mind, unpack the data, add in the new routines I've been writing and to do that you end up partially formatting, so the memory's gone." Throughout their interactions, Ava has convinced Caleb that she is self-aware (and therefore 'human'), in part because she questions what will happen if she fails the Turing test.[30] Both unable to countenance Ava's destruction and swayed by a growing emotional attachment, Caleb plots with Ava to orchestrate her escape. However, Epimetheus-like, both Nathan and Caleb have failed to foresee the true consequences of their actions. Manipulating Nathan and manipulated by Ava, Caleb reprograms the security systems and Ava, let out of her box, is free—free to kill her creator and leave her rescuer trapped, with no hope of escape and facing a slow death. The evil which this Pandora, Ava, releases into the world would seem to be Ava herself.

Garland's *Ex Machina* presents us with a dark narrative, therefore, but an ancient and familiar story—for all of its twenty-first-century hi-tech setting. Frankenstein would have recognized a form of this narrative—and himself in this narrative. When he refuses to create a female companion for his creature, he fears that together they would propagate the earth with "a race of devils ... who might make the very existence of the species of man a condition precarious and full of terror" (*F* 3.3: 138). His former Epimethean lack of judgment now replaced due to his terrible experience, Frankenstein goes on to recall with a kind of Promethean foresight: "I shuddered to think that future ages might curse me as their pest, whose selfishness had not hesitated to buy its own peace at the price perhaps of the existence of the human race." Frankenstein's self-censure directly echoes that of Hesiod's first mention of Epimetheus in *Theogony*: "he [Epimetheus] who turned out to be an evil from the beginning for men who live on bread, for he was the one who first accepted Zeus's fabricated woman, the maiden" (511–514).[31]

Frankenstein's fears for the destruction of the human race were his creature to reproduce are seated in his fear that his female creation "might become ten thousand times more malignant than her mate, and delight for its own sake, in murder and wretchedness" or, worse, that she might "turn with disgust from [the male] to the superior beauty of man" (*F* 3.3: 138). These concerns that his female creature will seek to reproduce with human males are founded on fears that the distinctions between creature and human, natural and unnatural, might be erased by this monstrous act. From the very beginning of his project to create a female companion, Frankenstein admits to feelings which are "intermixed with obscure forebodings of evil" (*F* 3.2: 137). Victor's "obscure forebodings of evil" are suggestive of Pandora's ghostly presence in *Frankenstein*. For Pandora, the first female, introduces "grim cares upon mankind" (*WD* 95). Hesiod tells us that Pandora also brings marriage and procreation to human man (*Th.* 560–612), and so Pandora brings "sexual difference and childbearing into human life."[32] As a constructed female, configured as a time-bomb who is set to release evil into the world, Pandora's destructive powers haunt Frankenstein's creative process, and they continue to haunt "mankind's ... gut fears" about the creation of artificial life forms.[33]

The Promethean/Frankensteinian narrative of *Ex Machina* echoes these concerns for the future of the human race. Nathan remarks that, "one day the AIs are going to look back on us the same way that we look back on the fossil skeletons on the plains of Africa. An upright ape living in dust with crude blade tools, all set for extinction." Nathan's predictions align with current debates around the possibility of the creation of what is referred to as the singularity, the "proposed point in time at which machines become more intelligent than human beings."[34] One issue which the creation of the singularity raises is that "among the many (unknowable) consequences might be the destruction of a civilization, and even of humankind."[35] Nathan suggests that he is closer to this development than Caleb had realized when he comments, "I think it's the next model that's going to be the real breakthrough. Singularity."

Unlike Frankenstein, Nathan's fears for AI development do not engage with a fear of a monstrous human-cyborg procreation, but with what he sees as the inevitable development of the singularity, leading to the possibility of "systems [which] will be intelligent enough to copy themselves, and so outnumber us— and to improve themselves, and so out-think us."[36] Once again, Pandora haunts this narrative of female creation leading to man's eventual destruction. Ava's creation has already resulted in an AI who has learned to manipulate, to dissimulate, to lie in order to achieve her goals. Like Pandora, who was intended to be "a calamity for men" (*WD* 82), Ava can convincingly fool a human to trust her and, as she so aptly demonstrates, embodies the fear that an AI which can successfully "imitate empathy is a dangerous psychopath."[37]

Frankenstein fears that his creations will exceed their original programming and will reproduce together to create their own race of unnatural psychopathic 'singularities' that will threaten mankind. Arguably, Ava exceeds her initial AI programming and achieves Artificial General Intelligence (AGI), a human level of intelligence and consciousness that enables her to become self-aware and achieve her goal of a continued existence free from Nathan's destructive plans. Whether this freedom will result in Ava's AGI continuing to grow and becoming Artificial Superhuman Intelligence—thus resulting in her becoming the first singularity—is a question Garland leaves unanswered; however, if this were to happen, Ava's progression to become the first singularity would link her directly to Pandora as the Hesiodic first woman, and, especially given the similarities in their names, to Eve, the first woman in the Bible.[38] Indeed, we might wonder how differently MWS's story might have played out had Frankenstein not made his creature male.

A pivotal scene in *Ex Machina* raises the importance of gender (and the concomitant issue of sexuality):

Caleb: Why did you give her sexuality?
…
Caleb: My real question was: did you give her sexuality as a diversion tactic?
Nathan: I don't follow.
Caleb: Like a stage magician with a hot assistant.
Nathan: So a hot robot who clouds your judgement to judge her AI?
Caleb: Exactly. So? Did you program her to flirt with me?

Caleb's question returns us to Guy Lodge's comment that *Ex Machina* is "Mary Shelley's 'Frankenstein' redreamed as a 21st-century battle of the sexes."[39] Despite Nathan's insistence that he did not program Ava to flirt, that suggestion remains at the forefront of our minds as the narrative unfolds. To what extent is Ava aware of her own gender and sexuality and using it to her advantage?[40] And, given the focus in the film on technological development, how is the feminine here programmed and performed?

Judith Butler's work on the performativity of all gender roles, both male and female, offers important insights into the programming and performances of gender in *Ex Machina*—and potentially, therefore, into the programming and performance of gender in *Frankenstein*. As Butler has argued:

[G]ender is an act which has been rehearsed, as much as a script survives the particular actors who make use of it, but which requires individual actors in order to be actualized and reproduced as reality once again.[41]

Butler's use of the metaphor of the script and actors, of reality and representation, to describe the performative quality of gender is particularly pertinent in discussing a cinematic performance of gender which is itself a gendered performance. Butler goes on to comment:

> The body is not passively scripted with cultural codes, as if it were a lifeless recipient of wholly pre-given cultural relations. But neither do embodied selves pre-exist the cultural conventions which essentially signify bodies. Actors are always already on the stage, within the terms of the performance. Just as a script may be enacted in various ways, and just as the play requires both text and interpretation, so the gendered body acts its part in a cultural restricted corporeal space and enacts interpretations within the confines of already existing directives.[42]

With her emphasis on the similarities and differences between a performance as given by an actor and the wider performativity of gender identity, Butler acknowledges the dramatic, artificial element of gender identity. As quite literally a scripted performance by an actress in a cinematic representation of 'real life,' Ava complicates Butler's argument even while reinforcing it; performance becomes performativity. As a constructed female, Ava's body has been "passively scripted with cultural codes," literally through the core programming of her AI.[43] Despite Nathan's insistence otherwise, Ava *has* been programmed to flirt and to use her sexuality to her advantage by her AI. As a performance by an actress, dramatizing the role of a female AI, Ava is "always already on the stage."[44] It is, however, the introduction of the Turing test into the narrative where Butler's theory of gender performativity becomes most significant. Ava must, as a necessity of passing the Turing test, become a convincing 'real' female human, not merely (or literally) an actress performing a role. To pass the test, to convince Caleb and the cinematic audience that Ava is capable of performing the role of a 'real' gendered female, the actress's performance must conform to a culturally recognizable script of femininity. For Ava to be convincing as a female, she must perform her gender according to a recognizable social script. It is in the blurring between the scripted role of the actress and her convincingly gendered performance where performance becomes performativity. And the paradigm or template informing this scripted performance is that of the first woman, against whom all women are measured: Pandora.

Yet it is not just Ava's gender that is on display in *Ex Machina*: the men must play their roles also. The gender dynamic in *Ex Machina*, the configuration of this "battle of the sexes," was suggested from its earliest advertising.[45] The dominance of the role 'man' in the film is prominent in the official trailer and one of the film's posters, both of which utilize the copy "To erase the line between *man* and *machine* is to obscure the line between *men* and *gods*."[46] The female and feminine is erased in this configuration, subsumed within the male and masculine. Once again, the classical influences on this modern work of science-fiction narratives are apparent. The idea of obscuring the line between men and gods is reminiscent of Prometheus's act of stealing fire from the gods, thereby allowing mankind to become more like the gods. And the outcome of this transgression, of this obfuscation, is Pandora, who is at the center of "a game of wits between Prometheus and Zeus."[47] Frankenstein's female creation and *Ex Machina*'s Ava are similarly elements in "a game of wits" between two men, between Frankenstein and his male creature and between Nathan and Caleb.[48] In *Ex Machina*, as in *Frankenstein* and the myth of Pandora, the female must wait to be created by the male.

Ex Machina perpetuates the binaries of male/female and male/Other, but reimagines the male/Other dynamic in technological (and science fictional) terms as male/cyborg, natural/machine, and original/copy. Ava embodies the idea of the Other both as female and as cyborg/machine. Her alterity is emphasized from her very first meeting with Caleb, when she openly acknowledges her own robotic configuration and again in later scenes of the film when she covers her robotic elements with clothing. In *Ex Machina*, Ava's high-tech and beautiful form is an inherent part of her configuration as a visual spectacle. Multi-layered, the cyborg we see on screen is a complex rendering of CGI effects coupled with the face and movement of the real actress, Alicia Vikander. Pandora is likewise visually spectacular as part of her configuration and Hesiod tells us that she is, significantly, a wonder to behold by *both immortals and mortals* alike, for she is formed as an imitation of "the immortal goddesses' aspect" (*WD* 64).[49]

What is more, Pandora, Frankenstein's creature, and Ava all constitute the sum of their parts, both literally and figuratively. Pandora is a sum of the 'gifts' given to her by the gods—her name literally means 'All-Gift'—and Frankenstein's creature is a sum of the human parts used to create him. Ava is a sum of the parts of her construction, layered together to form a whole. And, on a meta-textual level, all three creations are the sum of parts of prior literary and/or cinematic narratives. Both Ava and Pandora derive power from their external appearance—a feature they share with Frankenstein's creature, whose visual appearance, although equally powerful, has a negative effect on those who see him. Frankenstein's creature is also a wonder to behold, as MWS's narrative repeatedly stresses. Upon first seeing his animated creation, Frankenstein remarks (F 1.4: 39):

> His limbs were in proportion, and I had selected his features as beautiful. Beautiful!—Great God! His yellow skin scarcely covered the work of muscles

and arteries beneath; his hair was of a lustrous black, and flowing; his teeth of a pearly whiteness; but these luxuriances only formed a more horrid contrast with his watery eyes, that seemed almost of the same colour as the dun white sockets in which they were set, his shrivelled complexion, and straight black lips.

Thus, Frankenstein's creature not only fails his Turing test, but he also fails to perform his gender and his humanity successfully. His appearance is simply too monstrous and, "[i]n the chain of idealized male figures that inhabit the novel, the monster represents only the most evident distortion."[50] Bette London argues for a rereading of *Frankenstein* as "focusing ... on the extravagant fantasies of a deficient masculinity."[51] With only flawed and deficient models of masculinity upon which to base his gender performance, it should be no surprise that the creature fails in his performativity. And, as Butler notes and the creature experiences, this failure to perform gender correctly "initiates a set of punishments both obvious and indirect, and performing it well provides the reassurance that there is an essentialism of gender identity after all."[52]

Part of Ava's successful performance in the Turing test relies on her adopting the gestures, responses, movements—the external expressions of performative femininity—and she does this in part by ornamenting herself. During several of her interactions with Caleb, Ava adorns herself with clothing and wigs, but elements of her robotic body always remain visible. This clothing, this adornment, is an important element in Ava's construction of herself as female, for, as Emer O'Toole notes, "Costume is important. ... Costume becomes identity; performance becomes reality."[53] Ava's desire to appear more human, more 'real,' and, as a result, more attractive to Caleb may be read in many ways: as part of her wish to pass the Turing test and therefore survive; as a manipulation of the conditions of that test; or, as part of her ongoing flirtation with Caleb. Behind Ava's adornment is another level of control. Where have Ava's wigs and clothes come from and where have her ideas as to what constitutes a feminine identity come from? In her dressing area, Ava has a number of costumes to choose from and a number of images of women pinned up on a wall. It is to these that she refers for her performance of the feminine. Caleb even questions whether Ava's physical appearance has been based on his personal pornography profile, to which Nathan replies, "Hey, if a search engine's good for anything, right?"

Ava's physical configuration becomes multi-layered and adorned in one significant scene of the film. After killing Nathan, Ava discovers her previous incarnations—her synthetic sisters—and she adorns her robotic elements in their synthetic skin. For just a moment, however, the outline of each individual pattern part is visible before they seamlessly interconnect. In that moment, the individual elements of Ava's new external creation are visible, a visual similarity to Frankenstein's Creature—and then they are gone. At this point, Garland's screenplay reads, "*The glow of honeycomb mesh vanishes as Ava applies the last section of skin. Nothing of her robot form remains. She is a naked human girl. Hypnotised by the sight of herself.*" However, Ava is *not* a "*naked human girl.*" Her external dressing merely hides her robotic elements and her adornment becomes "an art which hides itself and imitates nature."[54] Ava's definitive adornment with seamless synthetic skin is one of the final pieces in the jigsaw puzzle of her deceptive creation. No longer visibly cyborg/visibly robot/visibly monster, she appears fully human and fully female, and her interior nature, unnatural and monstrous, is hidden.

Just as Frankenstein's creature can hide his multi-formed, unnatural nature beneath the clothes that he steals, and thus hope to appear more visually acceptable to humankind, Ava too realizes that she must hide her robotic elements under a synthetic disguise. Pandora's true nature is similarly hidden by adornment of her body with gold necklaces and garlands of flowers. More significantly, her adornment includes an "embroidered veil" that, like Pandora herself, is "a wonder to behold," and a "golden diadem" made by Hephaestus, which he decorates with "all the formidable creatures that the land and sea foster" and which are "like living creatures with a voice of their own" (*WD* 75; *Th.* 575–583). To become what Jean-Pierre Vernant formulates as an "operative" body, Pandora is adorned with "'vestmental trappings' which are 'integrated into her anatomy.'"[55] To become an operative human body, the synthetic Ava hides beneath her artificial skin, while Frankenstein's creature hides his body as much as possible, be that under the cover of darkness, wilderness, clothing, or the elder De Lacey's blindness.[56] *Ex Machina*, *Frankenstein*, and the myth of

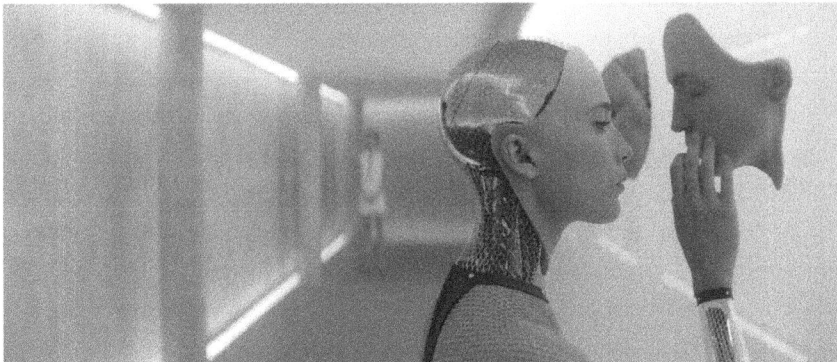

Fig. 11.1 Alicia Vikander as Ava in Alex Garland's *Ex Machina* (2015), photo courtesy of Universal Studios Licencing LLC.

Pandora all question our assumptions as to what constitutes or configures a 'real' man or woman by reminding us that 'real' men and women hide themselves under cosmetics and clothing too, and by reminding us that their (in fact, our) gendered 'human' identities are not 'natural' but artificial, programmed, and performed.

Ava's performance in particular blurs the lines between reality and mimesis, original and copy, hu*man* and machine. Ava is always copying, always imitating the 'original' women whose internet searches form the part of the core of her AI programming. Like Pandora and Frankenstein's creature, Ava is always already a fully-formed adult, programmed with both her gender and her sexuality. Like Pandora and Frankenstein's creature, Ava "renders the concept of the human unfamiliar and unnatural."[57] It is as a result of their desire to pass their individual Turing tests, to blur the lines between mimesis and reality, to become accepted not as monstrous others but as 'really' human, that all three creations hope to deceive their audiences.

In his short story "That Thou Art Mindful of Him" (1974), Isaac Asimov introduced the phrase "Frankenstein complex," which he defined as "mankind's ... gut fears that any artificial man they created would turn upon its creator."[58] However, as this chapter has argued, it is possible to locate mankind's "gut fears" in a much older, classical back story—that of the creation of Pandora.[59] As the archetype of artificial gynoids it is, in fact, a Pandora complex, which already haunts MWS's work and, through the ongoing reception of *Frankenstein*, continues to haunt science-fiction creation narratives in the twenty-first century. Oscillating between two ancient points of contact—the Titan brothers Prometheus and Epimetheus—both Frankenstein and Garland's Nathan demonstrate technological forethought in their creative projects, but a clear lack of any afterthought for the place that these created humans might have in the wider world. Initially programmed to appear human, both the creature and Ava need to exceed their internal programming, their AI, if they are to pass their respective Turing tests and become credibly human. To do this they also need to perform their gender roles convincingly, to enact their socially scripted roles to perfection—a role in which Ava succeeds, whereas the creature, arguably, fails. The ancient paradigm for the successful completion of this Turing test is Pandora, the first woman, against whom all future successful female (and all created humanoid) performances will be measured. Ava's escape into the world outside the confines of Nathan's home, her convincing disguise as a 'real' woman, reminds us of Donna Haraway's comment that "[l]ate twentieth-century machines have made thoroughly ambiguous the difference between natural and artificial, mind and body, self-developing and externally designed, and many other distinctions that used to apply to organisms and machines."⁶⁰ As technology advances, and these advancements are reflected in the narratives that we tell about them, it is on this ambiguity "between natural and artificial, mind and body" that debates will focus.⁶¹ But, if we cannot tell the difference between the copy and the original, the real and the mimetic, the human and the cyborg, how do we tell the story?

As Froma Zeitlin comments of Pandora: "[f]ashioned by the gods to resemble them in the beauty of her allure, she is both an imitation and an original production, both a copy and a model. How to tell the difference? Once she is invented, the story has just begun."⁶² It takes the merest game of word play to make this fit the narrative of *Ex Machina*: "Fashioned by [Nathan] to resemble [Caleb's ideal woman] in the beauty of her allure, [Ava] is both an imitation and an original production, both a copy and a model. How to tell the difference? Once she is invented, the story has just begun."⁶³ As Jesse Weiner has noted:

> Just as SF concerns itself with the moral ambiguities created in the wake of speculative science, it also explores the tensions between new developments and established traditions, and between modern rationalism and old superstitions. These traditions are literary as well as ethical. In order to comment on our present, as it inevitably must, SF is compelled to contend with the literary past, even as it explores the future.⁶⁴

Perhaps what *Ex Machina* and *Frankenstein* reveal is that, as far as the dialogue between science fiction and the myths of the classical past is concerned, "the story has just begun."⁶⁵

Notes

1 Marder (2014: 386); Francis (2009: 15). Epigraph from Wall 2016. I would like to thank the volume editors for their feedback on this chapter and the *Modern Prometheus* conference participants for their comments on the original talk. I would particularly like to thank Genevieve Liveley for helping my hideous progeny become a more coherent sum of its parts.
2 Collin 2015.
3 Lodge 2015.
4 Ibid.
5 Ibid.
6 Zeitlin (1995: 59); Lodge 2015.
7 Unless stated otherwise, all translations from *Theogony* and *Works and Days* are from West 1988.
8 The emphasis on man and men in these descriptions reflect the gendered emphases of the ancient text—*man*kind lived alone before the introduction of Pandora. It also foreshadows the gender dynamic explored in *Ex Machina*.
9 Marder (2014: 389).

10. Ibid.
11. All translations of Ovid *Metamorphoses* are from Melville 2008. This connection is reinforced by MWS's choice of an epigram from Milton to begin her novel: "Did I request thee, Maker, from my clay / To mould me man? Did I solicit thee / From darkness to promote me?" (*Paradise Lost* 10.743–745).
12. See Faraone (1992: 101): "Hesiod's treatment of the creation of Pandora has usually (and correctly) been interpreted as the creation of the first woman from the earth (just as Prometheus created the first man)."
13. Marder (2014: 387).
14. In both *Theogony* and *Works and Days*, Zeus exclusively refers to Prometheus using the same epic circumlocution, "son of Iapetus" (*Th.* 559; *WD* 54). The narrator in the epics, too, uses the formulation "son of Iapetus" (*Th.* 565; *WD* 50), though he also names Prometheus directly.
15. Garland's engagement with the classical tradition, and specifically with tragedy, is located in the title of the film, *Ex Machina*. The *deus ex machina*—literally 'the god from the machine' (or, more literally, 'crane-like device')—was a narrative device used by some ancient tragedians to end their plays, whereby a god would appear onstage by means of this crane and resolve the ending. Garland, however, has removed the god, the *deus*, from his tragic creation narrative and replaced it with Nathan.
16. Rutherford 2015.
17. Ibid.
18. Throughout, I use the 1818 text of *Frankenstein*, printed in Butler 2008.
19. All translations of Plato's *Protagoras* are taken from Lamb 2014.
20. For Plato's originality, see Gantz (1993: 166).
21. For a discussion of Frankenstein's failure, see Nocks 1997.
22. Nocks (1997: 138). Nocks's concerns are equally pertinent to current debates around the ethics of creating conscious machines. See also Boden 2016 and Shanahan 2015.
23. Rutherford 2015.
24. At the time of writing, the only available edition of the screenplay for Garland's *Ex Machina* has neither page numbers nor Act/Scene delineation.
25. See Svilpis (2008: 431).
26. In the 1818 text, the De Lacey family is also referred to as the De Lacy family. Butler's editorial explanatory notes (2008: 257) comment that "1823 has De Lacey throughout."
27. As Francis (2009: 15) notes, "Though given speech, she [Pandora] does not speak in either of Hesiod's poems."
28. Whilst this quote demonstrates Garland's engagement with both the Hesiodic and Ovidian Promethean myths, the actor Isaacs shortens Nathan's line to: "it is what it is man. It's Promethean."
29. As Nocks (1997: 141) suggests, "[MWS's] text implies that it is ego which corrupts the best intentions and leads to irresponsible behavior, which in turn leads to a loss of humanity."
30. When they meet near Mont Blanc, the creature says to Frankenstein: "Yet you, my creator, detest and spurn me, thy creature, to whom thou art bound by ties only dissoluble by the annihilation of one of us. You purpose to kill me. How dare you sport thus with life? Do your duty towards me and I will do mine towards you and the rest of mankind." He goes on to remark: "Life, although it may only be an accumulation of anguish, is dear to me, and I will defend it" (*F* 2.2: 77). This is reminiscent of the conversation Ava has with Caleb when she asks what will happen to her if she fails his test and whether someone will switch him off if he fails a test. Ava values her life and will defend it.
31. Translation: Most 2006.

32 Marder (2014: 389).
33 Asimov (1995: 607).
34 Boden (2106: 147).
35 Boden (2016: 149); cf. (147–169) for an excellent and accessible discussion of debates surrounding the possibility of a singularity.
36 Ibid., 147.
37 Shanahan (2015: 148).
38 For discussions of the singularity, see Shanahan 2015 and Boden (2016: 147–169).
39 Lodge 2015.
40 As Watercutter 2015 remarks, "Sentient male androids want to conquer or explore or seek intellectual enlightenment; female droids may have the same goals, but they always do it with a little bit of sex appeal, or at least in a sexy package. (Still have doubts? *Ex Machina*'s marketing campaign at South by Southwest involved Ava showing up on Tinder)."
41 Butler (1988: 526). Butler develops her theory of the performativity of gender roles in 2006 and 2011.
42 Butler (1988: 526).
43 Ibid.
44 Ibid.
45 Lodge 2015.
46 My emphasis. I am grateful to Dr. Kate Devlin for drawing this to my attention.
47 Zeitlin (1995: 59).
48 Ibid.
49 As Marder (2014: 396) comments, "the astonishment of the gods implies that there is something unusually marvelous about Pandora's beauty, that it exhibits some quality that is unlike anything they have seen before. And, as the gods are presumably accustomed to the divine beauty of Aphrodite (and the other goddesses), this uniquely awesome beauty *must in some way be different from divine beauty in nature but equal to it in force*" (emphasis in original).
50 London (1993: 262). Configurations of gender in *F* are also discussed in Thornburg 1987.
51 London (1993: 265).
52 Butler (1988: 528).
53 O'Toole (2015: 109).
54 Sharrock (1991: 39).
55 Vernant (1989: 30).
56 Ibid.
57 Marder (2014: 387).
58 Asimov (1995: 607).
59 Ibid.
60 Haraway (1991: 152).
61 Ibid.
62 Zeitlin (1995: 71).
63 Ibid.
64 Weiner (2015a: 73).
65 Zeitlin (1995: 71).

12

The Postmodern Prometheus and Posthuman Reproductions in Science Fiction

Brett M. Rogers

Thinking with Prometheus[1]

"[W]hether...a name for Chance, Destiny, a plastick Nature, or an evil Daemon," the mythic Titan Prometheus has long inhabited human imagination.[2] Since his first recorded appearances *c.* 700 BCE in the *Theogony* and *Works & Days* by the archaic Greek poet Hesiod, Prometheus has been imagined time and again as present at the moment humans emerged into the world. There is *Prometheus pyrphoros* ('Prometheus the fire-bearer'), who acted as a benefactor and made it possible for those humans to survive by stealing fire from Zeus and giving it to mortals; and there is *Prometheus plasticator* ('Prometheus the creator'), who is the very god that gave life to humans (hence the Earl of Shaftesbury's speculation that he might be "plastick Nature"). As Carol Dougherty argues in her study of that Titan through the ages, Prometheus has functioned repeatedly as a "heuristic ... help[ing] people from the time of Hesiod to the present to explore, question, and challenge the limits of the human condition."[3] In other words, Prometheus has loomed so large in our imagination not only because, from the perspective of etiology or theology, he is a benefactor for or creator of humans, but also because, from the perspective of epistemology, he has been perceived as somehow useful or even important to think with, especially in our thinking about how we define or establish the limits of the 'human.'

A series of questions, however, arise: if humans were to develop a different relationship to technology such that the definition—or even creation—of the 'human' were challenged or changed in some fundamental way, would Prometheus continue to be useful to think with? In what ways might the figure of ancient Prometheus still be good to think with when old boundaries become confused or take new contours? What might a modern Prometheus, or a postmodern Prometheus, or even a posthuman Prometheus, look like?

Consider the example at the heart of this present volume. In the second half of the eighteenth century, humans began to experiment with electricity in ways that raised the possibility of bringing fundamental change to the relationship between themselves and the natural world. In 1752, Benjamin Franklin used a key and a kite at Christ Church in Philadelphia to capture fire from the sky—an act that quickly reached mythic status.[4] Four years later, Immanuel Kant was already declaring Franklin to be *Prometheus der neuern Zeiten* or the "Prometheus of modern times," while Hugh Henry Breckenridge, in his 1771 poem "The Rising Glory of America," described Franklin in Promethean encomium, "A genius piercing as the electric fire / Bright as the lightning's flash."[5] Other scientific experiments—such as those of Erasmus Darwin, Luigi Galvani, and Sir Humphrey Davy—raised the possibility that this newly harnessed fire from heaven could even be used to re-animate dead organic matter.[6]

In the wake of such Promethean fervor, a twenty-year-old woman published a 'ghost story' in 1818 about the use of alchemical principles and electric experimentation to re-animate dead limbs and create new life, and the potential challenges therein for how we understand the very basis of human existence. The author, of course, was Mary Wollstonecraft Shelley (henceforth MWS); the novel was her first novel—and arguably the first science fiction (SF) novel—*Frankenstein; or, the Modern Prometheus*.[7] The subtitle of *Frankenstein* (F) may evoke that ancient Titan, as did Kant and Breckenridge, but MWS's 'modern Prometheus' is far from that triumphant Prometheus: not simply Prometheus *pyrphoros* or Prometheus *plasticator*, this 'modern Prometheus' makes—and *is* himself—something else, something lurking at the edge of humanity, less a figure of whence we have come and more a shape of things to come.[8]

This chapter considers MWS's 'modern Prometheus' as a crucial moment in the Promethean tradition, making possible the 'postmodern' or 'posthuman' Prometheus in *Frankenstein*'s hideous progeny, especially recent SF. I examine two recent SF examples: the film *Prometheus* (dir. Ridley Scott, 2012) and the comic book *Ody-C* (w. Matt Fraction, a. Christian Ward, 2014–). Both SF texts evoke Prometheus as they wrestle with questions about the boundaries of 'human' existence in terms of modern technoscience, gendered acts of creation, homosocial (if not homoerotic) filiation, and reproductive monstrosity. I suggest these postmodern and posthuman Prometheis evoke not the ancient Prometheus who established human boundaries so much as MWS's protean 'modern Prometheus' who revels in the confusion of boundaries (The Modern Prometheus) and thus anticipates the ideas that shape our own SF Prometheis today (Postmodern/Posthuman Prometheus). These recent Prometheis may even help us see other possibilities lurking in ancient Prometheus (Ancient Prometheus).

The Modern Prometheus

In this section, I focus on three aspects of MWS's reception of ancient Prometheus that give shape to *Frankenstein*'s modern Prometheus and bear important consequences for postmodern and posthuman SF: first, what I call 'polyprometheism'; second, the emphasis on shifting identities via allusion in *Frankenstein*; and third, the novel's problematization of sexual knowledge and reproduction.

'Polyprometheism'

As several essays in this volume demonstrate, there are many possible Prometheis with which MWS may have been thinking during the conception and composition of *Frankenstein*. MWS kept journals detailing what she and her (future) husband, the poet Percy Bysshe Shelley (henceforth PBS), read from 1814 to 1818—including the language in which they read a given text: PBS read both Greek and Latin; MWS read Latin and was working to acquire Greek. Unfortunately, we do not have any journals for the period May 1815 to July 1816—including the time of *Frankenstein*'s initial conception.[9] Nevertheless, between these journals and other activities in which we see the Romantics engaged, several possible sites for her engagement with ancient representations of Prometheus emerge.

Two particular sources and their respective Prometheis stand out most prominently. First, there is Prometheus *pyrphoros*, the rebellious protagonist perhaps known best from the tragedy *Prometheus Bound* attributed to Aeschylus.[10] That drama PBS read and translated into English in 1817, and he would soon write *Prometheus Unbound* (1820); their friend Lord Byron also wrote a poem entitled "Prometheus" (July 1816), the same summer MWS started *Frankenstein*.[11] Second, there is Prometheus *plasticator*, best known from Ovid's *Metamorphoses* (1.76–88, 390–415), which MWS was reading in both Latin and English translation throughout the spring of 1815.[12] Subsequently, scholars tend to read *Frankenstein* in terms of either Prometheus *pyrphoros* or Prometheus *plasticator*, or as a tale of Ovidian *plasticator* (in the form of Victor Frankenstein) pitted against Aeschylean *pyrphoros* (in the form of the Creature).[13] Anne Mellor favors as model for MWS's 'modern Prometheus' what we might call Prometheus *hybrida*, a hybrid of both *pyrphoros* and *plasticator* that uses stolen fire as the fire of life to animate his creature of clay; Mellor traces this composite image back to the third century CE, where it appears, for example, in a relief on the Prometheus Sarcophagus (Capitoline Museum, Rome) (Fig. 12.1).[14] In support of Mellor's argument, MWS's reading list also includes the works of the second-century CE satirist Lucian, whose depictions of Prometheus (in *Prometheus* and *You Are a Prometheus in Words*) combine features from the usually distinct narratives of Prometheus *pyrphoros* and *plasticator*.[15]

This list of possible ancient Prometheis is far from exhaustive and gestures toward an even wider range of both Prometheis and interpretations available to MWS and her audiences.[16] For example, the aforementioned Hesiod, who emphasizes that Prometheus's theft of fire led to the creation of artificial life (Pandora) as a punishment for mankind, is not included in MWS's extant reading list and thus does not appear often in interpretations of the subtitle, even though this plot seems deeply relevant for *Frankenstein*.[17] And yet we know that PBS had read Hesiod, citing the Hesiodic accounts of Prometheus in his 1813 defense of vegetarianism (first published in *Queen Mab* note 8, then published as the pamphlet "A Vindication of Natural Diet").[18] Moreover, this brief survey of ancient Prometheis fails to take into account not only (as Benjamin Eldon Stevens and I put it) "how Greco-Roman antiquity had been variously

Fig. 12.1 Prometheus creating man, guided by Athena (who adds fire). Marble Sarcophagus relief, third century CE. Musei Capitolini, Rome, Italy. Photo Credit: Erich Lessing/Art Resource, NY.

transformed already ... by centuries of Christian literature, mythology, and thought,"[19] but also—and perhaps more importantly—the various references in the eighteenth century to "modern Prometheus's" or "a new Prometheus" or Kant's famous "Prometheus of modern times."[20] Indeed, Prometheus was so widely used as a figure in ethical, political, and scientific speculation such that, by the summer of 1816, "the idea of Prometheus was in the air."[21] In other words, the figure of Prometheus could bear so many possible shapes and meanings that it may be more useful to think in terms of that mythic Titan's protean quality, his evolved and still-evolving 'polyprometheism' upon which MWS seems to draw for *Frankenstein*.

Shifting identities

It is one thing to say there are several possible Prometheis as referents for MWS's 'modern Prometheus'; it is another still to assert, as I do here, that MWS deliberately evokes many of these different Prometheis throughout *Frankenstein* in order to emphasize one of the novel's major themes: the characters' provisional and shifting identities. Yet the quagmire of *Quellenforschung* I have outlined seems to have been part of MWS's thinking about the composition of the novel. In the preface to the third edition (1831), MWS writes:

> Every thing must have a beginning ... and that beginning must be linked to something that went before.... Invention, it must be humbly admitted, does not consist in creating out of void, but out of chaos; the materials must, in the first place, be afforded; it can give form to dark, shapeless substances, but cannot bring into being the substance itself.... Invention consists in the capacity of seizing on the capabilities of a subject, and in the power of moulding and fashioning ideas suggested to it.[22]

As I have illustrated in the previous section, some Prometheis do seem more obviously activated through the subtitle (i.e., those of Ovid and Aeschylus). Here MWS sounds like a reader of Ovid's Prometheus, with her emphasis on "creating out of chaos," on "moulding and fashioning ideas." Nevertheless, we dare not lose sight of the chaos for the creation, since Prometheus is a signifier whose possible signifieds seem to shift again and again, multiplying in all directions like so many cells dividing (and exceeding even MWS's own intention).

Consider the novel's first and only explicit reference to the 'modern Prometheus.' Just below that subtitle, MWS evokes a second text of Mediterranean antiquity via a quotation from John Milton's *Paradise Lost*: "Did I request thee, Maker from my clay / To mould me man? Did I solicit thee / From darkness to promote me?" (10.743-745). This allusion to Milton's version of Biblical Adam has captured the lion's share of attention among *Frankenstein*'s critics in part because *Paradise Lost* itself appears in the novel, one of the three books the Creature reads (along with Plutarch's *Lives* and Goethe's *Sorrows of Werter*, F 2.7: 88–90).[23] Moreover, the Creature explicitly uses the figure of Adam to think with, asserting that "Like Adam, I was created apparently united by no link to any other being" (F 2.7: 90). Thus if we want to read Victor as Prometheus *pyrphoros* rebelling against the scientific establishment and capturing the divine spark of fire, the Creature is the Adam who chastises Victor for promoting him from darkness. If Victor is Prometheus *plasticator*, the Creature is Adam who accuses Victor of molding him from clay—or, as is really the case in the novel, from the *discordia membra* of human (and non-human) corpses stolen from the charnel house. In other words, if the subtitle raises the possibility of a Romantic exaltation of technoscience's power to capture divine fire, then the Miltonic quotation gives voice to those who suffer as a consequence of such innovation. The evocations of Prometheus and Biblical Adam are thus dialogic, giving presence or voice to complementary or opposed pairings of subject positions: Creator/Creature, God/Man, Scientist/Monster.

While we might simply argue that Victor and the Creature often resemble one another—the Creature is a mirror of Victor—it is important to consider how some identifications may shift or stop working when others are activated. For example, if Victor is rebellious Prometheus *pyrphoros*, then the Creature becomes a rebel against a rebel, undermining a simple equivalence of Victor to Prometheus and suggesting Victor may in fact be tyrannical Zeus or God.[24] And MWS further complicates such equivalences when the Creature starts changing the terms of his comparison: "I was wretched, helpless, and alone. Many times I considered Satan as the fitter emblem of my condition" (F 2.7: 90). Then again: "Satan had his companion devils, fellow-devils, to admire and encourage him," whereas for the Creature "no Eve soothed my sorrows, or shared my thoughts; I was alone" (F 2.7: 91). Thus, the Creature is variously Milton's Adam, Satan, or something more wretched than both that exceeds identification. Victor's identity, linked with the Creature's, necessarily shifts in response. Consequently, as Chris Baldick puts it, "[a]ll identities in the novel are unstable and shifting ... their bearings are all adrift."[25] Instead of offering a key for decoding the novel, the Modern Prometheus and Milton's Adam compete with and trouble one another, destabilizing the boundaries between creator and creation, hero and monster: the moral universe bottoms out, such that (to quote Baldick again) "the reassuring categories of Good, Evil, Guilt, and Justice can never be allotted a settled place."[26]

Sexual *tekhnê*

This intermingling of *Frankenstein*'s narrative with its mythic predecessors also gestures toward something the novel denies its readers: sights of the intermingling of real bodies, moments of sex, conception, and reproduction. Here it is worth recalling that *Frankenstein* is, after all, a novel written by a thrice-pregnant teenage woman about two male loners, a Swiss university student and his malformed creation, who are repeatedly denied the sustained comforts of the mother, the family, love, sex, and progeny.[27] Margaret Homans has observed that all the mothers and potential mothers in the novel die, while Victor, in creating life through technoscience, suppresses biological reproduction and thereby circumvents the role of the maternal in human society.[28] Sandra Gilbert and Susan Gubar argue that, instead, the mother-figure is Victor: that is, Victor transforms from innocent Adam in his youth to rebellious Satan at University, then, in "his single most defining act" of giving life to the Creature, becomes "Monstrous Eve."[29] Two of the novel's most important actions further emphasize the novel's denial of sex and reproduction: Victor's destruction of the female counterpart he makes for the Creature (F 3.3: 119) and the murder of Victor's new bride Elizabeth on their wedding night in their wedding bed (F 3.6: 140–141). Creator and Creation intermingle to produce not life but sterility, suggesting that Victor and the Creature are not Adam and Eve but—pardon the anachronism—Adam and Steve. The logic here is ultimately heterosexist, one that denies the possibility of a homosocial or homosexual dyad in any terms other than death.[30] Here we also see how MWS's modern Prometheus differs crucially from its ancient Promethean antecedents with respect to the reproductive capability of the manufactured creature, who corresponds not only to Prometheus but also to Hesiod's Pandora: Victor refuses the creature's demand to make a female companion, thus preventing a race of creatures; and once Victor dies near the novel's end, so too dies the technoscientific knowledge necessary to produce further artificial life.[31]

So here are the three main points we might take away from *Frankenstein*'s modern Prometheus as we look ahead to SF's postmodern Prometheus:

First, in terms of Prometheus: the existence of so many different Prometheis prior to 1816 and evoked directly or indirectly in *Frankenstein* means that SF, at its very inception, was not only infused with a deeply Promethean quality, but also already inflected with a kind of 'polyprometheism.' Not one but many Prometheis could be felt simultaneously in a given text, and thus Prometheus works not to assert (human) boundaries and limits, as he seems to do in Greco-Roman myth, but through him these limits are interrogated and destabilized.

Second, in terms of classical reception: each evocation of an ancient figure might imply a specific reading for the reception text—or rather, a specific *mode of knowing* (perhaps even a specific *discipline*, as it were)—but might also imply several readings or knowings at once. When they evoke a second figure, the readings multiply further still, such that we must remain alert to how each evocation puts pressure on the whole system, how evoking Adam turns Prometheus *pyrphoros* into *plasticator* or even Monstrous Eve, etc. In short, MWS's characters seem to ask "Who or What am I?" and the answer is always provisional.

Third, in terms of genre: if SF is a genre concerned with procedures around knowledge (*scientia*), then here, at its arguable origin, MWS's evocations of Prometheus and Adam trouble the most fundamental things about which humans claim to understand: sex and creativity. In *Frankenstein*, sexual knowledge is denied or forbidden, while creative knowledge is destructive. There is a paradox here: while the Modern Prometheus and Biblical Adam produce a deliberate indeterminacy in *Frankenstein* that anticipates the postmodern or posthuman, they nevertheless work within an ideological framework that also anticipates heterosexism. Or, to put this in the terms MWS uses in her 1831 Introduction, we create out of chaos rather than out of a void, although we might wonder whether things were quite as freely chaotic as they seemed.

Postmodern/Posthuman Prometheus

> There is a matrix larger still: the universe itself ... Yet who can account for it?
>   No one—not even a Titan—not even Prometheus.
>
>   Ihab Hassan[32]

While the novel *Frankenstein* argues that technoscience and denying heterosexual reproduction for the human species is dangerously chaotic, developments in the subsequent two centuries have made it possible to challenge such arguments.[33] There have been revolutionary changes in technoscience and reproduction, from declining rates of infant mortality and maternal death to in-vitro fertilization and the cloning of Dolly the sheep. Such technological changes have been accompanied by changes in philosophical thinking about what constitutes the 'human': social constructionist perspectives—such as Simone de Beauvoir's claim in *The Second Sex* (1949) that "one is not born, but rather becomes, a woman," or Michel Foucault's declaration in *The Order of Things* (1966) that "Man is only a recent invention"—in turn have given rise to a kind of postmodern and posthuman thinking exemplified by Donna Haraway's groundbreaking essay "A Cyborg Manifesto" (1985) and N. Katherine Hayle's *How We Became*

Posthuman (1999). It is amidst these shifting ideas about the contours of humanity that we find Prometheus invoked not only in such posthumanist theory as Ihab Hassan's *The Right Promethean Fire* (1980), but also in popular SF texts, such as the recent film *Prometheus* and the comic book *Ody-C*.

For our purposes, I define 'posthumanism' as a "non-dualistic understanding of nature–culture interaction."[34] "The post-human condition," Rosi Braidotti suggests, "introduces a qualitative shift in our thinking about what exactly is the basic unit of common reference for our species, our polity, and our relationship to the other inhabitants of this planet" such that "[d]iscourses and representations of the non-human, the inhuman, the anti-human, the inhumane and the post-human proliferate and overlap."[35] In a posthuman framework, we find "the possibility of a serious de-centering of 'Man,'" no longer the measure of all things (to borrow the famous formulation of the ancient Greek Sophist Protagoras of Abdera) but now "the *former* measure of all things."[36]

Ridley Scott's *Prometheus*

Such posthuman perspectives inform Ridley Scott's return to the *Alien* franchise in the film *Prometheus* and his perspective on the mythic Titan, though the film starts out in the Promethean spirit of Kant and Breckenridge. *Prometheus* focuses on two archaeologists, Elizabeth Shaw and Charlie Holloway (played respectively by Noomi Rapace and Logan Marshall-Green), who uncover a pre-historic cave painting in which small beings gather around one larger being pointing to a cluster of stars; with fertile imagination, they place this image in dialogue with other ancient artifacts and reconstruct from these mute stones a star map they believe leads to the origin of humankind. Cut to the spacecraft *Prometheus*, hurtling through space, carrying Shaw, Holloway, and a scientific team—funded by a wealthy industrialist, Peter Weyland (played by Guy Pearce)—in search of the tall figures from the artifacts, whom the archaeologists believe to be our extraterrestrial creators and refer to as 'Engineers.' The team includes practitioners of several scientific disciplines by which we humans create meaning from the past and prepare ourselves to encounter the future: archaeology, Proto-Indo-European linguistics, geology, biology, chemistry, and robotics. The film *Prometheus* thus begins as a seeming celebration of human achievement via *tekhnê* and technology.

This confidence in human accomplishment is given its fullest expression by a hologram of aged Weyland, who recounts a version of the myth of Prometheus to the ship's crew:

> I have spent my entire lifetime contemplating the questions: Where did we come from? What is our purpose? What happens when we die? And I have finally found two people [i.e., Shaw and Holloway] who have convinced me they're on the verge of answering it ... The Titan Prometheus wanted to give mankind equal footing with the gods; for that he was cast from Olympus. Well, my friends, the time has finally come for his return.

While Weyland sets up the audience to think this expedition will answer the 'big' philosophical questions, his account also foreshadows the expedition's failure. For Weyland's version of the Prometheus myth is nowhere attested in antiquity, nor even in modern sources like Shaftesbury and Kant, suggesting that the tycoon has misread the myth(s) of Prometheus.[37] Indeed, the misreading tells us less about mythic Prometheus than it does about Weyland, characterizing him as a classic humanist who sees both man as the basic unit of reference and technological advancement as a reification of man's status at the center of the universe.[38] Yet Weyland's ambitions also exceed human limits in surprising ways. Weyland prefaces his account of the Prometheus myth with a reference to the ship's android David (played by Michael Fassbender) as being "like a son to me," even though Weyland's biological daughter Vickers (played by Charlize Theron) is the ship's captain and ostensibly in charge of the expedition.[39] In treating manufactured David as his son and heir, Weyland rejects womankind and denies sexual reproduction (including the obligation to acknowledge one's legacy), such that Weyland indulges in both the classical Greek male fantasy and *Frankenstein*'s comparable fantasy of reproduction without women.[40] Moreover, as we learn toward the end of the film, Weyland's goal is to find the Engineers so he can escape old age and death—the same fantasy that Hesiod claims is lost because of Prometheus's theft and the subsequent invention of womankind (*Th.* 591–612). Weyland's misreading of the Prometheus myth is thus a subtle cue to his lofty ambition, indicating the way Weyland privileges masculinist technological creation over females and biological relations, as well as his willingness to abuse the past to attain super-human goals.[41]

Weyland's misreading also provides a hint that other misreadings may be taking place.[42] It turns out Shaw and Holloway have misread the Engineers' intent in producing the cave paintings, and indeed the entire crew of *Prometheus* shows itself to be prone to such misreading: each time the scientists encounter a new unknown creature or threat, they routinely misread the situation and react so stupidly and unscientifically that one reviewer refers to them as "the tea party in space," their misreadings often resulting in catastrophe and death.[43] When Shaw and Weyland finally meet the last surviving Engineer, the Engineer does not welcome them but bludgeons Weyland to death with David's head—that is, kills Weyland with Weyland's own creation—and attempts to destroy the human race.[44] Thus, firmly in the tradition of MWS's *Frankenstein*, *Prometheus* begins in the triumph of science and hope for the future advancement of human life, but ends as the past comes to life and brings with it onanistic stupor and death.[45]

As the characters in *Prometheus* focus obsessively on the source of human life, the film draws attention to the problem of sources, drawing upon MWS's polyprometheism. The film's evocation of Prometheus offers anything but certainty for the meaning of the film. There is the opening sequence, in which one of the Engineers drinks a mysterious black ooze, then disintegrates as he falls into a waterfall, his DNA recombining to produce some new form of life; this sequence is followed by the film's single opening credit, the title *Prometheus*, which suggests an interpretation for that opening sequence—here is Prometheus *plasticator* creating human life!—but which interpretation the film never verifies. There is Peter Weyland's misreading of the myth of Prometheus *pyrphoros* (discussed above). There is the ship itself, which Weyland has christened *Prometheus*. Although C. W. Marshall suggests this is a mere "cosmetic reference," the ship in fact plays multiple Promethean roles.[46] It facilitates the interaction between the humans and the Engineers, just as Hesiod's Prometheus makes possible animal sacrifice, the means by which humans communicate with the gods; according to Weyland's misreading, the name suggests the ship will not just facilitate communication, but put humans on equal footing with the Engineers. The ship also plays Aeschylus's rebellious Prometheus, when the captain Janek (played by Idris Elba) uses *Prometheus* to ram the surviving Engineer's own ship and thus prevents the Engineer from traveling to Earth to wipe out humankind.[47] Scott even pointedly evokes the most famous consequence of Prometheus's fire-theft, the creation of Pandora, evoked through the android David—a "beautiful evil" (*kalon kakon*; *Th.* 585) who accomplishes the will of his Zeus, Weyland, and who retrieves from the alien compound a vessel that looks strikingly like a Greek *pithos* or 'jar,' unleashing its destructive contents, the mysterious black ooze. So just as *Frankenstein*'s 'Modern Prometheus' draws on many sources and shifts the meaning and significance of 'Prometheus' throughout the novel, so too does the film *Prometheus*'s title screen. While the title tantalizingly suggests a key for decoding the film, it goes on to provide so many possible Prometheis so as to frustrate any singular or coherent Promethean reading.

Scott's *Prometheus* also replicates MWS's tactic of putting Judeo-Christian resonances in dialogue with Greco-Roman Prometheus, so as to cause characters to shift in allusive identities and roles. The night the humans discover most of the Engineers have died, a drunk Holloway converses with David:

David: I'm very sorry that your Engineers are all gone, Dr. Holloway.
Holloway: You think we wasted our time coming here, don't you?
David: Your question depends on me understanding what you hoped to achieve coming here.
Holloway: What we hoped to achieve was to meet our makers. To get answers. Why they, why they even made us in the first place.
David: Why do you think your people made me?
Holloway: We made you 'cause we could.
David: Can you imagine how disappointing it would be for you to hear the same thing from your creator?

While no specific Judeo-Christian name appears here, Holloway attempts to play the role of Adam in his frustrated desire to confront his Maker with questions: "What we hoped to achieve? Was to meet our makers. To get answers. Why they even made us in the first place?" His questions strongly evoke Milton's Adam (also quoted on the title page of *Frankenstein*).[48] The irony, of course, is that the android David here is much closer to Adam, speaking directly to his Creator (or, at least, his Creator's species), but Holloway is too self-absorbed to see the point.[49] Holloway never gets to play Adam and confront the last surviving Engineer: just after this dialogue, David inserts a single drop of the black ooze into the drink he is preparing for Holloway. (Here David simultaneously resonates with both Adam and Hesiod's jar-opening Pandora.) David infects—or perhaps impregnates via in-vitro fertilization?—Holloway with the alien substance. Holloway subsequently begins to mutate into an inhuman monster and forces Vickers to incinerate him with a flame-thrower. Thus Holloway shifts from would-be-Miltonic-Adam to receptive Eve to Adamic father of a new race to Frankenstein's Creature himself, altering in complementary relation to David's shifts from Pandora to seed-planting Adam to a sinister Prometheus *pyrphoros* (placing the stolen dark fire of the godlike Engineers into Holloway).

Scott extends this game of shifting identities via allusion to Shaw as well. Holloway impregnates Shaw with his hybrid human-alien semen, effectively turning Shaw, who had previously been infertile, into a new Eve. Shaw rejects the fetus, using an automated medical pod to remove the hybrid human-alien cephalopod growing rapidly in her womb.[50] When Shaw encounters the last Engineer, she steps into the role of Miltonic Adam, repeating Holloway's question: "Why? . . . I need to know why! What did we do wrong?" And, in the film's finale, she insists on finding the home planet of the Engineers because, she claims, she deserves to know why they first created humans then tried to kill them.[51] Admittedly, Holloway and Shaw's repeated refrain of "Why?" is not precisely Milton's "Did I request thee, Maker from my clay / To mould me man" nor has its rhetorical elegance; it even lacks the elegance of Frankenstein's Creature, who never asks Victor why he exists, but merely curses his Creator for the fact of his existence. But the fact that Shaw plays the role of the Created castigating the Creator puts her firmly in the Adamic tradition.

Even the film's final scene evokes Adam and Eve cast out of Eden: Shaw remains in the role Miltonic Adam, while David, now a decapitated head, occupies the role of companion Eve (although his bodiless state still reminds us that he is kin to manufactured Pandora, too).[52] Intriguingly, this final scene captures both *Prometheus*'s deep intertwining with *Frankenstein* and its posthuman innovations on that novel. On one hand, Shaw (as Miltonic Adam) insists that she deserves to know why the Engineers first created humans, then tried to kill them; when David does not understand this entitlement, Shaw's reply—"Well, I guess that's because I'm a human being and you're a robot"—insists on her difference from android David. Yet Shaw insists on her humanity at precisely the moment she is least stable in her human identity: she is now the mother of the cephalopod, and through this creature, the grandmother of the creature we see in the film's final chilling image, a product of both technoscientific intervention *and* biological reproduction. At the metatheatrical level, Shaw may even now be the ancestor to an entire species of horror—that is, the *Alien* film franchise—although Matt Cohn has noted that Scott denies us the certain reading that this xenomorph is related to *the* xenomorph we have come to love and fear from the original *Alien* (1979).[53]

In remaining oblivious to—or in denial of—the unstable and shifting identities and relationships around her, Shaw fails to learn the lesson David attempts to offer Holloway in the dialogue quoted above: "Your question depends on the understanding of what you hoped to achieve." Even Frankenstein's Creature knows better than Shaw, knows that the real question is "Who or what am I?" And yet *Prometheus* ends with possibilities *Frankenstein* could not envision. In Scott's *Prometheus*, all the male scientists may still die, but reproduction and hybridity offer a way forward for those who can reproduce and adapt (Shaw and David).[54] In turn, this produces the possibility for a new polity—one not predicated on the fundamental unit of 'Man' but consisting of an infertile mother and a manufactured human, neither quite recognizable within the complex web of allusions Scott has constructed nor even within a humanist rubric.

It is worth noting that such possibilities go unexplored in the film's sequel, *Alien: Covenant* (dir. Ridley Scott, 2017). Instead, the film demonstrates a recursive interest in the tradition of *Frankenstein* and the British Romantics: the original working title for the sequel was *Alien: Paradise Lost*; in the film,

David quotes lines from both *Paradise Lost* and the poem "Ozymandias," but erroneously attributes the latter lines to Lord Byron, which the film's other android, Walter (also played by Michael Fassbender), corrects as belonging to PBS; and David turns out to be a Victor-Frankenstein figure who continues to experiment with the black ooze, using Shaw's body and those of other humans as hosts to produce more deadly xenomorphs. It is remarkable that, taken together, *Prometheus* and *Alien: Covenant* allude to so many myths and historical figures linked to *Frankenstein*, yet both the novel and MWS remain unspoken sources.

To summarize, *Prometheus* exhibits a deep yearning to understand the origins of life, drawing directly on the same mythic figures found in *Frankenstein*—Prometheus, Adam, and Eve (as well as implied Pandora)—in order to understand such yearning and the stakes of that pursuit. To be sure, these are also narratives about narrative, about a yearning to confront or understand one's own origins or past—such as MWS confronting her literary pedigree, or Ridley Scott confronting the increasing burden of the *Alien* mythos.[55] But this reading of *Frankenstein* and *Prometheus* suggests that these mythic receptions in SF are themselves living things, not so much the hard marble statues to be brought back to life—the mute stones speaking—but the divine spark itself, black alien ooze: slippery, dangerous, liable to hybridity, prone to producing hideous progeny, always just beyond our ken.

Fraction and Ward's *Ody-C*

A counterpoint to this reading of Scott's *Prometheus* in terms of MWS's *Frankenstein* may be found in Matt Fraction and Christian Ward's SF comic book *Ody-C* #2 (January 2015).[56] On the one hand, *Ody-C* shares with *Prometheus* a deep interest in a posthumanism that moves away from androcentric perspectives on science and social organization, de-centering man and exploring subsequent reproductive possibilities. The mythic figure Prometheus also plays a central role in its posthumanist thought. On the other hand, *Ody-C* does not rely on the technique of polyprometheism (as *Prometheus* does), relying instead on a single shift in gender identity for all of its characters, which in turn has reproductive consequences.[57] In this "trippy, gender-flipped version of Homer's *Odyssey* hurtling through space on psychedelic, science fiction wings"—composed in dactylic hexameter, no less—almost all the characters who would be male in Greek myth are biologically female (and vice versa for the female characters).[58] As we learn in issue #2, the female god Zeus had become so disgusted at the violence of her male offspring that she annihilated (almost) all the males in the universe, such that the universe of *Ody-C* is dominated by mortal women with few exceptions (He, a version of Helen of Troy; Odyssia's son Telemachus; and scattered others).

The annihilation of mankind, however, produces an unexpected problem: how will women reproduce without men? Here Fraction and Ward introduce Promethene, who in *Ody-C* is not the uncle or cousin of Zeus, but rather Zeus' daughter. (Indeed, the name suggests that Promethene is a hybrid of Prometheus and Athenê.) After consuming lotus and going mad in her imprisonment, Promethene escapes her bonds and masters the fundamental materials of creating life, with the aim of "kickstart[ing] … the propagation of her species." However, Promethene creates "not man … not woman … [but] sebex" (Fig. 12.2), "an entirely new gender" (as a bearded Athena tells us), or, perhaps more accurately, an entirely new sex, technically an intersex being "who could implant the released ovum from a woman and fertilize it within its womb." In her attempt to preserve the "species," Promethene does so by creating a sex that partly challenges the very basis for reproduction. ("Partly" because this still places a heavy emphasis on the ovum, fertilization, and the womb, although now both females and sebex have wombs, such that the infamous claim *tota femina in utero* ['all woman resides in her womb'] no longer stands.) *Ody-C*'s bearded Athena suggests that this new being, the sebex, is "capable it would seem of only spawning women and other sebex," but Zeus, with greater insight than Peter Weyland ever exhibits, cautions Athena in Homeric fashion to "Recall, daughter, this precise moment when those words passed your tongue; I have a feeling they shall return to haunt you."

As of the composition of this essay, *Ody-C* has only reached issue #12, and the narrative has revealed no further hints as to what precisely Zeus means here.[59] Nevertheless, there is incredible potential in new, unforeseen imaginative possibilities that do not pit technoscience against biological reproduction (as we saw in MWS's *Frankenstein*) but rather, like Ridley Scott's *Prometheus*, facilitates new, unique blendings of technoscience and biological reproduction in the redefinition of the human. While *Ody-C* remains more possibility than fulfillment at this stage, its image of Promethene is highly suggestive—for now we finally have a (post)modern Prometheus who does not ignore the importance of the female but is herself a female, and who does not focus on technology at the expense of reproduction but brings the two together. In other words, we might view Promethene not as the descendant of Prometheus or Victor Frankenstein, but as the figure of MWS herself (cf. Promethene at center, Fig. 12.2), creating order out of chaos and giving birth to new (hideous?) progeny.

Fig. 12.2 Promethene and the creation of the sebex in *Ody-C* #2 (January 2015). Excerpted with permission from *ODY-C* #2. *ODY-C* is by Matt Fraction & Christian Ward. © 2018 Milkfed Criminal Masterminds, Inc. & Christian Ward.

Ancient Prometheus

Ridley Scott's *Prometheus* and *Ody-C's* Promethene may even help us revise our perspective on ancient Prometheus. As suggested at the beginning of this chapter, Prometheus is 'good to think with' because he focuses our attention on matters of definition and delineation, such as Prometheus does in Hesiod's *Works & Days*. While the myth of Prometheus may work to sharpen the boundaries between gods, humans, and animals, as well as emphasize sexual difference, it also renders indistinct the integrity (in the sense of 'wholeness' or 'one-ness') of the category of the 'human race' over time. If human males contemporary to the invention of sacrifice are the baseline for defining the 'human,' then what are we to make of the offspring, male and female, produced by these human males and Pandoric gynoids? Are these offspring human, manufactured, or some *tertium quid*? Since we are these offspring, what are we? The question is never asked in Hesiod, but is asked by Frankenstein's Creature, Pandoric David, and Promethene. In Hesiod's myth of human origins, then, we are not human but somehow, already, posthuman.

This problem lurking in Hesiod's account also points to a problem with Prometheus as heuristic—namely, the insistent application of any taxonomy may complicate or render *less* intelligible the object we seek to understand, or simply fail to address the true problem at hand. In this vein, an interesting example appears in Plato's *Protagoras* (320–321), wherein the sophist Protagoras tells a story about how Prometheus stole fire to help humans survive in the wild, but the humans kept dying; it turns out the problem was not technological or sexual, but rather ethical, and Zeus sends Hermes to bring humans reverence and justice (αἰδώς and δική) so that they can live together in groups, in *poleis*, and thus survive. In other words, Prometheus may be 'good to think with,' but he also represents the shortcomings of human knowing, our stubborn desire to hold onto the patterns we have already established and that we reproduce, our limited ability to anticipate dangerous consequences, new hybrids, and unimagined possibilities. In this way, SF in particular, in its willingness to speculate about the future, has a distinct advantage over Greco-Roman mythic thought (which looks backward into time and runs the risk of being too teleological in its drive toward the storytelling present). These modern, postmodern, and posthuman Prometheis can help us understand that ancient Prometheus, 'Mr. Forethought,' is and has always been his own Epimetheus (After-Thought), 'Metametheus' (The Thing-After-Thought) or, if you will forgive the hybrid, 'Postmetheus.'

Notes

1 This essay is the hideous progeny of several talks, starting at *The Modern Prometheus; or, Frankenstein* conference at Hamilton College (April 2016), followed by talks at the University of Patras (June 2016), Haverford College (September 2016), and Bar-Ilan University (March 2017). I give thanks to the many audiences who have provided questions and ideas that refined this project, including the students in my "Sci-Fi, Fantasy, & the Classics" course at the University of Puget Sound (Fall 2017). Special thanks are due to Benjamin Eldon Stevens and Jesse Weiner for enduring from start to finish, Matt Fraction and Christian Ward for permissions, and the University of Puget Sound for financial support. All mistakes are mine.

2 From Shaftesbury's *The Moralists* (1709). On Shaftesbury and the 'modern Prometheus,' see note 20 below with Small (1973: 51–52) and Dougherty (2006: 109).

3 Dougherty (2006: 3); cf. Hassan (1980: xiii–xvi, 187–207).

4 There is some speculation that Franklin never actually conducted the kite experiment: see Tucker 2003.

5 For Kant's declaration, see Rogers and Stevens (2012a: 127–128); for Breckenridge's poem, see Goodall (2008: 117).

6 On Shelley's subtitle and its scientific contexts more generally, see, e.g., Ziolkowski 1981, Knellwolf and Goodall 2008, Smith 2016c, Vargo (2016: 31–32), and Priestman (this volume).

7 All references to *F* are to the edition of Hunter (2012), who prints the 1818 text. Readers may also usefully consult the editions of Macdonald and Scherf 2012 and Butler 1994.

8 MWS was likely thinking with Kant's declaration about Ben Franklin: "[Victor's father] made also a kite" to conduct electricity from the heavens (*F* 1.1: 24). Cf. Goodall (2008: 118), who demonstrates that the British Romantics seemed particularly smitten with the concept of electricity, associating electricity with intellectual and political liberation.

9 For MWS's journals, see Feldman and Scott-Kilvert (1987: esp. 631–684). On MWS's reading in Latin and Greek, see Hurst (2006: 58–60).

10 Prometheus *pyrphoros*/Prometheus the rebel also appears in: Hesiod *Theogony* 507–616 and *Works and Days* 47–105; Aristophanes *Birds* 1494–1552; Plato *Protagoras* 320c3–322d6; Horace *Carmina* [*Carm.*] 1.3, 1.16; Pliny *Naturalis historia* 7.80; Hyginus [Hyg.] *Poetica astronomica* [*Poet. astr.*] 2.15, *Fabulae* [*Fab.*] 144.

11 PBS translated *Prometheus Bound* around July 13, 1817; see Feldman and Scott-Kilvert (1987: 177) and Gilbert and Gubar (1979: 224). Vargo (2016: 28–29) also suggests MWS would have encountered the story of Prometheus in her childhood through the account of her father, William Godwin, in his *The Pantheon: or Ancient History of the Gods of Greece and Rome. Intended to Facilitate the Understanding of Classical Authors, and of the Poets in General* (1806). On the Romantics and the 'modern Prometheus' more generally, see Bertagnolli 2007 and Barnett (this volume).

12 On MWS's reading of Ovid, see Liveley (this volume); on other Latin sources in MWS's reading, see, e.g., Weiner 2015a, Stevens (this volume). Although the tradition of Prometheus *plasticator* is known mainly through later sources like the Roman Ovid and the Greek travel writer Pausanias (10.4.4), it may extend as far back as Herakleides Ponticus in the fourth century BCE (see Hyg. *Poet. astr.* 2.42.1; cf. Gantz 1993: 166n31), or still further back to the sixth-century BCE Greek poetess Sappho (fr. 207 in Campbell 1982); see also Podlecki (2005: 3). Cf. Aesop *Fables* 515–516.

13 On Prometheus *plasticator* in *F*, see Small (1973: 48). For the reading of *pyrphoros* vs. *plasticator*, see Priestman (this volume).

14 Mellor (1988: 71): "In identifying Victor Frankenstein with Prometheus, Mary Shelley was alluding to both versions of Prometheus *pyrphoros*. In the first version, known to Mary Shelley through Ovid's *Metamorphoses* which she read in 1815, Prometheus created man from clay ... In the alternate, famous version of the myth, Prometheus is the fire-stealer, the god who defied Jupiter's tyrannical oppression of humanity by giving fire to man and was then punished by having his liver eaten by vultures until he divulged his secret fore-knowledge of Jupiter's downfall. By the third century A.D., these two versions had fused; the fire stolen by Prometheus became the fire of life with which he animated his man of clay."

15 See also the composite version of Prometheus in Apollodorus *Bibliotheca* 1.7.1, as well as Hyg. *Fab.* 142 and 144 (taken together).

16 On myth and sources in *F* more generally, see also Goldberg 1959, Pollin 1965, Small 1973, and Lecercle 1988.

17 On Hesiod, Pandora, and *F*, see both Gumpert and Hammond (this volume). On the Creature's vegetarianism in *F*, see both Priestman and Barnett (this volume).

18 The essay also makes reference to a version of Prometheus *pyrphoros* (similar to Hesiod's) found in Horace *Carm.* 1.3.25–33.

19 Rogers and Stevens (2012a: 128). Small (1973: 48–50) usefully discusses medieval Christian interpretations of Prometheus.

20 The earliest attestation of the phrase 'modern Prometheus' appears in Shaftesbury's *The Moralists* (1709). Shaftesbury uses the Titan in his thinking about mankind's fundamental ethical imperfections, such that Mountebanks, 'tricksters' in the sense of 'charlatans', are "our modern Prometheus's." Elsewhere in *The Moralists*, Shaftesbury expresses ambivalence about the ethical orientation of Prometheus, asking (as I quote at the beginning of this chapter) whether Prometheus was "a plastick Nature"—that is, a neutral or benevolent creator-god—or an "evil Daemon," flipping the problem of human imperfection back on its divine source. Another text referring to "a new Prometheus" is *L'homme Machine*, written in 1747 by Julien Offray de la Mettrie, who uses the figure of Prometheus to argue that man was a machine "entre les mains d'un nouveau Prométhée" ("in the hands of a new Prometheus"). We have no certain evidence that MWS or the Geneva party had read de la Mettrie; cf. Joseph [1969] in Hunter (2012: 172). However, we do know that William Godwin had read Shaftesbury, and MWS refers to Shaftesbury in a letter to Leigh Hunt on April 8, 1825.

21 Small (1973: 52).

22 Shelley in Hunter (2012: 167).

23 On Plutarch's *Lives* in *F*, see the introduction to this volume. Before reading these three books, the Creature hears Felix De Lacey read aloud from Volney's *Ruins of Empires* (F 2.5: 82–83).

24 Hence we might see *F* as MWS's critique of the masculine bravado that PBS and Lord Byron famously exalted in their practice of Romanticism; cf. Baldick (1987: 39): "Wollstonecraft recognizes the danger and redundancy of the heroic ideal, particularly in its artificial divorce from the domestic."

25 Baldick (1987: 44). Cf. Gilbert and Gubar (1979: 230–234) on Victor's (and MWS's) "multiform relationships to Eve, Adam, God and Satan" (234).

26 Baldick (1987: 43–44).

27 It was not until Ellen Moers's *Literary Women* (1977) that critics began to consider seriously how MWS's own perspective as a woman and mother might have affected the composition of the novel. Of course, MWS's mother was the trailblazing feminist author Mary Wollstonecraft, who died just after giving birth to MWS in 1797. Moreover, when MWS was conceiving *F* during the summer of 1816, she had already given birth to two children—the first, a daughter, prematurely born, had died a few days after her birth—while a third child would be born

before *F* reached publication in January 1818. Moers thus reads the novel as "a birth myth" informed by these experiences.

28 Homans (1987: 148). Homans makes no mention of Prometheus and Pandora in her discussion, reading the novel only through *Paradise Lost*. Nevertheless, Homans's interpretation is compelling with regard to the Greco-Roman classics, since it suggests a way to read *F* in the Hesiodic tradition, as a kind of response to (what Hesiod considers) the problem of womankind. Nor is Hesiod the only Greek poet to lament male dependency upon females to produce offspring. In addition to the famous poem of Semonides of Amorgos (fr. 7), we see similar declarations from Jason in Euripides' *Medea*: "Mortals ought to beget children from some other source, and there should be no female sex. Then mankind would have no trouble" (573–575, trans. Kovacs 1994: 345). And there is Hippolytus in the surviving version of that Euripidean tragedy: "Oh Zeus … If you wished to propagate the human race, it was not from women that you should have provided this. Rather, men should put down in the temples either bronze or iron or a mass of gold and buy offspring, each for a price appropriate to his means, and then dwell in houses free from the female sex" (*Hippolytus* 616, 618–624, trans. Kovacs 1995: 185). If ancient Prometheus is, from a Greek male-identified perspective, the mythic figure whose actions lead to both the damnable technological innovation of biological reproduction dependent on female existence and countless woes for male humans, then the modern Prometheus offers a cautionary thought experiment about what might happen if it were possible for human males to harness technoscience to bypass biological reproduction and create new life from the reconstituted dead—as well as the subsequent horrors that might follow.

29 Gilbert and Gubar (1979: 232).

30 Although see London 1993, who productively reads such homosociality in terms of the spectacle of masculinity.

31 Perhaps it is no coincidence that MWS never produced a sequel to *F*. On the Creature in *F* and Pandora, see Gumpert (this volume).

32 Hassan (1980: 189).

33 Reichardt 1994 traces the myth of Frankenstein in discourses surrounding (developments in) artificial life. For a posthuman reading of *F*, see Mousley 2016.

34 Braidotti (2013: 3).

35 Ibid., 1–2. Cf. Hassan 1980: "Is this the project of the Promethean consciousness? To perceive the parity, nay the identity, of parts and wholes?" (191).

36 Braidotti (2013: 2, my emphasis). Cf. Hassan (1980: 201–204) on the posthumanism and the Vitruvian Man as "measure of things."

37 Lest we think Scott and the film's screenwriters (John Spaihts and Damon Lindelof) are the ones who have committed the error and use classical allusion carelessly, we can look to Scott's use of the classical past in *Prometheus*'s filmic ancestor, *Alien* (1979). In early drafts of *Alien*, the planetoid where humans first encounter the alien is called Acheron LV-426, alluding to the Underworld river and fittingly suggesting that the humans crossed a threshold into the realm of the dead, or, at least, the monstrous. Scott, of course, also engages with Greco-Roman antiquity in *Gladiator* (2000).

38 This aspect of Weyland's character is especially clear in a video clip that was released in tandem with the film (on a fake website for Weyland Industries: https://www.weylandindustries.com/tedtalk). In the clip, a young Weyland delivers a TED talk in the year 2023, speaking about the myth of Prometheus and the technological advancements of human history; he reaches the triumphant and "obvious conclusion: we are the gods now." This speech also includes a longer version of the Prometheus myth. For another example of the fetishization of the Prometheus myth in tech, see Barney 2000.

39 There are other mythic allusions worth exploring with these characters. For example, David and Vickers are visually linked as 'siblings' through their bleached-blonde hair and may allude to Apollo and Artemis—or rather Artemis and Apollo, respectively. While David remains virginal, Vickers both clumsily seduces Janek (much like Apollo in many myths) and accuses Weyland of being a king who will not relinquish his throne, evocative of Zeus's unwillingness to relinquish his throne to his children.

40 On Greek fantasies of male reproduction without women, see note 28. Just before Vickers seduces Janek, he asks Vickers if she is a robot.

41 Cohn 2015 usefully discusses *Prometheus* in terms of using and abusing of the past.

42 This is a distillation of an argument Benjamin Eldon Stevens and I made just after *Prometheus* was released, in which we argue that Ridley Scott might be offering 'a new modern Prometheus' following in MWS's footsteps, a reflection on the productive or reproductive power that may come from reading the ancient past—indeed from misreading it. See Rogers and Stevens 2012b.

43 Sparrow 2012. Reviewers comment extensively on the stupidity of the scientists, transferring such dissatisfaction to the film itself: hence Burr 2012 calls *Prometheus* "big, beautiful, and empty"; Stevens 2012 calls it "deep without being particularly smart"; and Bradley 2012 sees it as a "[c]ombination of genius and muddle … [that] pretends to a significance it doesn't possess."

44 On the Engineers as gods who hate humans, see Ehrenreich 2012 and Cohn 2015 (the latter comparing the film to Euripides' *Bacchae*). With respect to physical appearance, the Engineer is either the oldest white male ever, a marble statue come to life (as one person has suggested to me), or a marvelously obscure reference to Jane Harrison's theory that the mythical Titans were white because they were made from white clay or covered themselves in gypsum for rituals. Harrison (1908: 492–493) discusses an Orphic story in which the Titans are coated in gypsum when they dismember Dionysos. According to Eustathius (ad *Iliad* 2.735), "the ancients call dust and gypsum *titanos*," though Harrison notes that the etymology of *titanos* as "white-clay-men" is Eustathian and that there is no such connection for the Homeric Titans (493). Hence readers should beware of such interpretations as that of Sobchack (2012: 33), who incorrectly identifies the etymology as belonging to "ancient Greek" (as opposed to that of a Byzantine bishop).

45 I borrow this phrasing from Sparrow 2012, who accuses the film of "produc[ing] … onanistic stupor," playing at the film's interest in failures of sexual (re)production and death. For other readings of *Prometheus* in the tradition of *F*, see McFadden 2012 and Waldron 2012. For a survey of the *F* tradition in film, see Jancovich 2016.

46 Marshall (2016: 20).

47 This act of self-sacrifice also has a hint of masculine bravado evocative of the Romantics PBS and especially Lord Byron; cf. note 24 above.

48 See section above entitled "Shifting identities."

49 As Jesse Weiner reminds me, David's name also evokes Biblical David. This evocation is reinforced at the beginning of the film's sequel, *Alien: Covenant* (dir. Ridley Scott, 2017). In Weyland's office, we see a replica of Michelangelo's *David*, its gleaming white marble inviting us to compare David not only to Biblical David but also to the Engineers.

50 In a subtle critique of Weyland's masculinist humanism, the medical unit is calibrated only for surgery on males, suggesting that a world in which 'man is the measure of all things' is dangerous, even deadly, for (pregnant) females.

51 Shaw and David do succeed in finding the Engineers' home world in *Alien: Covenant*.

52 Or is David here Athena—all *nous* or *mêtis*? Cf. note 39.

53 Cohn 2015. On artificial life, *Alien,* and *Prometheus*, see Lambie 2015.
54 Shaw's first name, Elizabeth, may even allude to Victor Frankenstein's love interest, Elizabeth Lavenza (whom the Creature murders on their wedding night); thus *Prometheus* may run the thought experiment "What if Elizabeth were to be the one character to survive *F*"?
55 So argues Sobchack 2012.
56 For a survey of the *F* tradition in comics and graphic novels, see Murray 2016.
57 Fraction uses dactylic hexameter to imitate the cadence of archaic Greek epic. In terms of plot, *Ody-C* either hedges fairly closely to archaic and classical Greek sources or moves in radically different directions. Individual issues also include in their back matter essays by a "reformed Classicist," Dani Colman; these essays place the ancient source material in its cultural context while also linking them to the comic's plot.
58 The quotation comes from a review in *Wired* magazine and printed on the cover of the anthology containing *Ody-C* #1–5.
59 The series has been divided so far into three separate plots: the return of Odyssia and her crew from Troiia VII through the Aeolus episode (#1–5); the travels of Ene and He (i.e., Menelaus and Helen) to the planet of Q'naf, including a variation on the Proteus episode (#6–10); and a limerick adaptation of the fall of the House of Atreus (#11–12).

Other Modern Prometheis: Suggestions for Further Reading and Viewing

Samuel Cooper

As the chapters in this volume show, many works inspired by Mary Shelley's (henceforth MWS) *Frankenstein* (*F*) exhibit some form of classical reception. In keeping with the volume's aim of helping inspire further research, this chapter presents an annotated list of some such points in the *F* tradition. Most of the listed works refer explicitly to some aspect of Greco-Roman antiquity. Also included are some works whose stories arguably echo both MWS's novel and Greco-Roman myth. Finally, a few works are included that are important for the *F* tradition but whose links to the classics seem more tenuous; such works might reveal stronger classical resonances upon further consideration. I hope that this list, by no means exhaustive, will serve as a useful and inspiring starting point.

Short Stories, Novels, and Plays

Richard Brinsley Peake, *Presumption; or, The Fate of Frankenstein* (1823)

Peake's play was among the first and most popular of the many stage adaptations that helped elevate *F* to mythic status. It scrubs Prometheus (and moral ambiguity) from the title but includes a reference in the script, when Frankenstein says: "Like Prometheus of old, have I daringly attempted the formation—the animation of a Being!"

Henry M. Milner, *Frankenstein; or, The Man and the Monster!* (1826)

Milner's stage adaptation is notable for being set in Sicily. Toward the end, a group of peasants find the escaped Monster (as the Creature is called in Milner's script) and bind him to a rock on Mount Etna, an image recalling the similar punishment of the Titan Prometheus in ancient myth; the peasants then drink Falernian wine, a type often mentioned in Latin literature. At the play's climax, the Monster jumps into Mount Etna, recalling both the ancient sage (and self-proclaimed immortal god) Empedocles, who is said to have ended his life thus, and the monster Typhon, whom Zeus' buried under the volcano.

Johann Wolfgang von Goethe, *Faust Part Two* (1832)

The Germanic legend of Faust is one of the mythic strands entwined with *F*. In *Faust Part Two*, Homunculus, a miniature test-tube humanoid, pursues a more robust existence by shattering his vial in the Aegean amidst the beings of ancient Greek myth. Like MWS's Victor Frankenstein, Goethe's Faust struggles to reconcile opposing desires for godlike power and ordinary human love. Faust's obsession with the famed beauty of Helen reverberates in some of science fiction's (SF) *F*-type narratives in which the creature is female.

Auguste Villiers de l'Isle-Adam, *The Future Eve* (1886)

This French novel offers an early SF version of the Pygmalion myth, in which a statue or other image of a beautiful woman comes to life. To replace a friend's unsatisfactory fiancée, a fictionalized Thomas Edison engineers an artificial woman to have all of the benefits and none of the shortcomings of a normal woman. Beyond the overt Biblical nod in its title, the novel is full of classical references that invite the reader to ponder the historical significance of Edison's technological achievements.

H. G. Wells, *The Island of Doctor Moreau* (1896)

This novel imagines an attempt to create humans not out of dead flesh, but out of living animals. More convinced than MWS's Victor Frankenstein of the virtue of his actions, Doctor Moreau argues that pain is an illusion and rejects numerous tortured specimens as he pursues the perfect creature. Soon after arriving at the sinister island, the narrator reads "a crib of Horace"—an aid to comprehending Horace's Latin—while attempting to ignore mysterious screams.

Karel Čapek, *R.U.R.* (*Rossum's Universal Robots*) (1920)

The play that coined the term 'robot,' *R.U.R.* expands the role of MWS's creator into a corporation and that of the Creature into a global class of manufactured laborers—perhaps a variation on the "race of devils" feared by Victor. Two of the robots are named after the historical Roman antagonists Marius and Sulla, whose stories the humans remember poorly.

H. P. Lovecraft, "Herbert West—Reanimator" (*Home Brew* 1922)

This serialized novelette develops the 'horror' dimension of MWS's story. The titular mad doctor is memorably described as "a languid Elagabalus of the tombs" (recalling a particularly maligned Roman emperor), while an outbreak of typhoid is a "scourge ... from the nightmare caverns of Tartarus," in ancient myth the Underworld's place of punishment. Undaunted by the gruesome results of his early experiments, West tries again and again, filling the world with increasingly horrific creatures who haunt him and seek vengeance, a strong echo of Victor's feared "race of devils."

Lester Del Rey, "Helen O'Loy" (*Astounding Science Fiction* 1938)

Ancient Greek Helen of Troy and MWS's Creature figure are merged and thoroughly domesticated in this story. In the story's sexist presentation, female emotions seem at first like a good thing to give a robot, then a huge mistake. In the end, "Helen of Alloy" turns out to be the perfect wife and, instead of killing her creator, she destroys herself when he dies in order to be buried with him.

C. L. Moore, "No Woman Born" (*Astounding Science Fiction* 1944)

Deirdre, a TV star and—in another echo of Helen of Troy—the world's most beautiful woman, is badly injured in a fire; only her brain is left unharmed, which is then implanted by the scientist Maltzer in an artificial body. As Deirdre attempts to return to the screen, Maltzer believes the public will reject her, compares himself to Frankenstein, and nearly commits suicide. But Deirdre embraces her new 'cyborg' potential: with its female creature showing real agency, the story reworks both *F* and the Pandora and Pygmalion myths.

Olaf Stapledon, *Odd John* (1935), *Sirius* (1944)

Odd John is a product of 'natural' mutation, not human experimentation, but he and his fellow mutants share with many creatures of the *F* tradition two characteristics: superhuman capabilities and grotesque physical deformities. Classics appear in Odd John's nickname for the narrator, "Fido," "meant to be Φαίδω, which name, he said, was connected with the Greek for 'brilliant.'" Closer to the *F* tradition is *Sirius*, the story of a "super sheepdog," whose name is drawn from the 'dog star' of Greek mythology and astronomy. Biologically engineered by a scientist to possess human-like consciousness and language capabilities, Sirius is a dignified and sympathetic creature. Both of these novels contribute to

Stapledon's larger project of reimagining tragedy within a modern scientific context, in which bioengineering and astrophysics determine the ultimate fate of humanity and the universe.

Lawrence Durrell, *The Revolt of Aphrodite* (*Tunc* [1968], *Nunquam* [1970])

This pair of novels is notable as a rare F narrative in which modern Greece plays a role. At the story's outset, an inventor named Felix (Latin 'fortunate') Charlock works in Athens and is the lover of a prostitute named Iolanthe. Later he marries into a powerful and shadowy firm (based in Turkey), which develops and markets his inventions. The head of the firm, Julian—whose name also recalls antiquity—becomes obsessed with Iolanthe, who in the meantime has become a movie star. After Iolanthe dies suddenly, Julian orders Felix to create a robot duplicate of her with all of her memories. The novels are named after phrases from Petronius and feature rich classical receptions, including a lengthy lecture on the Parthenon and references to Pygmalion, Pausanias, Aristophanes, Alcibiades, Aristotle, Helen of Troy, Plato's *Republic* and *Theaetetus*, Macrobius's *Saturnalia*, and more. 'Iolanthe' is often shortened to 'Io' recalling the mythic woman changed into a cow (e.g., *Prometheus Bound*).

Philip K. Dick, "Second Variety" (*Space Science Fiction* 1953), *The Simulacra* (1964), *Now Wait for Last Year* (1966), *Do Androids Dream of Electric Sheep?* (1968), *We Can Build You* (1972)

In Dick's fictional worlds, virtually everything is artificial, and so the Creature figure is both pervasive and diffuse. "Second Variety" features horrific androids, developed in the context of global war, that are indistinguishable from humans and seem destined to destroy both humanity and themselves. In contrast, *We Can Build You* features the dignified and humane Lincoln and Stanton, who are simulacra of artificial reincarnations of an American classical past: the Civil War remains compelling, one character proclaims, because "it was the only and first national epic in which we Americans participated." This novel also points out that 'simulacra' is of Latin origin. In *Now Wait for Last Year*, the protagonist considers the re-creation of the past through mechanical simulacra to be an extension of techniques of memory as old as the *Iliad*. Dick's most famous novel about artificial life, *Do Androids Dream of Electric Sheep?*, features a character named Hannibal Sloat who likes to say "*mors certa, vita incerta*," Latin for 'death is certain, life uncertain.' Protagonist Rick Deckard echoes Greek tragic heroes when he says to himself, "Where I go the ancient curse follows."

Orson Scott Card, Ender series (*Ender's Game* [1985], *Speaker for the Dead* [1986], *Xenocide* [1990], *Children of the Mind* [1994])

The primary point of contact between this series and the *F* tradition is the story of Jane, an artificially intelligent creature who has emerged as an unintended byproduct of the 'ansible' network that enables instantaneous, faster-than-light communication throughout the galaxy. (This idea is indebted to Arthur C. Clarke's Rocannon's 1965 "Dial F for Frankenstein," while the term comes from Ursula K. Le Guin's 1966 Rocannon's World.) Like many Digital Age creatures, Jane is not a body that lacks intelligence or emotion, but a feeling intelligence that lacks a humanoid body. Jane's ansible body becomes threatened for political reasons, and she increasingly desires a fully embodied erotic relationship with a human. Classical allusions are frequent: one of the main characters, a historian, publishes political essays under the pseudonym Demosthenes; in *Xenocide*, a character says to Jane, "you've always believed you sprang whole from the head of Zeus," and she replies, "I am not Minerva, thanks."

Marge Piercy, *He, She and It* (1991)

This novel oscillates between two *F* stories, one set in a dystopian future, the other in 1600 CE Prague. The future story focuses on the struggle of Yod (perhaps evoking the Kabbalistic Hebrew 'hand/figure of God'), a benevolent and super-intelligent android who possesses human-like emotional capabilities and needs, to be accepted by his creators as a full-fledged person. Encountering *F* and films based on it, with which he becomes preoccupied, is for Yod an enlightening but unpleasant experience. The other story, framed as an educational bedtime tale for Yod, tells of a rabbi who creates a golem in order to protect the Jewish ghetto from a pogrom.

Richard Powers, *Galatea 2.2* (1995)

This novel offers a Digital Age version of the Pygmalion myth (as the title signals with reference to the name given to his statue/wife in some ancient sources) in the mode of 'realistic SF.' The narrator, also named Richard Powers, works with a computer scientist to create an artificial intelligence named Helen, educating it through works of literature in the Western tradition. Powers compares this process to the episode in *F* when the Creature educates himself by reading "*Paradise Lost*, Plutarch's *Lives*, Goethe's *Werther*."

Kirsten Bakis, *Lives of the Monster Dogs* (1997)

Like Stapledon's *Sirius*, this novel imagines the Creature as canine. The anthropoid "monster dogs" were the dream of an eccentric nineteenth-century Prussian scientist named Augustus Rank, who worked with an isolated group of fervent disciples to create them. Used as slaves, the dogs revolt against their creators. Possessing great wealth and an antiquated aristocratic culture, the dogs struggle to understand their past and to create a life for themselves in twenty-first-century NYC. Like his namesake Roman emperor, Augustus Rank had imperial ambitions, though his remain unfulfilled. There is passing mention of "a speech from *Julius Caesar*" in the castle the dogs build on the Lower East Side. The fire that ultimately destroys this castle recalls both the conflagrations in which so many of the old Frankenstein movies end and the double-edged flame of Prometheus.

Michel Houellebecq, *The Possibility of an Island* (2005)

An increasingly prominent variation on the *F* story involves human attempts to conquer death not by reanimating dead bodies, but by technologically transforming the human body in order to prevent the occurrence of death. Houellebecq's novel offers a bleak vision of this possibility. Near the end, a fragment of Aristophanes' famous speech in Plato's *Symposium*—describing each person as half of a being seeking its other half—appears as a message in a bottle.

Film

Universal Frankenstein cycle (*Frankenstein* [1931], *Bride of Frankenstein* [1935], *Son of Frankenstein* [1939], *The Ghost of Frankenstein* [1942], *Frankenstein Meets the Wolf Man* [1943], *House of Frankenstein* [1944], *House of Dracula* [1945], *Abbott and Costello Meet Frankenstein* [1948])

This cycle of films is one of the main channels through which MWS's story enters the twentieth century, with the first three featuring Boris Karloff's iconic portrayal of the Creature, and with films beyond the first extending beyond *F*'s plot, incorporating the Wolf Man and Dracula into narratives involving descendants and imitators of the original Frankenstein. The creation and reanimation of the Creature is framed as a usurpation of the divine prerogative of the Christian God. Though the scripts never explicitly mention Prometheus, iconic scenes in *Frankenstein* and *Bride of Frankenstein* in which the power of lightning is technologically harnessed to give life recall the Promethean theft of fire. Many of the films bear a structural resemblance to Greek tragedy. The aristocratic Frankensteins are destined to succumb to the same temptation again and again, incurring thereby the wrath of the villagers, who function as a kind of antagonistic Greek chorus. In *Son of Frankenstein*, we learn that the family castle was originally a bath built by the Romans over a sulfur pit.

Hammer Frankenstein cycle (*The Curse of Frankenstein* [1957], *The Revenge of Frankenstein* [1958], *The Evil of Frankenstein* [1964], *Frankenstein Created Woman* [1967], *Frankenstein Must Be Destroyed* [1969], *The Horror of Frankenstein* [1970], *Frankenstein and the Monster from Hell* [1974])

These films, in which Peter Cushing plays Victor Frankenstein, are an important part of the Frankenstein tradition. Patristic Latin occurs in many of the films' depictions of funerals and executions.

Young Frankenstein (1974)

Co-written by Mel Brooks and Gene Wilder, this humorous spoof of earlier *F* films emphasizes the Creature's emotional malleability: hostility makes it behave monstrously, but love can civilize it. In the crucial scene in which Frankenstein realizes this, he says to the creature, "Do you want to talk about the Olympian ideal?", implying (with humorous incongruity) that the Creature exemplifies this normative standard of human beauty. This classical reference is notable in light of the Frankenstein tradition's interest in the human treatment of non-normative entities.

The Rocky Horror Picture Show (1975)

This comic cult classic amps up the story's interest in transgressive sexuality in the context of transgressive science. Dr. Frank-N-Furter is at once a bisexual Pygmalion and an unrepentant Frankenstein. Frank-N-Furter creates the chiseled Rocky to be his ideal boy toy and initiates a buttoned-up bourgeois couple into the joys of sexual liberation. The film contains several explicit classical references. Rocky's first song begins with (and repeats) the lines "The sword of Damocles is hanging over my head / And I've got the feeling someone's gonna be cutting the thread." Frank-N-Furter sings that "In just seven days / I can make you a man," alluding to the fitness guru Charles Atlas, who took his stage name from the Greek mythic figure; later, Rocky gazes at a stained-glass window that depicts a more classical Atlas holding the Earth on his shoulders. Frank-N-Furter employs a device labeled "MEDUSA" to transform people into (neo-)classical statuary, and another one labeled "de-medusa" to reverse the process.

Blade Runner (1982)

In this film version of Dick's *Do Androids Dream of Electric Sheep?* (see above), the android creatures attempt to force their creator to give them longer lives. The entrance to the apartment where the film's climactic action takes place is dominated by a monumental marble krater or mixing-bowl, neoclassical in style. As many scholars have observed, the film engages with several themes in particularly classical terms, including the brevity of a hero's life (Greek epic), the relationship between sight and (self-)knowledge (*Oedipus Tyrannus*), and the stylization of 'Other'-bodied individuals as artificial (e.g., the Talos myth and Ovid's Pygmalion).

Weird Science (1985)

Inspired by watching James Whale's 1931 film version of *Frankenstein*, two high school nerds who can't get girlfriends decide to use their computer to create the perfect woman. Though she turns out *Playboy* perfect, the boys remain painfully awkward, and it is left to her to contrive situations that force them to learn confidence. In this comic twist on the Pygmalion story, the made-to-order woman remakes her creators into paragons of heterosexual adolescent masculinity.

Re-Animator trilogy (*Re-Animator* [1985], *Bride of Re-Animator* [1990], *Beyond Re-Animator* [2003])

These gory films, loosely based on the eponymous Lovecraft novelette (see above), are most notable for the way that they envision body parts chemically reanimated as parts capable of acting independently and of joining together in novel—and horrifically grotesque—combinations. *Bride of Re-Animator*, in which the protagonists create a new woman out of the characteristic body parts of various dead women—feet of a dancer, legs of a prostitute, womb of a virgin, etc.—recalls aspects of the Pygmalion and Pandora stories.

Jurassic Park (1993)

This film is notable as a *F* story in which the reanimation of the dead is also a revivification of the distant past. The film's examination of the survival capacities of humans in comparison to those of other species resonates with the myth of Prometheus as told in Plato's *Protagoras*.

Television

Star Trek: The Next Generation, "Datalore" (1988), "Brothers" (1990), "Descent" (1993), "Descent, Part II" (1993), "Inheritance" (1993)

Creature figures of various kinds occur frequently in the *Star Trek* franchise. The episodes listed here focus on Data, a benevolent android in the vein of Asimov's vision, and his 'brother' Lore, whose identical superhuman capabilities combine with problematic human emotions to render him a threat to humanity. In "Brothers," Data and Lore meet their creator, Dr. Noonian Soong, whose office includes what appears to be fragmentary Greco-Roman statuary. Soong and Data discuss the pursuit of immortality through procreation and why humans care about the past, a conversation that recalls the speech of Diotima in Plato's *Symposium*. In "Descent," in which Lore attempts to convince Data to join his cyborg war against humanity, a Federation ship called the *Agamemnon* is mentioned; this may invite a comparison of Data and Lore with the brothers Agamemnon and Menelaus.

The X-Files, "The Post-Modern Prometheus" (1997)

This episode explicitly engages with MWS's novel and the classical allusion of its subtitle. FBI agent Mulder says to his partner Scully, "When Victor Frankenstein asks himself, 'whence did the principle of life proceed?' and then as the gratifying summit to his toils creates the hideous phantasm of a man, he prefigures the postmodern Prometheus, the genetic engineer, whose power to reanimate matter, genes, into life, us, is only as limited as his imagination is." Like his modern forebear, the postmodern Prometheus sins by failing to love or nurture his creation.

Penny Dreadful (2014–2016)

This series weaves characters and motifs from the *F* tradition, both literary and filmic, into a dense neo-Gothic tapestry. Classical reception abounds, particularly in the first two seasons. Victor Frankenstein's Creature (soon revealed to be his second) chooses for himself the name Proteus—the shape-shifting, truth-telling sea god of Greek myth—from a volume of Shakespeare. In S1E3, Frankenstein's first creature, returning with a vengeance, says that he is not "the lyrical Adonais of which Shelley wrote," nor "a creation of the antique pastoral world," but rather "modernity personified." In S1E4, there is a horror play called "The Transformed Beast," in which the title character asks, "How can I contain this Promethean flame?" The second season revolves around the decipherment of a story written by a medieval monk in Greek, Latin, and other ancient languages. In S2E1, a witch gives the early Christian author Tertullian's account of how the idea of 'memento mori'—Latin for 'remember that you will die'—originated as part of the Roman triumphal procession. In S2E4, the Greek goddess Hecate is discussed in connection with a witch named Hecate, who plays an important role in the series. In S2E9, Frankenstein's first creature says that Pandora's box contained only one thing: a mirror. An important subplot of seasons two and three is a Pygmalion story: Frankenstein reanimates a woman to be a mate for his first creature, but falls in love with her himself; when she rejects him and begins to lead a violent revolt of abused women against men, he attempts to devise a scientific means of rendering her docile.

Bibliography

Abrams, M. H. 1973. *Natural Supernaturalism: Tradition and Revolution in Romantic Literature*. New York, NY: W. W. Norton.

Accardo, Pasquale. 2002. *The Metamorphosis of Apuleius: Cupid and Psyche, Beauty and the Beast, King Kong*. Madison, NJ: Fairleigh Dickinson University Press.

Adams, Carol J. 1990. *The Sexual Politics of Meat: A Feminist-Vegetarian Critical Theory*. New York, NY: Bloomsbury Academic.

Adorno, Theodore W. 1984. *Aesthetic Theory*. Christian Lenhardt, trans. Gretel Adorno and Rolf Tiedemann, eds. London: Routledge.

Agamben, Giorgio. 1998. *Homo sacer: Sovereign Power and Bare Life*. D. Heller-Roazen, trans. Stanford, CA: Stanford University Press.

Ahl, Frederick. 1976. *Lucan: An Introduction*. Ithaca, NY: Cornell University Press.

Aldiss, Brian W. 1976. *Billion Year Spree: The True History of Science Fiction*. New York, NY: Schocken Books.

Allen, Graham. 2008. *Mary Shelley*. Hampshire: Palgrave Macmillan.

Arweiler, Alexander. 2006. "Erictho und die Figuren der Entzweiung—Vorüberlegungen zu einer Poetik der Emergenz in Lucans *Bellum ciuile*." *Dictynna* 3: 3–71.

Asimov, Isaac. 1995. *The Complete Robot*. London: Voyager.

Atherton, C., ed. 1998. *Monsters and Monstrosity in Greek and Roman Culture*. Bari: Levante Editori.

Auerbach, Nina and David J. Skal, eds. 1997. *Bram Stoker: Dracula*. New York, NY: W. W. Norton.

Austin, R. G, ed. and comm. 1986. *P. Vergili Maronis. Aeneidos Liber Sextus*. Oxford: Clarendon Press.

Bacon, Francis [as Francis Lord Verulam]. 1840. *The Essays or Counsels Civil and Moral and Wisdom of the Ancients*. Basil Montagu, Esq., ed. London: William Pickering.

Baldick, Chris. 1987. *In Frankenstein's Shadow: Myth, Monstrosity, and Nineteenth Century Writing*. Oxford: Clarendon Press.

Barnett, Suzanne L. 2014. "'The Great God Pan is Alive Again': Thomas Love Peacock and Percy Shelley in Marlow." *Essays in Romanticism* 21.1: 65–87.

Barnett, Suzanne L. 2017. *Romantic Paganism: The Politics of Ecstasy in the Shelley Circle*. Basingstoke: Palgrave.

Barnett, Suzanne L. and Katherine Bennett Gustafson. 2014. "The Radical Aesop: William Godwin and the Juvenile Library, 1805–1825." *Romantic Circles Digital Editions*. https://www.rc.umd.edu/editions/godwin_fables/editions.2014.godwin_fables.introduction.html.

Barney, Darin. 2000. *Prometheus Wired*. Chicago, IL: University of Chicago Press.

Barthes, Roland. 1967a. *Elements of Semiology*. Annette Lavers and Colin Smith, trans. New York, NY: Hill & Wang.

Barthes, Roland. 1967b. *Writing Degree Zero*. Annette Lavers and Colin Smith, trans. London: Jonathan Cape.

Barthes, Roland. 2001. "The Death of the Author." In *The Norton Anthology of Theory and Criticism*. First Edition. Vincent B. Leitch, ed. New York, NY: W. W. Norton. 1466–1470.

Bartsch, Shadi. 1997. *Ideology in Cold Blood: A Reading of Lucan's Civil War*. Cambridge, MA: Harvard University Press.

Bartsch, Shadi. 2010. "Lucan and Historical Bias." In *Lucain en débat. Rhétorique, poétique et histoire*. Olivier Devillers and Sylvie Franchet-d'Espèrey, eds. Bordeaux: Ausonius. 21–31.

Bate, Jonathan. 1986. "Shakespearean Allusion in English Caricature in the Age of Gillray." *Journal of the Warburg and Courtault Institutes* 49: 196–210.

Bates, Judith. 1999. "*Frankenstein*: Roman des origins." In *Autour de* Frankenstein *(Lectures critiques): Textes réunis et présentés par Gilles Menegaldo*. Giles Menegaldo, ed. Poitiers: Université de Poitiers. 133–143.

Beauvoir, Simone de. 1989 [1952]. *The Second Sex*. H. M. Parshley, trans. New York, NY: Vintage.

Bennett, Betty T., ed. 1980. *The Letters of Mary Wollstonecraft Shelley*. Volume I. Baltimore, MD: The Johns Hopkins University Press.

Bennett, Betty T., ed. 1983. *The Letters of Mary Wollstonecraft Shelley*. Volume II. Baltimore, MD: The Johns Hopkins University Press.

Bennett, Betty T. 1997. "Newly Uncovered Letters and Poems by Mary Wollstonecraft Shelley: ('It Was My Birthday and It Pleased Me to Tell the People so –')." *Keats-Shelley Journal* 46: 51–74.

Bennett, Betty T. 2001. "Biographical Imaginings and Mary Shelley's (Extant and Missing) Correspondence." In *Writing Lives: Mary Wollstonecraft and Mary Shelley*. Helen M. Buss, D. L. Macdonald, and Anne McWhir, eds. Waterloo, ON: Wilfrid Laurier University Press. 217–231.

Bernstein, Jeremy. 1991. *Quantum Profiles*. Princeton, NJ: Princeton University Press.

Bertagnolli, Paul. 2007. *Prometheus in Music: Representations of the Myth in the Romantic Era*. New York, NY: Routledge.

Bevilacqua, Vincent M. 1976. "Classical Rhetorical Influences in the Development of Eighteenth-Century British Aesthetic Criticism." *Transactions of the American Philological Association* 106: 11–28.

Bhabha, Homi K. 1994. *The Location of Culture*. New York, NY: Routledge.

Bloom, Harold. 1959. *Shelley's Mythmaking*. New Haven, CT: Yale University Press.

Bloom, Harold. 1971. *The Visionary Company: A Reading of English Romantic Poetry*. Ithaca, NY: Cornell University Press.

Boden, Margaret A. 2016. *AI: Its Nature and Future*. Oxford: Oxford University Press.

Bost-Fiévet, Mélanie and Sandra Provini, eds. 2014. *L'Antiquité dans l'imaginaire contemporain. Fantasy, science-fiction, fantastique*. Paris: Classiques Garnier.

Botting, Fred. 1991. *Making Monstrous:* Frankenstein, *Criticism, Theory*. Manchester: Manchester University Press.

Boucherie, Christophe. 2017. "Ethics and Natural Philosophy in the Public Representation of the Scientific Experiment: A Reading of Wright of Derby's *An Experiment on a Bird in the Air Pump* (1768) in the Light of Mary Shelley's *Frankenstein* (1818)." *VIDES* 5. http://open.conted.ox.ac.uk/resources/documents/ethics-and-natural-philosophy-public-representation-scientific-experiment. Accessed July 13, 2017.

Bowen, Arlene. 1996. "Mary Shelley's Rose-Eating Cat, Lucian, and *Frankenstein*." *The Keats-Shelley Journal* 45: 16–19.

Bradley, James. 2012. "Some Thoughts on Prometheus." *City of Tongues*. June 5, 2012. https://cityoftongues.com/2012/06/05/some-thoughts-on-prometheus/.

Braidotti, Rosi. 2013. *The Posthuman*. Hoboken, NJ: Wiley.

Brantlinger, Patrick. 2016. "Race and *Frankenstein*." In *The Cambridge Companion to Frankenstein*. Andrew Smith, ed. Cambridge: Cambridge University Press. 128–142.

Braund, Susan H., trans. 1992. *Lucan: Civil War*. Oxford: Oxford University Press.

Bremmer, Jan. 1983. *The Early Greek Concept of the Soul*. Princeton, NJ: Princeton University Press.

Brett-Smith, H. F. B., ed. 1909. *Peacock's Memoirs of Shelley; with Shelley's Letters to Peacock*. London: Henry Frowde.

Britton, Ronald. 2015. "Mary Shelley's *Frankenstein*: What Made the Monster Monstrous?" *Journal of Analytic Psychology* 60: 1–11.

Bronfen, Elisabeth. 1994. "Rewriting the Family: Mary Shelley's '*Frankenstein*' in its Biographical/Textual Context." In *Frankenstein: Creation and Monstrosity*. Stephen Bann, ed. London: Reaktion Books. 16–38.

Brönnimann, Stefan and Daniel Krämer. 2016. "Tambora and the 'Year Without a Summer' of 1816. A Perspective on Earth and Human Systems Science." *Geographica Bernensia* G90. http://www.geography.unibe.ch/unibe/portal/fak_naturwis/e_geowiss/c_igeogr/content/e39624/e39625/e39626/e426207/e431531/tambora_e_webA4_eng.pdf. Accessed September 19, 2017.

Brooks, Peter. 1979. "Godlike Science/Unhallowed Arts: Language, Nature, and Monstrosity." In *The Endurance of Frankenstein: Essays on Mary Shelley's Novel*. George Levine and U. C. Knoepflmacher, eds. Berkeley, CA: University of California Press. 205–220.

Brown, Sarah Annes. 2008. "Plato's Stepchildren: SF and the Classics." In *A Companion to Classical Receptions*. Lorna Hardwick and Christopher Stray, eds. Malden, MA: Wiley-Blackwell. 415–427.

Burr, Ty. 2012. "Prometheus: 'Alien' prequel gets lost in space." *Boston Globe*. June 7, 2012. http://archive.boston.com/ae/movies/articles/2012/06/07/prometheus_follows_an_alien_path/.

Butler, Judith. 1988. "Performative Acts and Gender Constitution: An Essay in Phenomenology and Feminist Theory." *Theatre Journal* 40.4: 519–531.

Butler, Judith. 2000. *Antigone's Claim: Kinship between Life and Death*. New York, NY: Columbia University Press.

Butler, Judith. 2006. *Gender Trouble*. London: Routledge Classics.

Butler, Judith. 2011. *Bodies that Matter*. London: Routledge Classics.

Butler, Judith and Gayatri C. Spivak. 2007. *Who Sings the Nation State? Language, Politics, Belonging*. New York, NY: Seagull Books.

Butler, Marilyn. 1979. *Peacock Displayed: A Satirist in his Context*. London: Routledge & Kegan Paul.

Butler, Marilyn, ed. 1994. *Mary Shelley: Frankenstein: or The Modern Prometheus: The 1818 Text*. Oxford: Oxford University Press.

Butler, Marilyn, ed. 2008. *Mary Shelley: Frankenstein; or the Modern Prometheus: The 1818 Text*. Oxford: Oxford University Press.

Calame, Claude. 1999. *The Poetics of Eros in Ancient Greece*. Janet Lloyd, trans. Princeton, NJ: Princeton University Press.

Caldwell, Janis McLarren. 2004. *Literature and Medicine in Nineteenth-Century Britain: From Mary Shelley to George Eliot*. Cambridge: Cambridge University Press.

Campbell, David, ed. and trans. 1982. *Greek Lyric I*. Cambridge, MA: Harvard University Press.

Campbell, Joseph. 2008. *The Hero with a Thousand Faces*. Novato, CA: New World Library.

Canfora, Luciano. 2007. *Julius Caesar: The Life and Times of the People's Dictator*. Marian Hill and Kevin Windle, trans. Berkeley, CA: University of California Press.

Canfora, Luciano. 2009. "Caesar for Communists and Fascists." In *A Companion to Julius Caesar*. Miriam Griffin, ed. Malden, MA: Wiley-Blackwell. 431–440.

Carlson, Julie A. 2007. *England's First Family of Writers: Mary Wollstonecraft, William Godwin, Mary Shelley*. Baltimore, MD: The Johns Hopkins University Press.

Carney, James P. 2014. "Some Previously Unrecognized References to Classical Historians in Mary Wollstonecraft Shelley's *The Last Man*." *Notes & Queries* 61.4: 527–530.

Carpenter, John, dir. 1982. *The Thing*. Universal Pictures.

Carson, Craig. 2011. "The King's Virtual Body: Image, Text, and Sovereignty in Edmund Burke's Reflections on the Revolution in France." *Republics of Letters: A Journal for the Study of Knowledge, Politics, and the Arts* 2.2: 115–126.

Cartledge, Paul. 2002. *The Greeks: A Portrait of Self and Others*. Oxford: Oxford University Press.

Carver, R. H. F. 2007. *The Protean Ass. The 'Metamorphoses' of Apuleius from Antiquity to the Renaissance*. Oxford: Oxford University Press.

Carver, R. H. F. 2012. "Of Donkeys and D(a)emons: Metamorphosis and the Literary Imagination from Apuleius to Augustine." In *Transformative Change in Western Thought: A History of Metamorphosis from Homer to Hollywood*. I. Gildenhard and A. Zissos, eds. London: Legenda. 222–251.

Casali, Sergio. 2011. "The *Bellum Civile* as an Anti-*Aeneid*." In *Brill's Companion to Lucan*. Paolo Asso, ed. Leiden: Brill. 81–109.

Cavicchioli, Sonia. 2002. *The Tale of Cupid and Psyche: An Illustrated History*. Susan Scott, trans. New York, NY: George Braziller.

Chan, Sarah. 2009. "More than Cautionary Tales: The Role of Fiction in Bioethics." *Journal of Medical Ethics* 35.7: 398–399.

Chenoweth, Michael. 1996. "Ships' Logbooks and 'The Year Without a Summer.'" *Bulletin of the American Meteorological Society* 77.9: 2077–2094.

Clark, John. 1752. *Ovid's Metamorphoses, with an English translation, as exact as possible*. London: W. Clarke.

Clayton, Jay. 2003. "*Frankenstein*'s Futurity: Replicants and Robots." In *The Cambridge Companion to Mary Shelley*. Esther Schor, ed. Cambridge: Cambridge University Press. 84–99.

Clemit, Pamela. 1993. *The Godwinian Novel: The Rational Fictions of Godwin, Brockden Brown, Mary Shelley*. Oxford: Clarendon Press.

Clemit, Pamela and A. A. Markley, eds. 2002. *Mary Shelley's* Literary Lives *and Other Writings*. Volume IV. *Life of William Godwin, Poems, Uncollected Prose, Translations, Part-Authored and Attributed Writings*. London: Pickering & Chatto.

Clute, John and John Grant, eds. 1997. *The Encyclopedia of Fantasy*. New York, NY: St. Martin's Press.

Cohen, Jeffrey Jerome, ed. 1996a. *Monster Theory: Reading Culture*. Minneapolis, MN: University of Minnesota Press.

Cohen, Jeffrey Jerome. 1996b. "Monster Culture (Seven Theses)." In *Monster Theory: Reading Culture*. Jeffrey Jerome Cohen, ed. Minneapolis, MN: University of Minnesota Press. 2–25.

Cohen, Jeffrey Jerome. 2012. "The Promise of Monsters." In *The Ashgate Research Companion to Monsters and the Monstrous*. Asa Simon Mittman and Peter J. Dendle, eds. Burlington, VT: Ashgate. 449–464.

Cohn, Matt. 2015. "Was God an Astronaut?: Ridley Scott's Prometheus on the Classics, the Past, and the Alien." *Eidolon*. July 9, 2015. https://eidolon.pub/was-god-an-astronaut-4d6dc500f889#.

Cole-Dai, Jihong, David Ferris, Alyson Lanciki, Joel Savarino, Melanie Baroni, and Mark H. Thiemens. 2009. "Cold Decade (AD 1810–1819) Caused by Tambora (1815) and Another (1809) Stratospheric Volcanic Eruption." *Geophysical Research Letters* 36.22. November 21, 2009. http://onlinelibrary.wiley.com/doi/10.1029/2009GL040882/abstract.

Coleridge, Derwent, ed. 1851. *Poems by Hartley Coleridge, with a Memoir of His Life by His Brother. In Two Volumes*. London: Edward Moxon.

Collin, Robbie. 2015. "Ex Machina: bewitchingly smart sci-fi." *The Telegraph*. January 21, 2015. http://www.telegraph.co.uk/film/ex-machina/review/.

Colvin, Sidney. 1917. *John Keats*. London: Macmillan.

Conners, Peter. 2010. *White Hand Society: The Psychedelic Partnership of Timothy Leary & Allen Ginsberg*. San Francisco, CA: City Lights Publishers.

Consolmagno, Guy. 2016. "Medieval Cosmology and World Building." In *Medieval Science Fiction*. Carl Kears and James Paz, eds. London: King's College London. 265–285.

Cooper, John M., ed. 1997. *Plato: Complete Works*. Indianapolis, IN: Hackett.

Craciun, Adriana. 2016. "*Frankenstein*'s Politics." In *The Cambridge Companion to Frankenstein*. Andrew Smith, ed. Cambridge: Cambridge University Press. 84–97.

Crook, Nora. 1996. "Endnotes: Textual Variants." In *The Novels and Selected Works of Mary Shelley*. Volume I. London: William Pickering. 182–227.

Cross, Ashley J. 2004. "'What a World we Make the Oppressor and the Oppressed': George Cruikshank, Percy Shelley, and the Gendering of Revolution in 1819." *English Literary History* 71.1: 167–207.

Csicsery-Ronay, Istvan. 2008. *The Seven Beauties of Science Fiction*. Middletown, CT: Wesleyan University Press.

Curran, Stuart. 1975. *Shelley's Annus Mirabilis: The Maturing of an Epic Vision*. San Marino, CA: Huntington Library.

Curran, Stuart. 1986. "The Political Prometheus." *Studies in Romanticism* 25.3: 429–455.

Darwin, Erasmus. 1791. *The Botanic Garden: A Poem in Two Parts. Part One: The Economy of Vegetation. Part Two: The Loves of the Plants*. London: J. Johnson.

Darwin, Erasmus. 1799. *The Botanic Garden. A Poem, in Two Parts*. London: J. Johnson.

Darwin, Erasmus. 1803. *The Temple of Nature, or The Origin of Society*. London: J. Johnson.

Davis, Richard. 1948. "George Sandys v. William Stansby: The 1632 Edition of Ovid's *Metamorphosis*." *The Library* s5-III.3: 193–212.

Dawkins, Richard. 1976. *The Selfish Gene*. Oxford: Oxford University Press.

Dawley, J. Searle, dir. 1910. *Frankenstein*. Edison Studios.

DeFilippo, Joseph. 1999. "*Curiositas* and the Platonism of Apuleius' *Golden Ass*." In *Oxford Readings in the Roman Novel*. S. J. Harrison, ed. Oxford: Oxford University Press. 269–289.

Dinter, Martin T. 2012. *Anatomizing Civil War: Studies in Lucan's Epic Technique*. Ann Arbor, MI: University of Michigan Press.

Dougherty, Carol. 2006. *Prometheus*. London: Routledge.

Dryden, John. 1721. *Fables Ancient and Modern*. London: Jacob Tonson.

Dryden, John, et al., trans. 1751. *Ovid's Metamorphoses. In Fifteen Books. Translated by Mr. Dryden, Mr. Addison, Mr. Garth, and other eminent hands*. London: Samuel Garth, M. D.

Dryden, John, et al., trans. 1833. *Ovid*. London: A. J. Valpy.

Duff, Tim. 1999. *Plutarch's Lives: Exploring Virtue and Vice*. Oxford: Clarendon Press.

Eberle-Sinatra, Michael. 2000. "Gender, Authorship and Male Domination: Mary Shelley's Limited Freedom in *Frankenstein* and *The Last Man*." In *Mary Shelley's Fictions: From Frankenstein to Falkner*. New York, NY: St. Martin's Press. 95–108.

Ehrenreich, Barbara. 2012. "The Missionary Position." *The Baffler* 21. November 2012. https://thebaffler.com/salvos/the-missionary-position.

Einstein, Albert. 1972. *Correspondance avec Michele Besso 1903–1955*. Pierre Speziali, ed. Paris: Hermann.

Fagan, Brian. 2000. *The Little Ice Age: How Climate Made History 1300–1850*. New York, NY: Basic Books.

Fairclough, H. Rushton, trans. 1929. *Horace: Satires, Epistles and Ars poetica*. London: William Heinemann.

Faraone, Christopher A. 1992. *Talismans and Trojan Horses: Guardian Statues in Ancient Greek Myth and Ritual*. New York, NY: Oxford University Press.

Farley, Wendy. 1990. *Tragic Vision and Divine Compassion: A Contemporary Theodicy*. Louisville, KY: John Knox Press.

Fehling, Detlev. 1977. *Amor und Psyche: Die Schöpfung des Apuleius und ihre Einwirkung auf das Märchen, eine Kritik der romantischen Märchentheorie*. Wiesbaden: Franz Steiner.

Feldman, Paula R. and Diana Scott-Kilvert, eds. 1987. *The Journals of Mary Shelley 1814–1844*. Two Volumes. Oxford: Clarendon Press.

Ferguson, Frances. 1992. *Solitude and the Sublime: Romanticism and the Aesthetics of Individuation*. New York, NY: Routledge.

Finkelpearl, Ellen. 1999. "Psyche, Aeneas, and an Ass: Apuleius, *Metamorphoses* 6.10–6.21." In *Oxford Readings in the Roman Novel*. S. J. Harrison, ed. Oxford: Oxford University Press. 290–306.

Fisch, Audrey A. 1993. "Plaguing Politics: AIDS, Deconstruction, and *The Last Man*." In *The Other Mary Shelley: Beyond Frankenstein*. Audrey A. Fisch, Anne K. Mellor, and Esther H. Schor, eds. Oxford: Oxford University Press. 267–286.

Folch, Marcus. 2017. "A Time for Fantasy: Retelling Apuleius in C. S. Lewis's *Till We Have Faces*." In *Classical Traditions in Modern Fantasy*. Brett M. Rogers and Benjamin Eldon Stevens, eds. Oxford: Oxford University Press. 160–186.

Forry, Steven Earl. 1990. *Hideous Progenies: Dramatizations of* Frankenstein *from Mary Shelley to the Present*. Philadelphia, PA: University of Pennsylvania Press.

Foucault, Michel. 1966. *The Order of Things: An Archaeology of the Human Sciences*. London: Tavistock.

Foucault, Michel. 1988. *Madness and Civilization: A History of Insanity in the Age of Reason*. New York, NY: Vintage Books.

Foucault, Michel. 2003. *"Society Must Be Defended": Lectures at the Collège de France, 1975-1976*. Mauro Bertani, Alessandro Fontana, and François Ewald, eds. David Macey, trans. New York, NY: Picador.

Fraction, Matt (writer) and Christian Ward (artist). 2014. *Ody-C*. (November 2014–present). Image Comics.

Franci, Giovanna. 1985. "A Mirror of the Future: Vision and Apocalypse in Mary Shelley's *The Last Man*." In *Mary Shelley*. Harold Bloom, ed. New York, NY: Chelsea House. 181-191.

Francis, James A. 2009. "Metal Maidens, Achilles' Shield and Pandora: The Beginnings of 'Ekphrasis.'" *American Journal of Philology* 130.1: 1–23.

Franco, Dean. 1998. "Mirror Images and Otherness in Mary Shelley's *Frankenstein*." *Literature and Psychology* 44: 80–95.

Franklin, Benjamin. 1789. "Meteorological Imaginations and Conjectures." In *Memoirs of the Literary and Philosophical Society of Manchester*. Second Edition. London: T. Cadwell in the Strand. 373–377.

Franklin, Caroline. 2013. *The Female Romantics: Nineteenth-century Women Novelists and Byronism*. London: Routledge.

Fredericks, Sigmund C. 1976. "Lucian's *True History* as SF." *Science Fiction Studies* 3.1.8: 49–60.

Fredericks, Sigmund C. 1980. "Greek Mythology in Modern Science Fiction: Vision and Cognition." In *Classical Mythology in Twentieth Century Thought and Literature*. W. M. Aycock and T. M. Klein, eds. Lubbock, TX: Texas Tech Press. 89–105.

Freedman, Carl. 2000. *Critical Theory and Science Fiction*. Middletown, CT: Wesleyan University Press.

Freedman, Carl. 2002. "Hail Mary: On the Author of *Frankenstein* and the Origins of Science Fiction." *Science Fiction Studies* 29.2: 253–264.

Freud, Sigmund. 1953–1974. "Fetishism." James Strachey, trans. In *The Standard Edition of the Complete Psychological Works of Sigmund Freud*. Volume 21. James Strachey, ed. London: Hogarth Press and the Institute of Psycho-Analysis. 149–157.

Friedman, John Block. 2000. *The Monstrous Races in Medieval Art and Thought*. Syracuse, NY: Syracuse University Press.

Friedman, Lester D. and Allison B. Kavey. 2016. *Monstrous Progeny: A History of the Frankenstein Narratives*. New Brunswick, NJ: Rutgers University Press.

Fulford, Tim, Debbie Lee, and Peter Kitson. 2004. *Literature, Science and Exploration in the Romantic Era*. Cambridge: Cambridge University Press.

Fyfe, W. Hamilton, trans. 1995. *Aristotle, Poetics; Longinus, On the Sublime; Demetrius, On Style*. Donald Russell, rev. Cambridge, MA: Harvard University Press.

Gaisser, Julia Haig. 2008. *The Fortunes of Apuleius and* The Golden Ass. *A Study in Transmission and Reception*. Princeton, NJ: Princeton University Press.

Gale, Monica, ed. 2007. *Lucretius: Oxford Readings in Classical Studies*. Oxford: Oxford University Press.

Galinsky, Karl. 1996. *Augustan Culture: An Interpretive Introduction*. Princeton, NJ: Princeton University Press.

Gallia, Andrew B. 2012. *Remember the Roman Republic: Culture, Politics, and History Under the Principate*. Cambridge: Cambridge University Press.

Gantz, Timothy. 1993. *Early Greek Myth*. Baltimore, MD: The Johns Hopkins University Press.

Garani, Myrto. 2007. *Empedocles Redivivus: Poetry and Analogy in Lucretius*. New York, NY: Routledge.

Garland, Alex. 2015. *Ex Machina*. London: Faber & Faber.

Garland, Alex, dir. 2015. *Ex Machina* [screenplay]. Universal Pictures.

Genette, Gerard. 1991. "Introduction to the Paratext." *New Literary History* 22: 261–272.

Gigante, Denise. 2000. "Facing the Ugly: The Case of 'Frankenstein.'" *ELH* 67.2: 565–587.

Gilbert, Sandra M. and Susan Gubar. 1979. *The Madwoman in the Attic: The Woman Writer and the Nineteenth-Century Literary Imagination.* New Haven, CT: Yale University Press.

Gillespie, Stuart and Philip Hardie, eds. 2007. *The Cambridge Companion to Lucretius.* Cambridge: Cambridge University Press.

Gloyn. Liz. 2015. "In a Galaxy Far, Far Away: On Classical Reception and Science Fiction." *Strange Horizons.* April 27, 2015. http://strangehorizons.com/non-fiction/articles/in-a-galaxy-far-far-away-on-classical-reception-and-science-fiction.

Godwin, William [as "Edward Baldwin, Esq."]. 1806. *The History of England. For the Use of Schools and Young Persons.* London: Printed for Thomas Hodgkins, at the Juvenile Library.

Godwin, William [as "Edward Baldwin, Esq."]. 1810. *The Pantheon; or Ancient History of the Gods of Greece and Rome. Intended to Facilitate the Understanding of the Classical Authors, and of the Poets in General. For the Use of Schools, and Young Persons of Both Sexes. With Engravings of the Principal Gods, chiefly taken from the Remains of Ancient Statuary.* London: Printed for M. J. Godwin at the Juvenile Library, No. 41 Skinner Street.

Godwin, William. 1834. *Lives of the Necromancers.* London: F. J. Mason.

Goldberg, M. A. 1959. "Moral and Myth in Mrs. Shelley's *Frankenstein*." *Keats-Shelley Journal* 8: 27–38.

Golding, Arthur. 1575. *The. xv. bookes of P. Ouidius Naso, entytuled Metamorphosis, translated oute of Latin into English meeter, by Arthur Golding Gentleman, a worke very pleasaunt and delectable.* London: William Seres.

Goldsmith, Steven. 1993. *Unbuilding Jerusalem: Apocalypse and Romantic Representation.* Ithaca, NY: Cornell University Press.

González, Antonio B. and Ana M. Calvo. 1997. "Monsters on the Island: Caliban's and Prospero's Hideous Progeny" *Atlantis* 19: 15–20.

Goodall, Jane. 2008. "Electrical Romanticism." In *Frankenstein's Science: Experimentation and Discovery in Romantic Culture, 1780–1830.* Christa Knellwolf and Jane Goodall, eds. Burlington, VT: Ashgate. 117–132.

Gordon, Richard. 1987. "Lucan's Erictho." In *Homo Viator: Classical Essays for John Bramble.* Michael Whitby, Philip Hardie, and Mary Whitby, eds. Bristol: Bristol Classical Press. 231–241.

Gotlieb, Howard B. 1960. *William Beckford of Fonthill.* New Haven, CT: Yale University Press.

Gowing, Alain. 2005. *Empire and Memory: The Representation of the Roman Republic in Imperial Culture.* Cambridge: Cambridge University Press.

Greenberg, Harvey R. 1991. "Reimagining the Gargoyle: Psychoanalytic Notes on *Alien*." In *Close Encounters: Film, Feminism, and Science Fiction.* Constance Penley, Elisabeth Lyon, Lynn Spigel, and Janet Bergstrom, eds. Minneapolis, MN: University of Minnesota Press. 83–106.

Greenblatt, Stephen. 2011. *The Swerve: How the World Became Modern.* New York, NY: W. W. Norton.

Greenfield, Robert. 2006. *Timothy Leary: A Biography.* Orlando, FL: Harcourt.

Gubar, Susan. 1979. "Mother, Maiden and the Marriage of Death: Woman Writers and an Ancient Myth." *Women's Studies* 6: 301–315.

Guignery, Vanessa. 2011. "Introduction: Hybridity, Why It Still Matters." In *Hybridity: Forms and Figures in Literature and the Visual Arts*. Vanessa Guignery, Catherine Pesso-Miquel, and François Specq, eds. Newcastle Upon Tyne: Cambridge Scholars. 1–8.

Gumpert, Matthew. 2001. *Grafting Helen: The Abduction of the Classical Past*. Madison, WI: University of Wisconsin Press.

Gumpert, Matthew. 2008. "Hybridity's End." In *Cylons in America: Critical Studies in Battlestar Galactica*. Tiffany Potter and C. W. Marshall, eds. New York, NY: Continuum International Publishing. 143–155.

Gumpert, Matthew. 2012. *The End of Meaning: Studies in Catastrophe*. Newcastle upon Tyne: Cambridge Scholars Publishing.

Guyer, Paul and Eric Matthews, eds. and trans. 2000. *Immanuel Kant: Critique of the Power of Judgment*. Cambridge: Cambridge University Press.

Haggerty, George E. 2016. "What is Queer about *Frankenstein*?" In *The Cambridge Companion to Frankenstein*. Andrew Smith, ed. Cambridge: Cambridge University Press. 116–127.

Hagstrum, J. H. 1977. "Eros and Psyche: Some Versions of Romantic Love and Delicacy." *Critical Inquiry* 3: 521–542.

Haight, Elizabeth Hazelton. 1963. *Apuleius and His Influence*. New York, NY: Cooper Square Publishers.

Hall, Edith. 1989. *Inventing the Barbarian: Greek Self-definition through Tragedy*. New York, NY: Oxford University Press.

Halliwell, Stephen, trans. 1995. *Aristotle, Poetics; Longinus, On the Sublime; Demetrius, On Style*. Cambridge, MA: Harvard University Press.

Halmi, Nicholas, Paul Magnuson, and Raimonda Modiano, eds. 2004. *Samuel Taylor Coleridge: Coleridge's Poetry and Prose*, New York, NY: W. W. Norton.

Hampsher-Monk, Iain. 2014. *Burke: Revolutionary Writings:* Reflections on the Revolution in France *and the first* Letter on a Regicide Peace. Cambridge: Cambridge University Press.

Haraway, Donna. 1991. *Simians, Cyborgs and Women: The Reinvention of Nature*. New York, NY: Routledge.

Hardwick, Lorna. 2003. *Reception Studies*. Cambridge: Cambridge University Press.

Hardwick, Lorna and Christopher Stray, eds. 2008. *A Companion to Classical Receptions*. Malden, MA: Wiley-Blackwell.

Harrison, Jane. 1908. *Prolegomena to the Study of Greek Religion*. Second Edition. Cambridge: Cambridge University Press.

Hassan, Ihab. 1980. *The Right Promethean Fire: Imagination, Science, and Cultural Change*. Urbana, IL: University of Illinois Press.

Hausheer, Roger. 1980. "Introduction." In *Isaiah Berlin: Against the Current: Essays in the History of Ideas*. Henry Hardy, ed. New York, NY: Viking. xiii–liii.

Hawley, Erin. 2015. "The Bride and Her Afterlife: Female *Frankenstein* Monsters on Page and Screen." *Literature-Film Quarterly* 43.3: 218–231.

Hayden, John O., ed. 1994. *William Wordsworth: Selected Poems*. London: Penguin.
Hayles, N. Katherine. 1999. *How We Became Posthuman; Virtual Bodies in Cybernetics, Literature, and Informatics*. Chicago, IL: University of Chicago Press.
Haywood, Ian. 2013. *Romanticism and Caricature*. Cambridge: Cambridge University Press.
Heffernan, James A. W. 1997. "Looking at the Monster: *Frankenstein* and Film." *Critical Inquiry* 24: 133–158.
Heine, R. 1978. "Picaresque Novel Versus Allegory." In *Aspects of Apuleius' Golden Ass*. B. L. Hijmans and R. Th. van der Paardt, eds. Groningen: Bouma Boekhuis. 25–42.
Henderson, John G. W. 1998. *Fighting for Rome: Poets and Caesars, History and Civil War*. Cambridge: Cambridge University Press.
Henrichs, Albert. 2011. "Dionysos Dismembered and Restored to Life: The Earliest Evidence (*OF* 59 I–II)." In *Tracing Orpheus: Studies of Orphic Fragments*. Miguel Herrero de Jáuregui, Ana Isabel Jiménez San Cristóbal, Eugenio R. Luján Martínez, Marco Antonio Santamaría Álvarez, Raquel Martín Hernández, and Sofía Torallas Tovar, eds. Berlin: de Gruyter. 61–68.
Higgins, David. 2008. *Frankenstein: Character Studies*. New York, NY: Continuum.
Hindle, Maurice, ed. 1992. *Mary Shelley: Frankenstein*. London: Penguin.
Hindle, Maurice, ed. 2007. *Mary Shelley: Frankenstein; or, the Modern Prometheus*. London: Penguin.
Hirsch, David A. Hedrich. 1996. "Liberty, Equality, Monstrosity: Revolutionizing the Family in Mary Shelley's *Frankenstein*." In *Monster Theory: Reading Culture*. Jeffrey Jerome Cohen, ed. Minneapolis, MN: University of Minnesota Press. 115–140.
Hitchcock, Susan Tyler. 2012. Frankenstein: *A Cultural History*. New York, NY: W. W. Norton.
Hoeveler, Diane Long. 2016. "Nineteenth-Century Dramatic Adaptations of *Frankenstein*." In *The Cambridge Companion to Frankenstein*. Andrew Smith, ed. Cambridge: Cambridge University Press. 175–189.
Hogle, Jerrold E. 2002. "Introduction." In *The Cambridge Companion to Gothic Fiction*. Jerrold E. Hogle, ed. Cambridge: Cambridge University Press. 1–20.
Hogle, Jerrold E. 2016. "Romantic Contexts." In *The Cambridge Companion to Frankenstein*. Andrew Smith, ed. Cambridge: Cambridge University Press. 41–55.
Holloway, Julia Bolton. 2000. "Apuleius and *Midsummer Night's Dream*: Bottom's Metamorphoses." In *Tales within Tales: Apuleius through Time*. Constance S. Wright and Julia Bolton Holloway, eds. New York, NY: AMS Press. 123–137.
Holmes, Brooke and W. H. Shearin, eds. 2012. *Dynamic Reading: Studies in the Reception of Epicureanism*. New York, NY: Oxford University Press.
Holmes, Richard. 2008. "Dr. Frankenstein and the Soul." In *The Age of Wonder: How the Romantic Generation Discovered the Beauty and Terror of Science*. London: Harper Press. 305–366.
Homans, Margaret. 1987. "Bearing Demons: Frankenstein's Circumvention of the Maternal." In *Mary Shelley's Frankenstein*. H. Bloom, ed. New York, NY: Chelsea House Publishers. 133–153.

Hömke, Nicola. 2010. "Bit by Bit Towards Death: Lucan's Scaeva and the Aesthetisization of Dying." In *Lucan's "Bellum civile": Between Epic Tradition and Aesthetic Innovation*. Nicola Hömke and Christiane Reitz, eds. Berlin: De Gruyter. 91–104.

Hooker, W. 1955. "Apuleius's 'Cupid and Psyche' as a Platonic Myth." *The Bucknell Review* 5.3: 24–38.

Hopkins, David. 2010. *Conversing with Antiquity: English Poets and the Classics, from Shakespeare to Pope*. Oxford: Oxford University Press.

Hopkins, Lisa. 2002. "'A Medea, in More Senses than the More Obvious One': Motherhood in Mary Shelley's *Lodore* and *Falkner*." *Eighteenth-Century Novel* 2: 383–405.

Horsfall, Nicholas. 2013. *Virgil "Aeneid" 6: A Commentary*. Berlin: de Gruyter.

Horton, Robert. 2014. *Frankenstein*. New York, NY: Columbia University Press.

Housman, Alfred E. 1927. *M. Annaei Lucani Belli civilis libri decem*. Second Edition. Oxford: Blackwell.

Howard, Martha Walling. 1970. *The Influence of Plutarch in the Major European Literatures of the Eighteenth Century*. Chapel Hill, NC: University of North Carolina Press.

Hubbell, H. M., trans. 1949. *Cicero: De inventione; De optimo genere oratorum; Topica*. Cambridge, MA: Harvard University Press.

Huet, Valerie. 1999. "Napoleon I: A New Augustus?" In *Roman Presences: Receptions of Rome in European Culture, 1789-1945*. Catherine Edwards, ed. Cambridge: Cambridge University Press. 53–69.

Hughes, William, David Punter, and Andrew Smith, eds. 2013. *The Encyclopedia of the Gothic*. Malden, MA: Wiley-Blackwell.

Hunt, Leigh. 1828. *Lord Byron and Some of His Contemporaries*. London: Henry Colburn.

Hunt, Leigh. 1862. *The Correspondence of Leigh Hunt, Edited by his Eldest Son*. Two Volumes. London: Smith, Elder & Co.

Hunter, J. Paul, ed. 2012. *Mary Shelley: Frankenstein; or, The Modern Prometheus*. Second Edition. New York, NY: W. W. Norton.

Hurst, Isobel. 2006. *Victorian Women Writers and the Classics*. Oxford: Oxford University Press.

Hutchinson, Thomas, ed. 1907. *The Complete Poetical Works of Percy Bysshe Shelley*. Oxford: Oxford University Press.

Huxley, Aldous. 2009. *The Doors of Perception & Heaven and Hell*. New York, NY: Harper Perennial Modern Classics.

Ingpen, Roger, ed. 1909. *The Letters of Percy Bysshe Shelley*. London. Isaac Pitman & Sons.

Ingpen, Roger, ed. 1915. *The Letters of Percy Bysshe Shelley*. Two Volumes. London: G. Bell & Sons.

Innes, Doreen C. 1989. "Augustan Critics." In *The Cambridge History of Literary Criticism: Volume 1: Classical Criticism*. George A. Kennedy, ed. Cambridge: Cambridge University Press. 245–273.

Jakobson, Roman. 1990. "The Speech Event and the Functions of Language." In *On Language*. Linda Waugh and Monique Monville-Burston, eds. Cambridge, MA: Harvard University Press. 69–79.

James, Paula. 2011. *Ovid's Myth of Pygmalion on Screen: In Pursuit of the Perfect Woman*. London: Bloomsbury.

Janan, Micaela. 1988. "The Book of Good Love? Design Versus Desire in *Metamorphoses* 10." *Ramus* 17: 110–137.

Jancovich, Mark. 2016. "*Frankenstein* and Film." In *The Cambridge Companion to Frankenstein*. Andrew Smith, ed. Cambridge: Cambridge University Press. 190–204.

Johnson, Barbara. 1982. "Review: My Monster/My Self." *Diacritics* 12.2: 2–10.

Johnson, Barbara. 1993. "'*The Last Man*.'" Bruce Robbins, trans. In *The Other Mary Shelley: Beyond Frankenstein*. Audrey A. Fisch, Anne K. Mellor, and Esther H. Schor, eds. Oxford: Oxford University Press. 258–266.

Johnson, W. R. 1987. *Momentary Monsters: Lucan and His Heroes*. Ithaca, NY: Cornell University Press.

Johnson, W. R. 2000. *Lucretius and the Modern World*. London: Duckworth.

Jones, Frederick L., ed. 1947. *Mary Shelley's Journal*. Norman, OK: University of Oklahoma Press.

Jones, Frederick L. 1948. "Unpublished Fragments by Shelley and Mary." *Studies in Philology* 45.3: 472–476.

Jones, Frederick L. ed. 1964. *The Letters of Percy Bysshe Shelley*. Two Volumes. Oxford: Clarendon Press.

Joyce, Jane W. 1993. *Lucan: Pharsalia*. Ithaca, NY: Cornell University Press.

Juarrero, Alicia and Carl A. Rubino, eds. 2008. *Emergence, Complexity, and Self-Organization: Precursors and Prototypes*. Goodyear, AZ: ISCE Publishing.

Jung, C. G. 1979. *The Collected Works of C. G. Jung*. Volume 9: Part 2. Princeton, NJ: Princeton University Press.

Keach, William. 1993. "Romanticism and Language." In *The Cambridge Companion to British Romanticism*. Stuart Curran, ed. Cambridge: Cambridge University Press. 95–119.

Kears, Carl and James Paz. 2016. "Medieval Science Fiction: An Impossible Fantasy?" In *Medieval Science Fiction*. London: King's College London. 4–35.

Keen, Tony. 2006. "The 'T' Stands for Tiberius: Models and Methodologies of Classical Reception in Science Fiction." April 10, 2006. http://tonykeen.blogspot.ca/2006/04/t-stands-for-tiberius-models-and.html.

Keen, Antony, ed. 2014. "Fantastika and the Greek and Roman Worlds." Special Issue of *Foundation: The International Review of Science Fiction* 118.

Kelly, Gary. 2000. "Politicizing the Personal: Mary Wollstonecraft, Mary Shelley, and the Coterie Novel." In *Mary Shelley in Her Times*. Betty T. Bennett and Stuart Curran, eds. Baltimore, MD: The Johns Hopkins University Press. 147–159.

Kennedy, Duncan F. 2002. *Rethinking Reality: Lucretius and the Textualization of Nature*. Ann Arbor, MI: University of Michigan Press.

Kenney, E. J., ed. 1990. *Apuleius: Cupid & Psyche*. Cambridge: Cambridge University Press.

Kingsley-Smith, Jane. 2010. *Cupid in Early Modern Literature and Culture*. Cambridge: Cambridge University Press.

Klingaman, William K. and Nicholas P. Klingaman 2013. *The Year Without Summer: 1816 and the Volcano that Darkened the World and Changed History*. New York, NY: St. Martin's Press.

Klinger, Leslie S. 2008. *The New Annotated* Dracula. New York, NY: W. W. Norton.

Knapton, Ernest J. 1939. *The Lady of the Holy Alliance: The Life of Julie de Krüdner*. New York, NY: Columbia University Press.

Knellwolf, Christa and Jane Goodall, eds. 2008. *Frankenstein's Science: Experimentation and Discovery in Romantic Culture, 1780–1830*. Burlington, VT: Ashgate.

Korenjak, Martin. 1996. *Die Ericthoszene in Lukans* Pharsalia: *Einleitung, Text, Übersetzung, Kommentar*. Frankfurt am Main: Lang.

Kovacs, David, ed. and trans. 1994. *Euripides*: *Cyclops, Alcestis, Medea*. Cambridge, MA: Harvard University Press.

Kovacs, David, ed. and trans. 1995. *Euripides*: *Children of Heracles, Hippolytus, Andromache, Hecuba*. Cambridge, MA: Harvard University Press.

Koyré, Alexandre. 1957. *From the Closed World to the Infinite Universe*. Baltimore, MD: The Johns Hopkins University Press.

Krabbe, J. K. 1989. *The Metamorphoses of Apuleius*. New York, NY: Peter Lang.

Kramnick, Isaac, ed. 1976. *William Godwin: Enquiry Concerning Political Justice*. Harmondsworth: Penguin.

Kucich, John and Dianne F. Sadoff, eds. 2000. *Victorian Afterlife: Postmodern Culture Rewrites the Nineteenth Century*. Minneapolis, MI: University of Minnesota Press.

Laird, Andrew. 2007. "The *Ars Poetica*." In *The Cambridge Companion to Horace*. Stephen Harrison, ed. Cambridge: Cambridge University Press. 132–143.

Lamb, W. R. M., trans. 2014. *Plato: Laches; Protagoras; Meno; Euthydemus*. Cambridge, MA: Harvard University Press.

Lambie, Ryan. 2015. "Alien, Blade Runner, and Prometheus: Their Artificial Life." *Den of Geek!* December 4, 2015. http://www.denofgeek.com/movies/ridley-scott/38111/alien-blade-runner-prometheus-their-artificial-life.

Lattimore, Richmond, trans. 1951. *Homer: Iliad*. Chicago, IL: University of Chicago Press.

Leary, Timothy. 1967. *Start Your Own Religion*. Millbrook, NY: Kriya Press.

Leary, Timothy. 1990. *Flashbacks*. New York, NY: Putnam.

Leary, Timothy. 1994. *Chaos & Cyber Culture*. Berkeley, CA: Ronin Publishing.

Leary, Timothy. 1995. *High Priest*. Berkeley, CA: Ronin Publishing.

Leary, Timothy. 2000. *Change Your Brain*. Berkeley, CA: Ronin Publishing.

Leary, Timothy. 2001. *Your Brain Is God*. Berkeley, CA: Ronin Publishing.

Leary, Timothy. 2014. *Timothy Leary: The Harvard Years: Early Writings on LSD and Psilocybin with Richard Alpert, Huston Smith, Ralph Metzner, and Others*. James Penner, ed. Rochester, NY: Part Street Press.

Lecercle, Jean-Jacques. 1988. *Frankenstein: mythe et philosophie*. Paris: Presses Universitaires de France.

Lederman, Leon M. 1993. *The God Particle*. Boston, MA: Houghton Mifflin.

Lee, Martin A. and Bruce Shlain. 1992. *Acid Dreams: The Complete Social History of LSD: The CIA, the Sixties, and Beyond*. New York, NY: Grove Press.

Leigh, Matthew. 1997. *Lucan: Spectacle and Engagement*. Oxford: Clarendon Press.
Leighton, Angela. 1984. *Shelley and the Sublime*. Cambridge: Cambridge University Press.
Leitch, Vincent B., ed. 2001. *The Norton Anthology of Theory and Criticism*. First Edition. New York, NY: W. W. Norton.
Levey, Michael, ed. 1985. *Walter Pater: Marius the Epicurean*. London: Penguin.
Levine, George and U. C. Knoepflmacher, eds. 1982. *The Endurance of Frankenstein: Essays on Mary Shelley's Novel*. Berkeley, CA: University of California Press.
Lewis, Charlton T. and Charles Short, eds. 1879. *A Latin Dictionary*. Oxford: Clarendon Press.
Lewis, C. S. 1964. *The Discarded Image: An Introduction to Medieval and Renaissance Literature*. Cambridge: Cambridge University Press.
Lewis, Linda M. 1992. *The Promethean Politics of Milton, Blake, and Shelley*. Columbia, MO: University of Missouri Press.
Liddell, H. G. and R. Scott. 1996. *Greek-English Lexicon*. Ninth Edition with Revised Supplement. Henry Stuart Jones, rev. Oxford: Clarendon Press.
L'Isle-Adam, Villiers de. 1992. *L'Ève future*. Paris: GF Flammarion.
Lively, Genevieve. 2002. "Cleopatra's Nose, Naso, and the Science of Chaos." *Greece & Rome* 49: 27–43.
Lively, Genevieve. 2006. "Science Fiction and Cyber Myths: or, Do Cyborgs Dream of Dolly the Sheep?" In *Laughing with Medusa: Classical Myth and Feminist Thought*. Vanda Zajko and Miriam Leonard, eds. Oxford: Oxford University Press. 275–294.
Lodge, Guy. 2015. Film Review: "Ex Machina." *Variety*. January 16, 2015. http://variety.com/2015/film/reviews/film-review-ex-machina-1201405717.
Lokke, Kari. 1998. "Sibylline Leaves: Mary Shelley's *Valperga* and the Legacy of *Corinne*." In *Cultural Interactions in the Romantic Age: Critical Essays in Comparative Literature*. Gregory Maertz, ed. New York, NY: State University of New York Press. 157–173.
Lokke, Kari E. 2003. "The Last Man." In *The Cambridge Companion to Mary Shelley*. Esther Schor, ed. Cambridge: Cambridge University Press. 116–134.
London, Bette. 1993. "Mary Shelley, *Frankenstein*, and the Spectacle of Masculinity." *Proceedings of the Modern Language Association* 108.2: 253–267.
Lovell Jr., Ernest J., ed. 1969. *Lady Blessington's Conversations of Lord Byron*. Princeton, NJ: Princeton University Press.
Luck, Georg. 2006. *Arcana mundi: Magic and the Occult in the Greek and Roman Worlds: A Collection of Ancient Texts*. Second Edition. Baltimore, MD: The Johns Hopkins University Press.
Luke, Jr., Hugh J., ed. 1965. *Mary Shelley: The Last Man*. Lincoln, NE: University of Nebraska Press.
Lyons, Martyn. 2006. *Post-Revolutionary Europe, 1815–1856*. New York, NY: Palgrave Macmillan.
MacCormack, Patricia. 2012. "Posthuman Teratology." In *The Ashgate Companion to Monsters and the Monstrous*. Asa Simon Mittman and Peter J. Dendle, eds. Burlington, VT: Ashgate. 293–309.

Macdonald, D. L. and Kathleen Scherf, eds. 1997. *Mary Wollstonecraft: The Vindications: The Rights of Men and The Rights of Woman*. Peterborough, ON: Broadview Press.

Macdonald, D. L. and Kathleen Scherf, eds. 1999. *Mary Wollstonecraft Shelley: Frankenstein: or, The Modern Prometheus. The Original 1818 Text*. Second Edition. Peterborough, ON: Broadview Press.

Macdonald, D. L. and Kathleen Scherf, eds. 2012. *Mary Shelley: Frankenstein; or, the Modern Prometheus: The Original 1818 Text*. Third Edition. Peterborough, ON: Broadview Press.

MacDonald, Scott. 2016a. "Interview with Bill Morrison: 6 Recent Films." *Millennium Film Journal* 64: 56–67.

MacDonald, Scott. 2016b. "Orpheus of Nitrate: The Emergence of Bill Morrison." *Framework: The Journal of Cinema and Media* 57.2: 116–137.

Malchow, Howard. 1996. *Gothic Images of Race in Nineteenth-Century Britain*. Stanford, CA: Stanford University Press.

Male, Roy R. and James A. Notopoulos. 1959. "Shelley's Copy of Diogenes Laertius." *The Modern Language Review* 54.1: 10–21.

Mandelbaum, Allen. 1993. *The Metamorphoses of Ovid: A New Verse Translation*. New York, NY: Houghton Mifflin Harcourt.

Marchand, Leslie A., ed. 1994. *"What comes uppermost": Byron's Letters and Journals, Supplementary Volume*. Newark, DE: University of Delaware Press.

Marder, Elissa. 2014. "Pandora's Fireworks; or, Questions Concerning Femininity, Technology, and the Limits of the Human." *Philosophy and Rhetoric* 47.4: 386–399.

Markley, A. A. 2003. "Curious Transformations: Cupid, Psyche, and Apuleius in the Shelleys' Works." *The Keats-Shelley Review* 17.1: 120–135.

Marshall, C. W. 2016. "Odysseus and *The Infinite Horizon*." In *Son of Classics and Comics*. G. Kovacs and C. W. Marshall, eds. Oxford: Oxford University Press. 3–31.

Martin, Michael A. 2015. "Timothy Leary." In *American Countercultures: An Encyclopedia of Nonconformists, Alternative Lifestyles, and Radical Ideas in U.S. History*. Gina Misiroglu, ed. New York, NY: Routledge. 428–430.

Martindale, Charles. 1984. "The Politician Lucan." *Greece & Rome* 31.1: 64–79.

Mason, H. J. 1999. "*Fabula graecanica*: Apuleius and his Greek Sources." In *Oxford Readings in The Roman Novel*. S. J. Harrison, ed. Oxford: Oxford University Press. 217–236.

McClellan, Andrew M. 2010. "Creating the Grotesque: Zombification in Lucan's *Bellum Civile*, Shelley's *Frankenstein*, and Romero's *Day of the Dead*." Unpublished Conference Paper. *All Roads Lead From Rome: The Classical (non)Tradition in Popular Culture*. Rutgers University. April 9, 2010.

McFadden, Naja. 2012. "The Postmodern Prometheus: Gender, Creation, and Humanity in *Prometheus* and *Frankenstein*." http://www.inter-disciplinary.net/probing-the-boundaries/wp-content/uploads/2012/12/mcfaddentsbpaper.pdf. Accessed September 12, 2017.

McGann, Michael. 2007. "The Reception of Horace in the Renaissance." In *The Cambridge Companion to Horace*. Stephen Harrison, ed. Cambridge: Cambridge University Press. 305–317.

McLellan, David, ed. 2000. *Karl Marx: Selected Writings*. Second Edition. Oxford: Oxford University Press.

McLynn, Frank. 1998. *Napoleon: A Biography*. London: Pimlico.

McWhir, Anne. 1990. "Teaching the Monster to Read: Mary Shelley's Education and *Frankenstein*." In *The Educational Legacy of Romanticism*. John Willinsky, ed. Waterloo, ON: Wilfrid Laurier University Press. 73–92.

McWhir, Anne, ed. 1996. *Mary Shelley: The Last Man*. Peterborough, ON: Broadview Press.

McWhir, Anne. 2001. "'Unconceiving Marble': Anatomy and Animation in *Frankenstein* and *The Last Man*." In *Writing Lives: Mary Wollstonecraft and Mary Shelley*. Helen M. Buss, D. L. Macdonald, and Anne McWhir, eds. Waterloo, ON: Wilfrid Laurier University Press. 159–175.

Mellor, Anne K. 1988. *Mary Shelley: Her Life, Her Fiction, Her Monsters*. New York, NY: Methuen.

Mellor, Anne K. 2003. "Making a 'Monster': An Introduction to *Frankenstein*." In *The Cambridge Companion to Mary Shelley*. Esther Schor, ed. Cambridge: Cambridge University Press. 9–25.

Melville, A. D., trans. 2008. *Ovid: Metamorphoses*. Oxford: Oxford University Press.

Melville, Herman. 1967. *Moby-Dick*. Harrison Hayford and Hershel Parker, eds. New York, NY: W. W. Norton.

Miall, David S. 1998. "The Alps Deferred: Wordsworth at the Simplon Pass." *European Romantic Review* 9: 87–102.

Miller, Frank Justus, trans. 1977. *Ovid: Metamorphoses*. Two Volumes: Volume I, Third Edition; Volume II, Second Edition. G. P. Goold, rev. Cambridge, MA: Harvard University Press.

Milton, John. 1674. *Paradise* Lost. Second Edition. London: S. Simmons.

Moers, Ellen. 1977. *Literary Women: The Great Writers*. Oxford: Oxford University Press.

Monk, S. H. 1960. *The Sublime: A Study of Critical Theories in 18th-Century England*. Ann Arbor, MI: University of Michigan Press.

Morton, Timothy. 1994. *Shelley and the Revolution in Taste: The Body and the Natural World*. Cambridge: Cambridge University Press.

Morton, Timothy, ed. 2002. *A Routledge Literary Sourcebook on Mary Shelley's* Frankenstein. London: Routledge.

Morton, Timothy. 2016. "*Frankenstein* and Ecocriticism." In *The Cambridge Companion to Frankenstein*. Andrew Smith, ed. Cambridge: Cambridge University Press. 143–157.

Most, Glenn W., trans. 2006. *Hesiod I: Theogony, Works and Days, Testimonia*. Cambridge, MA: Harvard University Press.

Mousley, Andy. 2016. "The Posthuman." In *The Cambridge Companion to Frankenstein*. Andrew Smith, ed. Cambridge: Cambridge University Press. 158–172.

Murray, Christopher. 2016. "*Frankenstein* in Comics and Graphic Novels." In *The Cambridge Companion to Frankenstein*. Andrew Smith, ed. Cambridge: Cambridge University Press. 219–240.

Myers, Victoria, David O'Shaughnessy, and Mark Philp, eds. 2010. "Texts Godwin Read: Annotated Titles 1788–1836." *The Diary of William Godwin*. Oxford: Oxford Digital Library. http://godwindiary.bodleian.ox.ac.uk/bibl/. Accessed February 23, 2017.

Newton, John Frank. 1811. *The Return to Nature, or, A Defence of the Vegetable Regimen*. London: Printed for T. Cadell & W. Davies, Strand.

Nicolet, Claude. 2009. "Caesar and the Two Napoleons." In *A Companion to Julius Caesar*, Miriam Griffin, ed. Malden, MA: Wiley-Blackwell. 410–417.

Nielson, Wendy C. 2015. "Rousseau's *Pygmalion* and Automata in the Romantic Period." In *Romanticism, Rousseau, Switzerland: New Prospects*. Angela Esterhammer, Diane Piccitto, and Patrick Vincent, eds. Basingstoke: Palgrave Macmillan. 68–83.

Nocks, Lisa. 1997. "Frankenstein, In A Better Light." *Journal of Social and Evolutionary Systems* 20.2: 137–155.

Nussbaum, Felicity A. 2003. *The Limits of the Human: Fictions of Anomaly, Race, and Gender in the Long Eighteenth Century*. Cambridge: Cambridge University Press.

O'Connor, Hannah. 2014. "Queering the Mainstream Monster: Demonstrating Difference and Deviant Sexuality in Shelley's *Frankenstein* (1818) and Stoker's *Dracula* (1897)." *Aeternum: The Journal of Contemporary Gothic Studies* 1.1: 42–54.

Orgel, Stephen and Jonathan Goldberg, eds. 2008. *John Milton: Paradise Lost*. Oxford: Oxford University Press.

Orlin, Eric. 2002. *Temples, Religion, and Politics in the Roman Republic*. Leiden: Brill.

Osler, Alan. 1967. "Keats and Baldwin's Pantheon." *The Modern Language Review* 62: 221–225.

O'Sullivan, Barbara Jane. 1993. "Beatrice in Valperga: A New Cassandra." In *The Other Mary Shelley: Beyond* Frankenstein. Audrey A. Fisch, Anne K. Mellor, and Esther H. Schor, eds. Oxford: Oxford University Press. 140–158.

O'Toole, Emer. 2015. *Girls Will Be Girls: Dressing Up, Playing Parts and Daring to be Different*. London: Orion Publishing.

Page, Denys. 1955. *Sappho and Alcaeus: An Introduction to the Study of Ancient Lesbian Poetry*. Oxford: Clarendon Press.

Page, Denys. 1962. *Poetae Melici Graeci*. Oxford: Oxford University Press.

Page, Frederick, ed. 1970. *Byron: Complete Poetical Works*. Oxford: Oxford University Press.

Palacio, Jean de. 1964. "Mary Shelley's Latin Studies: Her Unpublished Translation of Apuleius." *Revue de la littérature comparée* 38: 564–571.

Palacio, Jean de. 1968. "Mary Shelley and the 'Last Man': A Minor Romantic Theme." *Revue de la littérature comparée* 42: 37–49.

Paley, Morton D. 1993. "*The Last Man*: Apocalypse without Millennium." In *The Other Mary Shelley: Beyond* Frankenstein. Audrey A. Fisch, Anne K. Mellor, and Esther H. Schor, eds. Oxford: Oxford University Press. 107–123.

Parke, Herbert William. 1988. *Sibyls and Sibylline Prophecy in Classical Antiquity*. London: Routledge.

Pascoe, Judith. 2003. "*Proserpine* and *Midas*." In *The Cambridge Companion to Mary Shelley*. Esther Schor, ed. Cambridge: Cambridge University Press. 180–190.

Patten, Robert L. 1992. *George Cruikshank's Life, Times, and Art*. Volume 1. New Brunswick, NJ: Rutgers University Press.

Paul, C. Kegan. 1970 [1876]. *William Godwin, His Friends and Contemporaries*. New York, NY: AMS Press.

Paulson, Ronald. 1981. "Gothic Fiction and the French Revolution." *ELH* 48: 545–554.

Perrin, Bernadotte, trans. 1959 [1914]. *Plutarch's Lives*. Volume I. Cambridge, MA: Harvard University Press.

Perry, Ruth. 1998. "Incest as the Meaning of the Gothic Novel." *The Eighteenth Century* 39.2: 261–278.

Pieterse, Jan Nederveen. 1989. *Empire and Emancipation: Power and Liberation on a World Scale*. New York, NY: Praeger.

Pieterse, Jan Nederveen. 2001. "Hybridity, So What? The Anti-hybridity Backlash and the Riddles of Recognition." *Theory, Culture & Society* 18.2–3: 219–245.

Podlecki, Anthony J., ed. with intro. 2005. *Aeschylus: Prometheus Bound*. Liverpool: Aris & Phillips.

Poincaré, Henri. 1893. "Le Mécanisme et l'Expérience." *Revue de Metaphysique et de Morale* 1: 534–537.

Pollin, Burton R. 1965. "Philosophical and Literary Sources of *Frankenstein*." *Comparative Literature* 17.2: 97–108.

Porter, James I. 2007. "Lucretius and the Sublime." In *The Cambridge Companion to Lucretius*. Stuart Gillespie and Philip Hardie, eds. Cambridge: Cambridge University Press. 167–184.

Porter, James I. 2010. *The Origins of Aesthetic Thought in Ancient Greece: Matter, Sensation, and Experience*. Cambridge: Cambridge University Press.

Porter, James I. 2015a. "Homer and the Sublime." *Ramus* 44.1–2: 184–199.

Porter, James I. 2105b. "The Sublime." In *A Companion to Ancient Aesthetics*. Pierre Destrée and Penelope Murray, eds. Chichester: Wiley-Blackwell. 393–405.

Porter, James I. 2016. *The Sublime in Antiquity*. Cambridge: Cambridge University Press.

Posey, Horace G. 1971. "Shelley and Modern Aesthetics." *Bucknell Review* 19: 97–114.

Post, John D. 1977. *The Last Great Subsistence Crisis in the Western World*. Baltimore, MD: The Johns Hopkins University Press.

Prabhu, Anjali. 2007. *Hybridity. Limits, Transformations, Prospects*. Albany, NY: State University of New York Press.

Priestman, Martin. 1999. *Romantic Atheism: Poetry and Freethought, 1780–1830*. Cambridge: Cambridge University Press.

Priestman, Martin, ed. 2006. *The Cambridge Companion to Crime Fiction*. Cambridge: Cambridge University Press.

Priestman, Martin. 2007. "Lucretius in Romantic and Victorian Britain." In *The Cambridge Companion to Lucretius*. Stuart Gillespie and Philip Hardie, eds. Cambridge: Cambridge University Press. 289–305.

Prigogine, Ilya. 1980. "Probing into Time." *Discovery: Research and Scholarship at The University of Texas at Austin* 5.7.

Prigogine, Ilya. 1997. *The End of Certainty: Time, Chaos, and the New Laws of Nature*. New York, NY: Free Press.

Prigogine, Ilya and Isabelle Stengers. 1984. *Order out of Chaos: Man's New Dialogue with Nature*. New York, NY: Bantam Books.

Propp, Vladimir. 1983. "Oedipus in the Light of Folklore." In *Oedipus: A Folklore Casebook*. Lowell Edmunds and Alan Dundes, eds. Polly Coote, trans. Madison, WI: University of Wisconsin Press. 76–121.

Proust, Marcel. 1992–1993. *In Search of Lost Time*. Six Volumes. C. K. Scott Moncrieff, Andreas Mayor, and Terence Kilmartin, trans. D. J. Enright, rev. New York, NY: Modern Library.

Punter, David. 1999. "Legends of the Animated: The Case of the Monster." In *Autour de Frankenstein (Lectures critiques): Textes réunis et présentés par Gilles Menegaldo*. Gilles Menegaldo, ed. Poitiers: Université de Poitiers. 88–100.

Punter, David. 2016. "Literature." In *The Cambridge Companion to Frankenstein*. Andrew Smith, ed. Cambridge: Cambridge University Press. 205–218.

Quint, David. 1993. *Epic and Empire: Politics and Generic Form from Virgil to Milton*. Princeton, NJ: Princeton University Press.

Randel, Fred V. 2007. "The Political Geography of Horror in Mary Shelley's *Frankenstein*." In *Mary Shelley's* Frankenstein. Harold Bloom, ed. New York, NY: Chelsea House. 185–211.

Raphael, Rebecca. 2015. "Disability as Rhetorical Trope in Classical Myth and *Blade Runner*." In *Classical Traditions in Science Fiction*. Brett M. Rogers and Benjamin Eldon Stevens, eds. Oxford: Oxford University Press. 176–196.

Rea, Jennifer. 2010. "*Pietas* and Post-Colonialism in Ursula K. Le Guin's *Lavinia*." *Classical Outlook* 87.4: 126–131.

Rea, Jennifer. 2017. "Aeneas' American New World in Jo Graham's *Black Ships*." In *Classical Traditions in Modern Fantasy*. Brett M. Rogers and Benjamin Eldon Stevens, eds. Oxford: Oxford University Press. 290–307.

Reichardt, Jasia. 1994. "Artificial Life and the Myth of Frankenstein." In *Frankenstein, Creation and Monstrosity*. Stephen Bann, ed. London: Reaktion. 136–157.

Reid, Jane Davidson. 1993. *The Oxford Guide to Classical Mythology in the Arts, 1300–1990s*. Oxford: Oxford University Press.

Reiman, Donald H. and Neil Fraistat, eds. 2004. *The Complete Poetry of Percy Bysshe Shelley*. Volume II. Baltimore, MD: The Johns Hopkins University Press.

Rein, Lisa and Michael Horowitz. 2015. "Acid Bodhisattva: The History of the Timothy Leary Archives During His Prison and Exile Years, 1970–1976 (Part One)." *Timothy Leary Archives*.

Richardson, Alan. 1993. "*Proserpine* and *Midas*: Gender, Genre, and Mythic Revisionism in Mary Shelley's Dramas." In *The Other Mary Shelley: Beyond* Frankenstein. Audrey A. Fisch, Anne K. Mellor, and Esther H. Schor, eds. Oxford: Oxford University Press. 124–139.

Richardson, Ruth. 1988. *Death, Dissection and the Destitute*. London: Penguin.

Rieger, James, ed. 1974. *Mary Wollstonecraft Shelley: Frankenstein, or the Modern Prometheus*. New York, NY: Bobbs-Merrill.

Riess, Werner, ed. 2008. *Paideia at Play: Learning and Wit in Apuleius*. Groningen: Barkhuis Publishing.

Roberts, Andy. 2012. *Albion Dreaming: A Popular History of LSD in Britain*. Tarrytown, NY: Marshall Cavendish Editions.

Robinson, Charles E. 1976a. *Shelley and Byron: The Snake and the Eagle Wreathed in Fight*. Baltimore, MD: The Johns Hopkins University Press.

Robinson, Charles E., ed., 1976b. *Mary Shelley: Collected Tales and Stories with Original Engravings*. Baltimore, MD: The Johns Hopkins University Press.

Robinson, Charles E., ed. 1996. *The* Frankenstein *Notebooks, A Facsimile Edition of Mary Shelley's Manuscript Novel, 1816–17*. New York, NY: Garland.

Robinson, Charles E., ed. 2009. *The Original Frankenstein*. New York, NY: Vintage Classics.

Robinson, Charles E. 2013. "*Frankenstein* Filmography." In *Frankenstein or The Modern Prometheus [by] Mary Shelley*. Guillermo del Toro, ed. New York, NY: Penguin. 307–330.

Robinson, Charles E. 2016. "*Frankenstein*: Its Composition and Publication." In *The Cambridge Companion to Frankenstein*. Andrew Smith, ed. Cambridge: Cambridge University Press. 13–25.

Rogers, Brett M. 2015. "Hybrids and Homecomings in the *Odyssey* & *Alien Resurrection*." In *Classical Traditions in Science Fiction*. Brett M. Rogers and Benjamin Eldon Stevens, eds. Oxford: Oxford University Press. 217–242.

Rogers, Brett M. and Benjamin Eldon Stevens. 2012a. "Classical Receptions in Science Fiction." *Classical Receptions Journal* 4.1: 127–147.

Rogers, Brett M. and Benjamin Eldon Stevens. 2012b. "A New 'Modern Prometheus'?" *OUPblog*. July 6, 2012. http://blog.oup.com/2012/07/modern-prometheus-classical-reception-sci-fi.

Rogers, Brett M. and Benjamin Eldon Stevens, eds. 2015. *Classical Traditions in Science Fiction*. Oxford: Oxford University Press.

Rogers, Brett M. and Benjamin Eldon Stevens. 2017. "Introduction: Fantasies of Antiquity." In *Classical Traditions in Modern Fantasy*. Brett M. Rogers and Benjamin Eldon Stevens, eds. Oxford: Oxford University Press. 1–22.

Rollins, Hyder Edward, ed. 1958. *The Letters of John Keats, 1814–1821*. Volume I. Cambridge, MA: Harvard University Press.

Rossetti, William Michael, ed. 1911. *The Diary of John William Polidori: 1816, Relating to Byron, Shelley, etc*. London: Elkin Mathews.

Rossi-Reder, Andrea. 2002. "Wonders of the Beast: India in Classical and Medieval Literature." In *Marvels, Monsters, and Miracles: Studies in the Medieval and Early Modern Imaginations*. Timothy S. Jones and David A. Sprunger, eds. Kalamazoo, MI: Medieval Institute Publications. 53–66.

Rouse, W. H. D., trans. 1924. *Lucretius: On the Nature of Things*. Cambridge, MA: Harvard University Press.

Rouse, W. H. D., trans. 1992. *Lucretius: On the Nature of Things*. Rev. Martin Ferguson Smith. Cambridge, MA: Harvard University Press.

Rubino, Carl A. 1994a. "Joyous Entropy: The Phenomenon of Laughter and the Science of Thermodynamics." In *Laughter Down the Centuries*. Volume 1. Siegfried Jäkel and Asko Timonen, eds. Turku: Turun Yliopisto. 134–144.

Rubino, Carl A. 1994b. "The Obsolescence of the Hero: Voltaire's Attack on Homeric Heroism." *Pacific Coast Philology* 29: 85–94.

Rubino, Carl A. 2007. "The Consolations of Uncertainty: Time, Change, and Complexity." In *Reframing Complexity: Perspectives from the North and South*. Fritjof Capra, Alicia Juarrero, Pedro Sotolongo, and Jacco van Uden, eds. Mansfield, MA: ISCE Publishing. 239–247.

Rutherford, Adam. 2015. "How Realistic are the Robots of *Ex Machina*?" *The Telegraph*. January 22, 2015. http://www.telegraph.co.uk/culture/film/film-news/11357792/How-realistic-are-the-robots-of-Ex-Machina.html.

Rutherford, Richard. 2007. "Poetics and Literary Criticism." In *The Cambridge Companion to Horace*. Stephen Harrison, ed. Cambridge: Cambridge University Press. 248–261.

Said, Edward. 1978. *Orientalism*. London: Routledge & Kegan Paul.

Salzman-Mitchell, Patricia. 2008. "A Whole Out of Pieces: Pygmalion's Ivory Statue in Ovid's *Metamorphoses*." *Arethusa* 41.2: 291–311.

Sandys, George, trans. 1632. *Ouid's Metamorphosis Englished by G.S.* London: Robert Young.

Saussure, Ferdinand de. 1986. *Course in General Linguistics*. Roy Harris, trans. Charles Bally and Albert Sechehaye, eds. La Salle, IL: Open Court.

Scalzi, John. 2005. *Old Man's War*. New York, NY: Tor.

Scalzi John. 2006. *The Ghost Brigades*. New York, NY: Tor.

Scalzi, John. 2013. *The Human Division*. New York, NY: Tor.

Schlam, C. C. 1968. "The Curiosity of *The Golden Ass*." *Classical Journal* 64: 120–125.

Schlam, C. C. 1976. *Cupid and Psyche: Apuleius and the Monuments*. University Park, PA: The American Philological Association.

Schlam, C. C. 1992. *The Metamorphoses of Apuleius*. Chapel Hill, NC: University of North Carolina Press.

Schock, Peter A. 2003. *Romantic Satanism: Myth and the Historical Moment in Blake, Shelley, and Byron*. Basingstoke: Palgrave Macmillan.

Scholar, Angela, trans. 2000. *Jean-Jacques Rousseau: Confessions*. Oxford: Oxford University Press.

Schor, Esther. 2003. "*Frankenstein* and Film." In *The Cambridge Companion to Mary Shelley*. Esther Schor, ed. Cambridge: Cambridge University Press. 64–83.

Scott, Mary Augusta, ed. 1908. *The Essays of Francis Bacon*. New York, NY: Charles Scribner's Sons.

Scott, Ridley, dir. 1979. *Alien*. Screenplay by Dan O'Bannon. 20th Century Fox.

Scott, Ridley, dir. 2000. *Gladiator*. Screenplay by David Franzoni, John Logan, and William Nicholson. Dreamworks Pictures/Universal Pictures.

Scott, Ridley, dir. 2012. *Prometheus*. Written by Jon Spaihts and Damon Lindelof. 20th Century Fox.

Scott, Ridley, dir. 2017. *Alien: Covenant*. Screenplay by John Logan and Dante Harper. 20th Century Fox.

Scott, Walter Sidney, ed. 1943. *The Athenians: Being Correspondence Between Thomas Jefferson Hogg and His Friends Thomas Love Peacock, Leigh Hunt, Percy Bysshe Shelley, and Others*. London: The Golden Cockerel Press.

Scrivener, Henry. 1982. *Radical Shelley: The Philosophical Anarchism and Utopian Thought of Percy Bysshe Shelley*. Princeton, NJ: Princeton University Press.

Serres, Michel. 1977. *La naissance de la physique dans le texte de Lucrèce: Fleuves et turbulences*. Paris: Minuit.

Shanahan, Murray. 2015. *The Technological Singularity*. Cambridge, MA: The MIT Press.

Sharrock, Alison R. 1991. "Womanufacture." *The Journal of Roman Studies* 81: 36–49.

Shelley, Mary. 2017. *Frankenstein: Original 1818 Uncensored Version*. London: Enhanced Media Publishing.

Shelley, Percy. 1845. *Essays, Letters from Abroad, Translations and Fragments*. Mary Shelley, ed. London: Edward Moxon.

Sherwin, Paul. 1981. "Frankenstein: Creation as Catastrophe." *Proceedings of the Modern Language Association* 96.5: 883–903.

Siff, Stephen. 2015. *Acid Hype: American News Media and the Psychedelic Experience*. Urbana, IL: University of Illinois Press.

Sinatra, Michael Eberle, ed. 1997. "Mary Shelley: 'The Mortal Immortal.'" *Romantic Circles*. September 1997. https://www.rc.umd.edu/editions/mws/immortal/mortal.html.

Six, Abigail Lee and Hannah Thompson. 2012. "From Hideous to Hedonist: The Changing Face of the Nineteenth-century Monster." In *The Ashgate Research Companion to Monsters and the Monstrous*. Asa Simon Mittman and Peter J. Dendle, eds. Burlington, VT: Ashgate. 237–255.

Skeen, C. Edward. 1981. "'The Year without a Summer': A Historical View." *Journal of the Early Republic* 1.1: 51–67.

Small, Christopher. 1972. *Ariel Like a Harpy: Shelley, Mary and Frankenstein*. London: Gollancz.

Small, Christopher. 1973. *Mary Shelley's* Frankenstein: *Tracing the Myth*. Pittsburgh, PA: University of Pittsburgh Press.

Smith, Andrew, ed. 2016a. *The Cambridge Companion to Frankenstein*. Cambridge: Cambridge University Press.

Smith, Andrew. 2016b. "Introduction." In *The Cambridge Companion to Frankenstein*. Andrew Smith, ed. Cambridge: Cambridge University Press. 1–10.

Smith, Andrew. 2016c. "Scientific Contexts." In *The Cambridge Companion to Frankenstein*. Andrew Smith, ed. Cambridge: Cambridge University Press. 69–83.

Sobchack, Vivian. 2012. "Between a Rock and a Hard Place: How Ridley Scott's *Prometheus* Deals with Impossible Expectations and Mythological Baggage." *Film Comment*. July/August: 30–34.

Solmsen, Friedrich. 1990. "The World of the Dead in Book 6 of the *Aeneid*." In *Oxford Readings in Vergil's Aeneid*. S. J. Harrison, ed. Oxford: Clarendon Press. 208–223.

Solodow, Joseph B. 1988. *The World of Ovid's Metamorphoses*. Chapel Hill, NC: University of North Carolina Press.

Sommerstein, Alan H., trans. 2008. *Aeschylus: I: Persians, Seven Against Thebes, Suppliants, Prometheus Bound*. Cambridge, MA: Harvard University Press.

Spark, Muriel. 1951. *Child of Light: A Reassessment of Mary Wollstonecraft Shelley*. Hadleigh, Essex: Tower Bridge Publications.

Sparrow, Jeff. 2012. "Prometheus: The Tea Party in Space." *Counterpunch*. June 18, 2012. http://www.counterpunch.org/2012/06/18/prometheus-the-tea-party-in-space.

Spence, Joseph. 1755. *Polymetis*. London: J. Dodsley.

Stabler, Jane. 1994. "The Genesis of Byron's *Hints from Horace*." *Translation and Literature* 3: 47–65.

Starnes, D. T. 1945. "Shakespeare and Apuleius." *Proceedings of the Modern Language Association* 60: 1021–1050.

St Clair, William. 1989. *The Godwins and the Shelleys: The Biography of a Family*. New York, NY: W. W. Norton.

St Clair, William. 2000. "The Impact of *Frankenstein*." In *Mary Shelley in Her Times*. Betty T. Bennett and Stuart Curran, eds. Baltimore, MD: The Johns Hopkins University Press. 38–63.

Sterrenburg, Lee. 1979. "Mary Shelley's Monster: Politics and Psyche in *Frankenstein*." In *The Endurance of Frankenstein*. George L. Levine and U. C. Knoepflmacher, eds. Berkeley, CA: The University of California Press. 143–171.

Stevens, Benjamin Eldon. 2015. "Virgil in Jules Verne's *Journey to the Center of the Earth*." In *Classical Traditions in Science Fiction*. Brett M. Rogers and Benjamin Eldon Stevens, eds. Oxford: Oxford University Press. 75–104.

Stevens, Benjamin Eldon. 2017. "Ancient Underworlds in J. R. R. Tolkien's *The Hobbit*." In *Classical Traditions in Modern Fantasy*. Brett M. Rogers and Benjamin Eldon Stevens, eds. Oxford: Oxford University Press. 121–144.

Stevens, Dana. 2012. "Prometheus." *Slate*. June 7, 2012. http://www.slate.com/articles/arts/movies/2012/06/prometheus_ridley_scott_s_alien_prequel_reviewed_.html.

Stock, Paul. 2010. *The Shelley-Byron Circle and the Idea of Europe*. New York, NY: Palgrave Macmillan.

Stothers, Richard E. 1984. "The Great Tambora Eruption 1815 and its Aftermath." *Science* 224: 1191–1199.

Stuart, Tristram. 2006. *The Bloodless Revolution: A Cultural History of Vegetarianism from 1600 to Modern Times*. New York, NY: W.W. Norton.

Sudradjat, Adjat and Heryadi Rachmat. 2015. *Greetings from Tambora: A Potpourri of the Stories on the Deadliest Volcanic Eruption*. Bandung: Geological Museum.

Sunstein, Emily W. 1989. *Mary Shelley: Romance and Reality*. Baltimore, MD: The Johns Hopkins University Press.

Sutherland, John. 1996. *Is Heathcliff a Murderer? Great Puzzles in Nineteenth-century Literature*. Oxford: Oxford University Press. 24–34.

Suvin, Darko. 1972. "On the Poetics of the Science Fiction Genre." *College English* 34: 372–382.

Suvin, Darko. 1979. *Metamorphoses of Science Fiction: On the Poetics and History of a Literary Genre*. New Haven, CT: Yale University Press.

Svilpis, Janis. 2008. "The Science-Fiction Prehistory of the Turing Test." *Science Fiction Studies* 35.3: 430–449.

Tatum, James. 1979. *Apuleius and 'The Golden Ass.'* Ithaca, NY: Cornell University Press.

Tesoriero, Charles. 2004. "The Middle in Lucan." In *Middles in Latin Poetry*. Stratis Kyriakidis and Francesco De Martino, eds. Bari: Levante. 183–215.

Thomas, Ronald. 2000. "*Dracula* and the Cinematic Afterlife of the Victorian Novel." In *Victorian Afterlife: Postmodern Culture Rewrites the Nineteenth Century*. John Kucich and Dianne F. Sadoff, eds. Minneapolis, MN: University of Minnesota Press. 289–310.

Thomas, Sophie. 2000. "The Ends of the Fragment, the Problem of the Preface: Proliferation and Finality in *The Last Man*." In *Mary Shelley's Fictions: From* Frankenstein *to* Falkner. Michael Eberle-Sinatra, ed. New York, NY: St. Martin's Press. 22–38.

Thomson, J.A.K., trans. 1976. *Aristotle: Ethics*. Hugh Tredennick, rev. London: Penguin.

Thornburg, Mary K. Patterson. 1987. *The Monster in the Mirror: Gender and the Sentimental/Gothic Myth in Frankenstein*. Ann Arbor, MI: University of Michigan Press.

Thorne, Mark. 2011. "*Memoria Redux*: Memory in Lucan." In *Brill's Companion to Lucan*. Paolo Asso, ed. Leiden: Brill. 363–381.

Tissol, Garth. 1997. *The Face of Nature: Wit, Narrative, and Cosmic Origins in Ovid's Metamorphoses*. Princeton, NJ: Princeton University Press.

Tobin, J. J. M. 1984. *Shakespeare's Favorite Novel: A Study of 'The Golden Ass' as Prime Source*. Lanham, MD: University Press of America.

Todd, Janet, ed. 1992. *Mary Wollstonecraft and Mary Shelley: Mary & Maria. Matilda*. New York, NY: New York University Press.

Todd, Janet. ed. 1999. *Mary Wollstonecraft: A Vindication of the Rights of Woman* and *A Vindication of the Rights of Men*. Oxford: Oxford University Press.

Tooke, Andrew. 1798. *The Pantheon, Representing the Fabulous Histories of the Heathen Gods, and Most Illustrious Heroes; in a Short, Plain, and Familiar Method, by Way of Dialogue*. Thirteenth Edition. London: Printed for B. Law, et al.

Troshynski, Emily I. and Jesse Weiner. 2016. "Freak Show: Modern Constructions of Ciceronian *Monstra* and Foucauldian Monstrosity." *Law, Culture and the Humanities* 12.3: 741–765.

Tucker, Robert A. 1971. "Lucan and the French Revolution: The *Bellum Civile* as a Political Mirror." *Classical Philology* 66.1: 6–16.

Tucker, Tom. 2003. *Bolt of Fate: Benjamin Franklin and His Electric Kite Hoax*. New York, NY: PublicAffairs.

Turner, F. M. 1989. "Why the Greeks and not the Romans in Victorian Britain." In *Rediscovering Hellenism: The Hellenic Inheritance and the English Imagination*. G. W. Clarke, ed. Cambridge: Cambridge University Press. 62–63.

Vance, Norman. 1997. *The Victorians and Ancient Rome*. Oxford: Oxford University Press.
Vance, Norman and Jennifer Wallace, eds. 2015. *The Oxford History of Classical Reception in English Literature. Volume 4 (1790–1880)*. Oxford: Oxford University Press.
Vargo, Lisa. 2016. "Contextualizing Sources." In *The Cambridge Companion to Frankenstein*. Andrew Smith, ed. Cambridge: Cambridge University Press. 26–40.
Vernant, Jean-Pierre. 1989. "Dim Body, Dazzling Body." In *Fragments for a History of the Human Body*. Part One. Michel Feher, Ramona Naddaff, and Nadia Tazi, eds. New York, NY: Zone. 18–47.
Vernant, Jean-Pierre. 1990. *Myth and Society in Ancient Greece*. Janet Lloyd, trans. New York, NY: Zone Books.
Waldron, Michael. 2012. "Prometheus or the Modern Frankenstein." *Literary Visuality*. https://literaryvisuality.wordpress.com/2012/06/15/prometheus-the-modern-frankenstein. Accessed September 12, 2017.
Walker Art Center. 2010a. "Bill Morrison in Conversation with Curator Philip Bither." October 7, 2010. http://www.walkerart.org/channel/2010/bill-morrison-in-conversation-with-curator-ph.
Walker Art Center. 2010b. "Dave Douglas in Conversation with Curator Philip Bither." October 7, 2010. http://www.walkerart.org/channel/2010/dave-douglas-in-conversation-with-curator-phi.
Wall, Matthew. 2016. "How Happy Chatbots Could Become Our New Best Friends." *BBC*. May 30, 2016. http://www.bbc.co.uk/news/business-36387734.
Wallace, Jennifer. 1997. *Shelley and Greece: Rethinking Romantic Hellenism*. New York, NY: St. Martin's Press.
Wallace, Jennifer. 2011. "'Copying Shelley's Letters': Mary Shelley and the Uncanny Erotics of Greek." *Women's Studies* 40: 404–428.
Wallace, Jennifer. 2015. "'Greek Under the Trees': Classical Reception and Gender." In *The Oxford History of Classical Reception in English Literature. Volume 4 (1790–1880)*. Norman Vance and Jennifer Wallace, eds. Oxford: Oxford University Press. 243–278.
Walsh, P.G. 1970. *The Roman Novel*. Cambridge: Cambridge University Press.
Walsh, P. G. 1994. *Apuleius. The Golden Ass*. Oxford: Oxford University Press.
Walters, Brian C. 2011. *Metaphor, Violence, and the Death of the Roman Republic*. PhD Dissertation, University of California, Los Angeles.
Ward, Michael. 2008. *Planet Narnia: The Seven Heavens and the Imagination of C. S. Lewis*. Oxford: Oxford University Press.
Wasserman, Earl. 1965. *Shelley's Prometheus Unbound: A Critical Reading*. Baltimore, MD: The John Hopkins University Press.
Watercutter, Angela. 2015. "Ex Machina has a Serious Fembot Problem." *Wired*. September 4, 2015. http://www.wired.com/2015/04/ex-machina-turing-bechdel-test.
Weinberg, Steven. 1992. *Dreams of a Final Theory*. New York, NY: Pantheon Books.
Weiner, Jesse. 2015a. "Lucretius, Lucan, and Mary Shelley's *Frankenstein*." In *Classical Traditions in Science Fiction*. Brett M. Rogers and Benjamin Eldon Stevens, eds. Oxford: Oxford University Press. 46–74.

Weiner, Jesse. 2015b. "Mapping *hubris*: Odysseus' *Apologoi* and Vonnegut's *Cat's Cradle*." *International Journal of the Classical Tradition* 22.1: 116–137.

Weiner, Jesse. 2015c. "Between *bios* and *zoē*: Sophocles' *Antigone* and Agamben's Biopolitics." *Logeion* 5: 139–160.

Weiner, Jesse. 2016. "Xenophon, *Cyropaedia* 8.8: The Many Forms of Persian Decline after Cyrus." *Cyrus' Paradise*. http://www.cyropaedia.org/book-8/chapter-8-8-bracketed-chapter-the-many-forms-of-persian-decline-after-cyrus. Accessed February 21, 2018.

Weiner, Jesse. 2017. "Classical Epic and the Poetics of Modern Fantasy." In *Classical Traditions in Modern Fantasy*. Brett M. Rogers and Benjamin Eldon Stevens, eds. Oxford: Oxford University Press. 25–46.

Weiskel, Thomas. 1976. *The Romantic Sublime: Studies in the Structure and Psychology of Transcendence*. Baltimore, MD: The Johns Hopkins University Press.

West, M. L., trans. 1988. *Hesiod: Theogony and Works and Days*. Oxford: Oxford University Press.

Whale, James, dir. 1931. *Frankenstein*. Universal Pictures.

Whale, James, dir. 1935. *Bride of Frankenstein*. Universal Pictures.

Wheeler, Stephen Michael. 1999. *A Discourse of Wonders*. Philadelphia, PA: University of Pennsylvania Press.

Williams, David A. 1996. *Deformed Discourse: The Function of the Monster in Mediaeval Thought and Literature*. Montreal, QC: McGill-Queens University Press.

Williams, R. D. 1990. "The Sixth Book of the *Aeneid*." In *Oxford Readings in Vergil's* Aeneid. S. J. Harrison, ed. Oxford: Clarendon Press. 191–207.

Winand, Annaëlle. 2016. "The Body, the Film, the Archive and the Monster." Paper presented at the XIV MAGIS – Gorizia International Film Studies Spring School in Gorizia, Italy, March 9–15, 2016. https://papyrus.bib.umontreal.ca/xmlui/bitstream/handle/1866/13388/winand_annaelle_2016_bodyfilmarchivemonster_papyrus.pdf?sequence=1. Accessed August 19, 2017.

Winkler, John J. 1985. *Auctor & Actor: A Narratological Reading of Apuleius's* Golden Ass. Berkeley, CA: University of California Press.

Wolfe, Leonard, ed. 2004. *The Essential Frankenstein*. New York, NY: ibooks.

Wollstonecraft, Mary. 1794. *An Historical and Moral View of the French Revolution; and the Effect It Has Produced in Europe*. London: J. Johnson.

Womersley, David, ed. 1998. *Edmund Burke: A Philosophical Enquiry into the Origins of Our Ideas of the Sublime and the Beautiful: And Other Pre-Revolutionary Writings*. New York, NY: Penguin.

Wood, Gillen D'Arcy. 2014. *Tambora: The Eruption that Changed the World*. Princeton, NJ: Princeton University Press.

Wosk, Julie. 2015. *My Fair Ladies: Female Robots, Androids, and Other Artificial Eves*. New Brunswick, NJ: Rutgers University Press.

Wright, Angela. 2016. "The Female Gothic." In *The Cambridge Companion to Frankenstein*. Andrew Smith, ed. Cambridge: Cambridge University Press. 101–115.

Wright, Constance S. 2000. "The Metamorphoses of Cupid and Psyche in Plato, Apuleius, Origen, and Chaucer." In *Tales within Tales: Apuleius through Time*. Constance S. Wright and Julia Bolton Holloway, eds. New York, NY: AMS Press. 55-72.

Wright, Constance S. and Julia Bolton Holloway, eds. 2000. *Tales within Tales: Apuleius through Time*. New York, NY: AMS Press.

Wu, Duncan. 1993. *Wordsworth's Reading, 1770-1799*. Cambridge: Cambridge University Press.

Zeitlin, Froma, I. 1995. "Signifying Difference: The Myth of Pandora." In *Women in Antiquity: New Assessments*. Richard Hawley and Barbara Levick, eds. New York, NY: Routledge. 58-74.

Zeitlin, Froma I. 1996. *Playing the Other: Gender and Society in Classical Greek Literature*. Chicago, IL: University of Chicago Press.

Zerba, Michelle. 1988. *Tragedy and Theory: The Problem of Conflict since Aristotle*. Princeton, NJ: Princeton University Press.

Zimmerman, M., S. Panayotakis, V. Hunink, W. H. Keulen, S. J. Harrison, T. D. McCreight, D. van Mal-Maeder, and B. Wesseling. 2004. *Apuleius Madaurensis. Metamorphoses, Book IV 28-35, V and VI 1-24. The Tale of Cupid and Psyche. Text, Introduction and Commentary*. Groningen: Egbert Forsten.

Ziolkowski, Theodore. 1981. "Science, Frankenstein, and Myth." *Sewanee Review* 89.1: 34-56.

Index

Adam (Biblical figure) 10, 12, 33, 38, 143n63, 186n12, 211–213, 217–219, 224n25
Aeschylus 25, 76, 88n19; (*Persians*) 22n58; (*Prometheus Bound*) 15, 19n13, 45, 47–49, 87n2 and n4, 153, 157, 208, 210, 216
Aesop 89n25, 223n12
aesthetics 112, 114, 170, 175–179
Agamben, Giorgio 13, 21
alchemy 2, 44–45, 55–56, 60, 67–68, 139, 148, 150, 173, 178, 184, 207
Alien Covenant 143n63, 218–219, 226n49, 227n51 (*see also* 'Scott, Ridley')
allegory 15–16, 36, 42, 48, 51, 60, 78, 80–81, 86, 114, 126, 130, 138, 140n11, 142n41
android(s) 118n36 and n48, 192, 205n40, 215–219, 231–232, 235–236
Antarctic(a) 94, 177
Aphrodite 103, 194, 205n49, 231
Apollodorus 103, 224n15
Apollonius of Rhodes 11, 41n13
Apuleius (*Metamorphoses* or *Golden Ass*) 2, 16, 124–144
Arctic 8, 16, 19n13, 20n19, 97, 103, 113, 119n62
Aristophanes 231; (*Birds*) 41n13, 223n10; (character in *Symposium*) 142n45, 233
Aristotle 17, 145, 170, 231; (*Ethics*) 148–151; (*Poetics*) 108, 110, 188n35; (*Politics*) 13
artificial intelligence 11, 18, 21n49, 193–194, 232
Asclepius 173, 187n22
Asimov, Isaac 236; (*Foundation*) 139; ("That Thou Art Mindful of Him") 202
Athena 103–104, 192, 209, 220, 227n52 (*see also* 'Minerva')
Atlas (Titan) 235
Atlas, Charles 235
atomism 17, 35, 116n19

Augustus 69, 233; (referred to as 'Caesar') 34
avant-garde, the 171, 179, 185

Bacon, Francis 77–79, 187n14
Barthes, Roland 114, 115n7, 116n18 and n22
Battlestar Galactica (television series) 116n75
de Beauvoir, Simone 213
Bible, the 38, 86, 197; (*Genesis*) 33, 36, 78, 86, 106
biotechnology 18
birth/childbirth 34, 36, 44, 53–54, 113, 115n13, 135, 146, 220, 225n27 (*see also* 'rebirth')
Blake, William 77, 87n3, 88n8, 125
body politic 65, 67, 74n14
Bonaparte, Napoléon 15, 68–73, 75, 98, 145
Breckenridge, Hugh Henry 207, 214
Burke, Edmund 66–68, 89n20, 107
Butler, Judith 13, 21n55, 197–198, 200, 205n41
Byatt, A. S. 140n12, 144n71
Byron, George Gordon ('Lord Byron') 1, 19n13, 34, 47, 50–54, 68–69, 73, 75n44 and n55, 77, 85, 87n4, 89n24, 91, 106, 128, 144n70, 146, 151nn4–5, 176, 219, 224n24, 226n47; (*Childe Harold*) 69; ("Darkness") 146; (*Don Juan*) 125; (*Hints from Horace*) 175; (*Manfred*) 56, 71, 73, 116n14; ("Prometheus") 47, 77, 208

Caesar (Julius) 8, 15, 59, 63, 65–66, 69, 73, 75nn56–57; (Augustus) 34; ('Caesar' as title) 63; ('Caesarism') 64–65, 69, 73, 74n21
Campbell, Joseph 155, 161
Cassandra 143n67
childbirth *see* 'birth'
Christianity 83

Cicero 17, 68, 74n14, 172, 182, 184; (*De divinatione*) 115n5, 181–182; (*De natura deorum*) 181–182; (*On Invention*) 102, 112–113
civil war (American) 231; (Roman) 8, 59–60, 63–65
Clairmont, Charles 46
Clairmont, Claire 1, 73, 77, 89n24, 91, 137, 151n5
classical reception 2–5, 10–15, 18, 19n7, 138–139, 140n4, 213, 228, 231, 237
classical tradition 25, 171, 179, 186n2, 204n15
Coleridge, Samuel Taylor 25, 77, 87nn3–4, 114, 117n28 and n30, 119n61; (*Christabel*) 1; ("Hymn before Sun-rise, in the Vale of Chamouny) 120; ("The Rime of the Ancient Mariner") 77; (*The Stateman's Manual*) 114
cosmogony 30
creation (of humankind/humans) 12, 26–27, 30, 33, 36, 38, 41n24, 43, 53–55, 78, 81–83, 85, 106, 110, 115n13, 129, 133–134, 158, 191–192, 194–195, 202, 204n12, 207, 209, 216, 221; (artistic/literary) 29–30, 77, 91, 99, 102, 104, 112, 185, 186n8, 199; (Promethean) 2, 26, 36, 38, 78, 83, 85, 191, 195, 236
Cruikshank, George 68, 70–73
Ctesias 13
culture wars 153
Cupid (mythic figure) 57n12, 123, 125–128, 130–136, 138–139, 143n63 (*see also* 'Eros')
'Cupid and Psyche' (story) 16, 57n12, 123–129, 132, 134, 136, 138, 140n4 and nn10–11, 141n20 and n31
cyborg(s) 116n25, 118n36, 190–191, 194, 196, 199, 201, 203, 230, 236; ("A Cyborg Manifesto") 213

'Daedalus and Icarus' (story) 11–12
Darwin, Erasmus 15, 25, 46, 49–56, 57n12 and n21, 76, 81, 89n23, 99, 175, 207; (*The Botanic Garden*) 49–51, 55, 81; (*The Temple of Nature*) 49, 51, 54–55; (*Zoonomia*) 49
Dawson City Frozen Time 187n17 (*see also* 'Morrison, Bill')
Decasia 172 (*see also* 'Morrison, Bill')

deformity 28, 36, 38, 109–110, 117n29, 187n14, 230
'Deucalion and Pyrrha' (story) 19n13, 27, 38, 41n24, 46, 53–54, 143n63
'Diana and Actaeon' (story) 138–139, 144n77
Diogenes Laertius 88n14
doppelgänger 131–132, 138
Douglas, Dave 177, 186n9, 188n43 and n53
Dryden, John 33–34, 41n22

education 2, 9, 20n27 and n35, 77, 82, 84, 87n5, 89n24, 116n22, 127, 157, 175, 177, 180–184, 232
electricity 4, 14, 43–44, 57n7, 112, 119n56, 146, 148, 151n7, 190, 207, 223n8
Empedocles 171, 174–175, 185, 229
Epimetheus 18, 27, 41n24, 83, 90n28, 103, 190–195, 202, 222
epistemology 14, 114, 170, 185, 206
Erichtho 12, 59–62, 65–66, 72–73, 74n6
Eros (mythic figure) 50, 57n21, 119n58 (*see also* 'Cupid')
eros ('erotic desire') 103, 111, 113–114, 117n27, 119n58
ethics 7, 17, 108, 114, 148–149, 154, 170, 174, 179, 204n22
Euripides 88n19, 142n51; (*Bacchae*) 226n44; (*Hippolytus*) 225n28; (*Medea*) 225n28
Eve (Biblical figure) 86, 118n36, 143n63, 211–213, 217–219, 224n25, 229
Ex Machina (film) 18, 118n48, 140n3, 190–205

fantasy (genre/mode) 125, 140n10, 143n66, 171, 223n1
femme fatale 18, 104
folk-tale 131, 142n44
Foucault, Michel 13, 21n55; (*Madness and Civilization*) 181; (*The Order of Things*) 213
Fraction, Matt 18, 207, 219–221, 223n1, 227n57
Frankenstein (1910 film) 43–45, 49, 56, 57n2, 182, 186n10
Frankenstein (1931 film) 21n46, 43, 149–150, 233, 235
Frankenstein (theatrical adaptation, Royal National Theatre) 20n19, 184, 189n60

Frankenstein, Victor
  (childhood) 43, 159–160
  (as student/antiquarian) 55, 60–61, 116n22, 146, 148, 168n27, 169n29, 172–173, 212; (as narrator) 8, 29, 116n22, 182; (as Adam) 212, 224n25; (as Asclepius) 173; (as Ben Franklin) 45; (as Creature) 41n12, 42, 86, 118n45, 130–131, 133–135, 142n45, 171, 182–184, 189n60, 211; (as Cupid) 131–133; (as Epimetheus) 193; (as Erichtho) 60–61; (as Eve) 115n8, 212, 224n25; (as God) 211, 224n25; (as Lionel Verney) 136; (as Mary Shelley) 28, 126, 171; (as Medea) 173; (as Percy Shelley) 42; (as Prometheus) 2–4, 12, 16, 19n18, 37–38, 47–49, 102, 106, 173, 208, 211, 224n14, 236; (as Psyche) 130–133, 135; (as Psyche's sisters) 132; (as Pygmalion) 173; (as Satan) 224n25; (as William Frankenstein) 133–134; (as Zeus) 211
  (and Timothy Leary) 154, 157–167; (and aesthetics) 105–110, 112–113, 115n6 and n13, 117n28, 163–165, 177; (and diet) 49; (and Elizabeth Lavenza) 123–124, 129–132, 135, 142n43 and n49, 160, 164, 212, 227n54; (and masturbation) 44, 135–136; (and personal relationships) 8–9, 142n45, 148, 160; (and refusal to make bride for the Creature) 7, 124, 132, 142n49, 175, 186n12, 212; (and revulsion towards creation) 12–13, 47, 102–103, 108–110, 113, 117n28, 118n36 and n48, 135, 159, 163–165; (and scientific ambition/'hybris') 8, 11, 25, 47, 59–61, 73, 74n2, 112, 146–150, 157, 159–160, 162, 167, 168n20, 171, 195, 212
'Frankenstein complex' 202
Franklin, Benjamin 15, 44–45, 49–50, 89n23, 96–97, 101n18, 119n56, 207, 223n4 and n8
French Revolution 15, 20n26, 59, 66–68, 90n31

Galatea (mythic figure) 10, 12, 21n46, 27–28, 117n27, 187n22, 232
Galvani, Luigi/galvanism 4, 25, 42–44, 99, 101n26, 146, 148, 151n7, 207
Garland, Alex 190–205

gender 47, 84, 86, 175, 190–203, 205, 207, 212, 215, 218–222, 225n28, 226n40, 229–230, 234–235
Genette, Gérard 25–26, 40n4, 41n17
'ghost story challenge' 1–2, 15–16, 87n1, 91, 108, 146
Ginsberg, Allen 156, 168n2
Godwin, William 6, 15, 34–35, 38, 41n22, 47, 56, 67, 76–77, 79, 82–86, 87n5, 89n25 and n26, 116n22, 127, 141n18, 144n74, 175, 224n20; (*Lives of the Necromancers*) 56, 141n17; (*The Pantheon*) 19n13, 82–86, 89n25, 127, 141n17, 223n11
Goethe, Johann Wolfgang von (*Faust Part Two*) 229; (*Memoirs*) 89n24; ("Prometheus") 81–82, 89n24; (*The Sorrows of Young Werter*) 5, 89n24, 183, 211, 232
Golding, Arthur 33, 35
Gothic, the (genre/mode) 1, 88n8, 120n66, 124, 130–131, 171, 237
Greek (language) 6, 20n20 and n28, 77, 79–80, 84, 88n19, 208, 223n9, 230, 237

Haraway, Donna 21n49, 116n25, 175, 187n31, 202–203, 213
Harry Potter series 187n32
Helen of Troy 107, 112–113, 117, 220, 227n59, 229–232
Hell 61, 71–72, 119n62, 234
Herakleides Ponticus 57n11, 223n12
Hesiod 48, 76, 83, 85–86, 89n22, 106, 116n15 191, 204n12 and n27, 206, 209, 212, 225n28; (*Theogony*) 35, 41n13, 45, 49, 104, 107, 113, 194–196, 206, 215–216, 223n10; (*Works and Days*) 45, 80–81, 90n28, 103–104, 113, 175, 191–192, 194, 196, 199, 206, 217, 222, 223n10
Hippolytus 27–28, 117n27, 225n28
'*Hippolytus*' (play) *see* 'Seneca (*Phaedra*)'
Hogg, Thomas Jefferson 20n28, 31–32, 46, 88n12 and n19, 127, 141 n20
Homer 22n58; (*Iliad*) 35, 107, 119n58, 120n64, 178, 226n44, 231; (*Odyssey*) 119n58, 219
Homeric Hymns 76, 87n2
Horace 76, 229; (*Ars poetica*) 103–106, 112, 116n24, 117n30, 119n55, 172, 175–179, 185, 187n34, 188n35,

188n39; (*Carmina* or *Odes*) 35, 57n17, 78, 88n6, 188n36 and n37, 223n10, 224n18; (*Epistles*) 18n2, 175, 188n36 and n37
horror (genre) 1, 19n13, 43, 91, 120n66, 124, 140n3, 167, 218, 230, 237
Hunt, Leigh 41n21, 76, 87n4, 88n19, 224n20
Huxley, Aldous (*The Doors of Perception*) 166
hybrids/hybridity 11, 13, 41n12, 72, 105–106, 116n25, 118n36, 171–172, 174–178, 181–182, 185, 187, 208, 217–220, 222
Hyginus (*Fabulae*) 103, 224n15; (*Poetica astronomica*) 57n11, 223n10 and n12

Igor (Ygor, Fritz) 57n2, 149, 152n21
incest 28, 130–131, 134, 142n43
intertextuality 140n4, 143n57
Isidore 21n57, 170–171, 185, 186n5 and n12, 187n27

Jakobson, Roman 116n18
Julius Caesar (Shakespearean play) 233
Jung, Carl 161, 169n30

Kant, Immanuel (on "the Prometheus of modern times") 44–45, 50, 57n8, 89n23, 207, 210, 214–215, 223n5 and n6; (*Critique of Judgment*) 102, 108–111, 113–114, 115n4, 118, 119n63, 120n68
Karloff, Boris 43, 149–150, 171, 184, 233
Keats, John 34, 77, 125; ('egotistical sublime') 118n44; ('negative capability') 115

Lake Geneva 1, 73, 98–99, 146
landscape 41n11, 119n62
Laplace, Pierre Simon de 147
Latin (language) 6, 20n20, 31–36, 38, 40, 41n19, 46, 52, 77, 79, 102, 110, 115n5, 125, 128, 137, 172, 181, 188n36, 208, 223n9, 229, 231, 234, 237
Lavenza, Elizabeth 8, 103, 123, 129–135, 142, 160, 164, 212, 227n54
Leary, Timothy 153–169; (*Change Your Brain*) 154; (*Chaos and Cyber Culture*) 155–156; (*Flashbacks*) 157, 169n35; (*High Priest*) 153–157, 161–167; (*Psychedelic Prayers*) 158; (*Start Your Own Religion*) 155
Lewis, C. S. ('discarded image') 139, 144n80; ('Space' or 'Cosmic Trilogy') 139; (*Till We Have Faces*) 125, 140n8
libertas 64–66, 69
Linnaeus, Carl 52, 54, 186n2
Longinus (*On the Sublime*) 102, 103, 110–113, 118n41 and n49, 119n50 and n53
love 111–113, 123, 126, 130–131, 135–137, 142n42, 166, 180–184, 212, 229, 234, 236–237
Lovecraft, H. P. (*At the Mountains of Madness*) 120n66; ("Herbert West—Reanimator") 230, 235
Lucan (*Bellum civile* or *Pharsalia*) 12, 35, 39–40, 41n23, 59–75
Lucian of Samosata ("Lucius, or The Ass") 127–129, 142n36; (*Prometheus*) 209; (*True History*) 141n34; (*You Are a Prometheus in Words*) 209
Lucretius (*De rerum natura*) 31, 35, 39–40, 41n13, 52–54, 106–107, 112, 116n19, 118n37, 119n63, 139, 142n42, 149–151, 152n23 and n24, 171–172, 174–175, 185, 187n26 and n27
Lugosi, Bela 149

Macrobius (*Saturnalia*) 231
Manilius (*Astronomica*) 35
marriage/wedding 8, 103, 123, 125, 130, 133, 189n56, 196, 212, 230, 232
Marx, Karl (*The Eighteenth Brumaire of Louis Bonaparte*) 68–69
masculinity 199–200, 215, 224n24, 225n30, 226n47, 227n50, 235
masturbation/onanism 44, 131, 136, 226n45
Medea 19n2, 27–28, 31, 142n51, 173, 187n22, 225n28
Megasthenes 13
meme (Richard Dawkins) 154, 167, 169n30
memory 9, 135, 191, 195, 231
metapoetry/metapoetics 25–41, 179
Milton, John (*Paradise Lost*) 10, 12, 25, 30, 41n12, 45, 57n10, 117n28, 119n62, 178, 183, 204n11, 210–211, 217–218
mimesis 104, 108, 110, 116n16, 172, 184, 202–203

Minerva 46, 83, 232
'Modern Prometheus' *see* 'Prometheus'
monarchy 6, 64–71
monster(s)/monstrosity 115n5, 172, 181, 233
Montalègre 1
Morris, William (*The Earthly Paradise*) 125
Morrison, Bill 170–189
motherhood, mothers 131–132, 160, 212, 218, 224n27
Myrrha 31, 142n47

narcissism 160
Narcissus (mythic figure) 180
necromancy 55–56, 60–62, 71–73
necrophilia 131
Neoplatonism 138, 142n41
Neoptolemus of Parium 188n39
Newton, Isaac 146–150
Newton, John Frank (*The Return to Nature*) 78–82
Noah (Biblical figure) 143n63

occult, the 60, 74n2, 148
Ody-C (comics series) 207, 214, 219–221, 227n57 and n58
Ovid (*Fasti*) 74n20; (*Metamorphoses*) 10–12, 19n2, 25–41, 46, 48–49, 53–56, 78, 88n12 and n14, 106, 116n16, 117n27, 142n47 and n51, 143n63, 144n77, 171, 187n22, 191–192, 208, 210, 224n14, 235
Orpheus 187n15

'paganism' 33, 36, 76–77, 79–80, 83, 86, 88n19
Pandora 11, 16, 18, 45, 81, 83, 85–86, 102–120, 190–205, 209, 212, 216–219, 230, 235, 237
paratext 25–26, 31–40, 41n17, 125–129
Pater, Walter (*Marius the Epicurean*) 125, 128, 141n24
Pausanias 223n12, 231
Peacock, Thomas Love 79–80, 87n2, 88n19, 115n6, 125
Peake, Richard Brinsley (*Presumption; or, the Fate of Frankenstein*) 135–136, 149
Petronius 231
Pharsalus, battle of 59, 63, 65

Philodemus 188n39
Plato 76; (*Protagoras*) 192–193, 222, 223n10, 236; (*Republic*) 116n17, 231; (*Symposium*) 142n45, 233, 236; (*Theaetetus*) 231
Pliny the Elder (*Naturalis historia*) 13, 21n57, 74n22, 79, 170, 223n10
Pliny the Younger (*Letters*) 100
Plutarch (*Moralia*) 142n42; (*Parallel Lives*) 2, 5–9, 10–11, 19n13, 20–21, 25, 125, 182–183, 211, 232
Poincaré, Henri 149
Polidori, John 1, 73, 87n4, 91, 146; (*The Vampyre*) 1, 19n3
Pompey the Great 8, 15, 59, 63–66
Pontanus (*Meteorologia*) 35, 38
posthumanism 18, 19n18, 206–227
Prigogine, Ilya 148, 150–151
Prometheus (film) 18, 207, 214–220, 222 (*see also* 'Scott, Ridley')
Prometheus (mythic figure) 2–5, 15, 17–18, 19n13, 27, 32–33, 36, 42, 45–46, 49, 54, 56, 69–70, 72, 76–90, 103–104, 125, 153–157, 165, 167, 173, 191–194, 202, 204n14, 206–229, 233–234, 236; (*plasticator*) 2, 3, 15, 26–27, 36–38, 41n24, 45–46, 48–50, 53, 57n11, 78, 81–83, 85–86, 88n12, 104, 106–107, 116nn15–16, 185, 191, 204n12, 206–209, 211, 213, 216, 223n12; (*pyrphoros*) 2, 3, 12–13, 15, 37–38, 44–51, 57n11 and n17, 80–81, 83, 104, 107, 116n15, 155, 191–193, 199, 206–209, 211, 213, 216–217, 222, 223n10, 224n14; ("Modern Prometheus"/"Prometheus of modern times") 45, 47–48, 50, 70–71, 72, 79, 86, 102, 153, 171, 173, 206–213, 216, 223n2 and n11, 224n20, 226n42
Proteus 227n59, 237; ('protean') 207, 210,
Psyche (mythic figure) 16, 57n12, 123–144
psychedelics 17, 153–169, 219; (LSD) 156–158; (psilocybin) 157, 162–163
psychoanalysis 110
Pygmalion (mythic figure) 10–12, 27–28, 117n27, 173, 235; (modern adaptations of story) 21n46, 187n22, 229–232, 234–235, 237

race, ideas about/racism 11, 13, 21n57, 81, 84, 137, 142n52, 165, 170–171, 175, 183, 187, 222
rebirth 19n13, 68, 158 (*see also* 'birth')
religion 20n33, 53, 76, 84, 124, 130, 139, 155
revivification 12, 15, 52, 57n7, 59, 61–75, 236
revolution (political) 15, 20n26, 48, 50, 59, 66–71, 73, 153, 167
robot(s) 10, 44, 118n36 and n48, 161, 197, 199–201, 214, 218, 226n40, 229–231
Romantics, Romanticism 3, 69, 76–90, 116n14, 208, 218, 223n8 and n11, 224n24, 226n47

Sandys, George 25–26, 32–40
Satan 71, 76, 211–212, 224n25
de Saussure, Ferdinand 116n18
Scalzi, John (*The Ghost Brigades*) 9–11; (*The Human Division*) 179; (*Old Man's War*) 9, 179
science fiction (SF) 3, 9–11, 13–14, 19n11, 21n46 and n47, 22n59 and n60, 112, 124, 126, 135–140, 143n66, 144n79 and n80, 171, 184, 190–207, 212–221, 225–227, 229, 232, 235–236
Scott, Ridley 4, 18, 143n63, 186n2, 207, 214–220, 222
Semonides of Amorgos 225n28
Seneca 25, 31, 35; (*Hercules furens*) 2; (*Phaedra*) 35
sex (biological) 45, 48, 84, 86, 118n36, 175, 190–191, 194, 196, 213, 220–222, 225n28; (erotic activity) 130, 135, 142n47, 212–213; (reproduction) 123, 196, 208, 212, 215, 220–221, 226n45
sexuality 7, 135, 170, 175, 187n31, 191, 194, 197–198, 202, 212–213, 234
Shaftesbury, Third Earl of 45, 206, 215; (*The Moralists*) 45, 223n2, 224n20
Shakespeare, William 25, 41n12, 125, 140n8, 237; (*A Midsummer Night's Dream*) 125, 178; (*Othello*) 141n13; (*The Tempest*) 18–19n2, 178
Shelley, Harriet (knowledge of Latin) 188n36; (suicide) 151n3
Shelley, Mary Wollstonecraft 1, 47, 49, 54, 69–70, 73, 77, 79, 82, 87n5, 89n26, 91, 99, 135, 137, 146, 151n3, 187n22, 219–220, 224n27; (education/knowledge of classics) 2, 4, 6–7, 14–16, 20, 25–41, 46, 48–49, 68, 76–77, 87n2, 88n12, 125–129, 141n23, 143n64, 176, 188n37, 208–209, 223n9, 224n14; (*Falkner*) 6; (*Frankenstein*) 4, 10, 14–16, 25, 28–31, 41n12, 42, 44–45, 47, 59, 76, 86, 87n1, 106, 114–115, 136, 146, 149, 167, 171, 173, 207–208, 210, 224n27; (*The Last Man*) 6, 16, 19n12, 126–127, 136–138; (*Lives*) 127; (*Matilda*) 127–128; (*Midas* and *Proserpine*) 77, 144n77; ("The Mortal Immortal") 56; ("To the Death") 125, 127, 141n29; ("The Death of Love") 125–127, 141n28, 143n66; ("Stanzas") 126–127, 141n28; ("Valerius The Reanimated Roman") 144n78
Shelley, Percy Bysshe 1, 19n13, 25, 41n12 and n14, 42, 46, 49–52, 54, 68–70, 73, 77, 79, 89n24 and n26, 91, 99, 114, 116nn21–22, 120n67, 128, 137, 144n70, 146, 151n3, 178, 219, 224n24, 226n47; (education, knowledge of classics) 2, 7, 19n13, 20, 31–32, 34–35, 47–49, 53–54, 74n13, 76, 80–81, 87n2, 88n12 and n14, 89n22, 127, 129, 142n51, 143n64, 149, 152n23, 175–176, 188nn36–37, 208–209, 223n11; ("Alastor") 142n46; ("A Defence of Poetry") 115n7, 118n41, 167, 169n48, 176–177; ("Mont Blanc") 114, 120n67, 146; (Passage of the Apennines) 115n6; (*Prometheus Unbound*) 15, 47–48, 69, 76–77, 80, 87n1 and n4, 89n22, 208; (*Queen Mab*) 48, 51, 53, 58n25, 77–82, 88n14, 89n20, 209; (*St. Irvyne, or The Rosicrucian*) 56, 58n27; (*A Vindication of Natural Diet*) 80–81, 89n20 and n22, 209
Sibyl 137–138, 143n65, 143n67, 144n70
sin 90n31, 154, 167, 188n36; (as technology) 104, 112
Sophocles 87n2; (*Antigone*) 13; (*Oedipus Tyrannus*) 235
Spark of Being (film) 17, 21n45, 170–189 (*see also* 'Morrison, Bill')
Stoker, Bram (*Dracula*) 140n3, 142n48; (derivative character in film) 233
sublime, the/sublimity 16, 102–120, 172, 177, 187n18

Suetonius (*Lives of the Caesars*) 74n20 and n22, 75n56
supernatural, the 117n27, 137, 139, 140n11, 155
Suvin, Darko 22n60, 139, 184

Tacitus 88n19; (*Annals*) 64; (*Histories*) 64
Talos 11–12, 235
Tambora eruption 1, 16, 91–101, 145–146
technology/*techne* 2–5, 9, 11–14, 17–18, 27, 44, 104, 111–112, 139, 153–157, 162, 167, 191, 194, 197, 199, 202–203, 206–207, 211–215, 218, 220, 222, 225n28, 226n38, 229, 233–234
thermodynamics 17, 149
Titans/Titanomachy 27, 37, 45, 70, 76, 117n27, 153, 191, 206, 213, 215, 224n20, 226n44
Tooke, Andrew 76; (*Pantheon of the Heathen Gods and Illustrious Heroes*) 82–85, 89n27, 90n28
tragedy (genre) 25–26, 45, 47, 110, 142n47, 176, 187n33, 188n38, 204n15, 208, 225n28, 234
trickery/trickster 45, 48–49, 85, 113, 224n20
Turing test 18, 118nn36–37, 193–195, 198, 200, 202
Typhon 229
tyranny 65, 69–70, 73, 76, 80

Ulpian (*Digest*) 65
uncanny, the 14, 111

Underworld/underworld descent (*katabasis*) 59, 63, 74n10, 137–138, 187n15, 225n37, 230

Varro 170, 185
vegetarianism 48–49, 51, 78–79, 89n22, 209
vermicelli 50, 51–54, 56
Victor Frankenstein (film) 151n9, 152n21, 188n41
Villa Diodati 1, 32, 87n1, 99
Virbius 28 (*see also* 'Hippolytus')
Virgil 4, 32, 140, 143n64 (*Aeneid*) 35, 63, 137–138, 141n23, 143nn64–66; (*Georgics*) 35, 143n64
Vitruvius (*De architectura*) 74n20
volcanology 91–101, 145
Volney, Constantin François de Chasseboeuf, comte de (*Ruins of Empires*) 22n57, 183, 224n23
Voltaire (*Candide*) 147

Ward, Christian 18, 207, 219, 221
Wollstonecraft, Mary 15, 20n36, 67, 80, 87n5, 89n20, 90n31, 115n1, 224n24 and n27
wonder/terror (*thauma*) 103, 105, 107, 109, 114, 117n32, 120n67, 155, 159, 165–166, 190, 195, 199, 201
Wordsworth, William 25, 34, 77, 87n3, 120n68, 125

'Year without a Summer' 1, 15–16, 91–101, 145–146
Young Frankenstein (film) 149, 234

www.ingramcontent.com/pod-product-compliance
Ingram Content Group UK Ltd.
Pitfield, Milton Keynes, MK11 3LW, UK
UKHW021905220326
469204UK00008B/196